P9-AQE-469

GREAT CIRCLE DISTANCES IN STATUTE MILES (Approximate, Subject to Correction)

Scale along the Equator in Statute Miles

Van der Grinten Projection

Sea Distances shown in Nautical Miles

1 Nautical Mile = 1.15 Statute Miles

ALSO BY JAMES B. CONROY

Jefferson's White House: Monticello on the Potomac

Lincoln's White House: The People's House in Wartime

*Our One Common Country: Abraham Lincoln and
the Hampton Roads Peace Conference of 1865*

The

DEVILS WILL GET NO REST

FDR, CHURCHILL, AND THE PLAN THAT WON THE WAR

JAMES B. CONROY

SIMON & SCHUSTER

New York   London   Toronto   Sydney   New Delhi

Simon & Schuster
1230 Avenue of the Americas
New York, NY 10020

Copyright © 2023 by James B. Conroy

All rights reserved, including the right to reproduce this book
or portions thereof in any form whatsoever. For information, address
Simon & Schuster Subsidiary Rights Department,
1230 Avenue of the Americas, New York, NY 10020.

First Simon & Schuster hardcover edition June 2023

SIMON & SCHUSTER and colophon are registered trademarks of Simon & Schuster, Inc.

For information about special discounts for bulk purchases,
please contact Simon & Schuster Special Sales
at 1-866-506-1949 or business@simonandschuster.com.

The Simon & Schuster Speakers Bureau can bring authors to your live event.
For more information or to book an event,
contact the Simon & Schuster Speakers Bureau
at 1-866-248-3049 or visit our website at www.simonspeakers.com.

Interior design by Ruth Lee-Mui

Manufactured in the United States of America

1   3   5   7   9   10   8   6   4   2

Library of Congress Cataloging-in-Publication Data has been applied for.

ISBN 978-1-9821-6868-1
ISBN 978-1-9821-6870-4 (ebook)

For Delancey Mei

Contents

The Allied Military Cast at Casablanca

All ranks are as of the Casablanca Conference of January 1943.

THE BRITISH

GENERAL SIR HAROLD RUPERT LEOFRIC GEORGE ALEXANDER: The Allied Commander in Chief in the Middle East.

GENERAL SIR ALAN BROOKE: Chief of the Imperial General Staff and Chairman of the British Chiefs of Staff Committee.

ADMIRAL SIR ANDREW B. CUNNINGHAM: The popular Commander in Chief of all Allied forces in the Mediterranean, reporting to Eisenhower.

FIELD MARSHAL SIR JOHN DILL: Chief of the British Joint Staff Mission in Washington, Brooke's mentor, friend, and predecessor as Chief of the Imperial General Staff; a thoughtful, bridge-building man; Marshall's close friend and confidant.

BRIGADIER GENERAL VIVIAN DYKES: The popular, Cambridge-educated head of the secretariat of the British Joint Staff Mission in Washington, forty-four years old, the British Casablanca delegation's drafter of the minutes.

LIEUTENANT GENERAL SIR HASTINGS LIONEL "PUG" ISMAY: Prime Minister Winston Churchill's personal liaison to his Chiefs of Staff, Secretary to the Committee of Imperial Defense, Deputy Secretary (Military) to the War Cabinet, and head of the military wing of the combined secretariat, uniquely close to Churchill.

BRIGADIER GENERAL EDWARD IAN CLAUD JACOB: Assistant Secretary to the War Cabinet, forty-three years old, an observant wit, one of Churchill's favorite staff officers.

MAJOR GENERAL SIR JOHN NOBLE KENNEDY: Brooke's Director of Military Operations, in charge of the British Army's planning; Brooke's bird-watching friend.

GENERAL BERNARD MONTGOMERY: In field command of the British Eighth Army chasing Rommel through the Libyan desert, having driven him from Egypt at El Alamein.

VICE ADMIRAL LORD LOUIS FRANCIS ALBERT VICTOR NICHOLAS MOUNTBATTEN: The British Chiefs of Staff's Director of Combined Operations, a cousin of the King, a likable, brave, imaginative man of forty-two widely thought to be light on gravitas.

CAPTAIN R. P. PIM: An astute intelligence officer who briefed Churchill daily at Anfa on the latest war reports and oversaw his traveling map room.

CHIEF OF THE AIR STAFF, AIR CHIEF MARSHAL SIR CHARLES FREDERICK ALGERNON PORTAL: The brilliant upper-class commander of the RAF whom the Americans liked and particularly respected.

FIRST SEA LORD ADMIRAL SIR ALFRED DUDLEY PICKMAN ROGERS POUND: The aging senior officer of the Royal Navy, close to Churchill, often somnolent but for naval matters.

AIR VICE MARSHAL SIR JOHN COTESWORTH SLESSOR: Air Chief Marshal Portal's American whisperer and Assistant Chief of Air Staff for Plans, a dapper, witty man of forty-five who limped with the help of a cane.

BRIGADIER GENERAL GUY STEWART: Brooke's Director of Plans.

AIR CHIEF MARSHAL SIR ARTHUR TEDDER: In titular command of all Allied air forces in Africa, reporting to Eisenhower, appointed Air Commander in Chief, Mediterranean at Casablanca.

COMMANDER CHARLES THOMPSON: Churchill's personal aide.

THE AMERICANS

LIEUTENANT GENERAL FRANK MAXWELL ANDREWS: Based in Cairo in command of the U.S. Army Air Forces in the Middle East, brought in to help General Arnold at Anfa.

LIEUTENANT GENERAL HENRY "HAP" ARNOLD: Marshall's old friend in command of the United States Army Air Forces, a de facto member of the Joint Chiefs of Staff.

LIEUTENANT COMMANDER HARRY C. BUTCHER: Eisenhower's friend and forty-two-year-old naval aide, a reservist who managed a Washington radio station in civilian life.

LIEUTENANT GENERAL MARK CLARK: Commander of the Fifth Army, previously Eisenhower's Deputy Commander in Chief of Allied Forces in North Africa, a charming, courageous, highly ambitious backstabber.

MAJOR CHARLES CODMAN: A blue-blooded Boston reservist assigned as the French General Henri Giraud's translator at Anfa.

REAR ADMIRAL CHARLES M. COOKE JR.: Admiral King's Deputy Chief of Staff for Plans, a slight, Anglophobic Arkansan as bright and even more obnoxious than Admiral King.

BRIGADIER GENERAL JOHN R. DEANE: The American drafter of the minutes at the conference.

MAJOR GENERAL IRA EAKER: The Texas-born leader of the Eighth Bomber Command in England, called to Anfa to help persuade Churchill to endorse American day bombing.

LIEUTENANT GENERAL DWIGHT D. EISENHOWER: Commander in Chief of Allied Forces in North Africa, who had never been within hearing range of combat. The British liked him, appreciated his Anglo-American bridge-building, and considered him no strategist.

COLONEL CHARLES GAILEY: Flown to Casablanca several days into the conference to assist Marshall and Wedemeyer.

MAJOR GENERAL THOMAS T. HANDY: Marshall's Assistant Chief of Staff for Operations, who remained in Washington in telegraphic communication with Wedemeyer.

BRIGADIER GENERAL JOHN E. HULL: A highly regarded senior Army planner flown to Casablanca in midstream to support Marshall and Wedemeyer.

ADMIRAL ERNEST J. KING: The obnoxiously brilliant Chief of Naval Operations and Commander in Chief of the Fleet.

ADMIRAL WILLIAM D. LEAHY: President Franklin D. Roosevelt's friend and Chief of Staff.

COMMANDER RUTHVEN E. LIBBY: Admiral King's acerbic aide.

GENERAL GEORGE C. MARSHALL: The United States Army's unsparing Chief of Staff, brilliant at organization, thin on strategy, universally respected for strength of character.

CAPTAIN JOHN L. McCREA: Roosevelt's genial naval aide and all-purpose fixer.

CAPTAIN JAMES PARTON: General Eaker's thirty-year-old reservist aide, a Harvard-educated *Time* and *Life* junior executive in civilian life.

MAJOR GENERAL GEORGE S. PATTON JR.: The notoriously bombastic Commander of the Western Task Force in the Allied invasion of French North Africa, Commanding General of the First Armored Corps, responsible for the occupation of French Morocco and the Casablanca Conference's security and physical arrangements.

COLONEL JACOB E. SMART: An Army Air Forces planner who arrived at Casablanca on the conference's first day and helped Arnold carry his load.

LIEUTENANT GENERAL BREHON B. SOMERVELL: The U.S. Army's able Chief of Logistics.

MAJOR GENERAL CARL A. SPAATZ: Commanding all U.S. Army Air Forces in the European Theater.

BRIGADIER GENERAL ALBERT C. WEDEMEYER: An Anglophobic, right-wing Germanophile who called himself "Marshall's planner," Marshall's only senior aide at Casablanca.

BRIGADIER GENERAL WILLIAM H. WILBUR: De Gaulle's classmate at the French military academy, awarded the Medal of Honor by FDR at Anfa.

THE DEVILS WILL GET NO REST

EUROPEAN THEATER JANUARY 1943

LEGEND

 ALLIED LANDINGS IN AFRICA

 ALLIED NATIONS

 NEUTRAL NATIONS

 AXIS-CONTROLLED TERRITORY

 AXIS NATIONS

PACIFIC THEATER JANUARY 1943

UNION OF SOVIET SOCIALIST REPUBLICS

OUTER MONGOLIA

MANCHURIA

KURILE ISLANDS

INNER

MONGOLIA

KOREA

JAPAN

CHINA

TIBET

PACIFIC

INDIA

OKINAWA

Burma Road

Kunming

Lashio

TAIWAN

MARIANAS ISLANDS

OCEAN

BURMA

FRENCH

Hong Kong

THAILAND

Rangoon

INDOCHINA

PHILIPPINE

ISLANDS

CAROLINE ISLANDS

Truk

MALAYA

Singapore

BORNEO

Equator

SUMATRA

NEW IRELAND

NEW GUINEA

Rabaul

SOLOMON ISLANDS

NEW BRITAIN

Tulagi

Guadalcanal

AUSTRALIA

Scale of Miles

0   200   400   600   800   1000

PRELUDE

On the moonlit night of September 28, 1939, four weeks after a vast German army, swarms of panzer tanks, and waves of screaming warplanes fell on Poland like wolves on sheep, Lieutenant General Sir Alan Brooke crossed the English Channel on a camouflaged Belfast ferry with a flock of green recruits. The youngest son of an Anglo-Irish baronet, Brooke at fifty-six was a delicate man with a surgical mind, an effortless air of command, and the stare of a bird of prey. "Colonel Shrapnel," a subordinate called him, one of the last war's stars of the Royal Artillery, the living incarnation of "The Fighting Brookes of Brookeborough" who had bled for the crown for centuries.

On his way to take command of a corps of the BEF, the British Expeditionary Force in France, soon to comprise about 390,000 lightly trained men, Brooke began a diary in the form of a chat with his wife, Benita Blanche Brooke. "My evening talk with you on paper," he called it, a relief from the "awful futility of it all" as he faced his second war against the world's most lethal army with his country's life at stake. "It is all too ghastly even to be a nightmare."

The BEF had been ordered into line near the Belgian border under French command, which did not improve Brooke's mood. Born and raised in a country house in southwest France, Brooke had spoken French with a Gascon accent before he spoke English, but he knew firsthand the decay of the French and Belgian armies and "the utter efficiency of the Germans." Major General Bernard Montgomery, in command of one of Brooke's divisions of roughly 13,000 men, was not impressed with Anglo-French command and control. "The whole business was a complete dog's breakfast."

On his way to inspect the line he would defend with II Corps, Brooke stopped to see his mentor General Sir John Greer Dill, a fellow Ulsterman in command of I Corps, a decorated veteran of the Boer War and World War I and a Knight Commander of the Order of the Bath with the warmth of a kindly abbot. Orphaned as a boy, a bank manager's son taken into an uncle's parsonage in rustic County Down, Dill was the sort of man, a London sophisticate said, "who made no impression when he came into a room," but few British officers were more respected than Jack Dill, a tall, gray, gentlemanly man of fifty-eight with alert, appealing eyes, a wise, contemplative mind, and "as much charm and real goodness as any then living." Having reached the Army's heights, he had fallen just short of its pinnacles, passed over in quick succession for Chief of the Imperial General Staff and command of the BEF, disappointments made trivial by his troops' unpreparedness for war.

In conference with Lord Gort, the brass-knuckled aristocrat who led the BEF, Brooke and Dill contested the high command's plan, premised on Belgian-French politics, for the BEF to abandon its fortifications and move up into Belgium if the Germans breached her neutrality on their way into France. Gort brushed them off, unimpressed by the thought that letting political goals dictate military strategy invited disaster.

The last war had schooled them all on the subject of disaster. Dill had distinguished himself at the hideous Battle of Neuve Chapelle, the debacle at Aubers Ridge, and the slaughter at Arras, where the British had suffered 160,000 casualties. Brooke had lost an idolized older brother in the war's first month and fought at Neuve Chapelle, Vimy Ridge, Passchendaele, and the four-month Battle of the Somme that had left over 300,000 young men dead. Earning three decorations facing horrors beyond words, Brooke had felt blessed by the human incapacity to absorb it all.

A generation later, the ill-prepared and indifferently armed men and boys whose lives were in his hands were grossly overmatched by the cutting-edge German army and the vicious Luftwaffe, Hermann Göring's modern air force, accomplished in atrocity in Poland and the Spanish Civil War. In deadly combination they were the swiftest, best equipped, most violent human force in the history of the world. Whenever Brooke spoke with his regimental officers, he had the haunting feeling that someday his orders would kill them.

On November 11, an honor guard of men who were children or unborn when thousands of British and Canadian troops died at Vimy Ridge led a ceremony there on the twenty-first anniversary of the armistice. Returning to that blood-soaked ground, Brooke endured the helpless thought of fighting for it again. Perhaps it was "through such punishments that we shall eventually learn to 'love our neighbors as ourselves.'"

Two days later, Dill came to Brooke having failed to convince Gort that he was stretching the BEF thin, quite sure that Gort despised him for cold feet. Brooke credited Dill with twice Gort's vision, ten times his ability, and consistently superior judgment. The same could not be said for the judgment of General Montgomery, who had published to his commanders an exposition on venereal disease so obscene that the Army's senior chaplains had complained to the adjutant general and produced what Monty called "the father-and-mother of a row." Brooke informed him with the sharpest kind of clarity that he admired his military skills but not his literary talent, and his command could not survive another indiscretion. "He took it wonderfully well."

But for isolated incidents and enemy reconnaissance planes trolling hawklike overhead, Brooke's lines were quiet as he strengthened his defenses against the Wehrmacht, the combined Nazi forces, who were sure to attack in the spring. Whenever he had time, he indulged his love of birds and the "Sanctuary of Nature," often missing his sketchpad and camera. Gifted in the use of both, he had long since produced extraordinary bird photography, charming storybook drawings for his children, insightful sketches of friends and colleagues, beautifully illustrated letters to his mother, and evocative views of the natural world. In April, after a week's leave with Benita, he slipped away to a quiet wood "carpeted with wild anemones. I took you with me in spirit and we admired them together."

Four days later, Dill was made vice chief of the Imperial General Staff, the Army's second post, and ordered back to London, a personal blow to Brooke, who soon faced worse. His lovely first wife, Jane, had died in 1925 after he flipped their car when a cyclist dashed in front of it. Crushed by grief and guilt, he blamed himself for their children's loss of their mother. On April 25, 1940, Tom Brooke, Jane's son and his, a twenty-year-old BEF artillery officer, woke up in agony with a burst appendix. He survived emergency surgery, but his father was told that gangrene and peritonitis might kill him. His life ebbed and flowed for nearly a fortnight before his father's eyes until the general found him near death on the 8th of May. His surgeon gave him "a good fighting chance."

Just after dawn on May 10, the punctuated din of antiaircraft fire jolted Brooke awake as the Luftwaffe hit French targets and overwhelming German forces descended on the Low Countries. Luxembourg fell in a day as armored Wehrmacht spearheads shattered Dutch and Belgian defenses. For out-of-date armies built for static wars, the shocking violence of charging panzers, heavy bombers, self-propelled artillery, motorized infantry, and shrieking Stuka dive-bombers was next to irresistible. With terrifying sirens on their wings, plunging Stukas dropped bombs on streams of refugees, leveled off at ten feet, and strafed them into ditches, spreading chaos on the roads. Blitzkrieg, the Germans called it, lightning war.

Following the plan that Brooke and Dill had challenged, the BEF left its French fortifications and moved north into Belgium, where panicked refugees slowed them down and incompetent Belgian commanders blocked them. On May 14, Brooke was conferring with Gort when a message arrived from the front. Seven world-class panzer divisions had punched through the French defenses east and southeast of the BEF, supported by massive airpower and waves of mobile infantry and artillery. A telegram handed to Brooke that day said his boy was "just holding his own." For the next two weeks he would have no word of him.

Winston Churchill had succeeded Neville Chamberlain as Britain's prime minister on May 10, the day of the German attack. On the morning of May 15, a telephone call from the French premier, Paul Reynaud, awakened him. "We have been defeated," Reynaud said. Churchill was too stunned to reply. "We are beaten," the Frenchman said. "We have lost the battle." Armored German columns had cut the French armies in two and were dashing through open country with nothing to stop them. Churchill said France could not be conquered so fast. Reynaud repeated himself.

As Dill briefed the War Cabinet on the enemy breakthrough and a plan to evacuate the BEF, Churchill sprang from his seat. The very idea that France could be defeated in days was absurd. He would go to Reynaud himself. Churchill flew to Paris that afternoon in a small RAF plane escorted by a dozen Spitfires, the first of five such flights. With him came his longtime friend and right-hand staff officer, Lieutenant General Sir Hastings Lionel Ismay, and Jack Dill. France's broken leaders told Churchill she was lost, unmoved by his exhortations. The Dutch surrendered that day, freeing still more German divisions to rush south.

On May 17 the BEF began a five-day withdrawal to its French fortifications, often under fire, sometimes only minutes ahead of the Wehrmacht, on nightmarish roads clogged with refugees—terrified mothers made lame from carrying children for miles, old men and women struggling to keep up, exhausted little girls "hugging their dolls." In the hot days ahead, a ceaseless flood of calamities, sleep-deprived decisions, and the deaths of friends and aides hit Brooke so hard and fast "that life becomes a blur and fails to cut a groove on one's memory." "Whatever happens," he wrote Benita, "they can never take away from me our years of paradise."

On the 18th and 20th of May, as the Germans pushed down through

Belgium and west across northern France, Churchill telegrammed President Franklin D. Roosevelt pleading for help from the neutral United States. FDR itched to oblige, but his hands were tied by his people's dread of war. Some Americans expected the magnificent Royal Navy to steam to Canada and Australia if all else was lost, to defend the British Commonwealth and support the United States after Britain was gone, but Churchill told Roosevelt that the British would "fight on to the end in this island," very likely to the death of its leaders. If their successors "came in to parlay among the ruins" the fleet would be their only bargaining chip, and "no one would have the right to blame those then responsible if they made the best terms they could for the surviving inhabitants."

On May 19, in a rare burst of French élan, a colonel named Charles de Gaulle nearly took General Heinz Guderian's 2nd Panzer Division headquarters with a few tanks before he was ordered to withdraw. On May 20, Wehrmacht spearheads reached the Channel and took Calais. The BEF made it back to its fortifications, but the Germans had surrounded two French armies, the Belgian army, and the BEF and pinned them against the sea. "Nothing but a miracle can save the BEF now," Brooke wrote, "and the end cannot be very far off!" Like many British officers, Brooke often called the Germans the Boche, a contagious French epithet, but far from despising them he marveled at their shattering assault on four great nations' armies defending their homes and families. "There is no doubt that they are the most wonderful soldiers."

Some of Brooke's peers took blows too hard to absorb. General Michael Barker suffered a nervous breakdown in command of I Corps. General Sir Henry Charles Loyd fainted and gave up his division's command. A key French general phoned Brooke in a foaming panic and abruptly disappeared. General Edmund Ironside, Chief of the Imperial General Staff, flew to France to coordinate plans with Generals Gaston Billotte and Georges Blanchard and discovered that they *had* no plans but to tremble and berate each other. Ironside took Billotte by the buttons and shook him. Brooke was sure the catastrophe would have broken him too had it not left him numb.

Late on the night of May 24–25, with the BEF "bent back like a long hairpin" across a hundred-mile front, the Belgians began to give way, and Gort prepared to fight his way to the Channel, more than forty miles up the narrow corridor still under Anglo-French control. Brooke and his fellow commanders contrived a desperate plan, never doubting it would take the hand of God to save a quarter of their men. There was no question of saving their vehicles and heavy weapons or British formations in Brittany. As the troops at the bottom of the BEF's lines moved north toward Dunkirk, four divisions facing west held off one German army while Brooke and four others facing east fought another with inferior tanks and artillery and .50 caliber bullets aimed at panzers that "bounced back like peas off a windowpane."

Violent death and terrible wounds ripped the BEF. With its phone lines down and radio transmissions banned to avoid interception, Brooke could only guess what was happening beyond his eyes, ears, and couriers. On the edge of his capacities, he projected calm command to the frightened young men around him, easing the fear of death with humor he could barely summon and confidence he did not feel. Huddled with Montgomery in a series of fragile command posts with "bombs flying about like wasps," an aide later wrote, Brooke rolled under a fence as dozens of German bombers flew low overhead. "Otherwise, he was really rather silly" with his personal safety.

Near a village called Le Paradis, ninety-nine British infantrymen who had slowed a German advance ran out of ammunition and surrendered to an SS company who machine-gunned and bludgeoned them to death. Other SS troops matched their crime. As another British unit moved up a rural lane past hundreds of families fleeing through the fields, a flight of Stukas spreading panic ignored the helpless troops, attacked the screaming crowd on one side of the path, swung around to hit the other, and blithely flew away. Elsewhere, a teenaged English soldier spotted three women's corpses in a field. Looking away from their faces, he pulled them to the side of the road, put two dead children in their arms, and cried his way back to his unit.

On May 27, Churchill relieved Ironside and replaced him as Chief of the Imperial General Staff with Dill, who soon advised Lord Gort that the War Office was chaotic, "and I'm not sure that Winston isn't the greatest menace." He was "full of ideas, many brilliant, but most of them impracticable. He has such drive and personality that no one seems able to stand up to him." Least of all the cautious Jack Dill, soon known to Churchill out of earshot as "Dilly-Dally."

On the same day Dill took over the War Office, Charles de Gaulle, now the youngest brigadier general in the French army, led a successful counterattack before he was forced to withdraw, and Brooke began to lead the BEF's I and II Corps to Dunkirk, pushing through broken French troops fit for nothing but blocking the roads. After Brooke left his driver at the gate of his temporary headquarters and rushed in to grab some papers he returned to find a body in the gutter. "They have just shot that chap," an officer said. A lawless band of French soldiers had called him a spy and killed him for his cognac.

With the Germans in position to pour through a gap between the British and Belgian armies and roll up the retreating British column, Brooke ordered Montgomery to lead his 3rd Division thirty-six miles up a country road in the dark, slip past three embattled divisions, and fill the deadly hole. Headlights out, every man behind the wheel of a staff car, lorry, or troop carrier followed the axle in front of him, painted white so he could see it. As Brooke watched Monty's division move "down a pergola of artillery," it seemed to plod along at a heavy-footed nightmare pace. A single flight of bombers could be fatal.

Under fire from his rear and both flanks, Brooke kept his column moving north, anxiously scanning the sky, leapfrogging battered formations to cover gaps and losses, resting one division while stretching another, edging through waves of refugees. The Belgians surrendered on May 28, exposing the BEF's flank, but Montgomery linked up with a French division and the defensive line held. Reduced by deaths and wounds, penetrated in several places, Brooke's 5th Division, "thank God," had "held on by its eyelids." As Brooke neared the sea, pushing exhausted troops, sliding depleted units like bleeding chessmen from one spot to another, the BEF's artillery held the enemy at bay with what little help the Royal Air Force, the intrepid RAF, could give.

At a meeting of senior cabinet members in London, Churchill reviewed the BEF's desperate plight and "all that was in the balance," and then said, "quite casually, and not treating it as a point of special significance," that of course whatever happened at Dunkirk "we shall fight on." Some of his colleagues rushed to his side, shouting and slapping his back.

In sight of the Channel on May 29, hardly believing he had saved the great bulk of his command, let alone the entire BEF, Brooke was ordered home ahead of them, too valuable to be risked, and could not talk his way into staying. As his column reached Dunkirk under constant bombardment, frantic men clawed the sand, wounded planes fell into the sea, and Brooke stayed to plan a defensive perimeter and keep his troops in order. A thrown-together medley of warships, merchantmen, fishing boats, and yachts, the unsinkable "Mosquito Armada" as Churchill called it later, was coming to take them home.

Churchill insisted on saving as many French troops as possible, which complicated things. Brooke ordered a French division under his command to cover his flank as II Corps was evacuated and was told that General Blanchard had ordered them to evacuate ten miles away. Brooke wrote an order to Blanchard not to move the division until midnight and had it delivered with a message. If he disobeyed the order, Brooke would do his best to have him shot.

After all Brooke could do had been done without contempt for his orders to evacuate, he shook Montgomery's hand and broke down in tears on his shoulder. An hour before dark he was carried to an open boat on the back of his aide Captain Albany Kennett Charlesworth, the Eton- and Oxford-educated son of a member of Parliament. Helped by a younger officer, they paddled to a British destroyer that lingered and was strafed for hours as exhausted troops tried to reach it, some successfully, some not, before it pulled away full of prayerful men. Only after reaching

Dover in the morning was Brooke informed that his son, half dead when he saw him last, had been safely evacuated.

Almost afraid to believe that a terrifying dream was over, Brooke went home to Benita, their children, and their country house in Hampshire, amazed by the simple ordinariness of it all, and slept for a day and a half. Waking up on June 2 to a charming English spring, bright with the thrill of deliverance, he was driven to London to report to the Chief of the Imperial General Staff, walked with light steps into Dill's office, and asked where he was wanted. The answer barely registered: Lead a second expeditionary force to France.

"To be sent back into that cauldron," Brooke wrote, was not to have a chance to win but to waste young lives for nothing. Nonetheless, the orders came from Churchill and could not be argued away. Brooke proposed to refit two of his divisions and return with seasoned troops, but Dill said there was no time. He would lead what remained of Britain's only armored division and the 51st (Highland) Division, both still in France, and two formations yet to leave England, the 52nd (Lowland) Division and a division of fresh Canadians, the only equipped divisions the British had left.

Dill told Brooke that Secretary of State for War Anthony Eden wished to see him. A highly polished product of Eton, Oxford, Parliament, and the Great War, the very model of a handsome English gentleman, Eden asked Brooke if he was satisfied with everything being done for him. "I think I astonished him," Brooke wrote. He was anything but satisfied, he said. His mission might have political value, which was not for him to judge, but it could only be a military disaster.

Charles de Gaulle flew to London on June 9 as France's undersecretary of state for war, seeking help in the form of the RAF. Churchill was impressed by this audacious young general stepping out from a crowd of beaten old men, six feet five and confidence itself. As he circled the Cabinet Room, towering over its occupants, distinguished British statesmen stroked an ego that needed no stroking, for no one admired Charles de Gaulle more than Charles de Gaulle. Churchill withheld any part of the RAF, Britain's only hope to repel invasion, but de Gaulle flew home convinced that the British, "led by such a fighter, would certainly not flinch. Mr. Churchill seemed to me to be equal to the rudest task, provided it also had greatness."

On one of Churchill's last-ditch trips to France, a senior British general took the measure of de Gaulle. "A strange-looking man, enormously tall," he captured the room with his height and held it sitting down, owing nothing to good looks. "No chin, a long, drooping, elephantine nose over a closely-cut moustache," an elongated head under "sparse black hair lying flat and neatly parted," thick lips on a small mouth that pouted as he swung his head slightly from side to side in search of the right word, understanding English but speaking it imperfectly. "His heavily hooded eyes were very shrewd." Churchill's physician Sir Charles Wilson considered him "an improbable creature, like a human giraffe, sniffing down his nostrils at mortals beneath his gaze."

In the first part of June, German armor mauled most of what was left of the French army, and Britain's 51st (Highland) Division was surrounded and forced to surrender. The French government abandoned Paris on June 10. Churchill flew to France the next day with Eden, Ismay, and Dill, met with Premier Reynaud, members of his government, and senior French generals near Orleans, and solemnly denied their plea to throw the RAF into the fight, for Britain's survival depended on its preservation. Churchill pledged that the British would fight on, exhorted the French leaders to defend their capital, and was told it would do no good to make Paris a ruin. The French were resigned to defeat.

Returning to the airfield on June 12 for their flight back to London, Churchill said to Ismay in a private talk between two old friends that it would seem "we fight alone." Energized by the thought of controlling their own fate against unnerving odds, Ismay said he was glad of it, and "we'll win the Battle of Britain." Churchill gave him a look. "You and I will be dead in three months' time."

"Quite possibly," Ismay replied, "but we'll have a hell of a good time those last seven days," which Churchill seemed to accept as a point well taken.

Not for publication, Ismay told a trusted American writer after the war, in essence, that when Churchill had pledged in his famous June 4, 1940, speech to fight the invading Germans on the beaches, in the streets, and in the hills, with victory the ultimate outcome, his words "were bold and brave, but he did not really believe the final hypothesis."

On the same day Churchill predicted his execution, Brooke watched Benita disappear around a corner and boarded at Southampton a filthy Dutch steamer bound for Cherbourg. Back in the same bad dream, he was driven through a terrified sea of refugees to Le Mans, where the French supreme commander, General Maxime Weygand, who had just met with Churchill, advised him of two developments. The French army had ceased to exist as a fighting force, and Brooke had been ordered to try to save Brittany by forming a line in front of Rennes. "Quite impossible," Brooke replied. He had nowhere near enough troops. Weygand agreed.

Brooke briefed Dill by phone, asked him to stop shipping troops across the Channel, which Dill had already done, and urged the evacuation of all British forces still in France. Dill called him back. The scheme to save Brittany was off. A second evacuation would begin. Brooke issued orders to every British and Canadian unit in France to start for the coast at once, but for the battered armored division, which would cover the withdrawal as best it could.

Dill phoned Brooke that night at his château headquarters on a barely audible line. With his ear pressed to the receiver, Brooke described the evacuation orders he had given, and Dill stunned him again. "The Prime Minister does not want you to do that," he said.

"What the hell does he want?"

"He wants to speak to you," Dill said, and handed the phone to Churchill. It was Brooke's first encounter with the prime minister, who told him he had been sent to France to fight, to make the French feel the

British were with them. Long past the point of deference, Brooke said a corpse could not be made to feel. The French army was dead, and more British deaths could not revive it. Churchill fought back and implied several times that Brooke had lost his nerve, which tested Brooke's ability to contain himself.

As Brooke battled Churchill, whose voice he could barely hear, he glanced out a window at two good Scots, old friends both, sitting on a bench in the garden. Major General James Syme Drew, a rich industrialist's son decorated for gallantry at the Battle of Loos in 1916, led the 52nd (Lowland) Division. Major General Sir John Noble Kennedy, a wounded Great War veteran in command of the division's artillery, was one of many children of a poor Church of Scotland minister, a likable man with five young children of his own who shared Brooke's love of birds and their walks in the woods with field glasses. As Brooke found the strength to resist Winston Churchill, he kept his friends in sight and focused on their lives and the lives of the youths they led as he attacked the prime minister's plan to make the French feel better. "You've lost one Scottish division," he said. "Do you want to lose another?" Churchill kept fighting until he ran out of steam. "All right," he finally said. "I agree with you."

Churchill's verbal storms broke many strong men, but a cabinet member envied Brooke's "great gift" of letting it all wash over him and "shaking himself like a dog coming out of the water." Having learned that Churchill's massive will and skill for argument had to be experienced before one could know what it took to resist, Brooke redoubled his orders and performed a second miracle. For four days and nights he let no man stay in France an hour longer than it took to get him out, but for the covering armor. Over 130,000 troops were evacuated.

Dill phoned Brooke on June 17 to tell him the French had stopped fighting, and Brooke got his staff on a wretched trawler bound for Plymouth, hoping the Luftwaffe would think it not worth bombing. The port was bombed three times before they sailed. Having rescued hundreds of survivors from His Majesty's Transport *Lancastria*, lost that day with more than 3,000 souls, the trawler's deck was fouled with oil-soaked clothes and gear. On the way across the Channel, a crewman who had pulled drowning men from the sea kept shouting about saving people and had to be held down.

Exhausted on the squalid deck, Brooke absorbed what he and his men had endured in his two French expeditions. It might have been politically sound to support an allied army to the end, he wrote, even as a sacrificial gesture, but any troops left in France would have been lost, and probably Great Britain too. More than 11,000 British soldiers were dead, over 14,000 wounded, and 41,000 imprisoned, but almost 225,000 had been saved, the indispensable core of the British Army. While Brooke steamed for home, Churchill addressed the nation. The Battle of France was over. The Battle of Britain had begun. Its people would persevere, "if necessary alone," and if the British Empire should last a thousand years, this would be their finest hour.

Churchill's inspired courage was crucial to its survival, but Britain might not last a hundred days. Brooke was tasked with defending southern England against an invasion most professionals thought would come within weeks and end British history. With no allies but its own dominions, driven out of France in its first match with the Wehrmacht, all but stripped of heavy arms, the British Army had lost or abandoned thousands of artillery pieces, tanks, and antiaircraft guns and mountains of ammunition to a ruthless, seemingly unstoppable enemy. For Brooke, the strength to project undaunted leadership and utter confidence while "wracked with doubts as to the soundness of one's dispositions" was almost too much to pray for.

As Britain faced national extinction, Brooke went to lunch at Downing Street and found Churchill full of courage and plans to launch offensives. "I wonder whether any historian of the future will ever be able to paint Winston in his true colors," he asked himself later, a man of "the most marvelous qualities and superhuman genius," willfully deaf and blind when he chose to be, "quite the most difficult man to work with that I have ever struck, but I should not have missed the chance of working with him for anything on earth!"

One

SIBLING RIVALS

After the fall of France, baffled by Churchill's refusal to consider a favorable peace in what Hitler called Britain's "militarily hopeless situation," the Führer ordered the Luftwaffe to deplete the RAF and win air superiority over the Channel, a precondition to invasion. German fighter planes outnumbered Britain's two to one, but cutting-edge radar, superior British Spitfire and Hurricane fighters, and fewer than 3,000 brave young pilots destroyed German planes in astonishing numbers in the months-long Battle of Britain, forcing Hitler to cancel the invasion in September. Churchill told Parliament, "Never in the field of human conflict was so much owed by so many to so few."

The British were still on the ropes in November nonetheless, with the United States "neutral" in their corner and the Soviet Union's Joseph Stalin in league with Hitler, when Admiral Harold Stark, Roosevelt's chief of naval operations, presented five scenarios for a likely American war. The British Empire's survival was vital in every case. If the British Isles fell, "we would find ourselves acting alone and at war with the world." Only the United States could eventually hope to match the Wehrmacht's war power, and only by a stretch. Nothing would be left for a probable war against Japan but a purely defensive stand until Germany was subdued.

Victory would not be sure, but the odds were "in our favor, particularly if we insist upon full equality in the political and military direction of the war." Stark recommended secret talks with the British military and other potential allies.

Churchill cabled Roosevelt a few weeks later. With winter roiling the Channel, he wrote, Britain's risk of falling to "a swift, overwhelming blow" had much diminished, replaced by the threat of a slower death from a steady bleed of shipping inflicted by the German navy. If the maritime attrition cut the British off from food and fuel and the ability to move and sustain their troops, "we may fall by the way" and cost the United States the time it needed to defend itself. Roosevelt read the message on a fishing cruise with Harry Hopkins.

Harry L. Hopkins, the up-front, unkempt, chain-smoking son of an Iowa harness maker, had begun his climb to power in 1912 as a nearly unpaid social worker in a New York City slum. Fresh from Grinnell College and its social justice mission, tall, gaunt, and brilliant, Hopkins had risen through the staffs of the American Red Cross, the Association for Improving the Condition of the Poor, and the New York Tuberculosis Association, a driven young man, its director said, who looked as if he slept in a hayloft. By 1933 he was Roosevelt's alter ego and the second man in Washington, so close to FDR he could read his nuanced thoughts in the subtleties of his eyebrows.

As governor of New York, Roosevelt had spotted Harry's skills at the head of a state relief agency and called him to Washington in 1933 to lead its federal counterpart through the ditch of the Great Depression. Almost overnight, Hopkins became a New Deal czar and FDR's key advisor on everything that mattered, foreign and domestic, military and civilian, a straight-talking, fast-learning star who could sort wheat from chaff at a glance and clear every hurdle but his health. In 1937 radical stomach cancer surgery saved him from death but not from chronic pain, malnutrition, and a debilitating blood disease. Roosevelt made him secretary of commerce nonetheless and groomed him as his successor until a close-run fight for his life forced his resignation. Frail before his time, he called himself "a bright young man who has spent five months in bed."

As the blitzkrieg fell on the BEF in 1940, Hopkins was still unwell when Roosevelt called him to his study to weigh Churchill's cries for help. Asked to come to dinner and spend the night, he lived and worked in the White House for the following three and a half years with FDR's perfect confidence. The president's chief of staff, Admiral William D. Leahy, enjoyed teasing Harry for his liberal views, "Pinko" he sometimes called him, and prized their collaborative friendship. "Hopkins had an excellent mind," Leahy later wrote. "His manner of approach was direct, and nobody could fool him, not even Churchill."

On December 29, 1940, newly reelected by an isolationist public, Roosevelt told the nation in a radio address that Nazi domination threatened the United States and would leave the world "no liberty, no religion, no hope." America must become "the arsenal of democracy." On January 10, 1941, a bill was introduced in Congress to authorize the president to lend or lease weapons and supplies to any nation whose defense he deemed essential to American security. By and large, "lend" and "lease" were legal fictions, without which the British were doomed.

In 1918, as assistant secretary of the navy at thirty-six, Roosevelt had met Churchill, Britain's minister of munitions, at a London dinner. Seven years his senior, Churchill had snubbed the less important man, and Roosevelt had not forgotten. Despite a cordial correspondence begun in 1939, informal reports to FDR that Churchill thought little of him and less of his New Deal did not amuse the president. Before he threw his country's thin resources into Britain's defense, he wanted Hopkins to take a sharp look at Churchill, Britain's will to win, and her chances to survive. He was sending Harry to London, he told a cabinet member, to "talk to Churchill like an Iowa farmer."

Hopkins was greeted in London with white-glove service and an air raid. Before he went to Churchill, he spoke with an American diplomat over antiaircraft fire. "We want to help them to the limit," he said, but the president wanted proof that the British were giving their all. When the CBS radio correspondent Edward R. Murrow asked Hopkins why he was in London, he supposed he had come as "a catalytic agent between two prima donnas."

Churchill had never heard of Harry Hopkins but gave him lunch at 10 Downing Street, bomb-damaged top to bottom, and quickly grasped his mission, for "here was an envoy from the President of supreme importance to our life." Hopkins looked him steadily in the eye. "The President is determined that we shall win the war together," he said. "Make no mistake about it. He will carry you through no matter what happens to him." Deeply moved by this oddly compelling man, visibly frail and uncommonly strong, fueled by Scotch and Chesterfields, Churchill promised him every fact, figure, and opinion he wanted. Britain would persevere with American help that would keep the RAF in command of the air, the prime minister said, "and then Germany with all her armies will be finished." Attuned to American fears of being pulled into another war, Churchill insisted that "this war will never see great forces massed against one another."

Hopkins told a friend he had never been so riveted. "God, what a force that man has." Churchill took him on a fact-finding tour, convinced him of British resolve, and charmed him with his family. "If you just came into a room and saw him sitting there," Churchill's daughter-in-law said of Harry, "you would feel sorry for him until he began to speak." Having worked and relaxed with FDR for years, Hopkins saw a telling difference in the two great men. Roosevelt did his job with detached serenity and shed his burdens at the cocktail hour, but tranquility was unknown to the prime minister. Wherever Churchill was, there was the battlefield.

On January 21, 1941, two American staff officers set an agenda for a secret rendezvous with the British, intending an assignation, not a marriage. "Never absent from British minds," they wrote, "are their postwar interests, commercial and military. We should likewise safeguard our own." Brave and more experienced these imperialists might be, but "We cannot afford, nor do we need, to entrust our national future to British direction."

It was on that wary ground that covert talks began in Washington, code-named "ABC" for American-British Conversations. For three furtive months, five senior British officers disguised in civilian clothes conferred with their U.S. counterparts. The Lend-Lease bill was pending on Capitol Hill, where news of active plans to send American boys to fight an English war could kill it. The British delegation began with the proposition that an Anglo-American war against Japan was probable, but Germany, the far stronger enemy and an existential threat, must be beaten first. As Churchill later wrote, Japan's defeat would not cripple Germany, but Hitler's would make "the finishing off of Japan merely a matter of time and trouble." On this the Americans agreed, but not on ways and means.

Reviving a centuries-old strategy, the British had a naval power's plan to defeat a stronger land power and avoid the horrific losses they had suffered in the last war. Deploying land, air, and sea power in the Mediterranean, the Middle East, and elsewhere on the German periphery, they would make the enemy spread his forces thin and wear him down by bombing, blockade, raids, and blows around the edges until he was weak enough to invade if invasion proved necessary. In sharp contrast, American doctrine was rooted in the bludgeoning style of Ulysses S. Grant. Americans won their wars with enormous wealth, industry, manpower, and hubris. They built a powerful army when the need arose, attacked the enemy's strength as quickly as possible, and took and inflicted casualties until he stopped struggling. Anything less was a distraction.

Two weeks after Roosevelt signed the Lend-Lease Act and made Hopkins its administrator, the ABC participants produced a secret report defining common ground and accommodating differences. Both nations quietly set up military missions in the other's capital with the long-range cooperation of Generals Dill and George C. Marshall, the United States Army's chief of staff.

•   •   •

George Catlett Marshall was born to modest wealth and local prominence on the last day of 1880 in Uniontown, Pennsylvania, a coke-producing town near the West Virginia border where Civil War veterans ran things, Civil War generals owned them, and character was their currency. Northern or Southern origins had little to do with friendship or success. George's regal, loving mother had wellborn Virginia roots and so did his popular father, a coke and iron entrepreneur whose three older brothers had fought for the Confederacy. An important man in town, he was proud of his collateral ancestor the great Chief Justice John Marshall and a bit too fond of respect.

Privileged though it was, George's boyhood was touched with a whiff of Mark Twain. Fishing with his friends, hauling hay for fun, concocting rustic pranks at the head of the local miscreants with a certain detached reserve, more impressed by family lore of a pirate in its past than its kinship with a Founding Father, he could have been Tom Sawyer were it not for the maid and the cook. He showed no love of learning at the local private academy and neither did its genteel mistress, more concerned about breeding than reading. Removed to public school, he found himself behind, a condition that chafed his pride. "If it was history," he recalled in old age, "that was all right; I could star in history," and George Catlett Marshall wanted stardom.

On the edge of impressive riches, his father sold his business when George was ten and put the profits in a speculative venture that collapsed, dropping the family lifestyle from prosperous to pinched. When they dined at a modest hotel, Mrs. Marshall would ask for kitchen scraps, to feed the dogs she said. George picked them up at closing time, and the shame never quite burned off.

In 1897 a 25,000-man army with no enemies was not an obvious choice for a budding star's career, but George was enticed for reasons lost even to him when he thought about it decades later. Barred from West Point by spotty grades and local politics, he followed his older brother to the Virginia Military Institute, a uniformed, stiff-necked affair whose heroes were young Confederates killed as cadets at the Battle of New Market in 1864. When George overheard his brother beg his mother not to send him to VMI for fear that the family slacker would blot the Marshall name, he "decided right then I was going to wipe his eye."

Admitted on the strength of his "great Virginia name," Marshall found at VMI the life he was meant to live, an exacting life of discipline, he later said, and "the problem of managing men." His academic grades were middling, his performance in command superb. Honored every year as the top cadet officer in his class, speaking in a voice that expected to be obeyed, he bore down academically, finished fifth in civil engineering, led the football team as an All-Southern 145-pound tackle, and married Lily Coles, a Virginia society belle. Looking back, he understood that "ambition had set in."

Commissioned in 1902, Marshall was sent to an infantry regiment suppressing the Philippine Insurrection, arrived a few days after its leader surrendered, chased diehards through the jungle, and never heard an angry shot. After a year and a half in the Oklahoma Territory that challenged his choice of careers he won a coveted spot at the Army staff school in Leavenworth, Kansas, graduated first in his class, and distinguished himself as a stony-faced instructor. When the United States declared war on Germany in April 1917 Marshall was a captain on the staff of the unprepared 1st Division. Two months later he persuaded its commander, General William L. Sibert, to take him as his aide on a troopship bound for Europe with a deck gun and no ammunition. Sibert was the first American soldier to step ashore in France. Marshall was the second.

Barely trained in basic drill, let alone in savage trench warfare, the division set up camp under the overall command of General John J. Pershing, who observed a botched attack on a mock trench and expressed himself to the staff. "He just gave everybody hell." When Marshall began to speak, Pershing brushed him off and turned away. To the horror of his friends, the angry captain put a hand on the angry general's arm and stopped him, "mad all over." Pershing heard him out on the division's equipment shortage and constraints imposed by Pershing's staff and told him he must appreciate the Army's difficulties. "We have them every day," Marshall said, "and they have to be solved before night." He expected retribution, but Pershing sought him out for the unpaved truth whenever he came again.

Working from a château basement under artillery fire that hit "like the end of the world," Marshall planned the movements of the first Americans in combat in France. He often rode horseback through shelling, operated behind enemy lines at night, found himself in combat in a fight for a French village, and earned a Silver Star, a Distinguished Service Medal, four battle stars, and three quick promotions. In collaboration with the French as chief of operations of the adjacent American army, he helped design the offensives that won the war and contrived rapid movements that the Supreme Allied Commander General Ferdinand Foch had thought impossible. "The Wizard," Foch called him. Masterful though it was, all of his work was tactical and logistic, none of it strategic.

At the victory celebrations in London, Colonel Marshall escorted Winston Churchill, Britain's secretary of state for war, who all but ignored him. The Americans had contributed 3,000 decorated troops to the parade, but when Marshall fished for compliments, Churchill only grunted. With Prohibition in the wings in America, the Englishman finally turned to his escort as the Yanks marched by: "What a magnificent body of men," he said, "and never to look forward to another drink."

As the postwar Army's chief of staff, Pershing made Marshall his aide, a powerful learning experience. Next came Tianjin, China, a great commercial city protected from bandits and civil war by Japanese, European, and U.S. troops. Overmatched by French at VMI, Marshall attacked Chinese and acquired a certain fluency. In 1927 he joined the War College faculty in Washington, where Lily died of heart failure. A childless, cheerless widower at forty-five, Marshall lost himself in work at the Infantry School at Fort Benning, Georgia, and met his second wife, Katherine Boyce Tupper Brown, a veteran of the London stage, the Kentucky-born widow of a wealthy Baltimore lawyer shot by a disappointed client.

Marshall won his first star in 1936, leading and instructing men in a skeleton peacetime army, and rose with stunning speed and "seldom smiling" eyes. Named chief of the Army's War Plans Division in 1938, he was deputy chief of staff three months later. Never the chummy type, he distanced himself still further in high command, called colleagues and subordinates by their last names or ranks, almost never Tom or Bill, and expected to be called General Marshall even by friends.

With a second world war in the wind, Roosevelt called a dozen VIPs to the White House and declared his firm intention to expand the Army's airpower at the cost of its strength on the ground. Marshall later recalled how every bobbing head agreed in turn that the president's plan was sound. Then he "finally came around to me" with a familiar form of address that would have flattered almost anyone. "Don't you think so, George?" Marshall replied with an ice blue stare. "I am sorry, Mr. President, but I don't agree with that at all." Roosevelt was startled, and "that ended the conference." Marshall later recalled that after they left the room his colleagues "all bade me goodbye," but his candor had raised his stock. Even so, though Roosevelt trusted and admired Marshall they never warmed to each other. A hard man to warm to, the general's reaction to the sound of his first name was not lost on his commander in chief. "I don't think he ever did it again."

When the Army's chief of staff retired in 1939, Roosevelt summoned Marshall and told him he had the job. Rather than melting in gratitude, Marshall replied that he wanted to say what he thought "and it would often be unpleasing." Was that all right? FDR said of course, and Marshall poked him again: "You said 'yes' pleasantly, but it may be unpleasant." The president took the risk. "Never got too friendly with Roosevelt," Marshall said years later, "made a point of never laughing at his jokes." He may have been the only man in America who avoided invitations to Hyde Park, the president's inherited Hudson River estate. His detachment cost him influence, offset by his closeness to Harry Hopkins, to whom he owed his post. The United States Army's air wing was not a separate service like the RAF or the Luftwaffe, but Marshall made its commander Major General Henry H. Arnold his deputy and a de facto chief of staff, a longtime friend he trusted implicitly.

Marshall took command in the tired old Munitions Building on the Washington Mall and set about the task of turning a feeble army into an earthshaking force of millions of well-trained men. A clear, careful thinker but no intellectual, he was steeped in "the practice of arms," he later said, "and not the theory." Like most American flag officers of his day, he was strong on tactics, organization, and logistics, light on strategy, politics, and foreign affairs. Relying on forty years of disciplined study, rigorous planning, and strong advisors, he was never mistaken for an orator but took charge of a room by walking into it, in full command of the language, the facts, and his point. Any officer who slouched or tried a wisecrack in his presence regretted it on the spot, and a "foul mouth" was anathema. "He could laugh," a subordinate later recalled, "but he never gave evidence of a deep-seated pleasure in life" and no one got so far as "the beginnings of familiarity with George Catlett Marshall."

A merciless perfectionist who had seen horrific combat, he felt the "terrific strain" on the cusp of a world war and grew still less forgiving and companionable. It was said that his rage burned the paint off the walls, but officers who disappointed him met silence more often than anger and rarely got a second chance. He often showed kindness in private—after wartime trips abroad he always phoned the wives of officers he had seen—but suppressed it in command. "Once in the machine," he told a friend, "it is very difficult to spare anybody, because I have to work fast and rather ruthlessly." Officers called to his office to present a report learned to sit without a word while he finished what he was reading, sometimes for minutes, start talking when he looked up, stay riveted on point, answer questions crisply without evasion or excuse, and expect an abrupt dismissal. No time was wasted on families or sports. "He made you want to do your best," a former subordinate said, which many felt they had not, a view he often shared. Long after the war another aide who admired him called Marshall "a cold, impersonal individual" who earned respect, not affection. "Men love to say, 'I was with Patton,'" the officer went on. No one bragged about being with Marshall.

Others relieved the burdens of command over drinks with trusted colleagues, but Marshall was short of confidants. He had a few old friends but did not make new ones easily or care very much to do so. Relief came in walks with Katherine, but even to her it often seemed "he lived outside himself, and George Marshall was someone he was constantly appraising, advising, and training to meet a situation." Comfortably fixed by prudent savings, sound investments, and marrying well, he enjoyed light movies, social conversation, and Katherine's Virginia estate. His clear blue eyes could turn a man cold with a glance, but he was old-school charm itself at anyone's dinner table. "A magnificent looking man, courtly and cultured," a senior British officer found him to be. He had long since learned to treat politics like cholera. When asked which party he supported he would say "Episcopalian."

Having learned to pace himself, he typically came to work at 7:30, was driven home and back for a half hour lunch with Katherine, left a clean desk at five, and rode almost every day, turning problems in his mind. His bedtime reading inclined to popular history and biography, Western novels, and undemanding magazines on the order of *Reader's Digest* and *The Saturday Evening Post.* He went to bed early and would only come to the phone after dinner for a shirt-on-fire crisis, which discouraged his staff from disturbing him, not always for the best.

Admiral Leahy, an unassuming man close to FDR, was the titular head of the Chiefs of Staff but Marshall overshadowed him with sheer force of character. No shrinking violet himself, the future secretary of state Dean Acheson would later call Marshall's presence "a striking and communicated force."

Throughout the Second World War, the United States Navy was blessed and cursed by the leadership of Admiral Ernest J. King. As a gifted naval strategist King had no peer in the world and no senior American officer was more despised. In 1942, Brigadier General Dwight D. Eisenhower shared a fantasy with his diary: "One thing that might help win this war is to get someone to shoot King." Rife with talent, drive, and courage, Eisenhower wrote, the chief of naval operations was a bully, uncooperative as a matter of principle, petty beyond belief, obnoxious by design.

After King led the Navy from catastrophe to victory in the biggest naval war in history, nothing was named in his honor but a single destroyer and a few obscure buildings. Leaders are not admired for viciousness as recreation, and King was a schoolyard punk in a hand-tailored Brooks Brothers uniform. Sometimes capable of grace, he almost seemed ashamed of it, seeing courtesy as a form of weakness. FDR's genial naval aide Captain John L. McCrea was naturally intrigued when King told him he had the makings of a good officer but for "one outstanding weakness." What was that? McCrea asked. "You are not a son of a bitch," the admiral replied. "A good naval officer has to be a son of a bitch."

Brigadier General Vivian Dykes, a youthful leading member of the British military delegation in Washington, was said to have "a particular capacity for friendship." By way of first impressions, Dykes thought King had "a magnificent face, and I should say is pretty good" but soon learned the price "of having in such a high position a man of great strength of character with a very small brain. He certainly is a bastard."

Dykes had King's malignity right, but his brain was as big as they come. What made it seem small was his belligerent, single-minded focus on Ernest J. King and the United States Navy. Just over six feet tall, bald on top, close cropped on the sides, King was wary of his alliance with the United States Army, let alone the Royal Navy. King was "always sore at everybody," Marshall later said, especially the British, always "ready to fuss with them or us." Another American general said "King wouldn't give anyone the time of day. He'd sell you the time of day, but he wouldn't give it to you."

Ambition came early to King, who declared in old age "I was born with the idea of running things." His father, a former Great Lakes seaman, was a railroad repair shop foreman in the blue-collar town of Lorain, Ohio, when Ernie was born in 1878 on the edge of Lake Erie. His mother's death in his teens he recorded without comment. Growing up around ships and machinery, attracted to the Navy by an article in a boys' magazine, he outscored dozens of young Ohioans in a competitive examination for admission to the Naval Academy, where working-class origins were rare. From that day forth, his single-minded goal was a calculating climb to the top of the Navy, which he gladly let everyone know.

When America went to war with Spain in 1898, King and a few other plebes finagled summer billets on the cruiser *San Francisco*, which drew fire without effect off Havana and made them Academy heroes. King was battalion commander in his final year, the highest-ranking cadet officer, a feat that launched careers, but to graduate first in one's class was to shoulder expectations, while third or fourth won the glow without the glare. King graduated fourth in 1901 and married Mattie Egerton, a chaperoned star on the Annapolis scene who put home and family first and showed little interest in her husband's career, a regrettable match for a man who cared for little else. An able junior officer, fond of carousing and philandering ashore and returning drunk and disorderly with an anchor tattoo on one arm and a dagger on the other, Ensign King often clashed with superiors who mistook his sense of manliness for "stubbornness, belligerence, and arrogant insubordination." Confinement for days to an ensign's tiny quarters was to "go under hatches." King went under hatches more than once.

An up-and-coming lieutenant nonetheless, King published an article in the United States Naval Institute's *Proceedings* that proposed important shipboard reforms, chided the Navy for "clinging to things because they are old," ruffled feathers in high nests, and won a gold medal for the best submission of the year, which did not change his view that his opinions, however ill-received by lesser minds, were invariably right. Many years after an advanced naval ordnance school rejected his application, he admitted a disqualifying flaw: "I think I was too smart."

In 1915, King won a spot on Vice Admiral Henry T. Mayo's staff. Two years later, when America entered the war with no major role for its fleet, he crossed the Atlantic with Mayo to liaise with the Royal Navy, whose class-conscious officers soured him on their tribe. As an observer on His Majesty's ships King rarely came under fire, but most

American naval officers never did, and he came home a captain with a Navy Cross. In prestigious command of the Naval Postgraduate School, he developed a new approach to officer training that has guided the Navy ever since.

After several years in skillful command of destroyers—the swift, agile warships thrilled him—King took command of the New London, Connecticut, submarine base and won national acclaim directing the recovery of a submarine lost at sea. In 1927 he learned to fly at forty-nine and was running the Norfolk Naval Air Station a year later. Having rounded all three of the Navy's bases—surface ships, submarines, and aviation—he took command in 1930 of the aircraft carrier *Lexington* and directed its majestic movements "with imperious disdain for nearby ships."

Protective of his sailors, forgiving of ensigns' mistakes, he would not sit still for a superior's slight but hardly ever praised his own officers, and then only grudgingly in private, and ripped them almost violently in front of whoever was there. One of a group of Army officers observing flight operations on the *Lexington* never forgot how King gave a mid-ranking naval officer "immortal hell" in front of them. "It was embarrassing for us." King was the only man a colleague ever knew who would curse his subordinates. Small talk was foreign to him, humor almost vanishingly rare. A Marshall protégé who worked with King described them both as cold, impersonal men with a telling difference. Marshall rarely socialized with fellow officers and never embarrassed himself, but King wanted to be liked in a sophomoric way, despite his taste for tyranny. Unimpressed by Prohibition, he was one of the boys on liberty, sharing hip flasks with junior officers who loathed him and called him Uncle Ernie behind his back. Nimble hands under dinner party tables caused some of their wives to avoid him but he cuckolded brother officers when he could, sometimes flaunting the humiliation.

In 1932 King relinquished command of the *Lexington* and spent ten months at Newport's elite Naval War College. His thesis identified American altruism and democracy as weaknesses, elected officeholders' interference in war as a misfortune, and Britain as a hostile sea power.

Promoted to rear admiral in 1933, he commanded a dozen seaplane patrol squadrons and pressed his pilots to fly beside him through deadly weather as war would have them do. After a terrifying flight through an ice storm, he pressed a squadron commander to tell him what he had been thinking. The pilot said he had been wondering "whether you knew enough to be scared."

In 1938, King reached the rank of vice admiral in command of the carrier fleet, in sight of his ultimate goal, but Roosevelt crushed his hopes in 1939 by making Admiral Stark chief of naval operations. Nonetheless, the president liked salty old sea dogs. Early in 1941, as German surface ships and submarines—U-boats they were called, *Unterseeboots* in German—devastated British shipping, FDR created a new Atlantic Fleet, gave it to King, and made him a four-star admiral.

From his office in the worn-out Navy Building next to Marshall's matching post on the Washington Mall, King worked himself closer to FDR than Marshall ever wished to be, but the admiral's contempt for democracy was exceptional even in the officer corps, where right-wing opinions were the norm. In an ideal America, King said, civilians would be told nothing about a war until it ended, and then only who had won.

On June 22, 1941, Hitler broke his nonaggression pact with Stalin and sent three and a half million troops across the Russian border. The British were relieved that the blow had not fallen on them, but the Red Army's chances looked slim despite its massive size and Russia's vast spaces. Hopkins flew to Moscow to measure Stalin's will and stopped on the way in London, where he met Major General John Noble Kennedy, General Brooke's Scottish birdwatching friend. "I took to him at once," Kennedy wrote. He spoke "with great intelligence and spirit, though he looked a physical wreck."

Sitting in the sun in the garden at 10 Downing Street, Hopkins told Churchill that Roosevelt would like to meet him "in some lonely bay or other." The prime minister needed no coaxing. After Hopkins flew back from Moscow in an RAF bomber, Churchill left for Newfoundland in the battleship *Prince of Wales* with his Chiefs of Staff to rendezvous with Roosevelt and his. They brought Harry with them.

On August 9, 1941, Roosevelt welcomed Churchill to King's flagship, where what Churchill later called "a dear and cherished friendship" began. Nearly as important, Dill and Marshall bonded on the spot. Dill was a careful, honorable man steeped in the art of the possible, a good match for Marshall but no match for Churchill, who a British general said was "always expecting rabbits to come out of empty hats." When King hosted lunch Churchill seemed to him to be doing all the talking, Roosevelt all the listening.

Meeting separately from the politicians, the well-prepared British Chiefs of Staff, far more experienced in modern warfare than their American peers after more than a year of fighting Hitler alone, tried to sell them on Britain's peripheral war against Germany. The Americans had prepared nothing, contributed little, and caught a whiff of imperial condescension three centuries old. While their Chiefs of Staff conferred, Roosevelt and Churchill prepared for public release a stately set of goals for a secure, self-governing world. Scorned in many quarters as an old-time imperialist, Churchill wrote proudly years later that the Atlantic Charter, as the seminal declaration of Anglo-American values was called, "was in its first draft a British production cast in my own words."

On Sunday morning the Americans came aboard the *Prince of Wales* for religious services. Roosevelt and Churchill sat side by side under four of the battleship's massive guns, surrounded by a standing congregation composed of their Chiefs of Staff and hundreds of British and American sailors and marines. Chaplains of both nations read familiar prayers from a pulpit draped with the Stars and Stripes and the Union Jack in identical shades of red, white, and blue. Churchill had chosen hymns well known to the English-speaking world, and the young men who sang them moved him. "Every word seemed to stir the heart. It was a great hour to live. Nearly half of those who sang were soon to die."

•   •   •

To his military staff, Churchill was a brilliant child with a scowl and a cigar, letting no one sleep through the night. Jack Dill, never ruthless or audacious enough for the prime minister, had exhausted himself through the grim spring and summer of 1940, his wife's prolonged death, and an unbroken string of defeats, none of them attributable to him. In a sharp exchange with Dill, Churchill said "it isn't only the good boys who help win wars. It is the sneaks and the stinkers as well." Dill was a notorious good boy, and when it came to a war for survival, Churchill was partial to stinkers. Brooke was partial to Dill, "the essence of straightforward-ness, blessed with the highest of principles and an unassailable integrity of character. I do not believe that any of these characteristics appealed to Winston."

British officers were obliged to retire at sixty, which Churchill waived for several favorites but not for Dill. On Sunday, November 16, 1941, Brooke built a goat cart for his children and was summoned to Che-quers, the Tudor country house at the disposal of prime ministers. Dill was a tired man, Churchill said, and he wanted to promote him to field marshal, relieve him as Chief of the Imperial General Staff on Christmas Day, his sixtieth birthday, make him governor of Bombay, and replace him with Brooke as CIGS. Knowing that Dill would be crushed, Brooke could not prevent it, and Churchill's tone could not have been kinder. Brooke had never sought or even wanted the position, and it took him a moment to accept. The very thought of failure was unspeakable, and the weight of the job knocked the wind out of him. He was not an exception-ally religious man but when Churchill left the room, Brooke knelt and prayed to God.

Dill was predictably gracious, and Brooke turned the War Office upside down. To the joy of General Kennedy, his director of military operations, he "infected" the place with vitality, but others found him less than a workplace dream. He strode into the War Office like Henry V at Agincourt with a "gobble like an irate turkey" and a habit of snapping pencils in half while telling startled generals "I *flatly* disagree."

A London hostess invited him to her country house with Churchill.

"I don't know how he is going to get on with Winston," she wrote, for they spent the afternoon on a sofa, and Brooke "seemed all the time to be saying, 'No, no, sir, you can't.'" They skirmished almost daily in the underground Cabinet War Rooms. Sometimes after Brooke crossed him Churchill would turn to General Ismay with a hand cupped to his ear: "I cannot hear what he says." Ismay would repeat it, loudly enough for the room. "Oh," Churchill would say. "*Oh!* So that's what he says. *Oh!* I see," and say no more. As the meeting wound down, having had time to think about it, he would grab it by the throat like a Doberman Pinscher.

Churchill had served in his military youth with two of Brooke's older brothers. "I know these Brookes," he said, "stiff-necked Ulstermen, and there's no one worse to deal with than that," good friends though they had been. "When I thump the table," he wrote of Alan Brooke, "and push my face towards him, what does he do? Thumps the table harder and glares back at me."

"Dear Brookie," Churchill called him.

On December 10, 1941, three days after the Japanese attacked Pearl Harbor, Hong Kong, and other British and American targets, Japanese torpedo planes sank the *Prince of Wales* and the battlecruiser HMS *Repulse* off the coast of Malaya, leaving 840 British dead and Japan in control of the South China Sea and ascendant in the Pacific in the first week of its war on the Anglo-American world. Though no treaty with Japan required it, Hitler and Italy's fascist dictator Benito Mussolini declared war on the United States on December 11, a triumph of hubris over reason. Relieved beyond words by American belligerency, Churchill left for Washington the next day on the battleship *Duke of York*. With him came a cast of junior and senior stars like the RAF's brilliant Chief of the Air Staff, Air Chief Marshal Sir Charles Frederick Algernon Portal, the aging First Sea Lord Admiral Sir Alfred Dudley Pickman Rogers Pound, and Field Marshal Dill, whom Brooke had persuaded Churchill to bring to Washington to head the British military mission, a rather more important post than Bombay. Admiral King soon described Dill correctly as "a kind of 'over-all' Chief of Staff for Mr. Churchill in Washington." Churchill left Brooke in London "to grip the tremendous problems that awaited him."

Besieged by such problems though all of them were, there was no more important need than to embrace and guide the Americans, without whom, Churchill knew, "nothing but ruin faced the world." With the American battleship fleet still settling at the bottom of Pearl Harbor it was natural for the American people, not to mention the American military, to throw everything they had at Japan and leave Hitler and Mussolini catastrophically to the Brits.

For three weeks after his party reached Washington on December 22, Churchill lived in the White House and worked on Roosevelt and Hopkins while their high commands conferred. Already close to Hopkins and comfortable with FDR, Churchill wooed the president shamelessly and nuzzled his evolving military views toward his own. Every evening before dinner, Churchill later wrote, "I wheeled him in his chair from the drawing room to the lift as a mark of respect and thinking also of Sir Walter Raleigh spreading his cloak before Queen Elizabeth. I formed a very strong affection, which grew with our years of comradeship." Roosevelt admired Churchill and his strategic expertise but never let him wonder which hand held the whip. Churchill called Roosevelt "Mr. President." To FDR the prime minister was "Winston."

Despite their developing bonds, Churchill the conservative imperialist and Roosevelt the liberal anticolonialist understood their national differences. In a broadcast to his desperate people earlier in the year, Churchill had given them hope of rescue by "the most powerful state and community in the world." The Americans spoke the same language, he said, "and very largely think the same thoughts, or anyhow think a lot of the same thoughts." Very largely was too much to say.

On December 26, not neglecting the need to bond with the American people and their elected representatives, Churchill addressed a joint session of Congress with his hands on his lapels and opened with a guaranteed laugh. If his father had been American and his mother British "instead of the other way around, I might have got here on my own." Excoriating Hitler, mocking Mussolini, he rocked the room when he came to the Japanese: "What kind of people do they think we are?"

The Anglo-American military brass, now brothers in arms and sibling rivals, made no specific plans at their Washington conference but sketched out a general strategy. Dependent though the British were on American wealth and military-industrial capacity, they played the elders' role after more than two years at war and more than two centuries as a great power. Roosevelt's naval aide, Captain McCrea, was duly impressed: The British "knew their stuff. They all talked exceedingly well and made much sense," and their military reports were "masterful." The Americans were a far less experienced team, but Roosevelt, King, and Marshall were no blushing freshmen and even King thought Hopkins "did a grand job" as referee. "He did a lot to keep the President on the beam and even more to keep Churchill on the beam. I've seldom seen a man whose head was screwed on so tight." Not for nothing would Churchill later say that Hopkins should be raised to the British nobility and dubbed "Lord Root of the Matter."

To their great relief, Marshall told the British that Germany was still the prime American enemy, but disputed their peripheral strategy in the Mediterranean and other "subsidiary theaters." Sooner or later the war must be won by crushing the German armies on the Continent, preceded by a cross-Channel attack, though none had succeeded since 1066, let alone against the Wehrmacht. Years later, Marshall said his team understood that a landing in France risked catastrophe. They were simply convinced, American style, that they could do it, which the British did not find compelling.

Two weeks after their guests arrived, their welcome had worn thin for Brigadier General Eisenhower, a rising Marshall protégé, a cardplaying, chain-smoking Kansan with a winning smile, new to Washington and his assignment as a senior Army war planner. His request to fight in France had been denied in 1917, and he had climbed the ladder steadily as a politically astute staff officer. True to form, Marshall called him Eisenhower, but his friends liked Ike, and he spoke for his fellow planners in his diary: "The conversations with the British grow wearisome. They're difficult to talk to, apparently afraid someone is trying to tell them what to do and how to do it." As for their peripheral strategy, "Their practice of war is dilatory."

Their pitch to capture French North Africa landed well with FDR nonetheless, for the region had long since struck him as easy pickings and a chance to get the French back into the war. Under the terms of their 1940 armistice with the French, the Germans occupied the northern half of France and a wide swath along the rest of its Atlantic coast. The remainder was governed quasi-independently from the resort town of Vichy under Marshal Philippe Pétain, an octogenarian hero of World War I whose fascist regime kept France's fleet and colonial empire, including nearly all of Northwest Africa and its 125,000 troops and 200,000 reservists, most of them native to the region, all of them led by French officers. Lacking sensible alternatives, Roosevelt's government had recognized the Vichy government to preserve American influence and communications with the French, including their governors and military leaders in North and West Africa.

In the end, after much contentious debate in Washington, some of it well heated, the Anglo-Americans agreed that only "the minimum forces necessary" should be diverted to the Pacific until Germany was defeated. A European offensive would almost surely be premature in 1942 but might be possible in 1943. In the meantime, the "closing and tightening of the ring around Germany" would include a heavy bombing campaign, material support for the hard-pressed Russians, and "gaining possession of the whole North African coast" in 1942. This was broadly British thinking, soon to be challenged by further Japanese advances, but thanks to their vast potential power and Marshall's organizational skills, the Americans prevailed in the pivotal sphere of command and control, having started from something like chaos.

Just turned forty-three, temporarily blinded in his teens by a mustard gas attack in France, the popular, Cambridge-educated Brigadier

General Vivian Dykes led the British military mission's secretariat in Washington, where he had come to understand that the U.S. Army and Navy had a "long history, proudly nurtured, of mutual suspicion and rivalry." Truer words were never uttered. Both American services planned independently of the other and hawked the results to the president as adversaries in separate sessions. Unfortunately for the Army, Roosevelt had long since bonded with the Navy. Marshall thought himself lucky to dissuade his commander in chief from calling the Navy "us" and the Army "them." Dykes too was frustrated. The Americans could not have been friendlier, but their interservice conflicts were crippling and their military secretariat useless. "Light relief" was provided by their record of a White House meeting. "It read just like a child's comic story."

In enviable contrast, every cog of the British system meshed with all the others like the wheels of a fine Swiss watch. London had its logjams—according to a senior RAF officer the bureaucracy considered war "administratively impossible"—but the system was order itself, from the prime minister and his War Cabinet, accountable to the House of Commons, to the three Chiefs of Staff who led the Army, the Navy, and the RAF in close collaboration, to the expert committees who served all three. Written plans and analyses were prepared for every contingency and every serious issue or idea produced from above or below was vetted in a memo to the Chiefs of Staff. A respected secretariat of highly trained officers made minutes of every meeting at every level and kept the paper moving, giving every player his voice. Fully armed with salient facts and keen analysis, the British Chiefs of Staff resolved their differences before they saw Churchill and argued their way to concurrence with him. Only then did the Brits broach strategy with the Yanks, united and superbly prepared.

The Americans had nothing like it.

The British Chiefs of Staff met in Great George Street once or twice a day every day but Sunday. They briefed and were questioned by the War Cabinet every Monday evening and conferred with the Joint Intelligence Committee every Tuesday morning. Barring some emergency, the American chiefs met once a week at best, never saw a politician, and rarely shared intelligence. The British Chiefs of Staff had immediate access to any government official they thought it convenient to see. The Americans had none.

Churchill grappled with his Chiefs of Staff nearly every day and long into many nights and inspected every facet of the war like a jeweler with a loupe, from land, air, and naval strategy to the insides of mortars. Kept informed of the war's events almost hourly, he dropped in unannounced on low-level planners to challenge and cajole. A veteran of several wars, trained at the Royal Military Academy at Sandhurst, he had savored strategic complexities for half a century and written two dozen volumes of military history since 1898. Having played a major role in designing British strategy during and after World War I as First Lord of the Admiralty and secretary of state for war, he directed it in World War II.

Roosevelt absorbed the big picture, rarely saw his Chiefs of Staff, and dropped in on no one. His generals and admirals resented the "drug store strategists" he kept about him, old friends and wise men with no military qualifications. Secretary of State Cordell Hull knew FDR "loved the military side of events and liked to hold them in his own hand," but he had never worn a uniform, understood naval strategy but had never shaped it, and knew less about ground and air power, though he had boned up since 1939. He did not pretend to be a serious strategist and seldom took firm positions on military issues, which Churchill did twice before breakfast. Even when he made up his mind, FDR often kept its contents from his Chiefs of Staff, but Churchill's never had to guess what he was thinking. Marshall later told Brooke that at any given point he might not see Roosevelt for six weeks. Brooke replied that "I was fortunate if I did not see Winston for six hours."

King may have been the best naval strategist on earth, but few other Americans were accused of strategic genius, unlike Churchill and several captains of his team. The brilliant Air Chief Marshal Portal, "greatly liked and admired in the War Office," General Kennedy wrote, had been instrumental in keeping Hitler on his side of the Channel in 1940, a

"magnificent" leader of the RAF whom the Army often "ruefully reflected was much too good" at moving the prime minister. The equally
exceptional Brooke had immersed himself in strategy as a student and
instructor at Britain's finest war colleges and designed its defense against
invasion. Fluent in French and German, competent in Urdu and Farsi,
he had studied the world's strategic thought for decades on His Majesty's
time and his own, perfected British artillery strategy in World War I, commanded an infantry brigade and an armored division between the wars,
led a corps in action in 1940, and saved the British Army at Dunkirk.
"He had done all these things," Marshall said years later, "and while I had
been chief of operations in an army in the first war, I had done nothing
like it. So they felt I didn't understand the problems."

Most American staff officers stood no comparison to their British
counterparts, whose "long ingrained traditional skill," as Marshall put it
later, exposed their allies' "freshman innocence." Major General Thomas
T. Handy, a native of Spring City, Tennessee, recalled his side's surprise
when Churchill came to Washington "with a whole gang of people" and
assumed they were equally prepared: "We were more or less babes in the
wood on this planning and joint business with the British. They'd been
doing it for years. They were experts at it, and we were just starting."
Handy was much impressed that the British had "found a way to get
along between the services." Shocked by the Americans' organization,
if such it could be called, their lack of strategic depth, their ill-prepared
forces, and their ham-handed talk of going back to France to lick the
Hun, Dill sent Brooke a cable: "This country has not—repeat not—the
slightest conception of what the war means, and their armed forces are
more unready for war than it is possible to imagine."

Proud as they were of their system, the Brits were shocked again
when Marshall proposed a Washington-based replica in control not
only of America's defense but also of their own. Subject only to the
president and the prime minister, a Combined Chiefs of Staff composed
of the British and American chiefs, the latter reconfigured as the Joint
Chiefs of Staff—"joint" referred to interservice affairs, "combined" to

inter-allied—would set a common strategy, allocate resources, and run the war together.

With support personnel from both countries, the Combined Chiefs of Staff—the CCS for short—would meet every week in Washington, where the British chiefs would rarely be. In close contact with London, very senior officers of each British service and Dill at the head of the British Joint Staff Mission would ordinarily represent their chiefs. In every theater of war, a Supreme Allied Commander, British or American, depending on the preponderance of local forces, would have overall command, with deputies running the land, sea, and air wars. The CCS would make decisions for the United States, the entire British Commonwealth, and the free expatriate forces of Holland, Belgium, Denmark, and Norway, all of which had fallen in 1940.

Marshall had convinced the president to accept the idea, not without a struggle, and they both worked with Hopkins to persuade the prime minister, an even greater test of talent had the British been in a position to say no. At first, they said no anyway. Churchill had come to Washington to take control of the alliance, his traveling physician Dr. Wilson wrote, and to "show the President how to run the war. It has not worked out quite like that." After what Hopkins called "a hell of a row," Marshall got what he wanted. Only weeks after Pearl Harbor, he later wrote, the Anglo-Americans had accomplished "the most complete unification of military effort ever achieved by two Allied nations." It was not his last victory shared with Hopkins. Had it not been for Harry, Marshall said after the war, it would have lasted two years longer "and we might have lost it."

Still stuck in London, already anxious about Churchill loose in Washington, Brooke was kept apprised of the budding new command arrangement and failed to see its charm. Furious about the "wild and half-baked" scheme cooking up without him, he was sure it gave the Americans more power than they knew how to use, but he was thousands of miles away, new as Chief of the Imperial General Staff, and in no position to resist. Dr. Wilson thought the British missed Brooke's strength of will. "The peace-loving Dill is no substitute. What he lacks is the he-man stuff. That is why he is no longer C.I.G.S."

The Anglo-Americans were informally known as the Allies, but on January 1, 1942, twenty-six countries allied against Hitler endorsed the Atlantic Charter and called themselves the United Nations. When the prime minister and his team left Washington two weeks later, Roosevelt's farewell to Churchill could not have been simpler: "Trust me to the bitter end."

Led by Jack Dill, who was thoroughly liked and trusted at the highest levels of the U.S. military, the British Joint Staff Mission stayed behind to guide the alliance, whose painted-over stains seeped quickly to the surface. The harder the Americans looked at taking North Africa in 1942, a prime British goal, the clearer it became that the assets it would drain could prevent a Channel crossing in 1943, an American fixation. Marshall's planners thought control of North Africa's coast, which would open the Mediterranean to Allied shipping and threaten Italy and most of occupied Europe, would be "tremendously favorable" to the Allies but only an "indirect contribution to the defeat of the Nazis," as if punching the Wehrmacht in the face were the only thing worth doing. Eisenhower told his diary that "stiff-necked" British resistance to a head-on collision with the Germans "is wearing me down. We've got to go to Europe and fight." A continental invasion would "be one h - - - of a job, but so what? We can't win by sitting on our fannies and giving our stuff in driblets all over the world with no theater getting enough."

It is hard to say what the friction might have burned had it not been for Marshall's friendship with Dill, which deepened into something like matrimonial trust. They spoke or exchanged notes almost daily and attacked any sins against Anglo-American unity in either camp with the candor of the confessional and the zeal of the Inquisition. Dill kept Marshall informed of British thought and shared telegrams between Roosevelt and Churchill that Marshall had not seen. "He would bring stuff to me and read it," Marshall later said. "I would react—I am ashamed to say, with curse words." Marshall matched Dill's transparency. Over lunch before every CCS meeting, they spotted touchy issues and often solved them in advance. When Marshall suspected that Churchill might relieve Dill, he arranged to have five American colleges grant him honorary degrees and sent Churchill flattering articles about him "so he wouldn't dare recall him." Nothing if not astute, Dill called his soulmate Marshall, not George. Marshall called him Dill.

Subordinate to Dill at the head of the British secretariat in Washington, Vivian Dykes, inevitably known as "Dumbie" to his British friends, for Sir Walter Scott's amusing Laird of Dumbiedykes, was a talented mimic of stately men who promoted Allied fellowship with a keen sense of humor. Code names were required to communicate with London, and Dumbie made them count. Marshall was "Tom Mix," a square-jawed star of American cowboy films. King was "Captain Kettle," a pugnacious little seaman in adventure books for boys who sneered at the writers of adventure books for boys. Brooke was "Colonel Shrapnel," a British artillerist in the Napoleonic Wars who invented exploding shells shooting lead in every direction. The aliases stuck surreptitiously in both capitals.

While the Washington talks were under way, the Japanese had taken Hong Kong and Kuala Lumpur from the British and Manila and Wake Island from the Americans, followed swiftly by control of the Southwest Pacific. Churchill called the fall of Singapore on February 15 the worst disaster in British military history. American reinforcements rushed desperately to the Pacific left little for the European theater. Churchill wired Roosevelt on March 5, hoping Japan could be contained "without prejudice to the plans against Hitler," but King informed the president that Australia and New Zealand were in jeopardy, "white man's countries" whose fall would cause "repercussions among the non-white races." On March 7, a telegram from Roosevelt and Marshall dropped like a bomb in London. The Pacific was in critical condition. Troop movements to Britain must be limited, European operations curtailed, a North African invasion ruled out. The Japanese took Rangoon the next day and the rest of Burma in the spring.

At just that point, the Combined Chiefs of Staff's two strongest personalities got stronger. Churchill appointed Brooke to chair his Chiefs of Staff, and Roosevelt made King chief of naval operations and retained him as commander in chief of the fleet, an unprecedented concentration of power. Eisenhower told his diary two days later that Marshall's deputy General Arnold had sent King an important message that a clerk mistakenly addressed to "Rear Admiral King" instead of "Admiral King." The envelope came back unopened, Ike wrote, with a bold arrow aimed at the demotion. "And that's the size of the man the navy has at its head."

Marshall said after the war he had "one or two pretty mean fights" with King, but they avoided confrontations when they could. An unwritten understanding evolved. With occasional exceptions, King supported Marshall on Europe and Marshall deferred to King on the Pacific. Leaving wars of their own unfought was a reasonable price to pay for winning World War II.

Two

THE ROAD TO CASABLANCA

In a memo to Marshall sent on March 25, 1942, Eisenhower, his assistant chief of staff for the Operations Division, pointed up "the tremendous importance of agreeing on some major objective," if not a continental invasion, then an all-out push against Japan. Meeting that day at the White House with his Joint Chiefs of Staff and Secretary of War Henry L. Stimson, FDR swept the air with what Marshall called his "cigarette holder gesture" and wandered about the Mediterranean in search of a target. Stimson called it "the wildest kind of dispersion debauch." Marshall pulled him back to the English Channel, the shortest route to Berlin and the best way to pull Germans from Russia, which could not be allowed to fall, for the Russians were absorbing the shock of the German war machine. Roosevelt asked for a plan.

Two days later Eisenhower gave Marshall a broad-brush European strategy that he and FDR approved immediately. An enormous push to build landing craft, ships, and warplanes would accompany "constant raiding" of the German-held coast, a rapid buildup of U.S. forces in England soon code-named Operation Bolero, and the achievement of air superiority over northwest Europe, culminating by April of 1943 in Operation Roundup, a full-scale continental invasion. In the alternative, Operation

Sledgehammer, a much smaller attack in 1942, chillingly described as "a sacrifice in the common good," would pull Germans off the Red Army if it started to collapse before Roundup was ready. A third possibility, launching Sledgehammer against German defenses in France so weakened by Allied bombing or diversions of enemy troops and planes to Russia that a modest force could tip them over, was considered highly unlikely.

Roosevelt wired Churchill that he was sending Marshall and Hopkins to London with a plan that "has my heart and <u>mind</u> in it." British hearts were with him. British minds were not. General Kennedy told his diary that the British, of course, would support an all-out invasion in 1943 if they were sure it would win the war. "But the fundamental difficulty is that we cannot be sure," not nearly sure enough to take "the most colossal gamble in history" and strip the British Isles, the Middle East, and the Indian Ocean of their defenses, which was what it would take. "We are not prepared to risk everything—and it would be everything— on this one throw." As for the sacrificial version of Operation Sledgehammer, a small, shiny object designed to lure enemy forces from Russia to be destroyed from the air, the British thought the Germans would not bite. With their might in France alone they "could turn on us at their leisure and wipe us out."

Introduced to Marshall at a Downing Street dinner, Brooke found him gracious "if rather overfilled with his own importance. But I should not put him down as a great man." Several evenings later he had Marshall to dinner at his London flat and discovered that he liked him. Two days after that, having failed to convince him that a cross-Channel attack against unbroken Germans would be suicide, Marshall had become "a very dangerous man whilst being a very charming one!" Both generals admired the other's strengths and mistook his weaknesses for a lack of high intelligence. There was "a great charm and dignity about Marshall," Brooke thought, "a very great gentleman who inspired trust but did not impress me by the ability of his brain." Marshall told Hopkins that Brooke might be a fighter but "he hasn't got Dill's brains."

Two senior Army planners accompanied Marshall and Hopkins, the intelligent Colonel John E. Hull and the acidic Colonel Albert C. Wedemeyer. A tall, German-speaking, sandy-haired Nebraskan brined in Anglophobia from childhood, Wedemeyer brought to Downing Street the awkward combination of a bitter distaste for the British and an unfashionable affection for the Germans. For Wedemeyer, the cunning Brits were bent on spending American lives to save their empire while the Germans were Western civilization's bulwark against communism, sadly misunderstood. As an exchange student at Berlin's war college in 1936–38, Wedemeyer had studied German military theory and Nazi doctrine and met Hitler's inner circle. He disapproved of Hitler's methods, though the Führer, he thought, had done Germany much good, but German values, German officers, and German designs on Russia he liked. Communism, he wrote years later, was a "danger to the Republic far greater than Nazi Germany ever constituted except in the fevered imagination of Roosevelt and his speech writers." FDR was a left-wing fraud surrounded by "soft on communism eggheads" and Jews who "actually felt bitter against the Germans." Once the "power-drunk leaders" of the West provoked World War II it was Wedemeyer's misfortune to plan "a war I did not want."

He had not charmed the British in Washington. Vivian Dykes understood he "had to be pulled up some time ago for undue admiration of the Germans." Dykes being Dykes, Wedemeyer liked him, but Dykes found Wedemeyer "extraordinarily offensive," throwing British defeats "in the teeth of our people, announcing that he always had a witness present in discussions with British officers," calling them to their faces "the most ungrateful people on earth."

At the time he brought Wedemeyer to London, Marshall later wrote, "the Red Army was slowly falling back under the full fury of the German assault" and almost anything the Allies could do to help simply had to be done. The fall of the Soviet Union would free millions of German troops to turn west in battle-hardened hordes and crown a Nazi conquest of Europe never to be reversed. It was under that cloud, in which Wedemeyer saw the death of communism as a bright silver lining, that the Americans brought their Channel crossing plan to a Downing Street meeting.

Struggling with the devilish question of how to defeat the Boche, Brigadier General Sir Leslie Hollis, number two to Churchill's right hand, General Ismay, had hoped for an American plan of "revolutionary originality" but found it "almost childish in its simplicity." The American Colonel Hull laid it out "as though he were propounding some new theory." To defeat the Germans, he began, "we must get ashore on the Continent and fight them," and then, as Hollis told it, he looked around the room as if he wondered why the British were still in their seats. The first unanswerable question was how. The shipping and naval escorts required to move a vast American army across the U-boat-infested Atlantic and the landing craft required to put them on the beach did not exist and could not be thrown together, never mind the unbroken fortifications and unflinching German troops the invaders would face if they somehow got there. "This we tried to point out as patiently as we could." The British had been pushed back into the sea in France, Greece, Norway, and Crete, but the Americans "earnestly believed" that once they were ashore "they could go right on" to Berlin.

For Brooke the American plan came to "castles in the air." Marshall "only touched the fringe" of its implementation, and the thought of attacking an entrenched German army with raw, outnumbered troops seemed not to bother him. He had focused on the forces to be thrown into France, General Kennedy wrote, "but had no idea what was to be done next and what the plan of campaign should be and what the chances were of carrying it out." He cast the proposed invasion as the war's decisive thrust and defined its objectives broadly, but when Brooke asked him over dinner in which direction the invaders would move after they landed, he said he had not yet thought about it. "Whether we are to play baccarat" at Le Touquet, Brooke told his diary, or bathe in the Seine in Paris "is not stipulated." The whole thing was "just fantastic."

The British never scoffed at it, Wedemeyer wrote. They made "polite suggestions that there might be difficulties." Quite out of character,

Brooke spoke slowly and gently, as if teaching children. Northwest Europe must be invaded eventually, he said, almost surely, and the planning should start now, but Axis control of the central Mediterranean, which choked the required shipping, must be broken first. Vital maritime traffic to and from India and the Persian Gulf, Britain's crucial source of oil, had to steam around the Cape of Good Hope instead of through the Suez Canal, wasting vast amounts of shipping, the Allies' most critical shortage, but once the Mediterranean was opened and the Russians wore the Germans down, the Channel could be crossed "almost unimpeded."

Having been told that Marshall was insisting on invading northwest France as soon as possible nonetheless, Churchill's friend Dr. Wilson reminded him of Britain's appalling losses in the Great War: "You are fighting the dead on the Somme." But the Americans would not budge. Desperate to keep them from abandoning Europe for the Pacific and eager for a fresh U.S. army in England to ward off a German invasion, the Brits had little choice but to endorse a Bolero buildup of American forces in the U.K., accept the idea of a Roundup invasion of France in the following year, and expose its impracticability over time. Roundup was penciled in for the summer of 1943 and a small-scale Sledgehammer attack set aside, only to be reconsidered if the Russians seemed at risk of caving in.

In a cable to FDR responding to the American plan, Churchill praised "your masterly document," which Brooke had found absurd, and accepted it in principle, pending his Chiefs of Staff's review. "If, as our experts believe, we can carry this whole plan through successfully, it will be one of the grand events in all the history of war."

This was disingenuous at best. Churchill loved historic grandeur and itched to hit the enemy wherever he could and often where he could not, but his experts believed an assault on unbroken Germans in France could very well lose the war. Beneath the polite veneer, the British had neither committed to a specific operation nor set a target date and had only agreed to start planning. Wedemeyer was grudgingly impressed by his British peers, who endorsed the idea of a decisive invasion but, "for reasons inexplicable at the time," he later recalled, "I had misgivings. Not enough questions had been asked" and too many well-bred heads had shaken gently over details, with "a faint but definitely perceptible lack of enthusiasm." Marshall wrote a deputy that many British officers "if not most hold reservations regarding this or that," and only "great firmness" could head off "further dispersions."

No man was closer to Churchill than General Ismay, his personal liaison to his Chiefs of Staff, secretary to the Committee of Imperial Defense, deputy secretary to the War Cabinet. Born in the Himalayas, the son of a "Kentish squire" who had gambled his wealth away and started fresh in India in the robes of an imperial judge, Ismay was a Great War veteran of the Somaliland Camel Corps, a tough desert strike force as exotic as it sounds. A loyal, intelligent man with a broad snub nose, a striking pair of big gray eyes, and a sunny disposition, Ismay was known as "Pug" for his supposed resemblance to the breed. What made him indispensable to his master was an almost supernatural gift for making complexity simple, calming angry men, and bridging unbridgeable gaps. "Ismay straightened things out for us time after time," Marshall later said. "I was fond of him." Everyone loved Pug Ismay.

When Marshall and Hopkins met with the Committee of Imperial Defense, Ismay endorsed their "momentous proposal" with the subtle remark that "it remained to work out the details." Years later he regretted the error. Marshall and his team had yet to face the Wehrmacht anywhere, and the British had underplayed the catastrophic risk of hitting them in the teeth before they were staggering. "Our American friends went happily homewards under the mistaken impression that we had committed ourselves" and soon had cause to think "we had broken faith with them."

The British should have taken them to dinner, Ismay wrote, and spoken to Marshall plainly about hurling raw recruits at fortified Germans across an open beach laced with obstacles and barbed wire. "Look here old boy," they should have said, "that sounds lovely," but surely he was talking about weakening them first. "We are frankly horrified because of what we have been through in our lifetime," having seen their generation shattered in 1914–18 and been driven from France in 1940 with their tails between their legs and their country on the rim of extinction. "We who had survived had got that into our minds. Never again, you see. We are not going into this until it is a cast-iron certainty."

Nothing had been settled in London. Marshall told Dill "I have so many battles to fight I am never quite sure whether I am fighting you or the President or the Navy." Vivian Dykes found combined planning next to impossible with the U.S. Navy hell-bent for the Pacific and the Army for the Channel. On May 4, 1942, with Japanese aggression on a menacing upswing, King wrote his American peers that important as a buildup in Britain might be, "the Pacific problem is no less so, and is certainly the more urgent—it must be faced now." Marshall tipped Dill to a memo he had sent to the president. As Dykes understood it, "Marshall stated bluntly that if the South-West Pacific is to win the day, it's only right to tell the British so at once."

The pivotal Battle of the Coral Sea began that day, the U.S. Navy's first strategic victory over Japanese forces. One month later the Americans sank four enemy aircraft carriers off the Central Pacific Island of Midway and lost just one. In two quick strokes they had stopped the rise of the Rising Sun and left the Japanese incapable of a major offensive. King was determined to hit them again while they were reeling.

On May 28, convinced by his Chiefs of Staff that the Continent was out of reach for a long time to come, Churchill cabled FDR and began to back away from the Channel with vague talk of Norway, North Africa, and "the difficulties of 1942." On the following day FDR promised Stalin's foreign minister nonetheless a second front in Europe before the year was out.

As Churchill and his Chiefs of Staff prepared to return to Washington, Vice Admiral Lord Louis Francis Albert Victor Nicholas Mountbatten, their director of combined operations, arrived two weeks ahead of them, presaging Churchill's message, as Wedemeyer had it later, in the role of John the Baptist. Only among the British upper class could a man with six names, none of them Richard, be known to his friends as Dickie. Photographed in his infancy in the lap of his great-grandmother Queen Victoria, decorated in command of destroyers early in the war, Dickie Mountbatten was every bit as confident, charming, and articulate as a film-star-handsome cousin of the king should be. Churchill admired his courage, ingenuity, and optimism in command of men of all three services in commando raids and amphibious warfare and had made him not only a vice admiral of the Royal Navy but also a lieutenant general of the Army and an air marshal of the RAF, to give him a bit of weight. He was not yet forty-two.

In early June, Mountbatten met at the White House with Roosevelt and Hopkins, casting shade on the English Channel. No American officers were invited. Given the landing craft shortage, Mountbatten said, and enemy strength in France, a small-scale Sledgehammer attack on northwest Europe (some irreverent officers called it "Tack Hammer") could not be big enough to pull Germans from Russia in 1942. Roosevelt said he feared that if a continental invasion was as hard as all that it might also be impossible in 1943, and he had to get Americans fighting Germans soon. The public would not stand for a year of preparation in Europe and a defensive crouch in the Pacific.

Before Churchill left for Washington, his Chiefs of Staff thought they had him convinced that a near-term Channel crossing would be a debacle when he suddenly erupted not only with an invasion of France but also with retaking Burma from the Japanese and the North Cape of Norway from the Germans. Any one of these was unachievable in 1942, let alone together. "We consumed a great deal of time and energy in pointing out these facts," General Kennedy wrote. North Africa, however, they left on the table, grave misgivings notwithstanding. Disturbed by Dill's reports on the direction of London's winds, Marshall told FDR that a resource-draining, high-risk North African invasion in 1942 would cripple Bolero's buildup in the U.K. and bar a full-scale invasion of France in 1943. The American Chiefs of Staff were against it.

• • •

Churchill and his Chiefs of Staff reached Washington on June 18, and the prime minister flew to FDR's Hyde Park home the next day. The CCS, British and American alike, were anxious to a man about leaving him alone with Roosevelt and Hopkins. Marshall complained years later that the president often dropped a carefully chosen strategy, "particularly when Churchill got hold of him."

Churchill wrote after the war, "I had made a careful study of the President's mind and its reactions." Roosevelt was fixed on fighting Germans *somewhere* by October, winning the off year congressional elections in November, keeping the American public in the war against Hitler. His interest in a North African invasion, code-named Gymnast, was still keen, and Churchill worked on him and Hopkins with no British or American minders in the room. From that day forth, in Wedemeyer's view, "the virtuoso Churchill led the Anglo-American orchestra, although we furnished practically all of the instruments and most of the musicians."

Facing insurmountable obstacles, including the lack of enough landing craft to launch six or seven Allied divisions against five times as many Germans—a division averaged 15,000 men—Churchill told Roosevelt in writing that no responsible British authority had been able to plan a Sledgehammer attack in northwest Europe with the slimmest chance to succeed in 1942 "unless the Germans become utterly demoralized, of which there is no likelihood." If the Americans had such a plan, where was it? The Allies could not sit idle for a year, the prime minister wrote, singing Roosevelt's tune and his own. Operation Gymnast's invasion of French North Africa was the only big thing they could do in the European Theater in 1942, and Gymnast it must be.

In Washington, the CCS met for the first time with the British members present. Overwhelmed with urgencies, King sent a substitute and the others coalesced against Gymnast. Marshall said an all-out invasion of France was impossible in 1943 unless a Bolero buildup started now, and Gymnast would "probably achieve nothing." Brooke was keen on Gymnast *and* Bolero, but with the brilliant General Erwin Rommel's

German Afrika Korps backed by large Italian forces threatening Egypt and the Suez Canal, barely checked by the British Eighth Army, the British chiefs agreed that Bolero should proceed but Gymnast would soak up too much force. Ismay expected "a great explosion from the PM," which the CCS prepared to withstand. Introduced to King the next day, Brooke formed a strong first impression, but King was convinced that the Brits were stringing the Yanks along. They would never go back to France, he told Wedemeyer, except behind a bagpipe band.

After Roosevelt and Churchill returned to Washington in combined support of Gymnast, Ismay broke the news to Churchill that the CCS were against it and absorbed his wrath. His mood had improved to peevish by the time Brooke talked him down and accompanied him to the White House to meet the president. Brooke was no easy man to charm, but Roosevelt, famously credited by Supreme Court Justice Oliver Wendell Holmes Jr. with a second-class mind and a first-class temperament, charmed him on the spot. Later, at lunch with Churchill and Mrs. Roosevelt, FDR shared with Brooke a touching childhood memory of meeting his father and lamented eldest brother as his own father's Hyde Park guests. Brooke was deeply moved.

That afternoon, Brooke was standing by the president's desk with Churchill, Dill, Ismay, and Hopkins when Marshall came in with a pink sheet of paper. Rommel and the Italians had taken Libya's strategic port of Tobruk, which positioned them to take the entire Middle East. Churchill and Brooke were visibly staggered, then moved once again by Roosevelt's heartfelt empathy and Marshall's noble pledge to send the British Eighth Army hundreds of tanks and self-propelled guns just delivered to a needy American division. Hopkins suggested a private talk with Brooke, who expected to be led to Harry's office and found himself in his room, "where we sat on the edge of his bed looking at his shaving brush and toothbrush" as Hopkins, who had no office, trusted him with some of the president's deepest thoughts.

As Ismay had foreseen, Churchill would not accept rejecting Gymnast for an "idle" year of bombing and preparation. Nor would FDR.

After a heated exchange with Roosevelt and Churchill on one side and their Chiefs of Staff on the other, Ismay produced a solution based on Churchill's ideas without calling them such. Bolero's buildup in the UK would proceed, anticipating Roundup in 1943, but if events proved Roundup unlikely to succeed, alternatives would be found, of which Gymnast seemed the best, a polite British poke in Marshall's eye. Marshall raised again with his indignant American peers the heretical thought of "turning our backs upon the eastern Atlantic and going full out as quickly as possible against Japan." The best that can be said of the Washington meetings is their indecisive end.

Brooke left happier than usual nonetheless, comfortable with King and close to Roosevelt and Marshall. The president, he thought, was "a most attractive personality" with a "wonderful charm about him," sharp political instincts, and thin strategic credentials that left him prone to impractical ideas. Still, blessedly aware that FDR knew his limits, Brooke trusted Marshall to disabuse him of "wildish plans" while Churchill "never had the slightest doubt that he had inherited all the military genius of his great ancestor Marlborough! His military plans and ideas varied from the most brilliant conceptions at one end to the wildest and most dangerous ideas on the other," which Brooke seldom managed to dispel.

Marshall sent Eisenhower to London in June 1942 to command the U.S. Army's European Theater of Operations, where no American had dropped a bomb or fired a shot six months into America's war. Churchill called him Ike and welcomed him to lunch once a week with "explosive greetings," genuinely glad to see him and gladder to make a project of this seemingly guileless American who was not in Kansas anymore. Early on, the general spent a heady weekend at Chequers, where the PM gave him Cromwell's bed and nudged him toward North Africa and Norway. A near term invasion of France "would be slaughter," Churchill said. "We are not strong enough." The Germans would stop it "the second it started," but the French would not fight Americans in North Africa. Ike disagreed, still committed to the earliest possible invasion of France.

On July 8 Churchill wrote FDR that no continental invasion could be mounted before autumn, when the Channel would swallow landing craft. The taking of French North Africa in Operation Gymnast, he wrote, a predominantly American show, possibly unopposed, was the best chance to pull Germans from Russia and elect Democrats in November. Even Stalin might be satisfied. "This has been all along in harmony with your ideas," Churchill wrote. "In fact, it is your commanding idea," as if he needed schooling on the content of his mind. The prime minister's word was final. With Bolero's American buildup just begun in the U.K., British troops and landing craft would dominate an invasion of northwest Europe in 1942, which could only be launched from England. Secretary of War Stimson knew in any case that Roosevelt had been in Churchill's boat all along. North Africa was "his secret war baby."

It had taken Churchill months to accept that Gymnast could be mounted in 1942 or Roundup in 1943 but not both. Marshall and King knew it well, and Gymnast would impoverish the war on Japan. France was Marshall's war baby, King's the Pacific, and together they sent a memo to the president. If the British would not support a Channel crossing "we should turn to the Pacific and strike decisively against Japan." Marshall was bluffing, King meant every word, and it mattered neither way. In a phone call from Hyde Park, Roosevelt demanded to see *that day* their detailed plan for an all-out Pacific offensive, knowing that none existed. They slapped one together with staff and had it flown to FDR. "My first impression," he replied, "is that it is exactly what Germany hoped the United States would do following Pearl Harbor," that American troops would not fight "except in a lot of islands," which could not save the Russians or the Middle East. "Therefore it is disapproved as of the present. Roosevelt C in C." The signature line reminded them who was commander in chief and who was not.

Roosevelt sent Marshall, King, and Hopkins to London at once and told them to return in a week with something big on the books for 1942, a Sledgehammer assault on northwest Europe specifically, unless they were convinced it was impossible. There would only be an all-out push against Japan if *no* European or North African offensive could be worked out with the British. "Defeat of Germany means the defeat of Japan," the president wrote, "probably without firing a shot or losing a life."

Brooke thought the Americans would make "a queer party," with Marshall for Europe, King for the Pacific, and Hopkins for North Africa. Dill wired Churchill that a Channel crossing was Marshall's first love, convinced as he was that unless it came soon Russia would be lost and Germany too strong to invade. "We can then go on pummeling each other by air, but the possibility of a decision will have gone," leaving nothing but a stalemate to hope for. "Unless you can convince him of your unswerving devotion to Bolero," Marshall might turn toward Japan and leave the British "to make out as best we can against Germany."

Warmly received in London, Marshall, King, and Hopkins fought a three-day battle on Downing Street and lost. The British side's commitment to Bolero was unswerving indeed, but so was their rejection of invading northwest Europe any time soon, which Brooke called the loss of six divisions for no gain. Brooke told his diary that Marshall argued hard while King contributed "a face like a Sphinx, and only one idea," full speed against Japan. None of it changed the facts in the elegant British briefing books. After the argument played out, North Africa was the only option on the president's list as well as the prime minister's.

On July 22, the Americans gave in. Bolero would proceed, but the taking of French North Africa, renamed Operation Torch to confuse the enemy, was on for 1942, almost surely pushing a decisive invasion of the Continent into 1944. The British denied it but Marshall and King insisted on recording it, along with a declaration that the Allies had chosen "a defensive, encircling line of action" for continental Europe but for bombing and blockade. Convinced that the Russians would collapse in 1943, leaving Nazi Germany the permanent master of Europe, Eisenhower told an aide that July 22, 1942, might go down as "the blackest day in history." But Marshall said years later that he knew the Continent was out of reach for many months and accepted Torch grudgingly as "the only thing we could think of that could be done at an early date," and Roosevelt could not afford the political price of a year of preparation. Marshall had learned, he wrote, "that the leader in a democracy has to keep the people entertained. That may sound like the wrong word but it conveys the thought." When a democracy fights a war, the people "demand action. We couldn't wait to be completely ready."

To try to keep Stalin as happy as they could, sullen but not mutinous, Churchill and Brooke flew to Moscow, disappointed him with the sheer impossibility of a second front in France in 1942, and argued their case for Torch. Fearful that Stalin might make a separate peace with Hitler under life-threatening pressure, literal and figurative, Churchill assured him that preparations were under way to cross the Channel in 1943 with fifty divisions, and Stalin was not a man to disappoint twice.

Planning Torch under Eisenhower's supreme command, in concert if not always in harmony, British and American officers pulled together in three months the biggest amphibious invasion the world had ever seen, the first combined Allied operation of the war. Neutral Spanish Morocco, abutting the Strait of Gibraltar, would be left alone. The target was the 1,200-mile stretch of the French Empire from Morocco's Atlantic coast through Algeria and Tunisia to the western shore of the Mediterranean narrows between Tunis and Sicily. The entire region was defended by a Vichy French army whose officers were inclined to detest the Boche and despise the British. In July 1940, a British naval task force had devastated France's Algerian fleet to keep it from the Germans, killing almost 1,300 French sailors when its commander defied an ultimatum to cooperate with the British. Torch was therefore planned as a visibly American operation with Britain's heavy contribution hidden as best it could be.

The U.S. Navy would carry 35,000 soldiers directly from the United States to Casablanca and beaches on Morocco's Atlantic coast while the Royal Navy landed 65,000 American and British troops in Algeria near Oran and Algiers. Hopes were high for token opposition or none. The invaders would then move east into Tunisia while the British Eighth

Army pushed Rommel and the Italians west from Egypt, catching them in between. Successfully executed, Torch would take those Axis forces off the board, open the Mediterranean, add the French North African military to the cause, secure the Middle East and West Africa, strike a devasting psychological blow, and set up the next offensive.

Eisenhower treated his Anglo-American staff identically, regardless of nationality, and quashed the slightest friction, but Allied relations in Washington were strained. As American resources were earmarked for Torch and flowed to the Red Army through Persia and the northern Russian ports of Archangel and Murmansk but merely trickled into Bolero, it seemed to Albert Wedemeyer, now a brigadier general, that "our top men," meaning Roosevelt and Hopkins, were "kowtowing and genuflecting" to the British and the Russians when they ought to be putting America first.

On August 7, thousands of United States marines landed on Guadalcanal and other Solomon Islands, the first American offensive of the war, which spoke to the British more loudly than words. Dill told Marshall he detected a certain lack of enthusiasm about Torch in Washington, and Marshall reassured him, but Wedemeyer hid a recorder under his desk, purportedly with Marshall's knowledge, and tripped it with his knee when he spoke with British officers.

In September, Vivian Dykes sent a message from Washington to the British Chiefs of Staff. As soon as North Africa was taken, a broader strategy must be found, he wrote, truly shared with the Americans, starting from scratch with open minds. "It may be too much to hope that we shall walk exactly in step with the US, for though they have the same basic tongue as our own, they differ from us widely in outlook, temperament, and methods. But if we cannot walk in step, we must at least travel the same road and not take divergent courses." By October Dykes could see that too many cooks in Torch's kitchen were reading the recipes differently. British planning documents "perfectly intelligible to an Englishman may be obscure to an American." Worse, the list of disputed points was getting longer, tempers were getting shorter, and brotherly love was thin.

Unilateral American moves that the CCS should have worked out together provoked the British Chiefs of Staff, and Brooke was barking mad
at the whole arrangement. In Washington, Dykes wrote, the cold civil
war between the U.S. Army and Navy was "simply incredible." He had all
but given up on combined planning, and it looked to him as if Roosevelt
had too. "I must say we are certainly on a falling market just now."

As Torch's consumption of resources made it plainer all the time that
no big invasion of France could come before 1944, American talk reached
British ears that if the Allies must play defense in Europe through 1943
the Americans must play offense in the Pacific and keep more strength
for themselves. A *friendly* American officer told Dykes the United States
must be "the dictating power after the war" and therefore the strongest.
Dykes had had enough of Washington. "We certainly are in for some
very difficult times with the Yanks," he wrote. "I should love to get away
from here."

And then there were the French.

It was important to the North African invasion's military and political success to improve the considerable odds that the local French forces
would oppose it only symbolically if at all. Robert D. Murphy, the senior
U.S. diplomat in Vichy, had gathered intelligence in French North Africa
that most of its high command would resist in earnest, while the officers
at large would gladly join the Allies if properly ordered. Some respected
general or admiral would have to give those orders, and it fell to Murphy
to find one. General Charles de Gaulle was not his choice.

In June 1940, de Gaulle had pressed Premier Reynaud to send the
French fleet to North Africa and continue the war from there. "The defeated," he said, "are those who accept defeat." Reynaud resigned two
days later, succeeded by the elderly Philippe Pétain, who accepted just
that. In defiance of his orders, de Gaulle flew to England in adventure
film style, won Churchill's prompt support for a "Free French" movement, and broadcast a call to arms on the BBC that drew a few thousand
military evacuees and expatriates and some loose warships. Armed and

supplied by the British, de Gaulle's tiny forces were under his command, subject only to the British Chiefs of Staff.

De Gaulle foretold that "Churchill will launch me like a new brand of soap," which is just what he did. Londoners cheered the French general in the streets. Schoolchildren mailed him their shillings. War widows sent him their wedding rings. The adulation did not upset him. Previously apolitical, though groomed in right-wing authoritarianism, he saw himself at first as a purely military leader, but when no exiled statesman stepped forward to lead his movement, de Gaulle filled the void as the very personification of France—"*Moi, je suis la France!*"—and Churchill's government recognized him as the leader of Free France if not quite France incarnate. Vichy sentenced him to death for treason. Vichy, de Gaulle replied, was "subject to the invader." He would exercise power in the name of France and be judged by her people's representatives "when it will be possible for them to judge freely."

In the meantime he had a lot for a hero to work with—his London-based National Committee of distinguished French exiles, his miniature armed forces, his inspirational status with the brave French Resistance, his literally towering personality, a BBC microphone, broad support in France born of his rejection of defeat, an American Lend-Lease account, and His Majesty's Exchequer. Hungry for a charismatic leader, many Frenchmen embraced him. Others did not. Some denied his legitimacy or rejected his populist politics or his messianic vision. The governors of several French colonies put them under his wing, but an attempt to add the great French naval base at Dakar on the western tip of Africa failed when its Vichy commander repelled British and Free French warships instead of welcoming them. De Gaulle's attack on Dakar's French flag turned many French officers against him who did not already call him a deserter.

Churchill often expressed immense admiration for de Gaulle but not for his megalomania and still less for his Anglophobia, which his dependence on London perversely inflamed. He joined forces with the British against Axis and Vichy armies in Syria, but the military marriage cracked, and de Gaulle confronted the commanding British general: "You think I am interested in England winning the war? I am not. I am only interested in France's victory." The Englishman said they were one and the same. "Not at all," said de Gaulle, "not at all in my view."

After 1940 Churchill seldom stopped battling de Gaulle over one thing or another and never stopped admiring him. As they fought Adolf Hitler together, often moved by each other's courage, de Gaulle would call the prime minister a gangster and Churchill would threaten to accommodate de Gaulle in the Tower of London. As Churchill raged against the Frenchman in a talk with a member of Parliament, his friend replied that he might be right, but de Gaulle was a great man. Churchill nearly exploded. "A great man? Why, he's selfish, he's arrogant, he thinks he's the centre of the universe . . . he . . . You're right. He's a great man!"

De Gaulle's unconcealed political ambitions would have ruled him out as Torch's French general even if he were otherwise acceptable, and the American diplomat Robert Murphy never considered him for the role. Roosevelt would help no man anoint himself as France's future leader before France could choose one, let alone de Gaulle, whom FDR had typed as a dictator. He had not helped his cause by crossing Secretary of State Cordell Hull irretrievably. The mere mention of his name was said to draw from Hull "an outburst of skillful Tennessee denunciation." Nor did French politics break in his favor. The French electorate leaned left, and de Gaulle, a quick learner, promised France a leftist postwar government, but most of French Africa's officers were conservative if not reactionary.

Murphy picked as America's man General Henri Giraud, a pro-American, youthfully fit old-timer with an antique bearing and a turn-of-the-century mustache. With the strong recommendation of a French industrialist in Giraud's right-wing circle, Murphy chose him "almost in desperation" as the only credible alternative to de Gaulle who had not cozied up to the Nazis or aspired to public office. An officer of great courage and small intelligence, Giraud had been shot through a lung and left for dead leading a bayonet charge in 1914 and famously escaped captivity disguised as a magician in a traveling circus. In command of the Seventh French Army in 1940, cut off by German forces, his last message to headquarters reported himself surrounded by a hundred tanks, which he expected to destroy one by one. Captured again he escaped again, in cinematic fashion. The particulars included a Tyrolean hat acquired in a chocolate transaction, rappelling down a 150-foot wall from a German castle prison on braided string and wire in a downpour in the dark at sixty-three years of age, and a hairsbreadth evasion on a train. Now he was living as a hero in Vichy France, to which he had been obliged to swear allegiance after inquiring what arrangements had been made to resist any German encroachments.

Reactionary instincts and advisors aside, Giraud was politically a child, which Murphy considered a credential, along with his fame in France, not a second's collaboration with the Germans, a conservative core that attracted French officers, and no more interest in politics than in haute couture. His single-minded goal was to throw a North African army against the Boche, manned by Muslim troops, trained by French officers, armed with American weapons, led by Henri Giraud.

Murphy had often dealt with volatile French temperaments, none of them improved by "feelings of defeat, humiliation, pride, and exile," de Gaulle's and Giraud's included. The two French generals shared heroic war records, heroic egos, a grudgingly mutual respect, a passion for liberating France, a hatred for Germans acquired in two wars, and a narcissistic habit of referring to themselves in the third person. Giraud was known to call himself "the Great General Giraud" with no hint of humor. Neither Roosevelt nor Churchill was in love with either man, and neither were the Frenchmen with each other, but their love for themselves was unconditional.

Less than three weeks before the landings, Eisenhower sent his deputy, the extravagantly ambitious forty-six-year-old Major General Mark Clark, to a secret meeting with General Charles Emmanuel Mast, a Giraud confidant in command of a French corps in Algiers who had signaled a willingness to cooperate. Known at West Point as "Contraband" for his candy-smuggling skills, Clark climbed out of a British submarine off a dark Algerian beach, paddled a rubber boat ashore with a few other officers and Murphy, and misled Mast on key particulars of the pending invasion. Not the least of these was Giraud's expectation, grandiose to the point of disorder, that Giraud would set the invasion date, Giraud would command the French North African troops *and* the Anglo-Americans after they landed, and southern France would be invaded on the same day, also under Giraud's command. Clark evaded or dissembled on every point.

Giraud sent a confirming message to Murphy, whose diplomatic training induced him to reply a touch more honestly than Clark. He would forward Giraud's "suggestion" up the line and assured him that an "acceptable formula" would be found. Until French North Africa was secure (an undefined term), the operation would be under American command, but France's sovereignty over all her colonies would be restored "as soon as possible" (another diplomatic ambiguity), and American authorities would not interfere with its exercise, which far exceeded Murphy's authority.

On October 23, Montgomery led the British Eighth Army in the opening drive of its pivotal offensive against Rommel and the Italians in the Egyptian desert. If it failed, Brooke told his diary, he would not know how to bear it.

On the following day, a vast American fleet steamed east from Hampton Roads, Virginia, with an infant army led by the little known Major General George S. Patton Jr., a wealthy, French-speaking Southern Californian and a former Olympic pentathlete. In a message to his troops, he regretted the unfortunate prospect of fighting "the gallant French who are at heart sympathetic toward us." All resistance would be destroyed, but any surrendering troops deserved "the respect due a brave opponent and future ally. Remember, the French are not Nazis or Japs." A cursing comic book warlord with a high-pitched voice, as if nature had played a trick on him, Patton had told his subordinate commanders that if they failed to accomplish their missions, he did not wish to see them alive. If he failed in his, he said, he would come home in a box.

Several months earlier, Marshall had reviewed his plans for the Torch invasion with FDR. Knowing the political cost of the Army's absence from the war against Hitler, the president raised his hands in an attitude of prayer: "Please make it before Election Day." But on the eve of the fleet's departure he approved a delay that pushed the landings five days past the voting, a decision for the responsible commander, he said, not for the Democratic National Committee. While the fleet was at sea on November 3, the electorate sharply reduced his senate and house majorities, having no idea that Patton's troops were on their way.

On November 4 in Egypt, Montgomery drove Rommel into full retreat from El Alamein and began to push him west. On November 7, the day before the North African landings, Eisenhower and Clark spent four precious hours in their command post under the Rock of Gibraltar bargaining with Giraud, smuggled out of France by submarine, and continued the next day. Giraud let them know they were talking to "the incarnation of French resistance" to the Boche, "the one man who could attract to his person" France's will and power to prevail, and Giraud would withdraw from the whole affair unless he commanded the invaders. Ike stroked his ego with a politician's skill, sidestepped his silliest demands, promised him command of French North Africa's forces and its civil affairs too, and pledged to restore the French to full control "as soon as practicable," yet another vague idea. Giraud shook his hand with the landings under way.

Far from being asked to participate, de Gaulle was not told that the landings were coming. Even if Roosevelt had trusted his discretion, which was not exemplary, it was out of the question to gamble on his leaky National Committee or risk Frenchmen killing Frenchmen in North Africa as they had at Dakar and in Syria.

Just before dawn on November 8, the vast American fleet broke through the mist off Casablanca as if by magic as British and American troops landed in Morocco and Algeria. Pyrotechnics displayed the Stars and Stripes and the BBC transmitted Roosevelt's pledge, recorded in prep school French, that the Americans had come as friends to begin the liberation of France, but Admiral François Darlan, in command of the local Vichy forces, obeyed Pétain's orders to resist. Casablanca's French fleet was annihilated, some 1,300 Frenchmen were killed, and nearly as many British and Americans. No longer just lenders and leasers in Britain's ground war against Germany, the Americans had joined the fight.

Hitler reacted instantly. On the morning after the assault, with the closest Allied invasion force 560 miles away in Algeria—a landing in Tunisia had been judged impracticable—the Luftwaffe took airfields in and near Tunis unopposed by Tunisia's small French garrison. German and Italian troops, planes, and heavy weapons poured freely in from Sicily and swelled into a formidable army. Few Italian troops had ever been excited about the war, fewer still by now, having suffered repeated defeats, and many despised Mussolini, their strategically inept fascist leader, none of which improved their fighting qualities, but some of the German troops and tanks were among Hitler's best. His move into Tunisia would later be called a "decision to reinforce failure," and the Allies understood it as such, but their hopes for a rapid taking of the whole North African coast were gone.

Code-named Kingpin by the Americans, Giraud flew to Algeria on November 9 but could not stop the French from fighting. Some kingpin. French resistance was clearly futile nonetheless, and Churchill informed his Chiefs of Staff that very day that Torch was "no excuse for lying down during 1943, content with descents on Sicily and Sardinia" and the occasional raid. If North Africa became an excuse for locking up an army "it would be better not to have gone there at all."

On November 10, with the French still resisting in and near Casablanca, Clark persuaded Darlan to order a cease-fire in Pétain's name and cooperate with the Allies in return for his appointment as high commissioner of French North Africa, despite his elaborate record as a Nazi collaborator. Giraud would command the region's French armed forces. Darlan's subordinates followed his orders, most of them gladly, and

Eisenhower approved the transaction. Neither the British nor de Gaulle were consulted.

On November 11, German and Italian troops poured into Vichy France unopposed, completing Hitler's French occupation, but before the month was out, the French scuttled their fleet at Toulon when the Germans tried to seize it. Churchill cabled Roosevelt that the British were under "solemn obligations to de Gaulle and his Movement," and two rival French governments in exile, one in London backed by the United Kingdom, the other in North Africa supported by the United States, must be avoided at all costs. Roosevelt agreed but allowed no room for doubt about who was driving: "In regard to de Gaulle I have hitherto enjoyed a quiet satisfaction in leaving him in your hands. Apparently, I have now acquired a similar problem in Brother Giraud," who was proving himself difficult, exacerbated by a "cat fight in progress" with Darlan over control of French Africa's military. None of it mattered. "The principal thought to be driven home to all three of these prima donnas is that the situation is today solely in the military field, and that any decision by any one of them, or by all of them, is subject to review and approval by Eisenhower."

Under Eisenhower's supreme command from his Algiers headquarters, Allied forces pushed deep into Tunisia until heavy seasonal rains, mud thick enough to drown in, and fierce German resistance bogged them down. The Americans had raised their standing in British eyes with their successful North African landings, but their novice Tunisian campaign was brave, bold, and hapless, as novice campaigns will be. By the end of the year the United States Army had fought just a few small engagements with the Germans in Tunisia, almost all of them lost. A British after-action report on a combined operation called an American regiment "unfitted and unprepared for the task they were asked to perform." Marshall said after the war that the Americans could not field so much as "workmanlike divisions" in Tunisia, for lack of thorough training. Behind their backs, British officers were known to call them "our Italians."

Clark's negotiation with Darlan had saved many lives and made allies of the French North Africans, but Roosevelt took a hard political hit when much of the British and American press attacked "the Darlan deal" as a marriage with a Nazi stooge. Churchill too came under pressure. When the Germans attacked the Soviet Union in 1941, he had told the House of Commons in secret session that if Hitler invaded hell, he would find something good to say about Satan, but he cabled FDR that Eisenhower's embrace of Darlan was deeply resented in Britain and could only be called a temporary expedient. Roosevelt summoned the press and called it just that, which undermined French confidence in American fidelity.

Eisenhower signed a formal pact with Darlan despite the hostile press, reassuring his new French friends. The Americans kept control of the occupied region's military bases, ports, and airfields, and the French stayed in charge of their civic affairs and their own armed forces, conditioned on cooperation. Nothing was said about repealing their anti-Semitic laws or disbanding their local replica of the Gestapo, which enforced them energetically, or letting Jews and Arabs vote, or releasing political prisoners from concentration camps.

The Anglo-American press erupted, led by some of Roosevelt's most ardent supporters. Churchill tried to calm the House of Commons: "Since 1776, we have not been in the position of being able to decide the policy of the United States" and "the Almighty in His infinite wisdom did not see fit to create Frenchmen in the image of Englishmen."

Here were sown new seeds of Allied conflict. With the battle for all North Africa not yet won, de Gaulle, Giraud, and Darlan each pictured himself the hero to lead the liberation of France and restore her as a great power. De Gaulle was Churchill's reluctant choice for both holy missions, and he and the three French divas shared a beatific vision of the French and British empires revived, but Roosevelt, the ardent anticolonialist, had a sharply different view: Ike was Julius Caesar, conqueror of the Gauls.

Three

THE BIRTH OF THE
CASABLANCA CONFERENCE

n mid-November 1942, less than a week after Torch's success, the U.S.
Navy won a crucial victory at the naval battle of Guadalcanal in the
Southwest Pacific. Two days later, Montgomery was chasing Rommel
through Libya and the Russians were preparing a counterattack at Stalingrad when the president gave a speech in New York. The turning point of
the war might at last have been reached, he said. "But this is no time for
exultation. There is no time now for anything but fighting and working
to win."

The question was where to fight next. For the British, an Allied
army in North Africa made a Mediterranean strategy clearer than ever,
but Averell Harriman, Roosevelt's friend since childhood, found clarity
scarce in Washington. A handsome graduate of Groton and Yale, the
cultivated heir to a fabulous railroad fortune, he had spent his prewar
time on polo, thoroughbred horses, investment banking, and developing a pioneering ski resort in Sun Valley, Idaho, but no American was a
better match for the British ruling class than Averell Harriman, a future
governor of New York. Roosevelt had sent him to London as his special
representative overseeing the U.S.'s Lend-Lease program well before Pearl

Harbor, the news of which Harriman and Churchill heard together on the BBC. Now he was nearly as close to the prime minister as he was to the president. Visiting Washington soon after Torch, Harriman found it adrift in "indecision and divided counsels in high places."

Sharply tuned to Anglophobia in several such places, Churchill sent a white-hot memo to his Chiefs of Staff. He had made a commitment to Marshall in July, "solemnly undertaken," to cross the Channel in 1943, and "I cannot give this up without a massive presentation of facts and figures which prove physical impossibility." The Allies had meant North Africa to be "a springboard, not a sofa," but now it seemed that "the sum of all American fears is to be multiplied by the sum of all British fears, faithfully contributed by each Service." The British had "pulled in our horns," the staff had turned sour on a second front in France, "and I cannot imagine what the Russians will say or do when they realize it."

Keenly aware of what they might do, a separate peace included, Roosevelt sent Stalin a message. The British and American military were considering their options and he and Churchill hoped to consult the Soviet leader and his staff, for "whatever we do next in the Mediterranean will have a definite bearing on your magnificent campaign and your proposed moves this coming winter." Four days later the Russians surrounded the German Sixth Army at Stalingrad.

Churchill had told Anthony Eden, now his foreign secretary, that if Stalin drove the Germans from Russia, he must be stopped from overrunning the West. "It would be a measureless disaster if Russian barbarism overlaid the culture and independence of the ancient states of Europe." But Churchill sent Stalin a message that read like Soviet propaganda and did not mention barbarism: "The glorious news of your offensive is streaming in. We are watching it with breathless attention." The Allies, Churchill wrote, were building massive airpower and an invasion force in England that kept many German divisions pinned near Calais. "And all the time our bombers will be blasting Germany with ever increasing violence. Thus the halter will tighten upon the guilty doomed." The American deal with "the rogue Darlan" was no cause for alarm, and he and Roosevelt would like to send senior officers to Moscow to make aggressive plans.

Stalin lost no sleep fretting about Darlan. If it helped kill Germans, he replied, the Americans could do business with the devil and his grandma. Hoping, he wrote, that pinning Germans near Calais did not imply a substitute for the promised second front, he was ready to receive Allied officers in the Kremlin.

In the meantime, Churchill wrestled with his Chiefs of Staff and committed his short-term ambitions to paper: The Allies must first clear the enemy from Tunisia, open the Mediterranean, and ring its southern coast with air and sea power. Next, they must strike from North Africa "at the under-belly of the Axis" and bomb Italy out of the war. If bombing failed to separate the Italians from the Germans, an invasion of Italy would, and neutral Turkey should be pushed into belligerency. None of this ruled out a continental invasion in 1943, he wrote, if the Germans began to crumble.

Undecided on where next to strike, Roosevelt suggested to Churchill a secret meeting of senior British, American, and Soviet officers. Churchill saw scant worth in that but proposed a Big Three conference, privately confident of handling Stalin and seducing FDR. Hopkins convinced the president that Churchill was right. The top men alone could and should make the big decisions.

Roosevelt told Harriman over lunch that a high-level conference was afoot and asked him to come, but he wanted "no ringers," by which he meant diplomats. His secretary of state Cordell Hull, the most distinguished ringer, would be left at home, and Harriman must persuade Churchill to leave Eden. It would be a military conference, not a seminar on foreign affairs. Some sort of union of de Gaulle and Giraud would be the only diplomatic issue, and Roosevelt's chief of staff Admiral Leahy, his former ambassador to Vichy, would be there to advise him. He designed his foreign policy with Hopkins anyway, and neither of them admired diplomats as a class; "cookie-pushers," Harry called them, "old maids" and "pansies."

On December 2, Churchill wired Roosevelt that before they saw the Russians they should decide between themselves when to cross the Channel, which was almost all that Stalin would want to know, and asked the president to send Marshall and King to London, "if possible with Harry." Roosevelt replied that Stalin would suspect a stacked deck if the English speakers met alone. He and Churchill understood each other, and with "a very small staff" of senior officers they could work things out with Stalin, perhaps at a desert oasis in North Africa or Khartoum. "I don't like mosquitoes."

Delighted by the thought of a "supreme war conference," Churchill replied that he would bring Eden, his Chiefs of Staff, and a cast of expert officers, "supported by a powerful secretariat, cypher staff, map room, etc., say about twenty-five." Harriman called it "the typically British view of having everybody come along." Churchill would urge Stalin to come but would not send his Chiefs of Staff to Moscow. "It will only lead to a deadlock and queer the pitch." The American Chiefs of Staff should come to London first, he said again, for Stalin would have one question: "Have you then no plan for the second front in Europe you promised me for 1943?" The PM vouched for Marrakech as a conference venue and pushed for an early date. Any chance to do something big in 1943 depended on a quick decision.

Roosevelt invited Stalin to meet with him and Churchill, who enticed the Soviet czar with a message of his own. Before the Big Three convened, he wrote, the Anglo-Americans would decide "at the earliest possible moment the best way of attacking Germany in Europe with all possible force in 1943." What was possible was grist for debate, and Churchill was running whim-powered meetings with his Chiefs of Staff. One minute, Brooke complained to his diary, "we are reducing our forces, and the next we are invading the Continent with vast armies for which there is no hope of finding the shipping." At just that point, Churchill told his Chiefs of Staff to prepare to cross the Channel that summer, a ruinous operation in their educated view, having crossed the Channel before. The Germans had forty divisions in France and could quickly throw in more. The British could muster four, the Americans less, and the landing craft did not exist. Churchill was unmoved, and his planners spent two irreplaceable weeks digging up facts to move him.

In Washington, the CCS's combined planners were unable to frame a post-Torch plan for lack of agreement at the top, with Marshall fixed on the Channel, King on the Pacific, and the British Chiefs of Staff making different choices from the Mediterranean menu. Brooke liked Sicily. It was closest to the Anglo-American armies in North Africa, its geography, ports, and airfields would put the Allies in the best position to reopen the Mediterranean, and the tempting toe of Italy was two miles away. Others preferred Sardinia. Its airfields were in range of Axis industry, raids could be launched from its coast up and down the boot, and with no Germans there only light opposition was expected on its beaches. Some believed that if Sardinia were taken "Sicily might fall an easy prey soon after."

Neither island satisfied the prime minister. Having endorsed his Chiefs of Staffs' proposal in late November to take Sicily or Sardinia next, Churchill berated Brooke for it two weeks later: "You must not think that you can get off with your 'sardines' in 1943; no—we must establish a Western front, and what is more we promised Stalin we should do so when in Moscow." Brooke looked him in the eye. "No," he said, "*we* did not promise." Churchill stared back and said no more.

Brooke reflected on the end of his first twelve months as Chief of the Imperial General Staff, a year of incessant defeats before November, and looked forward to better things in 1943. Churchill was "desperately trying at times" but the "privilege to work with such a man" made him easy to forgive.

Any chance for a Big Three conference vanished on December 5 when Stalin wired Roosevelt that the Stalingrad campaign would not let him leave his post. For the Allies it was just as well. The Russians could bring little to the table but a louder demand for a second front. The Anglo-Americans were working together like acrobats, dangerous slips included, but there was little to coordinate with Moscow. Except for sporadic naval protection for Allied convoys approaching Russian ports with Lend-Lease munitions, no Soviet forces were deployed beside their British or American counterparts.

Early in December, Roosevelt told his naval aide and all-purpose fixer, the fifty-two-year-old Captain John McCrea, that he might be meeting Churchill in Africa and was leaning toward Casablanca. Vivian Dykes had called McCrea "a very nice fellow," the flaw King had spotted in his character, and McCrea balked hard at the risks, all the harder when FDR said he would fly rather than sail. The troops were taking risks, the president said, why shouldn't their commander in chief? McCrea thought otherwise. Flying the Atlantic was no small thing. Flying Franklin Roosevelt into a war zone was shocking. Polio had left him wheelchair bound since 1921, and no incumbent president had ever flown before, or traveled so far from the country, or left it in wartime, let alone flown into the war. Roosevelt laughed when McCrea said North Africa was full of assassins who would take him out for ten dollars. He was plainly going anyway, and it was up to McCrea and Mike Reilly, who led his Secret Service detail, to make him as safe as possible. Reilly blanched too when FDR told him. Behind a show of bravado, the president seemed worried and promised to play it Reilly's way.

Roosevelt liked to work with the smallest staffs he could get away with, trusting his own judgment and abhorring leaks, but Churchill liked mobs of specialists. Harriman told the president he had pressed the PM repeatedly to trim his party, and "I have been thoroughly beaten up, but he finally understands." Since Cordell Hull was staying home, Churchill would do without Anthony Eden, but in addition to his Chiefs of Staff, he simply had to have their senior advisors, much of his own inner circle, his minister of war transport, assorted teams of experts, and his personal entourage. Anxious about Stalin, he still wanted Marshall in London first, or the conference might produce no "plans satisfactory to our friend."

On December 10, FDR called his Joint Chiefs of Staff to the White House to start making plans satisfactory to themselves. King was in California with Admiral Chester Nimitz, a mastermind of the Pacific war, and nothing much came of the meeting. Marshall urged the president to resist the British yen for "dabbling" in the Mediterranean. Roosevelt observed that as American forces gathered strength in Britain and North Africa there should be no need for months to decide where to use them. On the following day, Dill wired Brooke what the latter called "an insight into Marshall's brain": After North Africa was cleared of the enemy (as everyone was sure it would be) the focus, Marshall thought, should be fixed on northwest France and a movement through Turkey into the Balkans. Brooke was sure that Marshall was wrong about France.

Roosevelt cabled Churchill on December 11: "There will be a commotion in this country if it is discovered that I have flown across any old seas," but he had just about decided to do it, despite the absence of "our Uncle Joe." The American people would "gasp but be satisfied when they hear about it after it's over." He and Churchill should meet in North Africa with a very small staff, again a very small staff. Perhaps "your three top men and my three top men" could meet separately for a few days before the two of them arrived.

That same day, Roosevelt's three top men approved Pacific offensives in the Solomon Islands and the Bismarck Archipelago and a campaign to retake Burma. Burma had been part of the British Empire since 1824, but its recapture was an American priority. Japan had been warring on China for six years, and Generalissimo Chiang Kai-shek's Chinese army, huge though unevenly capable, depended on American arms and supplies, but the Japanese controlled every Chinese seaport and had closed the Burma Road, a 700-mile supply route from the Bay of Bengal to southwest China over mountainous terrain. Only a trickle of supplies came by air from India "over the Hump" of the Himalayas. The Americans would push the British to retake the Burma Road and all of Burma.

On December 15 the British Chiefs of Staff sent Churchill a memorandum that rejected a continental invasion as unachievable in 1943, and the prime minister called them in to vet it. Expecting a Churchillian storm, Brooke brought facts and statistics that met the burden of proof the PM had defined—physical impossibility. To Brooke's great surprise,

Churchill accepted defeat. Now he was "fairly safe," the general told his diary, "but I have still the Americans to convince first, then Stalin next!!" Churchill's calm surrender led Brooke's director of plans General Kennedy to suspect the PM of demanding a Channel crossing in 1943 to prove it impossible and void his pledge to Marshall.

The British Chiefs of Staff now turned to the upcoming conference and what Kennedy called in his diary "a crystallization of the difference between us and the Americans on the strategy for 1943 and the increasing distrust of Eisenhower's conduct of operations in North Africa." With "little military insight" Ike was planning an attack on the Tunisian port of Sfax that would defer the decisive battle "and perhaps expose him to defeat on his main front, where he is very thin." On the global stage, the Americans seemed fixed on Pacific offensives and a Roundup invasion of France, while the British would push for land, sea, and air attacks in the Mediterranean and "put the residue into the UK pending the time when we feel we can get back into the continent without the certainty of defeat." Apart from their ambition to coax Turkey into the war, "we want to know more about the Pacific operations and to cut them to the minimum required to hold Japan till Germany is defeated."

Dill wrote his peers from Washington that "Life is not easy here." The Americans were framing a poor global strategy for the conference "and we are not in a strong position to guide them." Marshall was openminded but King was unshakably "Pacific-minded," claiming "no one else is Pacific-minded at all." All he wanted, King was saying, was to keep Japan contained until Germany's defeat, which demanded a two-thirds Europe, one-third Pacific split of assets. Dill thought he might take less.

On December 21, Roosevelt informed Churchill that a safe place to meet had been found near Casablanca. "It might be wise for some of our military men to precede us by a few days to clear the ground," after which four or five days "could clear up all of our business." Churchill replied immediately: "The sooner the better. I am greatly relieved," and secrecy was vital.

Within days, a Washington cab driver phoned the White House and asked to speak to someone about "the President's trip." Minutes later he was sitting with Mike Reilly. The driver told the Secret Service man he had just been taking two Englishwomen to a fancy address when one informed the other that Roosevelt would soon be meeting Churchill in Casablanca, "but don't tell a soul," apparently unconcerned about telling a cabbie. Reilly tracked the address to an English journalist, and the mortified British ambassador promised to plug the leak. Other rumors had the president on his way to Baghdad or Siberia.

Roosevelt told Captain McCrea he was taking him to Casablanca and asked him to make secret travel arrangements. The president's physician Admiral Ross T. McIntire was not pleased to hear that his patient would be taking a twenty-four-hour train ride to Miami followed by risky flights to the Caribbean, Brazil, and West Africa. McIntire called the latter "tsetse fly country," but Bathurst, British Gambia's capital, would make a tolerable overnight stay in a U.S. warship.

Three events marked Christmas Eve, none of them festive. Eisenhower canceled a Tunisian offensive, stopped by filthy weather; Brooke eviscerated Ike's "very bad plan for the capture of Sardinia"; and a young French royalist shot and killed Darlan in the high commissioner's office in Algiers, expecting to be cheered. Giraud stepped into the void and ordered a drumhead trial in suspicious haste. As Churchill later wrote, the assassin was shot on December 26, "much to his surprise." Roosevelt said one word when told that Darlan was dead. "Unfortunate." Others found it fortunate indeed. Darlan had served his purpose, and his removal cleared the field for de Gaulle as well as Giraud and took pressure off the Allies.

Years later, de Gaulle recalled his reaction to Darlan's murder: "I would have to turn it to my advantage." White House staff and many Frenchmen suspected him as its author, and de Gaulle was on his way to a military flight to Washington to meet with FDR when the president postponed it. The Darlan deal had empowered the French to choose their own leaders, but Eisenhower made it clear to French North Africa's Imperial Council that their choice was Giraud, who succeeded Darlan on December 26 and retained his military command. Churchill was not consulted and nor was de Gaulle, whose party was persecuted by Giraud's administration, which accused some of its leaders of complicity in Darlan's killing and jailed them. For the sake of Allied unity, Churchill endorsed Giraud's appointment in a message to Roosevelt. He would see de Gaulle that day, the PM wrote, to coax him to unite with Giraud.

Preparations for the Allied conference continued. On December 26, U.S. Army planners identified three potential paths to victory in Europe: massive bombing, a continental invasion, and new Mediterranean operations. Bombing was necessary but not sufficient. A Channel crossing was essential but probably impossible in 1943 except to take a bridgehead from which to launch a full-scale invasion in 1944. The planners concluded that the realist's choice for 1943 was a devastating bombing campaign and an assault in the Mediterranean designed to reopen it to shipping and perhaps knock Italy out of the war. In this they agreed with the British. Marshall and Hopkins still liked the Channel. Roosevelt's mind was open.

On December 27 de Gaulle sent Giraud an invitation to meet on French colonial soil to discuss a unification. Giraud endorsed the idea in principle and asked de Gaulle to send him a liaison officer but declined to meet in a post-assassination environment where every tête-à-tête was a conspiracy. De Gaulle replied that he and his National Committee had a different sense of urgency.

The bespectacled forty-three-year-old Brigadier General Edward Ian Claud Jacob, assistant secretary to the War Cabinet, was one of Churchill's favorites. The articulate son of a field marshal, educated at the Royal Military Academy, Woolwich, Ian Jacob had been commissioned into the Royal Engineers at eighteen, too late for the Great War, and had risen to support the Committee of Imperial Defense as one of Pug Ismay's deputies. An irreverent sense of humor notwithstanding, his meticulous efficiency inspired a colleague to call him "Iron Pants," a title "conferred with admiration."

At Churchill's request, Jacob left London on Christmas Day to inspect the Moroccan city of Fedala, the American choice for a conference venue, and consider alternatives. Given everything he asked for at Eisenhower's Algiers headquarters, Jacob took two officers, one British and one American, on a flight to Casablanca and found nearby Fedala unworthy and unsafe, with ample good cause. Churchill had touted Marrakech, having fallen in love with the place in 1937, but it was barely defended and full of Axis spies. Jacob left it alone despite the prime minister's wishes, for "excellent accommodation could be found, and I did not want to give him a loop-hole."

Acting on a young American officer's tip, Jacob and his companions drove to a lovely outer district of Casablanca called Anfa, an elegantly planned community of European and Moroccan grandees, where they found what they needed in the hilltop Anfa Hotel overlooking the sea, which Patton had commandeered for his headquarters, and the fourteen "Moroccan Modern" villas that curled around it, each of which had a name. As the diplomat Robert Murphy later wrote, "no place in Casablanca was really safe," and a decision was made that the conferees "might as well be comfortable."

The spectacular Villa Maas had been home to the Nazi thug who ran the local Gestapo and the German Armistice Commission, which enforced French compliance with the 1940 surrender terms limiting North African forces. Its occupants had thought it wise to leave in a hurry with no time to loot its furnishings when the Americans appeared in the harbor. A Boston Brahmin major thought it tasteless, but Patton called it "the most ostentatiously magnificent house I have ever seen" and found it fit for his personal occupation. The British officer accompanying Jacob got a glimpse of Yankee worldliness in a courtesy call on Patton. When an aide came to the door, the officer introduced himself in a regional British accent and asked to see General Patton. The American shouted back into the room: "Is there anyone here who understands French?"

Jacob found in Patton the rare American officer who impressed him. "He certainly is a magnificent looking man," Jacob told his diary, well

over six feet tall, "evidently very fit and tough," white hair notwithstanding, "with an exceedingly cold grey eye." Jacob declined Patton's offer
to donate Villa Maas to the conferees but asked him to make his guest
quarters available to VIPs and perhaps entertain senior officers. Patton
was more than glad to display his spoils of war.

Passing again through Eisenhower's Algiers headquarters on his way back
to London, Jacob found its British and American officers "inextricably
fused" in teamwork and wondered how they did it. There was no tribal
friction at all, but inconsistent methods and terminology cut efficiency
in half. Jacob thought the whole affair was tinged with Yankee amateurism and lacked the dignity of a British HQ. To the Englishman's military
eye, many Americans seemed "dressed up as soldiers." British officers said
they were apt to be green and ignorant, though many were "admirable,
cooperative, and loyal friends." Jacob himself took a liking to an American colonel. "Such an honest, simple-minded chap."

Churchill was pleased with Jacob's choice of a conference venue,
though "obviously still hankering after Marrakesh." The PM wired Roosevelt that an admirable site had been found, and Eisenhower agreed.
Anfa's aloof detachment from its less fortunate Arab neighbors made it
easier to protect, but even before the Allied high command assembled
within range of German airpower, Casablanca and its harbor were packed
with bomb-worthy warships, munitions, and fuel.

The Luftwaffe struck on New Year's Eve. Awakened in the night
by moaning sirens, rosy-pink fingers of antiaircraft fire, and low-flying
four-engine bombers roaring through shafts of light with black German
crosses under their wings, Patton ran up to his roof as bomb fragments
shot past Villa Maas. Finding it all "really lovely to watch," the general
dashed back up when a second wave struck, leaving room-sized craters.
Trapped in a searchlight beam, a bomber dropped to a gun crew's cheers,
leveled off trailing smoke, and "disappeared into the mist" before it hit
the water. No Americans were killed, but eleven were wounded and dozens of Moroccans lost their lives.

Earlier that night, the Roosevelts had hosted a New Year's Eve dinner party at the White House, where the president planted a joke that could not be appreciated for weeks. A moody new film was shown starring Humphrey Bogart and Ingrid Bergman. *Casablanca* it was called.

On New Year's Day in London Averell Harriman wondered whether the president had reconsidered telling Churchill who to bring to Casablanca and who to leave home and sent Hopkins a cable: "Does the Boss still want me to see that no ringers are in the party?" Was Harriman himself still coming? "You can well understand my concern as to the manner in which our decisions are put up to our gallant allies." Roosevelt cabled Churchill, who declared himself "delighted to bring Averell."

Ian Jacob was glad to hear that Mountbatten was sending a 6,000-ton headquarters ship to Casablanca. With HMS *Bulolo* in the harbor, stocked with every pertinent War Office file, teams of military experts, and instant communications with London, the British could perform "exactly as if we were in Great George Street," but Jacob was appalled by the size of the British herd. In addition to the prime minister's Chiefs of Staff, their senior subordinates, and Ismay, the British were taking several echelons of planners, the War Cabinet's secretariat, Churchill's minister of war transport Lord Leathers, a former self-made shipping line executive christened Frederick Leathers, whose lordly title honored his key role in the war, two of his lordship's staff, assorted specialists, secretaries, clerks, and technicians, and Churchill's nine-man entourage. All told, sixty-two British officers were coming, sixteen stenographers, sixty guards and orderlies of the Royal Marines, and six batmen, uniformed servants to high-ranking officers. Due to limited housing, the officers were informed, "all batmen will have to live in HMS *Bulolo*. Arrangements have been made for their transport from the ship daily."

Jacob had been told that the Americans would field a small team—nine officers as it turned out, the president's Joint Chiefs of Staff included—and advised the PM not to outman, out-paper, and embarrass them. Churchill had agreed, but his Chiefs of Staff decided on what

Jacob called "a full bag of clubs, leaving some of them concealed, as it were, in the locker, i.e., the ship." Throughout the conference, beautifully educated British staff officers with perfect English speech outnumbered the homespun Americans six to one and knocked them off their pins with impeccable memoranda on every key issue, mostly prepared in advance, presented in red-leather folders. The Americans brought three loose-leaf binders, one of them devoted to people and places they might see on the trip.

The conference was code-named Symbol, and Roosevelt wired Churchill the "aliases" he had chosen for himself and Hopkins—Don Quixote and Sancho Panza. In reply Churchill wondered how he had contrived so "impenetrable a disguise" and successfully suggested "Admiral Q" and "Mr. P." instead. Churchill would be Air Commodore Frankland. Roosevelt's 1940 Republican opponent and onetime London envoy Wendell Willkie had lately begun to attack him, and Churchill advised the president that if he happened to bring Willkie his code name should be Windmill.

The American Chiefs of Staff sent the British in advance a workmanlike, fancifully ambitious negotiating position called "Basic Strategic Plan for 1943." An offensive "directly against Germany" would begin with stupendous bombing and a rapid shipment of troops from the United States and North Africa to England, followed by a Channel crossing. Italy too would be bombed. The Russians would be supported to the utmost. An attempt would be made to coax Turkey into the war, to acquire a bombing platform and access to the Black Sea. After the enemy was cleared from North Africa, there would be no Mediterranean offensives but for bombing. The Burma Road would be reopened. Defensive *and* offensive operations in the Pacific would keep Japan contained until Germany's defeat.

The British sent two papers in reply, a masterly outline of their positions and a brilliant memorandum in support. No lawyer ever wrote a more persuasive brief, grounded in the facts, propelled by incisive analysis, crafted for American readers. "The days of plugging holes are over," it began. "We must now agree on a plan that will lead to victory, quickly and decisively," two favorite Yankee words. The paper endorsed the American positions on bombing, the Russians, Turkey, and the Burma Road but just a minimal Pacific war and aggressive Mediterranean operations. A modest Sledgehammer invasion of the Continent by September, before the Channel became too risky to cross, would only be launched if the Germans had been gravely weakened.

General Kennedy saw progress in this candid exchange of views. "The next thing was to convince the Americans that ours were right and theirs were wrong. The fact that Marshall was opposed to our policy did not carry much weight with us, for we were absolutely convinced that we were right, and that Marshall's policy would lead to disaster."

Disturbed by the British memoranda, angered in the case of King, the American Chiefs of Staff had an agitated talk in which a key word was "adamant." The British, Marshall said, were adamant about delaying an invasion of northwest France, Marshall was adamant about accelerating it, and King was adamant about pressuring Japan.

Meanwhile, De Gaulle urged Giraud again to meet him on French colonial soil and Giraud declined again. In response, de Gaulle made the invitation public and added a call for a governing French authority in North Africa until "the nation has made known her will," which prompted the State Department to inform de Gaulle's man in Washington that his purview was exclusively military. Roosevelt skipped the euphemisms in a cable to American diplomats in Algiers. In North Africa "we have a military occupation," he wrote, with Eisenhower in "complete control of all affairs, both civilian and military. Our French friends must not be permitted to forget this for a moment."

At half past noon on January 7, Roosevelt delivered his eleventh State of the Union address to a joint session of Congress. As he made his way to the podium, heavily braced, swinging on the arm of an aide through a sea of outstretched hands, the ovation broke in waves of patriotism on both sides of the aisle and shook the room again whenever he spoke of the war. "The Axis powers knew," he said, that "they must win the war in 1942 or eventually lose everything. I do not need to tell you that our enemies did not win the war in 1942." A year on the defensive was over in the Pacific. "Now our aim is to force the Japanese to fight. Last year we stopped them. This year we intend to advance." So now he was committed, whatever the British thought. When Harriman read the speech in London, he underlined in red the part about advancing and wrote "Magnificent" on page one.

That afternoon FDR and his Joint Chiefs of Staff had their first and only meeting to prepare for Casablanca. Churchill and his high command had been gearing up for weeks. Roosevelt said he would visit front-line troops in North Africa, eat with them from mess kits, sleep with them in tents. He would also raise with Churchill the thought of giving Stalin a new assurance: Far from making a separate peace with Hitler, the Allies would demand the Axis powers' unconditional surrender. A State Department advisory group had proposed that audacious move, unprecedented in American history, and Stalin might be prompted to make the same pledge. The minutes include no discussion of the idea, which apparently made no strong impression. Roosevelt mentioned in passing that instead of endorsing the French North African Imperial Council's appointment of Giraud as Darlan's successor, Ike should have said there was no such thing as a French North African Imperial Council.

The president inquired whether his Chiefs of Staff had agreed to press the British to invade the Continent in 1943, a question he might have asked earlier. Marshall confessed division, particularly among the planners. The American Chiefs of Staff, he said, had coalesced around the Channel while the British preferred the Mediterranean, but the issue was open. Many precious ships would be lost taking Sicily or Sardinia, and the Germans might move quickly through Spain and close the Strait of Gibraltar, trapping the Allies in the middle sea. "Personally," Marshall said, he favored a limited invasion of northwest France, where the losses would be taken in troops. "To state it cruelly," men could be replaced more easily than ships. The Brest peninsula could be captured and held in a relatively modest Sledgehammer operation in 1943. Even if the Germans dislodged the bridgehead, the battle would weaken them for Roundup in 1944.

Marshall said the British thought the Germans were too strong in France to attack them there in 1943, and it would be hard to reach agreement on the point, let alone on how much force to throw against Japan. Even if the Americans accepted a Mediterranean target, they would choose to make it Sicily while the British seemed to like Sardinia, and either operation would beggar Bolero's pre-invasion buildup in the U.K. King said Sardinia's capture would do little to reopen Mediterranean shipping, but Sicily's would be "decisive." If we took Sardinia, Roosevelt said, "we could shout Hooray," followed by "Where do we go from here?" Would it not be wise, he asked again, to build up forces in England, make plans for the Mediterranean *and* the Channel, and choose between them later? Probably not, Marshall said, but Admiral Leahy liked the idea.

A united Anglo-American strategy had been stretched out thin and could snap if the conference went wrong, but Roosevelt and his Chiefs of Staff were adrift on its salient points a week before it began. "The British will have a plan and stick to it," Roosevelt said, but there was no American plan to stick to, which bothered him not at all, having gotten where he was by playing his cards as they were dealt, rarely showing them, and keeping his options open. The discussion petered out without a coherent strategy and the meeting turned to other things. It had started at three and was over by four, when the president sat for a portrait artist's sketch. On his face was pure serenity.

The Americans handled secrecy about as well as planning. General Wedemeyer attended a dinner party that night, where a columnist told a senator a conference was afoot in Casablanca. Where was Casablanca, the senator asked? The columnist smiled. "Ask Wedemeyer."

In London, the British Chiefs of Staff discussed how to get to Africa. Churchill suggested a cruiser until the First Sea Lord, Admiral Pound, reported U-boat sightings. They would fly to Casablanca for the conference. Brooke told his diary, "I feel that we shall have a difficult time."

Four

THE GATHERING OF THE TRIBES

Hopkins made notes when the muse of history moved him. The president was going to Casablanca, Harry wrote, "because he wanted to make a trip. He was tired of having other people, particularly myself, speak for him around the world. He wanted to see our troops, he was sick of people telling him that it was dangerous to ride in airplanes. He liked the drama of it. But above all, he wanted to make a trip." All of this was true, but Margaret Suckley, FDR's cousin and longtime confidante, "Daisy" to him since childhood, was privy to his fears. No one knew better than he what he would suffer on a five-day trek to a war zone and back, disabled on the cusp of sixty-one, a prime German target. "He is going," Daisy wrote, "because he feels he must go."

Shortly after ten on Saturday night, January 9, 1943, he was driven through quiet streets from the White House to the Bureau of Engraving and Printing, where a private train was waiting at an underground siding meant for loading bales of cash. The president's armored railway car, ingeniously designed for him and his inner circle, had a miniature first-class kitchen and separate plush compartments built for work, relaxation, dining, and sleep. The rest of his party made do in a standard coach and a Pullman sleeper. A Signal Corps radio car kept him in touch with the world. Run by an engineer who was not told where he was going, the train headed north toward FDR's Hyde Park home, turned around in Baltimore, and ran back through Washington toward Miami.

Hopkins and Admiral Leahy traveled with FDR, but his other Chiefs of Staff flew from Washington's Bolling Field in two huge C-54 Skymaster transports, stocked with small arms and survival gear and fitted up for first-class travel. Should one plane go down to mishap or the Luftwaffe, it was hoped that the other would not. Secret documents were stowed in locked steel boxes rigged with explosives. One of the stately Skymasters carried, among others, Marshall, his British guests Dill and Dykes—both of whom Marshall, not Churchill, had invited—and the genial commander of the Army Air Forces Lieutenant General Henry H. Arnold. In the other were King, his waspish deputy chief of staff for plans Rear Admiral Charles M. Cooke Jr., Wedemeyer, and Lieutenant General Brehon B. Somervell, the Army's able chief of logistics, enthusiastic Anglophobes all.

When they stopped in Puerto Rico at an airbase to refuel and spend the night King's plane arrived first, but a radio message from Marshall instructed its pilot to let *him* land first and receive the senior officer's honors. King loudly disapproved of wasting wartime fuel "for a bit of blasted protocol," and "blasted" was surely bowdlerized. "How dare that goddamned pillar of virtue pull rank on me?" Marshall was not pleased when King confronted him. Years later, King called Marshall a very able man with a sturdy ego; "born that way, thought and believed he could do any damn thing."

The Skymasters took off for Brazil the next morning, and General Arnold took the lead plane's controls for a two-hour shift. An engine started missing and coughed for 500 miles, which spoiled the general's mood, particularly "in view of my passenger list and the unsettled jungle beneath us." As the planes refueled at Natal, Brazil, where a small American base served bombers crossing the Atlantic, Arnold was told that a secret meeting of the CCS was the talk of every airfield in Africa.

• • •

Should any need arise to establish his credentials as a pioneer military aviator, General Arnold had a drop-dead line. The Wright brothers had taught him to fly. Raised in a posh Philadelphia suburb, the son of a grim physician who pushed him into West Point, he had barely noticed the flight at Kitty Hawk in his plebe year of 1903 and graduated in 1907 in the middle of his class. After a stint in the Philippines, he failed the Ordnance Department's entrance examination and asked a superior's advice about joining the aviation program. "If you want to commit suicide," the officer replied, "go ahead." In 1911, after three hours and forty-eight minutes with Wilbur and Orville Wright in contraptions like bicycles with wings, Arnold was one of the Army's two aviators. In the program's first four years eighteen of its twenty-four fliers crashed and died.

As a moonlighting stunt pilot in silent films, Arnold's cheerful disposition, oddly combined with a dominant personality, earned him the nickname "Hap." A near-death experience spooked him into the infantry, but he returned to the air in 1916 as a protégé of General Billy Mitchell, the Army's controversial champion of aviation. After reaching France only days late for World War I, Arnold rose to command the Army Air Corps as a brigadier general and built a world-class air force. He admired the heroic RAF but begrudged FDR's diversion of warplanes to Britain in her hour of need at the cost of American airpower and made it public. Roosevelt came close to forcing his retirement, but at Hopkins's request Marshall sent him to London in April 1941 to see what the Brits were up against.

From the moment he arrived, Arnold's British hosts gave him what Hopkins called the treatment. He started a London diary with a moving tour of two dozen blocks of shattered family homes. The next Luftwaffe raid left nightmarish streetscapes, tragic loss of life, and defiant "Britain back at work." Admiral Pound welcomed Arnold to the Admiralty with its windows and doors blown out. An airmen's talk with ordinary RAF pilots escorted by Pug Ismay and Jack Dill was mutually rewarding, and Air Chief Marshal Portal turned out to be "a brilliant man who does things." Churchill swept Arnold away. Capping his two-week treatment,

Hap sat down at Buckingham Palace with King George VI and a "fine gentleman" he found him to be, though he wondered after half an hour's chat why no one had told "a fellow how to leave a king."

Eyes wide open, Arnold went home a zealous convert and praised the RAF and its use of American planes in a well-reported speech. Portal wrote him in "deep appreciation for your keenness to help us" at the sacrifice of equipping his own service. FDR called his report on Britain's peril the best he had seen and made him a lieutenant general a few days after Pearl Harbor. Now he was Roosevelt's man and the RAF's, not just Marshall's and his own.

No one ever suspected Arnold of brilliance. The future Pulitzer Prize–winning novelist James Gould Cozzens, the reservist who wrote his speeches, had him classed as "really dumb" but more than a match for the Luftwaffe's intellectuals. Ismay got it right: "Arnold's paramount interest was to bomb Germany by day as well as by night every day of the week and every week of the month from all points of the compass."

Admiral King flocked with birds of a feather, and Rear Admiral "Savvy" Cooke, the capable, intelligent, slightly built, scowling Arkansan who led the Navy's strategic planners and lived on King's official yacht with King, was a prime example. Vivian Dykes thought Cooke was anything but savvy, "that bloody little man" who made things hard for the fun of it, a "common little squirt." Jack Dill had discovered that Cooke could "out-King King," which Cooke would prove again at Casablanca. King also brought his flag secretary Commander Ruthven E. Libby, another honors graduate of the King school of charm. Libby had recently replied to a subordinate's request for comments on a draft press release: "Briefly and succinctly, I think it stinks." A longer review followed.

Before they left for Africa, King had tried and failed to persuade Marshall and Arnold to support his grand design—a major Pacific offensive followed by others in time—and had grudgingly lined up with keeping Japan in check until Germany's defeat. On their overnight flight to Africa, King discussed with Cooke and Wedemeyer what purpose might be served by sending more troops to North Africa. None, they thought. Torch had accomplished its mission. Allied air and naval bases on the North African coast would open a Mediterranean sea lane, and the threat to the Suez Canal was gone. When King asked if Marshall agreed Wedemeyer said he did.

Cooke later wrote that as for invading France in 1943, "I knew that King was still supporting Marshall, that Wedemeyer was going along with Marshall, but what they proposed to do was not practicable." Cooke told King in flight that "to finish up the campaign in Africa and then turn around a million men, their supplies and equipment and land them in England" from Africa and America in time to cross the Channel by September was impossible. "King agreed after some delay, but it was some days before Marshall and Wedemeyer allowed themselves to be convinced." Concerning the war in Europe, Cooke "was in complete agreement with the British point of view" and had staked himself out two months earlier: "Our main amphibious operations in 1943 should be conducted in the Mediterranean."

In a memo shared with the Americans, the British had concluded that a large-scale invasion of France "against unbroken German forces is not a practical operation of war." It would surely fail, and its failure would be catastrophic. "Probably correct," Cooke had written, "but no indication is made as to how German military power will be broken." It would break under constant pressure, and "the drain on their ammunition and fuel production should be unrelenting."

As the Skymasters neared the African coast, a star flare popped from the sea, an international call for help that U-boats often sent to lure Allied planes to their antiaircraft guns. The Skymasters flew into the clouds and radioed the rescue authorities.

The Americans landed at the U.S. Army airfield at Bathurst, the wretched capital of the British Gambia Colony and Protectorate, which protected its wealth from the Gambians. With tsetse flies in mind, Marshall deplaned in gloves, boots, and a beekeeper's veil, to be greeted by British officers in shorts and half-sleeve shirts. On the Americans' way into town, laborers marched by in columns with right-shouldered picks and shovels, swinging their left arms like British soldiers. They earned less than two shillings and half a cup of rice a day.

Lifting off later from a steel mesh runway roamed by leopards and baboons, the Americans flew northeast for five hours over yellow-brown desert, empty but for the odd camel caravan, until they approached the snowcapped Atlas Mountains and the ancient oasis town of Marrakech, walled in the Middle Ages. The party's senior members spent the night at the stunning Moorish mansion leased by an American widow to the State Department for the use of Kenneth Pendar, its resident diplomat.

Pendar was in the business of entertaining VIPs, but this batch set him back: "I was struck at once," he wrote, "with the thoughtfulness and simplicity of General Marshall," who made just one request: "Would you be so kind as to show me the room you have assigned to Field Marshal Dill? You know he is my guest, and I want to make sure that he is comfortable." Pendar was taken with Jack Dill, "a great friend of the United States," and also with Vivian Dykes, "a delightful man who loved America deeply and sincerely." Pendar's eclectic tastes even encompassed King on his best behavior, "so grudgingly good-humored and so wonderfully tough. I could picture him barking orders from his flag ship and having the oceans themselves change position."

The shades were drawn for the daylight run on the president's train to Miami, but he left one up and caught himself waving to a man on a platform. His escape had done him good. "Yesterday," he wrote Daisy, "seems so far away." When the train reached Miami after midnight, two huge "flying boats," Pan American Airways Clippers chartered to the Navy for the trip, were waiting in the harbor. The world's most luxurious aircraft, with kitchens manned by gourmet cooks, dining rooms seating fourteen, comfortable sitting rooms, and cabined beds, they were also the safest ocean crossers, taking off and landing on water. The second plane carried Roosevelt's junior entourage and flew in sight of the first, ready to rescue its passengers if it ditched.

For security's sake, arrivals and departures were timed for the dark of night, and the president was carried before dawn to the *Dixie Clipper's* pier. The crew, he told Daisy, knew nothing of their passengers until he came aboard, "and then they had a fit." He had not flown a mile in a decade, and what could be more exciting than a flying boat? As the plane skimmed the waves and rose into the sky, Hopkins watched him act like a boy. First thrill aside, he was not fond of ordinary flight. He could not stretch his legs, walk the aisle, or quickly escape a wreck. As his secretary wrote, he had "bounced around some in the old World War I flying machines" in France as assistant secretary of the navy and had never tried it again until he flew to Chicago in 1932 to accept his presidential nomination. Many scolding letters followed.

The travelers landed off Trinidad after ten hours in the air and were up at four a.m. for Brazil, but Admiral Leahy had developed bronchitis and had to be left behind, a blow to Roosevelt's hopes to manage the French. No one else on the trip knew as much about them as he. Refueling in Brazil they started a nineteen-hour flight to Africa over water. The Luftwaffe hunted the flight path, and the Secret Service detail included a former Olympic swimmer "just in case." Months earlier, Churchill had flown to Washington in a Boeing Clipper, in "the bridal suite," he wrote, and recommended Eden to succeed him "In case of my death on this journey." Apart from interception, every aircraft was at risk in 1943. An engine had quit in mid-ocean on Marshall and Hopkins's April flight to London, three planes carrying generals to or from conferences never arrived, and Brooke thought recurring funerals did not sustain "one's flying nerves."

Hopkins spotted three U.S. Navy ships tracking the president's path and scrawled another note: After months of indecision, temperature-raising arguments, and trust-shaking changes of minds, "we are off to decide where we shall fight next. King, Marshall, and their aides are ahead of us by two days to iron out all possible differences." Two days of ironing was wishful thought indeed.

• • •

Patton wrote his wife from Villa Maas, his grandiose commandeered home in the shadow of the Anfa Hotel: "There is a great and very hush hush conference going on here, which I am not in—thank God. I think it is a mess as are many other things." The mess, it seems, was French. Roosevelt and Churchill considered Morocco a conquered country, Patton told his diary, "which it is not. The French have been told nothing and when they find out, as they will, it is going to take a hell of a lot of talk to restore their confidence." Inordinately fond of the French and hostile to the Brits, Patton was convinced that the latter were "pulling hell out of our leg, and no one knows it," scheming to turn the Arabs against France and steal her colonies. He had talked General Clark out of posting troops beside a French artillery unit to discourage them from shelling Anfa, an obvious sign of distrust, and put an American fieldpiece within range of their position.

Lieutenant Colonel Elliott Roosevelt, a thirty-two-year-old photographic reconnaissance pilot based near Algiers, was ordered to fly an admiral to Casablanca and report to the airfield's colonel. The colonel had a wonderful time teasing out his father's secret, but Elliott was not surprised. His mother had given him a hint.

On Tuesday evening, January 12, Pug Ismay dined early at White's, London's oldest club, and then "I sneaked away like a thief in the night." The British Chiefs of Staff assembled inconspicuously and were driven to an RAF aerodrome, headlights off in deference to the Luftwaffe. To help conceal their absence, the minutes of their daily meetings, read by many officers, would continue to show them speaking while they were away. Subordinates would speak in their places.

The Chiefs of Staff were briefed at the aerodrome on the literal ins and outs of parachutes, life vests, forced desert landings, and the art of plunging into the sea. Ismay and the others were told that a dew-collecting gadget could save them from death by thirst "if we were clever enough to use it properly." Engraved cards in English and Arabic—"Greetings and Peace be upon you"—bore the royal coat of arms, identified the bearer as an officer of the British government and "a friend of all Arabs," and promised, in Ismay's words, to reward "any tribal cut-throat who might find us." He had never thought of air travel as dangerous. "This was evidently going to be an exception."

Brooke brought General Kennedy, his director of military operations, ten years his junior. In a stratified society, Queen Victoria had been godmother to Brooke's father and Kennedy had been raised in a threadbare Scottish vicarage, but their friendship outran class. A talented bird photographer like Brooke, Kennedy was a fellow officer of the Royal Artillery, they had both fought at the Somme, and their wry sense of humor, hidden sensibilities, and instinctive sense of decency overlapped. Every morning at Casablanca and again in the late afternoon, they would steal away in search of North African birds, "delighted," Kennedy wrote, by "a good many migrants from Europe."

Air Chief Marshal Portal brought Air Vice Marshal Sir John Cotesworth Slessor, his assistant chief of air staff for plans and self-styled American interpreter, a veteran of the ABC and Lend-Lease talks in Washington. A dapper, witty man, equal to a major general at forty-five, Jack Slessor was Portal's intellectual peer, which was saying something. Born in India to a soldiering family, a star of the RAF and the British Joint Planning Committee, he resembled the English actor David Niven, shared his gift for charming Americans, and walked with a limp and a cane. Lamed in both legs by childhood polio, Slessor was a twice-decorated World War I pilot, polio and all.

Allied generals often crossed war zones in American B-24 Liberator bombers, heavily armored and studded nose-to-tail with eight heavy machine guns. Slessor thought no one could call the "crudely converted" Liberator that brought the British Chiefs of Staff to Casablanca "a very comfortable conveyance for very senior officers of uncertain age." It occurred to Ian Jacob as he and the others were trussed in winter flying kit—fur-lined jackets, pants, and boots and Mae West life vests under parachute harness—that some "truss more easily than others." Ismay and Pound were not among them. As many as eight trussed men could pretend to sleep in a Liberator, a privileged few on cots in the bomb bay, one on a mattress in the tail, the rest on the flight deck in intimate proximity. Vivian Dykes called bomber travel "a grim and squalid business."

They took off at two a.m., swinging wide past France and the Luftwaffe. Ismay and Lord Leathers had the privilege of the bomb racks. "Sleep was out of the question," Ismay wrote, "and the next ten hours were acute discomfort." For Brooke they were a shoving match. The Chief of the Imperial General Staff lay down on the flight deck next to Dickie Mountbatten and "did not find him a pleasant bed companion. I had to use my elbows and knees to establish my rights."

Averell Harriman penciled notes of his trip to Casablanca in a blank address book: "The most elaborate plans had been made to cover up the P.M.'s departure," he wrote. Churchill's personal Liberator, a gift from General Arnold vaingloriously dubbed the *Commando*, had been reserved in Harriman's name at a blacked-out RAF aerodrome near Oxford, ostensibly for a flight to Algeria on Lend-Lease business. Churchill "was supposed to drive up quickly and slip into the plane" but his motorcade made a noisy midnight arrival, led by a blinding spotlight. "This was the P.M.'s secret departure. They had come up that way all the way from London—horns blowing, no stop at red lights etc. etc." An RAF officer wondered why they had not informed the press.

Portal and Harriman shared Churchill's flight, as did his physician Dr. Wilson, his personal aide Commander Charles "Tommy" Thompson, his fussy Cockney manservant Frank Sawyers, his two private secretaries Leslie Rowan and John Martin, and his bodyguard Walter Thompson, a tall Scotland Yard detective. As they boarded the *Commando*, Detective Thompson told Portal "with proper pride," Harriman thought, that his son had just been decorated after thirty-four missions over Germany.

The *Commando*'s American pilot hosted more than one visit from the curious prime minister before Churchill went to sleep on a bomb bay cot. Naked under a short silk nightshirt in keeping with his habit and his privilege, the PM was awakened by the red-hot coil of a makeshift heater in a space that reeked of fuel. It was "rather an unpleasant moment," he later felt "bound to say." It seemed to Dr. Wilson that, exposed below the waist, "the savior of the realm cut a memorable figure as he fumbled with the heater on his hands and knees." Churchill decided to freeze instead of burn and shivered the rest of the way at 8,000 feet in January.

Five

ANFA CAMP

General Kennedy woke up having performed the impressive trick of sleeping through the night in a Liberator and made his way aft to a porthole through the engine noise and fumes. "We had just emerged from a bank of fleecy white clouds, and there in front of us was a long stretch of sandy beach with a heavy surf breaking on it." Casablanca shone white in the sun on "a lovely balmy day," set off by fertile green land and a turquoise sea. The pilot spotted Churchill's plane and waited for it to land.

General Clark understood that Casablanca's ten-dollar asking price for murder was so reasonable that haggling was rare, but Churchill defied his bodyguard and the spies who infested the place, refused a sedan from the American officers who greeted him, shooed a Secret Service detail away, and chatted with mechanics "under cover" in an RAF officer's uniform. As the second Liberator taxied in, General Ismay looked down at the portly man with the big cigar waving up from the tarmac. "As any fool can see," he said, "that is an air commodore disguised as the Prime Minister."

Churchill strode up to the bomber as its high-ranking passengers, stiff, unwashed, and bleary-eyed, eased themselves down a ladder dropped from its belly: "Now tumble out, you young fellows, and get on parade." He shook all their hands and ignored the poor detective who kept beckoning him toward a van driven up close to the plane to take him quickly away, putting Ismay in mind of a nanny coaxing a child unsuccessfully from the sea. The United States Chiefs of Staff had just landed and been driven away. Awed by their luxurious Skymasters, a contrasting display of American wealth, Ian Jacob thought "they must have rattled around like peas in drums." The British were driven to Anfa as the Americans had been, with mud-smeared windows obscuring their identities. The soldiers who slung the mud were said to enjoy it like toddlers.

Atop a gentle hill sloping down to the beach stood the Streamline Moderne Anfa Hotel and the crescent of elegant villas that embraced it, scented with mimosa, dressed in bougainvillea, within sight and sound of the surf. Only days before, Patton's "Hell on Wheels" 2nd Armored Division had encircled the whole affair with a mile of fortified barbed wire festooned with pebble-filled cans that rattled when disturbed. Machine gun nests, bazooka teams, and antiaircraft guns protected its periphery. Tanks guarded the beach. The 30th Infantry's elite third battalion, several hundred heavily armed young men in gleaming boots and helmets, mostly from San Francisco, patrolled the compound day and night with "military snap," an American captain wrote, and "the highest degree of polish," abetted by police dogs and rooftop riflemen. Slit trenches dug by the hotel's door provided light protection from air raids. American day fighters and British night fighters circled overhead. Jack Slessor called the place "a sort of young fortress." Everyone called it Anfa Camp.

In Patton's unlikely role as cruise director—supplying room, board, entertainment, and security—he had done a thorough job, particularly with the latter. The compound had been swept with mine detectors and Geiger counters. Every villa and hotel room had been searched for weapons, bombs, and listening devices, several French or German models of which had been found and removed. Roosevelt's and Churchill's food and drink were tested and guarded. The phone lines were monitored, long-distance service was shut down, and scramblers were installed in senior officers' rooms. The British delegation was warned that "in the hotel and in each villa there are servants of whose affiliation and contacts we have no knowledge." Many were replaced by American GIs and British marines. The rest were confined within the wire. A pass was required to enter either of its two heavily guarded gates, where MPs and Secret Service men inspected every face. Anyone who seemed a touch out of plumb was at risk of being shot. Only some of the compound's residents were allowed to leave at all except on official business. The diplomat Bob Murphy called Anfa Camp "a luxurious prison."

"Naturally there are many local rumors," an American report to Eisenhower's headquarters said, "but none are accurate." Something was going on at Anfa, and many astute observers had deduced what it was. In addition to Roosevelt, Churchill, and de Gaulle, Spain's fascist dictator Francisco Franco was coming. So was the emperor of Ethiopia Haile Selassie and an Italian surrender mission led by King Victor Emmanuel and the pope. Thoughtful minds dismissed the ridiculous rumor that the Allies were risking their entire high command in one small space less than two weeks after its New Year's Eve bombing.

The Anfa Hotel hosted something like a military convention. The Germans had merrily looted its best accoutrements, but its furnishings were au courant. "A very swank hotel," King's aide Commander Libby called it. Its bustling ground floor included a handsome banquet room converted to a conference room for the occasion, separate British and American meeting rooms, partitioned space for U.S. Army clerks, a message room, a ground transportation center, and separate offices for the two secretariats. The British edition was crowded with staff and the odd senior officer popping in for news or to vet a breaking issue. Junior American officers manned the reception desk. Patton's spiffy soldiers tended a bar stocked with top-shelf liquor, beer, soft drinks, tobacco, candy, and gum, all free of charge. The Americans kept in touch with Washington by radio, the Brits spoke with London through HMS *Bulolo* in the harbor.

The CCS and most of the other officers were housed in the hotel.

Private rooms were provided for the top brass, doubles for the others. No gentle critic, Brooke was pleased with his. Every guestroom had a balcony overlooking the surf-tossed sea or distant golden hills and purple-pink snowcapped mountains. Royal Marine orderlies and American corporals were posted on every floor, "available for any service" twenty-four hours a day. Every British chief of staff had his batman, every American counterpart his orderly. Marshall's had been thoughtfully selected from the first company he commanded in his youth. The third floor's Restaurant Panoramique, also free, adjoined a rooftop garden. The elevator seldom worked and some of the officers had their beds rigged with mosquito nets but there was little other cause for complaint.

The U.S. Army had moved the villas' owners to a Casablanca hotel, respectfully no doubt, if not without the occasional scene, and assigned their homes to the president, the prime minister, their senior civilian advisors, some officers working in teams, and transient VIPs. The villas and hotel rooms "appeared to be made of elastic," Jacob wrote, for the officers in charge could "let out a fresh link" whenever the need arose. The British planners' villa had long since been improved with "a large library of decidedly doubtful books," which produced a small sensation, bound in Moroccan leather and written in French, regrettably for some, but "profusely illustrated."

Built in 1935, Roosevelt's striking white villa across from the hotel could have been designed for him. Its ground floor master bedroom suite featured an easily accessible sunken black marble tub, and its sleek modern dining room sat twelve. The double-height drawing room with a minstrels' gallery adjoined a white-pillared veranda draped in bougainvillea overlooking a lawn with a garden in bloom. Sliding steel shutters and a high adobe wall commended the whole affair to the Secret Service. Hopkins got one of the upstairs rooms, Elliott Roosevelt the other.

Ian Jacob had interviewed the villa's "flashy" French owner on his preliminary tour and guessed she was an actress and a thoroughbred racehorse owner, judging by the pictures on the walls and the "extremely exotic decoration." Slessor considered it a particularly "lovely villa, of which my main recollection is the zebra hide covers to the sofas and chairs." A British journalist later described it as "the very type of French colonial civilization—a discreet mixture of modern French and Moorish. . . . Everything a little over-sophisticated, a little decadent."

Its owner called it Villa Dar es Saada, "Abode of Divine Favor." Harry Hopkins called it a California bungalow. The U.S. Army called it Villa 2. Churchill called it the White House, which stuck. A smart marine always stood by the White House door. Other marines stopped callers at its gate, regardless of rank, unless the Secret Service cleared them. An armored sedan was kept ready for a sudden presidential departure. To rig a bomb shelter for Roosevelt and Churchill, the Army Corps of Engineers had overlaid the swimming pool with thick steel plates stripped from the new French battleship *Jean Bart*, "ripped like a sardine can" by American naval shells in the November landings. The villa was staffed by two officers and no fewer than fourteen carefully chosen and cleared GIs—a highly regarded mess sergeant, two handpicked cooks, a talented pastry chef, a head waiter, three subordinate waiters, and six orderlies.

Churchill was pleased with his Villa Mirador, guarded by British marines in battle dress, served by British orderlies, chosen for its auspicious entrance hall, impressive drawing room, commodious dining room, private garden, and proximity to the White House. In a letter to Lady Churchill, Clementine to him, the prime minister called his villa very nice and Roosevelt's magnificent. Here was another sign of who was who. So was Kennedy's disappointment that Casablanca's shops "have been cleaned out by the Americans."

The warm, pleasant weather turned comfortably cool at night, and Churchill wired Clement Attlee, the Labour Party leader and deputy prime minister in his coalition wartime government: "Conditions most agreeable. I wish I could say the same of the problems."

On his first day in the sun, Churchill walked the beach with Admiral Pound and other fugitives from wartime London, awed by fifteen-foot waves "roaring up terrible rocks" that "made one marvel that anybody could have got ashore at the landing." There was little for him to do before Roosevelt arrived but to host lunch for Marshall, Clark, and Harriman, who preserved the table talk's drift—"Talk of Japs mostly." Marshall was keen on bombing Japan into submission from China, "not fighting ant hill to ant hill." Churchill told Marshall, "You must educate me about the Pacific war while you are here. We must stay on long enough this time to come to conclusions everywhere." The PM spoke of Stalin beating him up in the Kremlin and how different things would be had Hitler invaded England instead of Russia. The French having scuttled their fleet at Toulon, perhaps it was best that Darlan had ignored Churchill's pleas in June of 1940 to sail it to North Africa and fight on from there, where "the Germans might have conquered him" with the British too weak to help. Harriman reminded him that he had called the scuttling a tragedy at the time and had prophesied that Hitler would strike elsewhere before he turned on Stalin. Churchill defended himself, "laughingly of course"— "You must tell about the times when I was right" as well as wrong.

For the first time since 1939, Churchill was almost on holiday. At a glance, he wrote Clementine, "you would not believe there was such a thing as war, and one might be on the Riviera." He was playing a lot of bezique with Harriman, who "pretended to be entirely ignorant but inflicted a number of defeats upon me." Growing bored and underemployed, he ordered a tour of the casbah, Casablanca's medieval quarter, famous for exotic performers and purveyors of Moroccan rugs, leather goods, and erotic experiences, a place too unsafe to take him even if his presence in Casablanca had not been secret. A young British intelligence officer assigned to dissuade him advised him against the invented risk of catching a disease and spreading it to the president. Churchill replied that he took it as a compliment "not easily ignored" to be suspected at his age of risking an indelicate infection in a dodgy part of town but declared himself "at a complete loss" as to how he might infect the president.

The prime minister was reading for pleasure for the first time in the war. *The Years of Endurance*, a popular history of Britain's war with France after the French Revolution, had just been published in London. Slessor gave Marshall a copy and Churchill was absorbed in his. Its author reminded his countrymen that their ancestors had prevailed, though the war had begun without "the slightest chance of victory and with very little of survival."

Summoned to their meeting room by the American Chiefs of Staff to discuss the president's safety, Mike Reilly—code-named "Copper" for the trip—said his Secret Service team had rejected Kenneth Pendar's Marrakech mansion as an overnight stop on the president's way to Casablanca, though Marshall's party had survived it. Roosevelt would be flown from Bathurst directly to Casablanca. Intelligence had come to Marshall, probably from Dill, that Churchill would invite FDR to visit Marrakech after the conference. This would be sharply discouraged. Everyone thought Roosevelt's demand to visit combat troops was imprudent but could not be denied.

After Reilly was dismissed, Marshall asked his peers how they wished to approach the conference, a question they had left to the day before it started. King said no specific operations should be considered until the British accepted the American plan for an aggressive war against Japan and a direct attack on Germany. Marshall said the British seemed fixed on taking Sardinia, "and their whole thought would be turned toward this." Neither Churchill nor Dill is a likely source of that impression, given that it was wrong.

Two weeks before he left for Casablanca, Churchill had sent his Chiefs of Staff a "Most Secret" memorandum. "A prime object" of Allied strategy in 1943 should be "to bring the maximum force" against the Germans on the ground and in the air. "Only in this way can we achieve the wearing down of the enemy's air force and play our part equally with the armies of our Russian ally." Torch had positioned the Allies to attack from the west *and* the south. Once North Africa was cleared, several targets would be attractive in the Mediterranean and the Middle East, but unless the Allies also attacked from the west, "we shall not be able to bring the most important part of our forces into play." The

Allies must determine whether "combined and concurrent operations" could be launched from both directions. If so, which theater should be the major and which the minor? In the Mediterranean, Churchill wrote, the case was stronger for Operation Husky, the capture of Sicily, than for Operation Brimstone, the taking of Sardinia.

Brooke too favored Sicily. Mountbatten was Brimstone's champion and no match for Churchill or Brooke, let alone both, but the British planners also liked Sardinia, and Ismay and Portal had leaned their way in London. Dill may have alerted Marshall to the Brimstone insurgency or Mountbatten may have buttonholed him.

Whatever the British wanted, King said, the Americans were the greater power and must seize the initiative and keep it. The British must be pushed to do more against the Japanese, pressure the Germans, and give missions to the French. No more troops, planes, or ships that could not be used immediately should be wasted in North Africa. The Americans should start the conference with a push for their global strategy and not let the British digress until they agreed to spend 30 percent of Allied assets on the war against Japan, twice the current 15 percent.

Fifteen percent was a figure of King's invention, and the Americans were giving lopsided weight to the war on Japan. The United States had over 85,000 more troops in the Pacific than it had in Europe and North Africa combined, at least three times the shipping, nearly 25 percent of its overseas air combat groups, and nearly every deployed marine. Moreover, King's identification of the United States as "the greater power" was a matter of potential, not of current capabilities in Europe. The Americans had 150,000 men in the Mediterranean theater. The British had three times as many, four times as many warships, and almost as many aircraft. The troops on hand for the next European operation, whether it came in the Mediterranean or on the Continent, would consist of four French divisions, nine American, and twenty-seven British.

Marshall called the shipping shortage uppermost in his mind. More than a thousand Allied ships had been sunk in 1942, many more than had been built. The silver-haired General Somervell, the U.S. Army's master of logistics, endorsed the British push for the Mediterranean and leaned toward Sicily. The capacity to move troops and cargo was crucial, he said, and an open Mediterranean would free over two million tons of shipping (some 240 ships) from the trek around the Cape of Good Hope. But General Clark said Admiral Sir Andrew B. Cunningham, in command of all Mediterranean naval operations, an exclusively British responsibility, had told him that Tunisian-based aircraft could protect that maritime traffic after North Africa was cleared.

King's caustic acolyte Admiral Cooke said it looked as if Tunisia would not be taken until the spring, when 500,000 Allied troops would be in North Africa, half of whom could hold it. The issue was whether to use the other half in the Mediterranean or carry them to England, draining precious shipping. Burnishing his credentials as a model Anglophobe, Cooke had written that America could avoid *conflict* with Britain only by conceding her supremacy in world trade. Now he challenged Cunningham's view that the ships to be lost taking Sicily or Sardinia would not be worth the price. But first things first. Whatever they proposed, the Americans must stand up to the British.

Clark raised the threat that the Germans might push quickly from France through Spain to the Strait of Gibraltar in response to a Mediterranean operation and plug the Allied forces in the Med like ships in a bottle. German support for Franco had won Spain's civil war in 1939, but Clark called the Spanish "a doubtful quantity." They were waiting to see what happened. Once the Allies took Tunisia, Franco would know where the war was going and resist a German invasion.

Wedemeyer, Cooke's competitive rival in the Anglophobic sweepstakes, said the British were misleading them. Sicily is what you take if you want to control the Med. The British wanted Sardinia to set up an invasion of Italy. Marshall agreed. He had not yet figured out what the president was thinking, he said (an astonishing handicap), but Churchill was working on him, and Churchill kept saying that after the Germans were swept from Africa, we must drive up the Italian boot. Wedemeyer asked how the British could justify impoverishing Bolero's buildup in the

U.K. and delaying a decisive invasion of France merely to take Sardinia. Marshall offered little hope of stopping them.

Despite their commitment to defeating Germany first, Ian Jacob wrote later, the Americans "didn't quite see how it was to be done. They were uncertain of an invasion of Northern France, but they had a deep suspicion of the Mediterranean," which they saw "as a kind of dark hole, into which one entered at one's peril." Jacob was only half right. Marshall was committed to invading France and indeed unsure of when, where, or how, and the Americans were leery of the Mediterranean, but they understood its value and Germany First was a wobbly proposition. King's commitment to the doctrine was fragile. Wedemeyer's was thin. Cooke's did not exist.

The Americans, in fact, were committed to very little. Roosevelt had no firm strategic ideas, Marshall's ambition to cross the Channel was not blind, and King's mind was open on Europe. No one recognized the worth of the Mediterranean better than he, but he begrudged every cent not spent in the Pacific. Arnold would go where Marshall led, but a bombing campaign to set up an invasion of France could not peak until 1944, and Sardinia was an excellent platform not only for bombing German and Italian factories but also the Romanian oil fields and refineries that fueled Hitler's war.

Quite apart from indecision, the American Chiefs of Staff were poorly armed for a clash with the Brits. The floating war college in HMS *Bulolo* and dozens of British experts were poised to overwhelm them. They could only lean for help on Somervell, Wedemeyer, Cooke, and sometimes Clark, who shuttled in and out from Algiers. Marshall said years later that Roosevelt had wanted "about five people" at the conference. "I was shooting off the cuff all the time," and "Dill had told me that the British would be ready." Unable to engage them as equals in staffing, preparation, experience, strategic thought, or current capability, "the greater power" was scandalously unprepared. Marshall's recollection speaks for itself: "Casablanca was our first full-scale conference. Our staff preparation was most incomplete. . . . We hoped to keep the British from getting out of hand at Casablanca. Wanted to block Churchill. Figure out what was wise. No rigid view."

General Arnold oversaw his country's only combat in Europe, where British and American airmen were fighting different wars. The RAF bombed German cities by night while the Americans hit military and industrial targets in occupied France and Holland by day. Churchill opposed the American approach, and Arnold had come to Anfa "bluff and hearty and barrel-chested," a junior officer said, with no strategy to defend his position and no one to help, hobbled by Roosevelt's call for a Lilliputian staff.

Having learned early in the war that daylight bombing beyond fighter escort range was prohibitively fatal to pilots and crews, the British had turned to bombing German cities in the dark, which required no precision and killed, unhoused, and demoralized war industry workers and their families. Morality was hardly an issue. At the onset of the war in 1939, Roosevelt had made an open plea to both sides to reject urban bombing, which Chamberlain endorsed, but after German bombs killed 30,000 men, women, and children in London alone in the fall of 1940, Churchill led a people whose passion to hit back was impossible to constrain even if he had wanted to, which he did not. Far more sleep was lost in London from German terror bombing than from turning it back on Germans. The question was what worked best. Air Marshal Sir Arthur Travers Harris made it simple: "What we want to do in addition to the horrors of fire is to bring the masonry crashing down on top of the Boche, to kill Boche, and to terrify Boche."

A vengeful view of German suffering was the norm on both sides of the Atlantic. *Time* magazine called Stalingrad "a graveyard for the *Herrenvolk*'s fresh young sons." But at this stage of the war the American high command, whose civilians were safe from the Luftwaffe, were inclined to take a more humane approach to depressing German morale and civilian war-abetting capabilities. Partly for that reason, the Americans had chosen a visual bombing doctrine in the 1930s, targeting factories, dams, refineries, and the like, and their planes were designed accordingly. A breakthrough bombsight made them capable of "precision" bombing by day, very far from "pickle barrel" accuracy but much more selective than British saturation bombing by night. Heavily armed and armored American bombers in huge formations devastated German fighters in daylight at altitudes most antiaircraft fire could not reach and hit targets the British could not find. But the Americans flew from England, and Churchill had started pressing FDR to abandon precision bombing and help the RAF level working-class neighborhoods at night. Arnold was sure that Churchill would lean on Roosevelt at Anfa, who in turn would lean on Marshall, and they would all "start bearing down on me."

With Somervell absorbed in logistics, Marshall's only help came from Wedemeyer, who faced what seemed like half of His Majesty's army, superbly prepared to a man. Almost as outnumbered, King, Cooke, and Libby made a capable, effectively sour naval triumvirate, but Arnold was alone and on the spot. He summoned from Cairo Lieutenant General Frank Maxwell Andrews, who led the U.S. Army Air Forces in the Middle East, and got Eisenhower's leave to have Major General Ira Eaker fly down from his VIII Bomber Command in London. Wedemeyer remained laughably outmanned after Colonel Charles Gailey and Brigadier General Hull came in off the bench halfway through the game, Hull having flown into a sandstorm in a plane that landed on its belly. For the Americans to come to Anfa with their shirttails out at the turning point of the war was nothing short of negligent.

Marshall and Arnold were summoning help when the Pan Am Clippers bearing Roosevelt and his party touched down in the waters off Bathurst, British Gambia's fetid capital. King had sent the light cruiser *Memphis* to accommodate them, and its captain lent his quarters to his commander in chief. Having settled in, FDR accepted a Royal Navy boat tour of the harbor and wrote again to Cousin Daisy. "I'm getting a wonderful mind rest," he wrote, but "this awful, pestiferous hole" confirmed his contempt for empires. An officer in his party was appalled by this "incredibly squalid, disease-ridden town" whose residents "dressed in weird assortments of rags." Rust-encrusted barges in the harbor overflowed with destitute families.

As FDR took a foul whiff of Bathurst, Jack Dill, fresh from Washington with the American brass, briefed his British peers in their Anfa Hotel meeting room on their allies' latest thinking. Having lived and worked with the Yanks for over a year, Dill understood them as his compatriots could not. Jacob later wrote that they wanted Dill's advice "on how to tackle the agenda, and incidentally the Americans." The British, like King, meant to set a global strategy then discuss its execution, but Jacob saw "the makings of a pretty little vicious circle here. One couldn't decide in detail what to do unless one knew what one's strategic aim was to be," which turned on the means to execute it. But Dill gave the Brits something like an unfair advantage, knowing the Americans' strengths, weaknesses, temperaments, and disputes and what and how they thought, having seen and heard it all literally up to the minute.

Simply put, Dill told his colleagues the Americans did not trust them. They resented British backtracking from the Channel, did not believe the Brits understood the war against Japan or took it seriously enough, and suspected that they "would not put our backs" into it after Germany's defeat. Dill said they still considered the Germans the prime enemy, favored the Channel over the Mediterranean, and thought it urgent to pressure Japan and recapture Burma to keep China in the war. Marshall seemed to be coming around on the Mediterranean and thought Italy soft and vulnerable but worried about a German thrust through Spain to Gibraltar. The Americans' interservice jealousies made them harder to deal with, not easier.

Even so, Dill said, Marshall was anxious about the Pacific drain on American resources and looking for ways to strike directly at Japan, devastate her shipping, and avoid a prolonged, bloody island-hopping campaign, but King controlled the landing craft, and would not let them sit in England for a year and a half waiting to cross the Channel. He needed them in the Pacific and begrudged their near-term use in the Mediterranean. Dill told Brooke later, "I am ashamed of a rather sneaking regard" for King, which he probably shared now, but King was always ready to think "he is being got at, no matter how simple the question one puts to him. In formal conference he is at his worst. 'Off the record' and by himself he can be understanding and helpful" but "he does not trust us a yard."

Little of Dill's report on the Americans was new. "We were still convinced that they were wrong and we were right," as Kennedy had it later. "Now our problem was to get them to accept our strategy" and abandon any thought of leaving the Germans to the British and going full bore against Japan. "They have organized this camp in the most wonderful way for us," Kennedy wrote at the time, "and their hospitality is overwhelming," Their military acuity was not. "We feel that the Americans have great drive and bigger ideas than ours," but they were "weak on staff work" and strategy, "owing to incomplete knowledge and examination," and their grip on modern war was thin. "We should do well."

The Americans had no match for Churchill, Brooke, or Dill, hardly any staff, scant preparation, and far less experience than the Brits. What they did have was extravagant land, sea, and air power, actual and potential; an embarrassment of riches in industry, raw materials, energy, and agriculture; a vast, unexhausted, fiercely patriotic population with boundless confidence in their country's divine favor; the political skills of Franklin D. Roosevelt; the toughness of Ernest J. King; and the presence of George C. Marshall.

After Dill's American seminar, the British chiefs crossed the street to Churchill's Villa Mirador, where Dill replayed his briefing and Brooke restated his case for Sicily, but Churchill wanted more. Before the end of the year the Allies must sweep the enemy from North Africa, capture Sicily, invade northwest France, "on a moderate scale perhaps," start retaking Burma, and let no Pacific operations interfere with any of it. "Only in this way would we be taking our fair share of the burden of the war," an allusion to the Russians, who were taking its savage brunt. The Allies' plan should seem beyond their capabilities, for that was "the least that could be thought worthy of two great powers." Churchill cautioned his team not to pressure the Americans. In ten to fourteen days they would come around and everything would fall into place. Give them a full discussion, he said, hear them out, let them take their time, as he would do with the president, making steady progress like "the dripping of water on a stone."

Welcoming dinners capped the night of that long day. Churchill hosted a sailor's supper for his shipping master Lord Leathers and Admirals King, Cooke, Pound, and Mountbatten, which triggered the savvy in Savvy Cooke: "I suspected that Mountbatten had arranged this dinner in order to put a certain amount of pressure on me," Cooke wrote, to send him more landing craft, an ambition for which Cooke was proud to be "the stumbling block to the British." No such pressure was applied. "My suspicions were somewhat confirmed," Cooke went on, "when I found myself sitting between Churchill and Mountbatten" but the Brits did not bring up "such controversial or prosaic matters." Mountbatten never worked on Cooke, and "Churchill was working on his Scotch highballs but not unduly rapidly."

Marshall had met Mountbatten in London and taken to him on the spot. Even Wedemeyer found him impossible to dislike. "He was too decent a guy." The U.S. diplomat Kenneth Pendar had discovered in Mountbatten "a buoyancy and gaiety that I have rarely seen," with "the sort of easy assurance that less gifted people often interpret as a lack of seriousness." Eisenhower, for one, called him "the pretty boy in the navy," but King considered him a "most interesting man." A serious man or not, which Brooke did not think he was, Mountbatten was a serious charmer. An English film, *In Which We Serve*, based on his exploits at sea, was a popular hit in London with the suave Noel Coward suitably cast in the lead. Charisma paired with grit was Mountbatten's strength. King's aide Commander Libby soon found that no one could "talk Lord Louis Mountbatten down" from the positions he took at Anfa. "He just wore everybody down," which amused rather than angered King. There could be no better evidence of his charm.

Brooke and Portal broke the ice with Marshall, Arnold, and Clark over dinner at the hotel. Ike rated Clark "an unusual individual," an astonishing, visionary thinker, one of the best he had, despite his tireless self-promotion. Brooke was not easily beguiled, and Clark beguiled him. Patton had given Clark a tour of his local installations. "He was not in the least interested. His whole mind is on Clark. We went to the house and for one hour he spent his time cutting Ike's throat. And Ike, poor fool, sent him here." A telegram to London headed "HUSH—MOST SECRET" in triple-sized red type, like most British wires from Anfa, suggested that some of the Brits were on to him already. Among the other Americans, it said, "Clark also is here temporarily horning in."

A telegram from Eisenhower pulled the American airman General Ira Eaker away from dinner guests at his home near London that night: "Proceed at earliest practicable time to Casablanca for conference, reporting upon arrival there to General Patton. Conference involves method of air operations from United Kingdom." There was no further guidance, not even who the conferees were.

Though Brooke's day had started at dawn on the deck of a Liberator, he met with Churchill at six to cement his support for Sicily, had a long talk with Marshall, sat down in his room at the Anfa Hotel, brought his diary up to date, and roughed out nothing less than his opening statement to the Combined Chiefs of Staff on the state of the global war and how to win it. General Kennedy went to bed, picked up the Anglo-Irish satirist Oscar Wilde's comic story "The Canterville Ghost," and came across this: "We have really everything in common with America nowadays except, of course, language." As Kennedy fell asleep, he "wished very much that that had been true."

Six

DAY ONE:
THURSDAY, JANUARY 14

O n the bright, balmy morning of opening day, the American Chiefs of Staff huddled in their room like a scrappy freshman squad getting up for a varsity scrimmage. King set the tone with a churlish snipe at the Royal Navy. At dinner last night, he said, Churchill and Pound had deplored the state of their Eastern fleet, freshly stripped of its destroyers and aircraft carriers. "Just where the carriers were was not stated," but for HMS *Victorious*, which the British had lent to the U.S. Navy after the Japanese sank an American carrier and crippled another, leaving just one in the Pacific. Not known for gratitude, King said the British may have lent them *Victorious* and its complement of "green pilots" and offered them a second carrier to immobilize the British fleet instead of using it, "which they now show no disposition to do." The Royal Navy "served no purpose" in the Pacific. "Pressure should be brought on them."

Marshall started with Sardinia, thinking the British would, and asked Clark if landing craft could be massed in North Africa unbeknownst to the Germans. No, Clark said, but they could not know the target. Once Allied forces cleared the enemy from North Africa, Clark went on, it would be more efficient to use them promptly in the Mediterranean than to ship them to England to cross the Channel later. That said, Clark agreed with Marshall that France's Brest peninsula was more valuable than Sardinia. Its capture would be "very hazardous," but American troops were "fully capable of standing up to the German defense," though many were untrained for battle. These were thoughts that did not fit, gentle punctures in Marshall's hopes to cross the Channel in 1943.

Arnold said fighter planes based in England could defeat enemy air defenses, and many German fighters were shot down over Holland and France attacking American bombers. "If they persist in these tactics, the German Air Force will be practically eliminated within a year." King called the British bid for more troops in the Mediterranean "a good out" for avoiding the Channel. Somervell said if the flow to North Africa stopped, another 300,000 troops could be shipped to England by September were it not for the U-boats in the North Atlantic. Unless U-boat facilities were heavily bombed and raided, fewer troops could be shipped in 1943 than in 1942. New ship construction could not make up the losses. It was crucial to relieve the shortage by reopening the Mediterranean.

King said again they must seize the initiative from the British, get them to accept the American global strategy "before permitting any discussion of details," and show them who the greater power was.

Long prepared for anything, the British had the morning off, but Brooke spent an hour and a half refining the opening statement he had outlined the night before. To produce in so little time a cogent review of the worldwide war and a taut set of arguments to keep the Americans strong in the Mediterranean, light in the Pacific, and away from the Channel would have been a feat had he not had it all in his head.

By 10:30 a.m. the CCS were seated in the first floor's hotel banquet room, a Moroccan Modern showpiece blessed with Moroccan light, which was not an insignificant thing. A drab, institutional, neon-lit room does not improve a meeting, let alone a days-long marathon, and the pleasant converted banquet room was a nice place for a confrontation. Slessor called it "the long room," last door on the left past the bar, anchored by a sweeping bow window with a semitropical view. At two rather narrow polished tables butted end to end over a vast Moroccan rug, Marshall and Arnold sat with Somervell and Wedemeyer, King with Savvy Cooke. On the opposite side of the ashtray-lined table (smoke-filled rooms were as natural as air) Brooke, Pound, and Portal had a stronger bench in Ismay and Dill and a wild card in Mountbatten. Smaller tables behind both delegations were available for staff. An American sentry stood just outside the room with a placard on its door: "Business: Chiefs of Staff Conference."

Only the chiefs would speak today. The others took notes, whispered to their principals, and watched opposing faces for unvoiced thoughts. In crisply tailored uniforms of barely different colors, cut, and style, speaking the same language, more or less, defending the same culture, to a degree, in search of the same victory if not the same results, admirable and flawed in their own individual ways, the military chiefs of the two great surviving democracies would decide in this makeshift room how to crush the most powerful evil forces the world had ever seen. Millions of men, women, and children would live or die, be freed or remain in bondage, depending on when, where, and how the blows would fall. The blessings of success were immeasurable, the consequences of failure too horrific to consider.

The brigadier generals who took notes and composed the minutes, Vivian Dykes for the British, John R. Deane for the Americans, had worked together in Washington in the combined secretariat. Wedemeyer thought highly of Deane and considered him "sound," but Dykes had told his diary that "Deane lets Cooke get away with conduct he would stop if he had the guts. But he *has* no guts." The minutes were expected to be improved with "the customary suppressions" and end up accurate but unprovocative, especially when a meeting had been anything but. What to record, how to phrase it, what to add, and what to leave out were negotiated terms, and Dykes had found Deane not as bold a sausage maker as Brigadier General Walter Bedell "Beetle" Smith had been until

Eisenhower made him his chief of staff. Smith had cooked the minutes "nobly" in the interests of all concerned, Dykes had told his diary, but "Deane will not stick his neck out like old Beetle used to," which complicated things. "We had a hell of a job with the minutes."

To make their lives still harder, Deane and Dykes had to draft the minutes overnight, not only for the CCS but also for their own delegations' respective daily meetings, a close to sleepless mission that an irreverent British scribe had captured in verse: "And so when the great ones repair to their dinner/ The secretary stays getting thinner and thinner/ Wracking his brains to record and report/ What he thinks they will think that they ought to have thought."

Read in cold print, the first day's minutes of the Casablanca Conference record a businesslike exchange, but Ismay was disturbed by the "veiled antipathy and mistrust" that filled the room. What the great ones ought to have thought was debatable, but they all seemed determined to "cling obstinately to their own preconceived ideas, and there seemed little hope of reaching agreement."

The Americans hosted the meeting as Casablanca's occupying power, and Marshall chaired it. In a terse opening statement reduced to two sentences in the minutes, he led off as King had wished. Defining the key issue as the allocation of resources between the European and Asian-Pacific theaters, he "suggested" a 70-30 split "as a concept on which to work," a softer sell than King may have liked, but King's position nonetheless. King's bid to erode Germany first, the rock on which British strategy was built, had become American policy in the meeting's first few minutes.

Marshall had barely begun when King jumped in and switched the American tone from suggestion to demand. According to his estimates, he said, unencumbered by any facts, the Allies were spending only 15 percent of their assets on the war against Japan, which gave the enemy space and time to fortify his conquests, check the American advance, and ship raw materials home. Strengthened at her leisure, Japan would be a tough tooth to pull after Germany's defeat. The CCS should fix the proportionate effort to devote to the theaters of war before they considered specific operations.

"We did not see many attractions about this kind of mathematical basis of strategy," Slessor later recalled, and Brooke said so, which did not flatter King or his team. Brooke, it has been said, seldom hid his "contempt for inadequacy," and the American Chiefs of Staff were unaccustomed to contempt. Still worse, King's game plan fell apart on the first play when Brooke stole the ball and ran with it. "In fixing this balance of effort," he said, it would be wise to "weigh up the enemy situation" first, and this he proceeded to do, without leave or interruption from the chair, with his facts laid before him like dental tools. What followed was a brilliant flow of military logic honed for months in fights with Churchill, a merciless sparring partner.

Brooke's conference room style was not among his strengths. His rapid speech, pedantic air, and persistent, cocksure righteousness got under American skins, and his round horn-rimmed readers made him look like a predatory owl. The effect was not improved by his forbidding, pinched demeanor, his abrupt birdlike movements (ironically enough), what Jacob called his "constant habit when talking of shooting his tongue out with the speed of a chameleon," and a pace too fast for comfort. Jacob had never met a man who "so tumbles over himself in speaking. . . . He cannot make his brain move slowly enough to fit his speech." All of this made him easy prey for Vivian Dykes, whose closed-door impressions of Brooke were tongue-darting, pencil-snapping, flatly disagreeing, horselaugh-producing stuff. Had he known, Brooke could not have fairly complained. Portal and many others enjoyed Brooke's own "delicious talent for mimicry" of powerful men, Churchill included.

No doubt more measured than usual, Brooke's compelling opening statement overcame it all, beginning with genuine compliments to his audience, ancient tools of the art of persuasion. The American Chiefs of Staff "would naturally know more" about the war against Japan than the British, who admired "the magnificent work" they had done in the Pacific "after the early disasters" there. The Japanese had seemed unstoppable until the Americans stopped them, which implied that they needed no more stopping. Brooke said not another word about Japan until he closed, and very little then.

Dill had surely told Brooke that Marshall's first concern was the shipping shortage, and that is where Brooke began. British strategy, he said, had always started with the security of the United States and Britain. The German threat to Britain had been dire, but the danger had subsided, and some forces stationed there could now go on the offensive, but the threat to British supply lines was severe, a U-boat threat primarily, and insufficient shipping constrained offensives everywhere. Brooke put the upshot bluntly. The U-boat must be defeated "or we might not be able to win the war."

Support for the Red Army was his second key to victory. The Germans were "staggering" under their second failed offensive on the Russian front, and a feeling must be growing in Berlin that they could not defeat Russia. (Judging by the minutes, no conferee had ever heard of the Soviet Union.) The Germans had only two chances, either push the Russians back at Stalingrad, a nearly impossible feat in winter, or retreat to a shorter line and take a hard psychological blow. Hitler's allies were struggling too. The Romanians were suffering in the Crimea, the Hungarians had never had much stomach for a fight, and the Italians were losing heart.

Ian Jacob later wrote that "the effect of being thrown violently out of the Mediterranean would be shattering for the Italians" and drive them out of the war. They were nothing like a terrifying force. Patton described his mission as "killing Germans and chasing Italians," but the British assigned great value to Italy's surrender. Apart from losing her fleet, her cannon fodder army, and her strategic geographic position, Hitler would have to leave Italy, Greece, and the Balkans to the Allies or replace their Italian occupation troops with Germans, which the British calculated would soak up fifty-four divisions and 2,250 planes.

The Germans were in a precarious state, Brooke said, which might make it possible to defeat them this year. The issue was how to use the

Allies' three main assets. First, Russia was the biggest land power on earth, and her strength was growing. The Allies must support her in every possible way "to get the best value out of her," a thought Brooke would have rephrased had Stalin been there. "Our second main weapon" was bombing, to be exploited in full. The third was superior sea power, which threatened to disrupt the enemy in several places at once and "compel him to disperse his forces." But once the Allies attacked a given spot he could concentrate against it. It was crucial to strike where he was least able to do so.

So now came the crucial choice, to attack in northwest Europe or the Mediterranean. "As a point of reentry to the Continent," France had great advantages. The Channel made the shortest crossing and English bases provided air cover, but the Germans were strongest in northwest France, and so was their ability to reinforce their defenses at the point of attack. Many railroads ran east and west across Europe. Few ran north and south. The Germans could move seven divisions from Russia to the Channel in ten to fourteen days and only one to the Mediterranean.

Sometime at Anfa, Churchill told King that the Channel would be "a river of blood" if they crossed it too soon. Montgomery, who wanted it crossed in 1943, was a British outlier. "I was pushed into the sea at Dunkirk," he told a public audience at Winchester College, and "the only thing to do with the Germans is to find a good sea and push them into it." But Monty was not at the table. Slessor wrote after the war that the Germans having bitten them hard in France in 1914–18 and again in 1940, the British "were twice shy about that particular dog. We knew we should have to go back sooner or later, but our experience of amphibious warfare and of fighting Germans had left us with fewer delusions than our relatively inexperienced American friends about just what an immensely formidable undertaking it would be."

Torch had shown what Anglo-American collaboration could do, Brooke said. Thanks to General Eisenhower's success in command of that operation, the captured North African shore threatened all of Southern Europe and made the Germans disperse their strength. Once Allied convoys could cross the Mediterranean protected from land and sea, the Germans must attack them from the air, pulling warplanes from Russia to destruction. There was "always some anxiety" that Spain would join the Axis, seize the Strait of Gibraltar, and "close the door behind us," but the Spanish seemed to be turning away from the Germans, and the more the Allies controlled the Mediterranean the more Spain would turn. With his own team split on *where* to strike in the Med, Brooke left the point alone.

It was important to bring Turkey into the war, Brooke said, to give the Allies access to the Black Sea and a platform for bombing Axis industry and Romanian oil. The Turks were reluctant to take the Germans on (understandably) but Allied conquests in the Mediterranean would encourage them, and Allied arms and training would strengthen their antiquated army.

All these things combined would pressure the Germans at every turn. The difficulty was that none of them could be done without taxing the others. Supplying the Russians by convoy, for example, took ships from amphibious landings. A balance must be struck, and a considerable loss of ships accepted, "providing these paid a good dividend." Having fought for Britain's life for years, Brooke had learned to speak of burning ships and drowning men as sound investments, and so had the Americans.

"We must be in a position to take advantage of a crack in Germany in the late summer," Brooke said. The Germans were moving troops from France to Russia already, and a continental invasion's prospects would improve if this continued. London's estimates had thirteen British and nine American divisions available to cross the Channel by August, whether a Mediterranean operation was launched or not. The determining factors were the scarcity of landing craft and trained crews to run them. The very idea of landing craft was an innovation. Marshall later said the only landing craft he ever heard of before the war was a rubber boat.

Brooke closed with Asia. Indian troops were taking a port in southwest Burma, but northern Burma was a tough place to fight, and "the Japs" (Germans were always Germans in the minutes) could not be expelled until the Allies controlled the Bay of Bengal and could attack Rangoon and Burmese airfields simultaneously. Troops "well adapted to jungle fighting" could be found in India and the African colonies. The difficulty was scraping up ships.

So ended Brooke's concise soliloquy with the very word Pacific unspoken. Wedemeyer was not surprised, knowing that the Brits saw Japan as mortally wounded prey set aside for the kill. The "bombshell," he thought, was Brooke's implication that a Mediterranean operation would do more for the Russians than a continental invasion, an absurd idea in Wedemeyer's view, though Torch's Mediterranean strike had already caused Hitler to pull warplanes and troops from Russia to Tunisia and Vichy France.

What came next was not an American rebuttal but a second British opening. Brooke turned to Admiral Pound for a report on Britain's naval war in Europe as Marshall sat silent in the chair.

Sir Alfred Dudley Pickman Rogers Pound was a small, bright man with twinkling blue eyes and a wry sense of humor, born to a barrister father and a Boston-bred mother from a line of Massachusetts seafarers. Unflappable Pound was too. In command of a battleship at Jutland in 1916 he had sunk a German ship as a sailor standing beside him lost an arm to a shell. Often spotted outside the Admiralty tinkering with his car on the Horse Guards Parade, Pound was sixty-five and seemed older after fifty-two years in the Royal Navy, which had started in 1890 at age thirteen. Churchill's principal secretary John "Jock" Colville described the First Sea Lord as "courageous, matter-of-fact in thought and word, and gifted with a fine precision of mind." Marshall later recalled how "affectionately fond of Pound" he had been, "as I think he was of me." Arthritis made him walk with a cane, and he was prone to close his eyes when conference talk turned from the sea. Admiral Leahy found that Pound only joined a discussion when it involved the British Navy, "about which he expressed very positive opinions." The prime minister, his friend and onetime predecessor as First Lord of the Admiralty, called him "necessary to me. His slow, unimpressive look is deceptive." It was said that Dudley Pound "feared neither God, man, nor Winston Churchill."

Pound's presentation covered over a hundred U-boats in the Atlantic operating from French ports, Italian battleships loose and unfound in the Mediterranean, the need to keep German warships from breaking out of the Baltic into the Atlantic, and stopping Japanese-German trade— Asian and Pacific raw materials shipped to Germany around the Cape of Good Hope in exchange for machines and parts. American warships, Pound said, were assembling off Brazil and British vessels off West Africa to attack that trade in the Atlantic narrows. Pound, like Brooke, said nothing about the Pacific.

The British kept the floor yet again when Pound passed it on without a word from Marshall to the RAF's intellectual Chief of the Air Staff, Air Chief Marshal Sir Charles Frederick Algernon Portal, known as Peter to family and friends, the youngest by far of the British Chiefs of Staff. In command of the RAF at forty-nine, born to aristocratic wealth, position, and confidence that went without saying, Portal was a tall, thin, unremarkable-looking man. A junior American officer described his "inordinately long cleaver of a nose, which from the profile looked like the bow of an Arctic icebreaker." Educated at Winchester and Oxford, Portal had joined the Army as a humble motorcycle dispatch rider four days after the Great War started and was blown through a door unharmed by a shell that killed five men. Decorated twice after joining the Royal Flying Corps, taking rifle shots from biplanes at German pilots, his "inevitable progress to the top" had been obvious to his peers though not to him, the reverse of King's experience.

At the head of the British Bomber Command, Portal had indirectly helped win the Battle of Britain and been given command of the RAF soon after it was won. A passionate fisherman, a lifelong falconer, and a deadeye shot, Portal had an equally keen eye for spotting holes in good ideas and fixing them. He spoke with a courteous air of "serene authority," good humor, and good sense, but he spoke not at all unless he had something useful to say. Jock Colville called him "a master of the art of reticence, disinclined to volunteer any opinion or information unless invited to do so." No social butterfly despite an elegant, well-connected wife, he arrived every day "in his large official Rolls-Royce for luncheon at the Traveler's Club in Pall Mall, marched upstairs, greeted nobody and ate a solitary meal," a function of introversion, not pride. And yet he "was a man with whom it was pleasant and indeed a privilege to be," born to lead and be admired. If Brooke had saved the British at Dunkirk, Portal's RAF had saved the British. Their relationship was contentious, Brooke being anything but reticent.

German airpower was in critical condition, Portal said now. The surviving pilots showed less interest in a fight, their training was slipping, and they could not win on two fronts. The Allies must "destroy and bleed them," keeping them in combat in the west while the Russians chewed them up in the east, taking "losses from which they cannot recover." Allied warplane production outpaced theirs four to one. Portal's remark that American daylight bombing was effective and should continue while the British carried on at night was a seismic shift in the British position and a wide-eyed godsend to Arnold. Portal too said not a word about the Pacific.

The three British monologues had consumed nearly two hours, and King's plan to seize the initiative had long since hit the rocks. Doubtless he was furious that Marshall had given it up without a word, let alone that the British had ignored his war, but Marshall replied only briefly to their initiative-seizing openings, with something close to deference. The United States Chiefs of Staff were "in full accord" with most of what they had said. The rub was in the Mediterranean and especially the Pacific. "The Japs" were digging in from the Solomons to New Guinea to Timor and strengthening in the air, and the United States Chiefs of Staff were eager to hit them from behind and on the flanks. Major operations in Burma would spread them thin and weaken them in the Pacific. The Americans were "most anxious" to retake the Burma Road.

Marshall closed with arguably too much gentlemanly tact, surely too much for King. The United States Chiefs of Staff (his habitual articulation) were "concerned" about whether Mediterranean operations "would bring advantages commensurate with the risk." The Americans were "inclined to look favorably" on invading northwest France with air support from England and supply from the United States. Ending on a point of agreement, Marshall said the U-boat was "our first concern" too. Next to no analysis came with any of this.

Portal said the British were "most grateful" for the twenty-one Liberators the Americans had lent them, and the U-boat was their bombing priority. Three kinds of targets were under RAF attack, U-boats at sea, the factories that made their parts, and their bases on the Bay of Biscay, which Portal proposed to destroy, an experiment to be tried for several months. Nothing was said of the surrounding French inhabitants.

King threw the day's first punches at Portal. Had the British considered bombing the shipyards that assembled U-boats, he asked, as if it might not have occurred to them. Portal said they were too small to hit at night. King shared his "personal impression" that Portal's antisubmarine campaign was sporadic, inconsistent, and poorly planned, and gave the British airman an American admiral's view of how he might improve. Ian Jacob was not the only British officer who found King "angular and stiff" and "hard to weigh up," always "on the look-out for slights or attempts to put something over on him." At some point at this table King said the American people would not accept certain things. "Then you will have to educate them," Brooke replied. King snapped back that the American people were just as well educated as the British. King seemed to wear "a protective covering of horn," Ian Jacob wrote, but one might be surprised by whatever lay underneath.

As if it were another incisive thought, Arnold suggested identifying crucial U-boat parts and focusing on bombing their factories. Portal was familiar with the idea. "Hammering on one link in the chain," he called it. Ball bearing factories were the weakest link, he said, but it was tactically impossible to destroy them. "General Arnold had trouble following the strategic arguments," Portal said after the war, and "never talked except on air. He had trouble holding the interest of the group." But the Englishman patted his head: "He was a grand fellow; never had any trouble with him."

The meeting broke for lunch, which Arnold enjoyed at the Restaurant Panoramique with a British cast of five: Brooke, Dill, Portal, Pound, and Ismay, any one of whom had him outsmarted, all of them hammering gently on one link in the chain.

When the CCS reconvened Brooke took the meeting over as if he chaired it. He would like to hear the American view of the situation in the Pacific, he said, a genuine wish to be educated as well as a calculation. Dill having told the British Chiefs of Staff that King did not believe they supported the war on Japan, Jacob wrote, they thought "'Uncle Ernie' would take a less jaundiced view of the rest of the world if he had been able to shoot his line about the Pacific and really get it all off his chest."

King had prepared an island-by-island review of the Pacific from New Guinea to Bora Bora as acute as Brooke's on Europe. Japanese resistance at Tulagi and Guadalcanal had been "more violent and sustained" than expected, he said, partly because the means to crush it swiftly had been "diverted" to North Africa, a pointed remark. The issue was where to strike next after the nearly finished Solomons campaign.

King called the American proposal to throw 30 percent of the war effort against Japan "a concept rather than an arithmetical computation," an inscrutable thought. It was not enough to hold the Japanese where they were, he said. Just as the Germans must be given no breathing room, neither the captured raw materials the Japanese were shipping to their home islands nor the "inner defense ring" they were building around them could be safely left alone. As one of King's staff had told him, "The defensive anywhere is a losing war." Years later, Wedemeyer admired King as the only "high-ranking American" at Anfa, Roosevelt seemingly included, who thought himself equal to his British peers, unembarrassed to rate the Pacific as important to the United States as the Mediterranean was to Britain. A "truly American position," Wedemeyer called it.

As King made his pitch, Wedemeyer watched the British squirm. Brooke was impatience in the flesh and the others were visibly annoyed. King's assessment of what he needed to pressure Japan did not upset them because it seemed wrong but because it seemed right. A British memorandum had concluded two months earlier that enough offensive action should be taken against Japan to keep her from attacking America's West Coast, Russia, India, Australia, or New Zealand. But King, the British knew, had more than that in mind. The British had lost Hong Kong, Burma, Singapore, and Malaya, thousands of lives, and many good friends to Japanese aggression and they did not mean to forget it, but Japan was half a world away in the able hands of the U.S. Navy while the Germans threated their national existence twenty-one miles from Dover. Germany simply must come first.

When King's exposition was done, Marshall remarked unhelpfully that with Japan on the defensive the United States Chiefs of Staff had more peace of mind than they had a year ago, but they worried about Japanese aircraft carriers, which could threaten their lines of communication and raid their West Coast. Victory would be a long time coming. The Japanese fought "with no idea of surrendering" and would not stop "until attrition has defeated them." None of it pleased the British.

Perhaps to ease the tension, someone changed the subject to the Russians, a shared source of resentment. Crucial though they were to defeating Germany, every man in the room despised their communist ideology, their Stalinist brutality, and their grudging, typically absent cooperation. At some point at Anfa, Churchill told FDR the Kremlin was "populated with wicked men," spitting "wicked" out of his mouth. Roosevelt replied with a mock rebuke: "Winston, do you realize you are talking about one of our allies?" Churchill had "considered that as well."

It was hard to get information out of them, Arnold said, and their paranoid suspicions were maddening. The Americans sent them 150 aircraft a month, soon to be 400. They were glad to take the planes but not "gossipy" Western airmen. Portal shared similar complaints. Pound said Russian destroyers sometimes ventured a few miles out to sea to lead Allied convoys into their ports but invariably claimed to be low on fuel and fled at speeds inconsistent with an arrow near empty. Why, Marshall asked, were they prepared to risk divisions but not warships? "They are a continental people," Pound replied, and "do not understand naval action." Brooke said their incompetence never deterred them from "silly advice."

Marshall went on to the construction of a vast U.S. Army, which was going well. Americans "veteranized" quickly in combat. Young officers and sergeants learned fast from mistakes. His jarring remark that the "deadly character" of the Pacific ground war was "particularly fortunate" may not have jarred his fellow professionals. Facing a fanatical enemy, Marshall said, the Americans learned to "kill or be killed," which produced "tremendous power for future operations."

The subject having returned to Japan, the room heated up again. The very idea of tremendous Pacific power raised Brooke's blood pressure with visible and audible effects that did not make him more persuasive. King described it later: He typically "talked so damn fast it was hard to understand what he was saying." Ismay thought it made the Americans think "he was trying to bounce them." He surely talked fast now, likely with darting tongue, glaring through owlish spectacles. How far forward did the Americans think they had to go to keep the Japanese from solidifying? Could the forces already in place not contain them? Hitting them hard would mean all-out war, and the Allies could not fight two at once.

King's disciple Admiral Cooke could hardly contain himself: "Naturally it made me very hot to have the British attempt to dictate in such a highhanded manner what we in the United States should do with our own resources." Some of the Brits could be sniffy. High-handed is close enough. But with Stalin in the Kremlin there were no dictators at Anfa. The concept of an Allied conference convened for the very purpose of rigorous debate and collective decision making was lost on Savvy Cooke.

Marshall supported King and contained his temper. It had been essential to take the offensive to stop the Japanese from advancing, he said. Short of a full-tilt push, the only way to keep them in check was a constant "whittling away" until they collapsed from exhaustion. Portal asked if it was possible "to stand on a line" and damage them when they tried to break it. Could bombing not defeat them? Arnold replied that the

Americans were operating from "two narrow salients" but the enemy was free to maneuver. Marshall conceded that Japan's wooden factories were so vulnerable that bombing might destroy her capacity to make war, but not yet. "Might have worked against a trembling people, like in Italy," Marshall said years later, "but the Germans and the Japanese were not that."

Rather than attacking King's 30 percent solution, Portal proposed to determine what the Japanese could not be permitted to do, then decide what was needed to stop them and see what remained to use elsewhere, a characteristically logical thought. But if anyone replied the minutes do not say so. "One of the greatest snags" in every Allied negotiation, Portal later said, was an American search "for hidden motives whenever we put up a plan. They were the victims of the common American impression that the British are frightfully cunning and will do you down at every turn . . . and they always seemed to us frightened of being trapped." The British were also aware of the common American belief, which Wedemeyer often expressed, that their war plans were based on imperial goals, "and we never really allayed this fear." The U.S. Chiefs of Staff were prepared to send American boys to die to save the British but not the British Empire.

King changed the subject to the Burma Road, which must be reopened forthwith or China might quit the war. These were not only his ideas, he said, the American Naval War College shared them. The whole U.S. Navy shared them. The British would not have been impressed. The Pacific had been an American sphere of influence for a hundred years, but Burma was British ground. Vivian Dykes was among the Brits who resented the Yanks "sticking their noses" in it, and Brooke had told Dill just that. Operation Anakim, Brooke said, a full-scale campaign to retake Rangoon and eventually all of Burma, would "cut across the main effort against Germany" but Operation Ravenous, a limited advance into northern Burma, was a "risk worth taking."

Perhaps provoked by Brooke's allusion to "the main effort against Germany," King asked an acerbic question. After Germany's defeat, which of the Allies would carry the heavy end of the load against Japan?

Many years later his aide Commander Libby still remembered how angry King was. Once the Germans were defeated, Brooke said, "practically all the British naval forces would be released for the war against Japan." Portal emphatically agreed, but Marshall said it was dangerous to depend on sea power alone. A single battle could reverse it. The U.S. Navy had won at Midway by getting its planes up first. "With a little ill fortune" the opposite could have happened and exposed the West Coast. The forces in the Pacific were already "stripped to the bone."

Pound proposed to let the Japanese fortify what "we did not mean to attack," and waste their capabilities. To retake the Philippines before the Germans were defeated was impossible, for example, and it was "all to the good if the Japanese locked up troops in these islands." King agreed, but the Japanese had to be softened up now and could not be left to do what they wanted. Wedemeyer watched the British go "particularly stuffy" at this point, and some stray provocation was too much for Cooke, who swung his head to Somervell with a loud profane remark. As he turned back around, he later wrote, "I noticed Sir John Dill looking at me very intently from across the table." Seeing King about to forget himself, Dill whispered to Brooke, who suggested a break, which Marshall quickly granted.

When the meeting reconvened another round of heat undid the cooling off, and the first day closed with a British victory. The Americans abandoned King's formula and accepted Portal's needs-based approach. The combined planners were instructed to prepare a report: Having agreed that Germany was the primary enemy "what situation do we wish to establish" in Asia and the Pacific in 1943 "and what forces will be necessary" to do it? Speaking privately with Brooke, Portal captured the British approach: "We are in the position of a testator who wishes to leave the bulk of his fortune to his mistress. He must however leave something to his wife, and his problem is to decide how little he can in decency set apart for her."

When the problem went to the combined planners, as nearly every

stubborn problem did, the British had a decisive advantage. Several echelons of top-notch British planners shone their light on every question,
backed by teams of experts on HMS *Bulolo* in the harbor, guided by Jack
Slessor. Before the British planners wrote their papers overnight, "usually
on rather inadequate riding orders," Slessor later recalled, he briefed them
on what the great ones had said in the long room and how and why they
had said it, "putting them more freely into the minds of their Chiefs,"
improving their grip on "what was really required of them," guiding their
production of convincing memoranda with which to subdue the Yanks.

The Americans had only Cooke and Wedemeyer, who sat with Marshall, King, and Arnold at the conference table and prepared them for the
next day, leaving little time to thwart the British planners, though Cooke
did his best. He alone in the combined planners' room knew anything
to speak of about the Pacific, and he told his British peers, as Jacob had
it, that he had "no intention of studying the problem in the abstract, im-
partially, so as to arrive at the ideal solution." The Pacific was America's
battleground and "it was nobody else's business what was done there." He
disclosed his navy's plans but not what was needed to execute them. He
would only say they could be accomplished with assets already earmarked
for the Pacific, which squared not at all with cuts.

The British planners too were short on objectivity. Brooke summoned them after tea, he wrote, not to open their minds but "to instruct
them on the line of action to take": The Americans "must be tied down"
to a specific objective, Brooke said. Operation Ravenous "suits us" by
diverting Japanese forces to northern Burma from the Pacific, slowing
the drain on American resources, but Operation Anakim's recapture of
Burma at large was too big a load before Germany's defeat. Brooke accepted the Americans' need to secure their lines of communication but
told his planners to limit even that. "I then went for a walk with John
Kennedy to the beach to look for birds."

Hap Arnold put the day in a mysteriously rosy light: "Meeting today not
bad. Everything seems to be smoothing out. I hope! British and US have

not as yet put all their cards on the table. Perhaps things will get worse then." And so they would.

Unsolicited nepotism caused Arnold's son Hank, an artillery lieutenant, to be ordered from Algiers to help at the Anfa Hotel. Pleasantly surprised, his father took him for a drive, an odd bit of leisure, outgunned as the general was by Portal, Slessor, and the high-end RAF planners. Late that afternoon, Colonel Jacob Smart arrived from Washington expecting to accompany Arnold to post-conference meetings, unaware of the general's short-staffed woes. Arnold told him he needed help and Smart was it: "Find Al Wedemeyer," get a briefing from him, and "keep me informed." With no files, staff, or preparation Smart was dumbstruck by what had befallen him. Wedemeyer told him what had transpired and what was expected, "and then—like Alice in Wonderland—to run in order to stay even." Smart put it simply later. "We Americans were unprepared." They blamed FDR for their tiny staff, overmatched by the British and their brilliant memoranda. "We felt that we had been duped."

Almost every respectable paper produced at Anfa came from British hands, and many such reports had long since been perfected in London. A generous British officer credited "a little assistance from the Americans." The U.S. diplomat Bob Murphy called the Yanks "a reluctant tail to the British kite." When the British challenged their positions, the Americans relied on memory or unraked raw material cabled from Washington. Error and frustration ensued.

What few memoranda the Americans did produce the British were prone to discount, even mock in private. Jacob and Dykes, the two youngest members of the British delegation not related to King George VI, entertained themselves in their room with the American papers' recurring incantation, "it is believed that." Jacob had come to expect that when a sentence began that way a declaration so inaccurate that it "takes one's breath away" was sure to follow. The Americans "calmly repeat any hare-brained report they hear, or any so-called fact that someone has palmed off on them, nearly always prefacing it with the great formula, 'It is believed that.'" To Dykes's great amusement, Jacob wrote, "I managed to work an 'it is believed that' into the final report of the Conference."

It is believed that the Americans could see, hear, and smell the imperial disdain, which was not to the Brits' advantage.

After Kennedy and his planners met with Cooke and Wedemeyer, London was told by wire that two "unexpected American views emerged." Despite considerable agreement on broad global strategy, the two leading Anglophobes made it plain that they suspected the British would abandon the war on Japan after Germany's defeat. The telegram's report that the point was unexpected exposes its inaccuracy. Cooke and Wedemeyer had also shared their fear that the American people would be war-weary when the Germans were finally beaten and unwilling to pay the expected horrific price of invading Japan.

Just past six that evening, Kennedy was walking the beach between meetings when several big planes flew up from the south with a strong fighter escort. "This was the President arriving."

"An amazing day" it had been, FDR wrote Daisy. Up before dawn in Bathurst on the USS *Memphis*, his party had flown to Casablanca across the African interior in the same two Skymasters that had brought his Chiefs of Staff. An officer had noted fish heads for sale on the potholed road to the airstrip and "gangly, undernourished children" emerging from their hovels. One of their British protectors said a team of dejected men on their way to the fields would be happier when the sun burned off the chill. Their life expectancy was less than thirty years. Their cattle lived longer. "On the whole," the president wrote, "I am glad the U.S. is not a great Colonial power."

After a long flight over desert, an oxygen-masked climb over the Atlas Mountains, and a descent over land that looked to Hopkins "like the Garden of Eden should look and probably doesn't," FDR's plane landed in dimming light a hundred feet from a bomb crater. For secrecy's sake, there was no honor guard, only Clark, a Secret Service detail, and Elliott Roosevelt, looking fit, his father thought, proud of his Distinguished

Flying Cross earned for photographic flights over enemy ground. The Roosevelts and Hopkins were hurried into a mud-smeared armored sedan under heavy guard for the short drive to Anfa.

With barely enough exceptions to prove the rule, FDR was in a holiday mood throughout his time at Anfa, despite the incongruous black armband in mourning for his mother nearly a year and a half gone. He soon gushed to Daisy about his "delightful villa," the home of a French woman whose husband was a prisoner of war. "She and her child were ejected as were the other cottage owners & sent to the hotel in town." Only a patrician could have called them cottages. For the next ten days it was rare to find fewer than two or three callers in his, British, French, or American. Few of his meetings with military stars seemed like work, but Patton advised the president's physician Admiral McIntire about his patient's health: "I hope you'll hurry up and get to hell out of here. The Jerries occupied this place for two years, and their bombers know how to hit it." They had done it two weeks earlier and "it's a cinch they'll be back."

FDR read screaming newspapers from home about Eisenhower's embrace of Nazi stooges in Algiers. To any astute politician, let alone Franklin Roosevelt, they underscored the point that the value of uniting the French was not just military.

Hopkins walked over to the Villa Mirador and returned to the Villa Dar es Saada with Churchill, on top of his game but looking older than he had in July, having earned it. Roosevelt greeted him warmly, and Churchill was delighted to see his friend and partner on the "conquered or liberated territory"—an aptly ambivalent phrase—they had taken so handily against military advice. They would deal with the French at Anfa like conquerors more than liberators, and Churchill would come to FDR so often every day that Roosevelt's aide Captain McCrea asked the marines to keep an eye on the prime minister's villa. When they saw him head their way, they would let McCrea know, "so I could welcome him at the president's door."

Churchill told his wife he found Roosevelt at his best after a five-day trek to Africa and eager to win the war, "plunging right into the matter straight away. I think he was delighted to see me." He was bent on visiting his troops and promised to stay for ten days if necessary. "After all, we have everybody here," Churchill wrote. "We have this tremendous opportunity. If we cannot settle things now how will we ever be able to?" Recently remarried after his second wife's death, Harry looked "extraordinarily well, and twice as fit as he was before the combined restoratives of blood transfusions and matrimony were administered to him."

Hopkins walked over to the hotel, perhaps for a pack of Chesterfields, and returned to tell the president he had found some Chiefs of Staff of mixed nationality at Le Bar Américain. Roosevelt sent him back to ask them all to dinner. Marshall was at Patton's table at Villa Maas when an invitation to dine with "A Number 1," as Patton called him, pulled Marshall away. He had been talking about the South Pacific, not North Africa or Europe, Patton's present and future concerns. The war against Japan was on his mind.

Elliott helped mix drinks as his father's well-picked cooks made an unexpected dinner for the president of the United States, his son, His Majesty's Prime Minister, their Combined Chiefs of Staff, Harry Hopkins, Averell Harriman, and Captain McCrea. With a faux dramatic flourish, FDR produced his "short snorter," a dollar bill signed by others who had made the daring crossing of the Atlantic by air, a wartime fad named for shots of liquor once consumed by Alaskan bush pilots on the job. Any airborne ocean crosser who failed to produce his short snorter on another's demand was obliged to buy a drink for every other survivor in the room or pay them each a dollar. "Luckily," Churchill wrote, "I was well prepared."

In the Moroccan Modern White House dining room Hopkins enjoyed "good talk of war—and families—and the French" and perhaps his drink of choice, which Slessor called a "high-explosive proportion of whiskey to soda." Churchill coached the officers: "This is the most important meeting so far. We must not relinquish the initiative, now that we have it. You men are the ones who have the facts and who will make plans for the future." The look on Brooke's face was not recorded.

A telegram to London said the evening "went with a swing" but both clans were wary despite the bonhomie. The Brits expected guilelessness from the Yanks, which tended to amuse them, but Kennedy found most Americans hard to know. "Under their hearty and friendly manner one feels there is suspicion and contempt in varying degrees according to personality." Jacob found them quick to "either take you or reject you wholeheartedly. When they take you, they make no bones about it." In Washington they had long since taken Dill "and Dumbie, of course," for Dykes was irresistible. At Anfa "they were captured by Portal." Of Brooke they seemed suspicious. "They like transparent honesty, and not too much obvious mental superiority."

Safety drove the evening's only arguments. The officers were worried about the Germans bombing Anfa Camp if they detected something worth hitting, and how could they not? Berlin radio had reported Anfa's barbed wire fortress and speculated about its residents. (Much to the future consternation of Reichsminister Joseph Goebbels, who knew that Roosevelt and Churchill, "these gangster bosses," were conferring but not where, a report to German intelligence from its Spanish station that they were meeting in Casablanca was translated from the Spanish by some wooden German officer as "the White House.")

Some of the British proposed to move to Marrakech, out of Luftwaffe range, but FDR was not going anywhere, happy where he was. Regardless of public shock about flying into a war zone, he said, he would still hold his office for two more years. Pound said that was more than anyone else at the table could say and regretted it when Churchill glowered. Everyone tried to dissuade the Western world's irreplaceable leaders from touring the front, but Roosevelt assigned the airmen, Portal, Arnold, and Elliott, to plan it. Elliott would have no vote, his father said, "you are merely secretary."

King had sworn off liquor for the war's duration but not wine, and Brooke was entertained when "King became nicely lit up towards the end of the evening." Progressively thick-tongued and insufferable, the admiral explained North African politics to Winston Churchill and Franklin

Roosevelt "with many gesticulations," told them how poorly they were running the war, and made choice observations about the British and French in general. Churchill "failed to appreciate fully the condition King was in," Brooke wrote, and took him on. "Most amusing to watch."

Despite the literally earthshaking problems that faced the Chiefs of Staff in the morning, the party rolled on past midnight. At half past one, the lights went out for an air raid alert and ten great men sat around the table talking by the light of six candles, an ordinary thing for the Londoners, a tale for the Americans to tell. It occurred to the photographer in Brooke that Roosevelt and Churchill would have made quite a picture huddled with their warlords in candlelight in Morocco. Churchill soon wrote Clementine that he and FDR had talked until two, careful to let her know he had not forgotten his manners. "I made several offers to go."

Seven

DAY TWO: FRIDAY, JANUARY 15

Brooke woke up to a gorgeous morning and took a walk with Kennedy, a "delightful" hour and a half with "warblers of all sorts" and "several kinds of waders." Another Chief of the Imperial General Staff might have prepared for a bruising day with briefing books and briefers. Having no need for either, Brooke cleared his mind with birds.

Sitting up in bed, Roosevelt asked his Chiefs of Staff and the ever-present Hopkins and Harriman if they thought he should see the sultan of Morocco and General Auguste Charles Noguès, French Morocco's governor and resident quisling who had orchestrated the deaths of hundreds of young Americans in Torch's November landings. Marshall referred the president to Eisenhower, but Noguès struck King as "rather tricky." Patton had him pegged as "a crook—a handsome one." On closer acquaintance Noguès was promoted to "a clever crook only moved by self-interest, but he knows I am his best interest for the moment."

Marshall told FDR that the four-or-five-day conference they had planned looked like ten, but however long the president stayed he should decline an invitation from the prime minister to see Marrakech. Marshall's declaration that "it would not be desirable" was not a suggestion. Far from Allied air and sea power, Marrakech was occupied by a single

American regiment, thousands of French troops recently "hostile to us," and countless Axis agents. It would not be wise to put the president in such a place. If the prime minister wished to go, he might bring Mr. Hopkins, which "would furnish good cover for the real location of the President." A laugh may have been involved in casting Mr. Hopkins as a death-defying decoy, but Marshall was no comedian.

King said the British were calling a campaign to reopen the Burma Road a "profitable gamble." Even a failure, Marshall said, would draw Japanese forces from the Southwest Pacific battleground, link two Chinese armies, and give them combat experience. Roosevelt pushed to double U.S. airpower in China and bomb Japan from there, but Arnold said the difficulty of supplying General Claire Chennault's China-based bomber force by air made its expansion impossible, only one urgent reason to reopen the Burma Road. Marshall confirmed that Churchill opposed daylight bombing. For now, the RAF had many more planes in Britain than the Americans did, and target selection and timing should be under British command, but the British "should not be permitted to dictate our procedure."

Marshall briefed FDR on the latest British thinking gleaned from yesterday's meetings and chats. The British were "extremely fearful" of returning to France before the Russians or massive bombing opened "a decided crack" in German strength, but once all North Africa was cleared, a powerful Allied force of amphibious warfare veterans would be poised to strike in the Mediterranean. "It must be understood, however," that it would "definitely retard" Bolero's buildup in the U.K. King threw in the Strait of Gibraltar's vulnerability to a German thrust through Spain. The British, Marshall said, were shifting their Mediterranean preference from Sardinia to Sicily. There was reason to believe the prime minister had inspired the change.

Frank talks with Clark and Mountbatten had inspired change in Marshall. It was clearer now than ever that U.S. troops were not yet fit to storm a fortified beach against "determined resistance," German resistance. More training was needed, and training took time. Clark had told Marshall that many "mishaps" overcome against French opposition would have been fatal against Germans, whose military skill and ferocity in Tunisia had convinced even Eisenhower that Roundup could not succeed before August 1944.

There was more drift than steer in the American wheelhouse, but an invasion of France was fading away. Marshall confessed years later, but not to the Brits at Anfa, "We did not consider the cross-Channel thing feasible in 1943."

The British Chiefs of Staff and their advisors assembled in their room. Dill called Sicily and Sardinia "steppingstones to Europe" and suggested that which to take, a thoroughly arguable call, might turn on which attack could start sooner and whether the Americans would supply the escorting warships. A Mountbatten subordinate said either operation demanded three weeks' amphibious training, and trainers were hard to come by, particularly since the United States Army and Marines did not work well together. Brooke raised the danger of "demanding too high a standard of training and equipment." Both had been "too haphazard" before. Now there was a risk of overdoing.

Since the war on Japan should "rest for the present," the British agreed to propose a combined planners' report on what was needed to secure the global sea lanes. "We should then know what was left for the campaign against Germany." Dill repeated Marshall's reluctance to commit to what the Americans called "the Mediterranean bottleneck." They must be sold on the "great opportunities" in the Mediterranean, the only chance to draw Germans from Russia soon. The debate should then turn to Sicily versus Sardinia and the chance to seize a bridgehead in France in 1943 and "open the gate" for 1944. Had the Americans been present, their suspicions about British intentions to cross the Channel when the time was right might have eased.

Partway through the discussion, Churchill walked in with an unlit cigar and a match stuck in one end, congratulated his Chiefs of Staff on their "strategic position near the bar," and asked how they were getting

on. His gray summer suit startled Kennedy, for the PM waged the war
in his one-piece zip-up "rompers" custom-tailored in assorted colors. "I
had almost come to think of him as possessing no other clothes." King
later called it "that damn Zoot suit he used to wear." Brooke briefed him
on yesterday's talks, the impasse on Japan, and the British negotiating
strategy. Churchill called a limited Sledgehammer invasion of northwest
France in 1943 "a residuary legatee" (one who gets the remaining assets
under a will after specific bequests are fulfilled) but "some operation of
this kind" was essential, to "broaden the area of the fighting" and use the
forces massed in England, which could not be used elsewhere. Contrary
to the move his chiefs had already made, he cautioned them not to be led
into weighing what was needed in the Pacific and taking what was left
for Europe. It would be "like carrying water from a well in a sieve—there
would be nothing left when we got home."

The Tunisia campaign was in good shape, he said, "in fact better than
if we had cleared it up quickly." They had to wear the Germans down
somewhere. It was better "if they came to us and did not wait for us to
go to them." If they attacked Montgomery in force, "we should have
more of them in the bag eventually than if they had not." He urged his
Chiefs of Staff to examine every way to strike them. "We should not be
impatient" with the Americans, he reminded them again. Negotiations
like these took time, probably ten days. When friends had arguments,
he told Clementine, it was best to let their differences "melt themselves
down." At Dill's request before the meeting closed, Churchill said he
would reassure the Americans that the Germans were unlikely to strike
through Spain. It would be "a great and difficult undertaking" and even
if it succeeded, shipping could be protected more easily in the Strait of
Gibraltar than in the open sea. It caused Jacob pain to see the Americans,
a "naturally gullible people," swallow "every cock and bull story put out
by the Axis" about how easily the Germans could close the strait. Slessor
called it "qualms of claustrophobia."

Brooke told Kennedy that Roosevelt and Churchill had decided
to invite de Gaulle and Giraud to Anfa to arrange some sort of shared

French authority. "They meant to knock their heads together to agree to some compromise" and consider which Frenchmen might join them.

In the meantime, Jacob wrote, Dill played the Anglo-American "go-between and general lubricator," speaking separately and together with officers on both sides uneasy with each other but trusting Jack Dill, whose canine nose for trouble helped them dodge it. He later described his role at Allied conferences as "bringing the young things together." Sir John, the Americans called him. "All our people thought the world of him," the American General Handy said later, "Marshall particularly, but all of them. Even people like old Ernie King who didn't love the British at all."

Summoned by Marshall, Eisenhower left Algiers for Casablanca in his B-17 Flying Fortress bomber with his naval aide Lieutenant Commander Harry C. Butcher, an affable forty-one-year-old reservist who knew a great deal more about public relations than he did about the Navy. A CBS radio executive in civilian life, Butcher and Ike, as he privately called him, had been friends since 1927. Butcher's wife and daughter lived with Mamie Eisenhower in Washington. Dykes called him "quite a good sort," Butcher having learned that Americans should reconsider what their schoolbooks had taught them. The British were "really not red-coated devils."

At Churchill's request, Harold Macmillan, Britain's minister resident in Northwest Africa, an insightful Churchill protégé and a diplomatic rookie previously ignorant of French politics, came along to work on the French. Attached to Eisenhower's staff but not part of it, Macmillan advised him of the British government's views on political affairs and kept Whitehall informed. A member of Parliament and a recent colonial undersecretary, stiff and often in pain from his third wound of World War I, Macmillan was forty-eight and a former junior partner of the London publishing house his grandfather had founded in 1843. With a trim mustache, a celebrated wit honed at Eton and Oxford, "a very British voice," and a socialite mother from Indiana, Macmillan was a classic English gentleman who called himself a Scot and a Hoosier.

On the flight to Casablanca, a commotion roused him from a doze. A crewman said an engine was acting up but wouldn't quit. "This did not give me much enlightenment," Macmillan later recalled, "but I observed that the oil from the motor was running out all over the wing, which seemed wrong." The other three engines looked fine, and the fuss seemed overblown until the pilot said something about bursting into flames and ordered everyone to stand by the doors in parachutes. When a second engine went bad the crew briefed the passengers on jumping technique. A "swimming hole dive" would do. "Feet or fanny first" was a matter of taste. Butcher breathed again when the pilot cut the last two engines and glided in, "ending a hundred miles of misery." Eisenhower knocked a star off his shoulder as he stripped off his chute, and Butcher's hands were still shaking as he put it back on. Had he never fastened a star before? Ike asked. "Yes sir," Butcher said, "but never with a parachute on, sir."

Patton met their plane in his GI-chauffeured Packard limousine and took them all to Anfa Camp, where they ran into King, whom Patton was surprised to find genial off duty. Eisenhower and Butcher lodged in Villa Maas with Patton, an old friend of Ike's, who lunched there with Marshall and King and reviewed his plans for a Tunisian offensive, not enough practice for the British grilling he would face in the morning.

No one could have embraced his British staff more completely than Eisenhower, whose team was *too* combined for Patton. Ike had gone native in London, Patton thought, loading his senior staff with British officers, calling gasoline petrol, Germans the Boche, antiaircraft fire flak: "I truly fear that London has conquered Abilene." Portal had found Ike "utterly dedicated to forgetting about nationalities, sometimes forgetting about rank, but always being on the side of the best plan and the best man, whatever his uniform, whatever his service." Ismay was impressed when he asked Eisenhower if his intelligence officer was British or American. "I can't remember," Ike said, "but he is very good at his job."

Butcher had little to do, which he gladly did with Patton, who showed him around Casablanca in his Packard as Ike's eyes and ears. Gutted French warships littered the harbor, sunken superstructures broke the waves, a dead cruiser leaned on the beach. Butcher was awed by the fate of the brand-new battleship *Jean Bart*, which had, "as advertised, been shot up proper." Sensitive to French pride, the general gave him only a glance. Patton was not known for sensitivity, but Butcher admired how he kept the French trusting and helpful. He was proud of the vast warehouse he had made of Casablanca, including a million sandbag covers, 90 million gallons of gasoline, and impressive stocks of lipstick and rouge.

Late that afternoon, Major General Ira Eaker, in command of the American Army Air Forces in England, arrived in his Flying Fortress with his aide Captain James Parton, a thirty-year-old reservist who had stuffed three briefcases with a rarity at Anfa Camp, an impressive American report on a centrally important issue. "The First 1,200 Sorties of the VIII Bomber Command" was a gold mine on the first six months of U.S. bombing. Its major weakness, Parton thought, was obvious in its title. The British had flown a thousand sorties in one night.

Having spoken of bringing de Gaulle and Giraud to Anfa, Roosevelt and Churchill began to air their differences on the best way to wrangle them. A British diplomat wrote that French North African turmoil inflamed by Darlan's murder had "a deadening effect on the war effort." Merging de Gaulle's forces with Giraud's in some respectably liberal entity was thought to be essential not only for the sake of the war but also to show the world "and France in particular that the principles of freedom and justice which were the declared policy of the Allies should be put in practice in North Africa," a "testing-ground of the practicability of those principles" in a liberated Europe.

The split concerned ways and means. Churchill wanted a provisional administration in Algiers, temporarily sovereign over the French Empire, accepted as one of the United Nations, led by some tame civilian with a touch of prestige, that would merge de Gaulle, Giraud, their military forces, and their compatriots. When Anthony Eden had proposed one in a cable to Cordell Hull the State Department had withheld the courtesy of a reply. Hopkins had told the British ambassador Lord Halifax that "important Americans" believed a provisional French authority, inevitably run by de Gaulle, as opposed to bureaucrats under Allied control, would produce a postwar dictatorship. Eden had told Churchill he was "not much impressed by Harry's argument. The Frenchman is a politically minded animal, and we shall have no peace until one authority speaks for all, and not much then."

Eden had advised the Americans through Halifax that London was not "backing de Gaulle for first place in North Africa. It is for him and Giraud to come to terms if they can." If de Gaulle had political ambitions, the liberated French people would consider them. In the meantime, he could "bring a valuable contribution to the common fund, namely a substantial part of the French Empire and a great and resounding name in France." Working with Eisenhower in Algiers, Macmillan and the American diplomat Bob Murphy, now Roosevelt's personal representative at Ike's headquarters, had become fast friends, and Macmillan told Murphy that self-interest, prestige, and honor "all demanded that the British government should support de Gaulle's political aspirations."

At lunch in the president's garden, improved by Moroccan weather if not by French politics, Roosevelt handed Churchill a telegram to Hull from a U.S. diplomat named Matthews. Eden had told Matthews, it said, that de Gaulle caused him more trouble than all the other allies put together. Matthews had replied that the British paid the general's bills and should be able to contain him, but Eden said de Gaulle was a hero in Britain with a large French following, "not like a quantity of gin that can be put in a bottle." Churchill had reportedly said that de Gaulle could not be consigned to a secondary role, for he "is more than a man. He is a movement and a symbol." Perhaps, Matthews wrote, the British are "jealous of our leading role in North Africa."

Churchill had taken the position that the French "cannot be wholly denied some form of national expression in their present phase," but de Gaulle and Giraud both insisted that France, shamefully conquered in weeks, Nazi occupied, with small, obsolescent forces under their splintered, exiled command, was entitled to great power status. Roosevelt was determined to deny de Gaulle *and* Giraud *any* political power, marginally useful though their forces might be. The people of France would choose their leaders when they were free, and no aspiring candidate, least of all de Gaulle, would get a head start from him.

The CCS reconvened at 2:30. "At present they are working on what is called 'off the record,'" Churchill told Clementine, "in an easy and non-committal fashion." They were surely speaking freely and making no commitments, but a record was being kept and not much was easy. Admiral Pound began the discussion. The only question about British plans to bomb U-boat ports was whether to warn the French inhabitants, he said, for nothing else was working.

Eisenhower joined the meeting at that point and did not enjoy it. Brooke simply took him apart. He had been no match for Brooke in London, and Patton was tired of hearing him say "how hard it is to be so high and never to have heard a hostile shot." Brooke had heard more than his share. To make matters worse, a month of flu, colds, stress, and exhaustion had worn Ike down, thickened his voice, and dropped bags under his eyes.

Brooke's impatience with flawed strategic thought was often expressed in the traditional green ink of a Chief of the Imperial General Staff. He had recently turned a subordinate's report a venomous shade of green and circled its final paragraph's number 13—"A most suitable ending to a really lamentable effort." Another such effort was the "Same old bloody plan that didn't run last time and won't run now." More politely to be sure, Brooke was about to make it clear that Ike's plan to outfox Rommel had no legs.

Eisenhower had three explanations for his stalled Tunisian campaign. First, no-fly weather and "the appalling condition of the airfields" let the Germans pour in reinforcements unopposed. Second, when Torch was being planned, French intentions to resist or cooperate had been unknown. The invasion force now fighting in Tunisia had therefore been designed and equipped for a contested amphibious landing, not a land offensive. Third, rain and mud in northern Tunisia had shut down his planned offensive, but his 1st Armored Division was concentrating in the south, and he now planned to take the port of Sfax on Tunisia's southeast coast, drive a wedge between General Hans-Jürgen von Arnim's army in northern Tunisia and Rommel's Afrika Korps and his Italian allies in Libya, and cut off their supplies. The attack would begin in nine days, with every reason to hope it would succeed.

Brooke thought not and swiftly tore it down. Harry Butcher had considered the plan "on the daring side." Brooke consigned it to the losing side. Like everyone else, Brooke liked Ike, admired his Anglo-American bridge-building, and respected his executive skills, but Brooke had recently told his diary that "Eisenhower as a general is hopeless! He submerges himself in politics and neglects his military duties, partly, I am afraid, because he knows little if anything about military matters."

Now Brooke schooled the Supreme Allied Commander in North Africa on the elementary need to coordinate his plan with his Scottish subordinate General Kenneth Anderson's First Army in Tunisia and Montgomery's Eighth Army in Libya. If Anderson bogged down in mud, "there seemed to be a danger" that Arnim could attack the Americans from the north while Rommel attacked them from the south with Montgomery hundreds of miles away, having just taken Tripoli, out of fuel with spent troops. Ike agreed that seasonal rain would stop quick northern movements for a month, but he would keep his 1st Armored Division in reserve and Montgomery would come on "as fast as possible," he "hoped." He could leave his forces idle or keep them engaged and take losses, the lesser of two evils. Brooke surely thought a debacle would be a greater evil. Having exposed the American plan as strategically flawed, Brooke started questioning its tactics, and Ike had no good answers.

His report on the French was not more inspiring. General Giraud's poorly trained and equipped colonial troops held the middle of the Allied front between the British to the north and the Americans to the south and defended the ports and supply lines. Their morale was low, desertions high, and "a serious situation would develop" if they buckled.

Giraud was hard to manage and not "a big enough man to carry the burden of civil government." He had no political sense in a politically charged environment, "no idea of administration," and a megalomaniac's ego "always ready to take offense."

The positive side was thin. With British help, air defenses were improving around Allied North African ports, night fighters had arrived from England, and radar had been installed. Portal questioned even that. Much of the radar was defective, he said, and he had arranged to improve it. When asked what airpower could be based around Sfax, Eisenhower said one airstrip was in range and another almost ready, but both were a hundred miles from the front, the Germans had two all-weather airfields, and it took 2,000 tons of steel mesh and a day's rail capacity over dangerously stretched supply lines to turn mud into a runway. When the rain stopped "all these difficulties would vanish."

"General Eisenhower withdrew at this point," the minutes say. Not one of his fellow Americans had said a recorded word.

After Ike's retreat, Brooke made a fluent presentation on two alternatives for 1943 after North Africa was cleared. Option one was to take a key Mediterranean target, launch massive continental bombing, and build an assault force in England that could seize a French bridgehead and lure German aircraft to destruction even if it could not be held for long. Option two was to accelerate Bolero's buildup in the U.K. and invade one of three French regions—Calais-Boulogne, heavily defended but the shortest Channel crossing, in easy range of English-based air cover; the Cherbourg peninsula, which a smaller force could capture; or the Brest peninsula, the most attractive target but impossible to take with fewer than fifteen divisions. Nothing could be done to execute option two before the Channel turned risky in mid-September, leaving the Russians unrelieved for the better part of a year.

Option one would give the Allied army in North Africa a good choice of targets: Sicily, Sardinia, Corsica, Crete, or the Dodecanese islands off Turkey. A simultaneous threat to them all would disperse German forces, and Italy could be bombed from any of them, possibly knocking her out of the war and bringing Turkey in. "Sicily would be the bigger prize" but also the bigger undertaking, which could not start until late summer. Sardinia or Corsica could be taken sooner and easier, and their airfields would be valuable. All in, the British Chiefs of Staff thought a southern strategy preferable to northwest France.

Brooke thought his case went down well, but it did not go unchallenged. The more we concentrate in the Mediterranean, King said, the more likely the Germans will take Spain and Gibraltar. Brooke replied that twenty German divisions would be required. Even then, the Allies could take Spanish Morocco and keep the strait open. Portal said Spain's dependence on Allied trade made her unlikely to join the Axis and wave the Germans through, and an Allied assault in the Mediterranean would drain German airpower, the scarcest enemy asset, but if the Allies invaded northwest France, the Germans could trust their ground defenses and move Mediterranean airpower to Russia.

The ups and downs of Sicily and Sardinia followed, focused on how quickly they could be attacked, keeping pressure on the enemy. Once North Africa was secure from Morocco to Egypt and its coast lined with air and naval bases, Pound said, a thirty-ship convoy could run through the Mediterranean every ten days even without Sicily in hand. Some fifteen ships a month were sunk on the African route. About nine would be lost in the Mediterranean, but Pound understood the American estimate was eighteen. If anyone questioned the disparity, Deane and Dykes left it out of the minutes.

At Roosevelt's request, Eisenhower had gone straight from his inglorious match with Brooke to the White House, where the atmospheric pressure dropped. The general's nerves were still raw, but he found FDR full of "optimism and buoyancy, amounting almost to lightheartedness," a transformation since they last met in June. Roosevelt was thrilled to see the enemy caught between the British and American armies and suggested by his manner more than words that Ike, as he called him, overstated the risks and underestimated the fight in U.S. troops. Ike explained his stalled Tunisian offensive without ducking the responsibility, including long supply lines and novice Americans fighting veteran Germans.

"No excuses, I take it," the president said.

"No Sir. Just hard work."

When pressed to predict when North Africa would be secure, Ike said May or June at best, which would make a Channel crossing nearly impossible by September. Roosevelt said a Mediterranean offensive would produce important results but only as preliminary steps toward a decisive invasion of France, which Eisenhower was relieved to hear. Ike had told Marshall informally that he favored the efficiency of using the forces in North Africa in the Mediterranean, but Roundup was for him the keystone of U.S. strategy.

The president and the general saw the French differently. Eisenhower considered himself their brother in arms in military control of a friendly territory, not strong enough in any case to give them orders and compel compliance with impunity. He had recently told Marshall, who passed it on to the president, that a withdrawal of French cooperation "would be catastrophic." In sharp contrast, Roosevelt cast the Americans as an occupying power and spoke of the region's governors, troops, and population as if he employed them. Ike reminded him that they were his allies, not his subjects. Of course, the president said, and continued to speak as their conqueror. An admirer of French culture but hostile to imperialism and negative on France's restoration as a great power, the president described his hopes to erase colonial empires from the postwar world, which the general could only see, understandably enough, as "the distant future."

Eisenhower said his decisions to make the Darlan deal and censor French political infighting had been "arbitrary," and political censorship was always a mistake. Generals could be fired for such decisions, but their governments could not. That was why generals should make them. Roosevelt laughed. Go ahead and make mistakes, he said, with "reasonable" assurance of his backing. He also made it clear that the Darlan deal was no mistake. Eisenhower was impressed by the president's memory and mastery of detail as he repeated word for word great chunks of Ike's report of months before on the deal's rationale and told him how useful the report had been as he went about "calming fears that all of us were turning fascist."

Roosevelt said he hoped to reconcile de Gaulle and Giraud, a subject under Eisenhower's purview. Ike had told Churchill he was in over his head in French affairs, with his hands more than full of "all the slickers with which this part of the world is so thickly populated." His education, experience, and innocence of French politics had not prepared him to grip its intrigues, much less unravel them, and Hopkins was impressed by his courage to admit it and take the blame for mistakes and failures, military and otherwise. As Captain McCrea showed the general to the door, he let him know that General Pershing had told the president that Marshall said Eisenhower would do all right in supreme command. Ike said he was glad to hear it; he needed all the friends he could get.

Roosevelt remarked to Hopkins that Ike had seemed jittery, not a high qualification for a supreme commander.

Harold Macmillan was summoned to Churchill's Villa Mirador, greeted warmly by "the genial secretaries." The great man himself was "in tremendous form." Churchill said he and the president were thinking of inviting de Gaulle and Giraud to Anfa, to help them find a path to cooperation. He had accepted the president's proposal for a more gradual approach than previously envisioned, he said, to avoid a French dispute that might disrupt the war. Rather than being combined, their two organizations would stay separate for now, but each would welcome the other's representatives and establish interlocking directorships. Macmillan and Murphy would advise Giraud and communicate Eisenhower's "wishes and requirements." Ike, of course, would retain his "ultimate, supreme" authority. Macmillan "expressed some doubt as to this plan," an exercise in British understatement.

Shortly after five, FDR summoned Murphy to the White House.

The subject was the French. To the diplomat's alarm, Roosevelt spoke of changing French law and French officials "as if these were matters for Americans to decide." The president treated him cordially but said in a "mildly reproachful" way that Murphy had "overdone things" in assuring Giraud before the Torch landings that France's colonies would be returned after the war. Murphy thought FDR failed to grasp "how abhorrent his attitude would be to all imperialist-minded Frenchmen, including de Gaulle," who called the colonies under his wing "*mes fiefs.*"

Murphy, Macmillan, and Harriman shared a villa, perhaps the first time a former streetcar conductor ever roomed with two aristocrats in Casablanca. Elliott Roosevelt found Murphy "suave and smooth," which was not a compliment but should have been. The rare career diplomat born to the working class, Murphy was tall, slim, and memorably warm, his subordinate Kenneth Pendar wrote, with "a tremendous gift for friendship." One of an immigrant railroad worker's many children, he had worked his way through high school and college on trolleys in Milwaukee, edged himself into the blue-blooded Foreign Service as a clerk, and acquired a polished, soft-spoken charm that suited him. He had kept tabs on Hitler in Munich in the 1920s, distinguished himself in Paris and Vichy, and knew more than any other American about French North Africa, where Roosevelt had sent him late in 1940 to weigh the feasibility of getting its army into the war. Eisenhower had decorated him for dangerous work on Torch with one scene played at gunpoint. Long before the landings, Marshall had sent him secretly to confer with Ike in London, where he was well known: "We'll disguise you in a lieutenant colonel's uniform," Marshall had said. "Nobody ever pays any attention to a lieutenant colonel." Murphy would have laughed had Marshall not been serious.

Having picked Giraud as America's French general, Murphy briefed the president on the problems he was causing—treating Allied generals like lieutenants, deploying his troops in Tunisia without consultation, ignoring his administrative duties—and why he should still be backed as a counter to de Gaulle, whom Murphy abhorred. Having not seen

Murphy since before the Darlan deal, Roosevelt assured him that he endorsed it despite the heat. It was crucial, he said, to stop French disputes that could interfere with victory. Giraud was a handful and de Gaulle seemed bent on civil war. On that happy note, Murphy and Macmillan went to work on their unification.

Roosevelt's aide Captain McCrea learned late that day that the destroyer USS *Mayrant* had just led a convoy into the harbor with her executive officer, Lieutenant Franklin D. Roosevelt Jr., decorated for bravery in November in the fight for Casablanca. McCrea had the lieutenant sent in ignorance to the Anfa Hotel where he spotted McCrea: "My God, Captain! Is Pa here?" Pleased to say he was, McCrea walked Franklin Jr. to a family reunion. The president's son James later wrote that his younger brother, respectfully known as "Big Moose" to the men who served under him, "came closest to being another FDR. He had father's looks, his speaking voice, his smile, his charm, and his charisma." Now he had his villa too, and moved in with Elliott.

Anfa Camp evoked for Macmillan a late-Roman scene with "the Emperor of the East and the Emperor of the West" in imperial conclave. Two Anglo-American social classes had formed. "The very smart ate their meals in the villas, the more ordinary in the hotel. The whole thing was rather like the *Normandie* or the *Queen Mary*," and a "certain rivalry naturally developed between the two groups."

Both tiers of Anfa society enjoyed excellent wines and meals, a paradisical treat for the London-based British. American officers sent to England had been warned that ordinary foods at home were luxuries in wartime Britain. One egg a week was the rule, and oranges, "few that there are, are saved for the sick and the needy." The British team in Washington had been spoiled, Dykes wrote, by "a colossal amount of very good food" and "terrifying" waste, but Moroccan fruit and American abundance delighted the Londoners at Anfa. Gorgeous oranges "lay about in platefuls everywhere," Jacob wrote. "One began to wonder if it were possible to do oneself harm by a surfeit."

The Brits were inclined to rise, eat, and go to bed later than their hosts, but the Yanks changed their ways "at close quarters with us." British and American officers enjoyed the Restaurant Panoramique together, four to six at a table, catch-as-catch-can, and a Black GI who called himself Shorty sometimes played the piano. Harriman watched friendships form and defenses come down, and "for the first time real willingness to be frank & work together with mutual confidence." Jacob observed "a general mixing of the clans," and "a genial warmth spread over our souls."

In their London and Washington meetings, the home team had scarcely mingled with the visitors. As soon as a session adjourned, the hosts fled to their desks and the foreigners to their hotels. At Anfa Camp, Jacob wrote, "British and Americans met round the bar, went for walks down to the beach together, and sat about in each other's rooms in the evenings. Mutual respect and understanding ripen in such surroundings, especially when the weather is lovely, the accommodation is good, and food and drink and smokes are unlimited and free." Macmillan wrote his wife that the grounds were "superbly beautiful. Every conceivable flower, of which you would have known the names but I did not, was out," with gorgeous shrubs in bloom. The whole affair was a curious marriage of "a cruise, a summer school and a conference." Hotel easels announced meeting rooms and times like college notice boards, and "when they got out of school at five o'clock or so," generals and admirals gathered surf-polished pebbles on the beach.

Nonetheless, the American reservist Captain Parton told his diary, informal work went on "in every villa at virtually every minute of the day" as British and American experts evaded the minute-takers and tackled "the entire collection of satellite problems." Somervell, Harriman, and Leathers met on shipping. Allied aviators vetted chains of command and various warplanes' peculiarities. Even King dropped his growls in productive chats with Cunningham and Pound, fellow sailors in Royal Navy uniforms. Dill befriended American clerks and walked the grounds with Marshall deep in conversation. Candor flourished off the record. Eisenhower told Marshall, preaching to the choir, "someday we have got to go across that Channel if we are going to whip Germany," but Arnold's subordinate General Andrews spouted heresy. Echoing the Brits, Andrews told Marshall an invasion of France would be "military suicide" and he did not know a single commander who would lead his men into it except under protest. No one could have thought Marshall liked what he heard, but the messenger and his message were sound. Jacob ascribed to "a neutral pitch" a large part of British success in "the gradual education of the Americans to our way of thinking."

The Harrow-educated General Sir Harold Rupert Leofric George Alexander, the Allied commander in chief in the Middle East, flew in from Libya in desert battle dress with a sun-browned face and a three-day beard, too busy chasing Rommel with his field commander Montgomery to shave for the occasion. It occurred to Elliott Roosevelt that here was the very "picture of a grim, tired, single-minded soldier." The third son of an earl, fifty-one years old, tall with a British mustache, Alexander had battle-weary bags under his eyes.

"One could not help being fond of Alex," Brooke wrote years later, a talented painter who had wanted to be a soldier since his privileged Northern Irish childhood. Trained at Sandhurst, gravely wounded with the Irish Guards at First Ypres in 1914, highly decorated at Loos and the Somme, Alexander was an instinctively courteous, exceptionally brave man who had led one of Brooke's divisions to Dunkirk. A hardened war correspondent called him "the most charming and picturesque person I have ever met." Brooke thought the regrettable part was a "deficiency of brains and character," by which he meant an unremarkable intellect and a tendency to be overborne by overbearing men less gracious than he. But for that, Alexander was the model British officer, a natural leader, a gentleman in every detail, respectful to every person in every walk of life, as calm in deadly combat as he was in the Regent's Park. "Alex was an unmistakable aristocrat," Jock Colville wrote after the war, "with a natural diffidence and modesty that his birth and established position provided no inducement to discard." According to a biographer he never indulged in introspection, for it "never occurred to him that he needed it." Hostile to class distinctions in and out of the Army, Colville later wrote, Alexander "invariably put duty before personal predilection. It was that as much as all his other graces and virtues that so endeared him to Churchill."

The pipe-smoking Air Chief Marshal Sir Arthur Tedder, a decorated World War I flier, a Scot who had studied history at Cambridge and Berlin, accompanied Alexander from the front. Looking more like a friendly Oxbridge don than a Knight Commander of the Order of the Bath in command of all Allied air forces in Africa, Tedder reported to Eisenhower, who rated him a "topflight" leader and an Anglo-American team builder.

The entire high command, civilian and military, met in FDR's villa, where Alexander and Tedder briefed them on the desert war in Libya. To Churchill's delight, Roosevelt was smitten by Alexander, but his swoon was unrequited. "Frankly I was rather disappointed," Tedder later wrote, and so was Alexander. The president was affable of course and asked a few "elementary questions," but "we did not draw from him the fresh inspiration we had looked for."

The two young Roosevelts watched like wide-eyed princes as Alexander and Tedder described their pursuit of the Afrika Korps. They hoped to take Tripoli in ten or so days, Alexander said, propelled by Montgomery's inspired idea to dismount one of their two armored corps and bring the other hell-bent against Rommel with both corps' armor. As Churchill read the room, everyone was taken by Alexander's grace and uplifted by his news, for his "unspoken confidence was contagious," even in this crowd of accomplished skeptics. Eisenhower condensed his afternoon report to the CCS and admired Alexander's "great boldness and rapidity, taking every kind of risk." With credit-sharing modesty Alexander reviewed the great victory he and Monty had won at El Alamein. Their "fine American Sherman tanks" and the "magnificent work" of Tedder's pilots had made it possible. In the first twelve days, Alexander said, the British had taken 16,000 casualties and Rommel an estimated 60,000 to 70,000.

Eisenhower asked Alexander if he could put enough pressure on Rommel to keep him from blocking an assault on Sfax. Alexander answered carefully, surely briefed on Ike's afternoon embarrassment. "Rommel was living very much hand to mouth" and would "certainly be trapped" if he lost his ports, but an attack on Sfax demanded "very careful study," and great care to avoid undue risk. Rommel would "react like lightning" and his plans would be as perfect as plans get. For the benefit of those who had missed it, Roosevelt included, Brooke contributed highlights of his afternoon roast of Eisenhower's less than perfect plans, whose results "might be unfortunate."

Ike explained his Tunisian air war's difficulties and proposed to put the entire front under British control, though the French refused to serve under British command. Seconded by Pound and echoing Cunningham, Tedder said North African–based aircraft could protect convoys passing through the Mediterranean, undercutting Brooke's pitch for Sicily. Churchill suggested that the opening of the Mediterranean and the protective proximity of the British Tenth Army, sent to Persia to meet the risk of a German thrust to capture oil that the enemy's failure at Stalingrad had eliminated, would educate the Turks on the wisdom of joining the war. Someone asked what special Allied units would make Turkey's dated army useful. Brooke said the Turks, notoriously fierce fighters, were "first-rate material as infantry" but "tended to misuse technical equipment." They would never be fit for a modern offensive but might keep the Germans out of Turkey, whose air force was good for nothing but handing over runways to the Allies.

Out of his depth, Roosevelt said little, except to endorse Mediterranean operations as the next offensive step, which was more than enough to say. His Chiefs of Staff had always known that Torch was a slippery slope into the Mediterranean but the moment FDR declared himself openly for the Med, any chance to get something from the British in return wilted on the spot. If Marshall, King, or Arnold said a word in the two-hour conversation it was not enough to make the minutes.

Eisenhower walked Churchill home and stayed until he left to dine with the president. Ike told his aide Harry Butcher that Marshall had "more-or-less bawled him out" for his performances on Anfa Camp's stage, but Hopkins thought Ike had done well at the Villa Dar es Saada, even in the shade of Alexander's tales of chasing Rommel through the desert with "ever-mounting success."

Arnold shared his biggest headache over dinner with Harriman and General Ira Eaker, the American bomber force commander in England. Eaker was a soft-spoken Texan, a tenant farmer's son, but his Harvard-educated aide, the reservist Captain Parton, only months from *Time* magazine's Manhattan executive suite, had learned from experience that when the general "chose to show displeasure, he left no doubt about it." Despite Portal's compliment to American "precision" bombing on the conference's opening day, Arnold told Eaker that Churchill was urging Roosevelt to switch to incinerating German cities by night, preferably under RAF control. Eaker's reply was not obscure. "Absurd," he said, "a complete disaster." Humanity was not the issue. His planes were not built for it, he said, and his fliers were not trained for it. They would lose more lives to English fog by night than to German defenses by day. Nothing was more likely to save the Luftwaffe and prevent a continental invasion. "If our leaders are that stupid, count me out. I don't want any part of such nonsense."

Arnold laughed and said all Eaker had to do was convince Churchill, who had spoken well of him. "Stand by and be ready." Arnold ran into the PM on a walk and asked him for a chance to address his concerns before they left Anfa, which he cheerfully granted. The news that the Japanese were being driven from Guadalcanal must have brightened their day, and a telegram from Stalin put a cap on it: "We are finishing the liquidation of the group of the German troops surrounded near Stalingrad."

FDR declared at dinner with Marshall, Eisenhower, Hopkins, Harriman, and the two young Roosevelts that he had gone up to the front in the last war as assistant secretary of the navy "and I'm going up front in this one too." Eisenhower and Marshall never hesitated. Out of the question, they said. Roosevelt asked how much danger there could *be* in Allied-controlled territory. Eisenhower said he had just flown in from Algiers in a sputtering bomber with a parachute on his back, and "there wasn't anybody very happy on that plane." Roosevelt turned to the pilot at the table, but with Marshall and Eisenhower glaring, Elliott pointed to a mouth full of food. "Coward," his father said. The president suggested a fighter escort, which Ike dismissed out of hand. Nothing drew Germans like an escorted plane. Marshall made it clear that if his commander in chief insisted on daring the Luftwaffe he would be obeyed, but on his own responsibility. A compromise was struck. He would review three of Clark's divisions near Rabat, fifty miles up the coast from Casablanca, from a heavily guarded motorcade. Unbeknownst to him the plans were already in place.

After his guests went home FDR amused his sons with a Kansas Republican congressman's speech. The president's boys, it seemed, were boozing in Manhattan nightclubs while other American sons were fighting far from home. Elliott and Franklin Jr. had earned medals in North Africa. One of their brothers was a naval officer, the other a knife-in-his-teeth commando. This war was being fought by the privileged as much as the poor. Katherine Marshall's son Allen, embraced by the childless general as his own, would be killed by a German sniper in 1944. It would fall to FDR to tell Hopkins that his youngest boy, Stephen, an eighteen-year-old marine, had died in battle. Churchill's bodyguard Walter Thompson, so proud of his young son Fred, learned just after leaving Anfa that Fred had lost his life in a bomber on his forty-third mission over Germany.

Churchill invited Brooke, Alexander, Portal, and Tedder to dinner, and Harriman and Hopkins dropped by. It seemed to Brooke that Harry was in "rather a bitter mood which I had not yet seen him in," soured, perhaps, by the conference's difficult turn. Having learned English as a second language growing up in France, Brooke was prone to the occasional syntactical lapse and made a diary entry that night that parses as congeniality but probably vented irony and frustration: "There is no doubt that we are too closely related to the Americans to make cooperation between us anything but easy."

In command of all Allied naval forces in the Mediterranean, reporting to Eisenhower, Admiral Sir Andrew B. Cunningham was a smiling man of sixty universally known as ABC. Comfortable in a fight, he had headed the British Admiralty delegation in Washington in early 1942 and delighted Vivian Dykes in a battle with King, "a magnificent show." At Anfa Camp, Cunningham was given a room in Patton's Villa Maas, to which Eisenhower's stay had drawn enhanced protection, prompting ABC to wryly tell his boss he was tired of having a GI put a tommy gun in his stomach whenever he walked its garden. Patton threw a dinner party to give Eisenhower a chance to relax with Marshall, King, Dill, and Mountbatten, but a command invitation to dine with FDR pulled Ike away, leaving Harry Butcher at "the aide's table," not as big as a kid's table, from which a fellow aide instructed GI waiters on the etiquette of the thing. Butcher told them when to pour the champagne, "not quite knowing myself."

After talks with Marshall and others ran past midnight at Villa Maas, Eisenhower went to the hotel bar with Patton and unburdened himself when they returned. "Ike was his old self," Patton wrote, "and listened." Clark was maneuvering against him, he said, and "his thread is about to be cut." Patton told him to ditch his desk and get to the front, but he felt he couldn't do it with his hands full of the French. He said he had discussed with Marshall letting Patton run the Tunisian campaign while he ran the politics. It was Marshall who had raised the idea, which must have made Ike doubt Marshall's faith in his generalship.

When Eisenhower and Patton had returned from the bar, Butcher had gotten up to give Ike some messages and gone back to bed for a nightmare born of war and the company of great men. The harbor he had toured with Patton was being bombed, and "the Germans were after the Anfa Camp and all of its distinguished and undistinguished occupants."

Eight

DAY THREE:
SATURDAY, JANUARY 16

German bombers launched from France toward Casablanca triggered a yellow alert and an anxious morning. Every fighter squadron in the vicinity warmed its engines. Antiaircraft crews readied their guns. The bombers changed course over the Mediterranean, but nerves had been set on edge and they tingled every day that the Allied high command lingered in Luftwaffe range. Even before the Americans left Washington, the Secret Service's director Frank Wilson had worried about "block buster bombs or some new terrific weapon which we felt Hitler might be saving for such an occasion." And yet, Roosevelt later told the press, "we were so comfortable in Casablanca, the accommodations were so delightful, that we decided to risk it and stay right there."

Physically and mentally drained by two long days and nights, Brooke pulled himself out of bed to reset the Tunisia campaign with Eisenhower, Marshall, Alexander, and Kennedy. Alexander explained that even if the Americans captured Sfax, the Germans would sabotage the port of Tripoli before his Eighth Army could take it, immobilizing them for weeks for lack of supplies. Ike canceled the attack. The French, he said along the way, caused more problems than they solved, and Giraud knew as much about logistics as a dog does about religion. It surely occurred to Brooke that Giraud was not alone.

Later in the day Ike conferred with Marshall and Arnold and had a long talk with Churchill, who cabled his War Cabinet: "It was fortunate indeed" that he had called Alexander to Anfa. Eisenhower had been on the edge of an attack on Sfax, "most daring and spirited but also most hazardous," that should have been planned with Alexander. They had gotten on well, alone and with Brooke and Marshall. "The result has been a perfect understanding." All four generals thought their chances in Tunisia were good, "provided we do not make a mistake."

Eisenhower, Murphy, and Macmillan, the French diplomacy team, called on FDR, the first of Macmillan's many visits to the Moroccan White House. If you approached it after dark, he later wrote, "searchlights were thrown upon you, and a horde of what I believe are called G-men, mostly retired Chicago gangsters, drew revolvers and covered you," but once you breached its defenses all was well. Macmillan arrived first and was led "through the dangerous approaches." He had never seen so many sentries armed with "such terrifying weapons."

Macmillan had met Roosevelt socially several times in America and found him sitting up in bed, as one often did at Anfa. "He was indeed a remarkable figure: the splendid head and torso full of vigor and vitality; below, concealed by the coverings, the terrible shrunken legs and feet." Hopkins and Harriman, "the court favorites," were there, and Churchill sat by the bed. FDR threw a hand up when Macmillan came in. "Hallo Harold," he called, "it is fine to see you—fine!" Churchill surely beamed at his protégé and made some jovial remark. The president was typically warm, and probably launched the first of many jests about Macmillan's distinction as his publisher and Churchill's too. Murphy joined them just as Eisenhower walked in and stood at the president's side like a sentinel. Elliott and Franklin Jr. dropped by, "the two sons who act as aides," Macmillan wrote, "and, tragic as it seems, almost as male nurses to this extraordinary figure."

They discussed the hostile press on Eisenhower's and Murphy's dealings with Hitler's French admirers and the odds of getting Giraud and de Gaulle to Anfa, "my problem child" and "your problem child" Roosevelt called them in chats with Churchill. Macmillan thought they might resent a summons to an armed Anglo-American camp on French soil. Giraud was a simple soldier and might be flattered, and "I naturally hoped that General de Gaulle might take the same view, but I believed it doubtful."

Eisenhower left with a smart salute as Macmillan whispered to Murphy, "Isn't he just like a Roman centurion!" Roosevelt had dropped a "Harold" or two in Ike's presence, which had not been lost on the general. "How strange you English are," he soon told Macmillan. Any American on a first-name basis with the president would have said so long ago. "Well, I'm not sure that I am," Macmillan replied, "not mutual." The president was just being friendly. Macmillan found that the incident served him well in adjusting the general's view of him.

Churchill had been the first to arrive and lingered after the others left. "The President's tendency to shift and handle things loosely and be influenced, particularly by the British, was one of our great problems," Marshall said years later. "Our whole idea was to keep the President on the course he had accepted. Always worried when the Prime Minister got near him."

The American Chiefs of Staff were literally all over the map at their morning meeting, shockingly thin on information, undecided on how to handle the day, never mind the war. How quickly could they turn against Japan after Germany's defeat? Could a modest Allied force invade the Continent in time to help the Russians before weather closed the Channel? Would a Mediterranean operation take northwest France off the board in 1943? No one had clear answers to any of these questions and more.

The central issue in the European theater was no longer whether an attack in the Med would precede a Channel crossing but when and where, and how to play the card with the Brits. The president had blessed the Mediterranean option; Clark and Mountbatten had told Marshall his troops would not be ready to win in France for many months even if the ships and landing craft were available, which they were not; tenacious German fighting in Tunisia had convinced Eisenhower that invading France would take twice as much force as he had thought, which he too had just told Marshall; and Tedder had said the Allies lacked the airpower. "It did not prove too hard to" get the Americans into the Mediterranean, Tedder later wrote, "for they had no real constructive alternative."

King conceded later that, like the British chiefs, "We all believed that we had to go either to Sicily or to Sardinia." Now he told his American peers he favored Sicily if the attack came soon enough to pull Germans from Russia by September, but the point should be traded, not given away. Cooke said the British had specific Mediterranean plans the Americans had a right to see, undeterred by his closemouthed approach to the Pacific in the combined planners' room. British promises to fight Japan after Germany was beaten meant little to Savvy Cooke, for they "do not say how or where."

Wedemeyer stuck with building up force for a Channel crossing, still against British plans to "disperse our forces" in the Mediterranean, an arena "neither vital nor final." The diversion could be tolerated if it produced big shipping gains, and Somervell repeated that it would, but Wedemeyer thought Admiral Cunningham's assurance to General Clark that convoys could be protected from North Africa made Sicily merely nice to have. King recalled Cunningham's caveat that the convoys would take heavy losses with Sicily in enemy hands.

Marshall insisted on blocking any operation that precluded any chance for a limited Channel crossing in 1943. A second front was "our main objective," crucial to keeping Russia in the war. "If we do Sicily, we might not have the means to do anything on the Continent before October," too late to help the Russians this year. King pointed out that if the Russians defeated the Germans alone, they would "dominate the peace table." Arnold fretted about his fear of losing daylight bombing, and

King said China's manpower and location were vital to Japan's defeat. The Burma Road and whatever else made the Chinese stronger were high priorities. He proposed to push the British for a war-winning plan and let them take the lead on Europe. Pulled in every direction, the Americans were incapable of leading.

Marshall followed King's approach when the CCS reconvened. The Americans, he said, were "anxious to learn the British concept as to how Germany is to be defeated." He reminded them of the "paramount importance" of bolstering the Russians and the British commitment to cross the Channel. Could the Allies take advantage of a crack in German strength in 1943 if they tied themselves up in the Mediterranean, "financed" by the troops in North Africa? Could bombing not impair the enemy's ability to move troops to France? What were the relative merits of taking Sicily or Sardinia and their impact on shipping and Bolero's buildup in the U.K.? Was Sicily part of a plan to win the war, or to be taken because it was there?

King piled on and threw elbows. Would the Russians *always* carry the European ground war's whole burden? Would the Allies *ever* invade the Continent? Would they form a step-by-step plan to win the war, or merely lunge for opportunities at random? Europe was in the British sphere of responsibility. He would like to hear British answers.

Marshall recalled that in the summer of 1942 the Allies had begun to prepare to take North Africa "on a shoestring," then switched to building up in the U.K. when the Russians seemed at risk of collapse, then switched back to Torch on the fly, taking great risks with "abnormally fortunate" results. Now they must chart the war's "main plot" and avoid every diversion like a "suction pump" pulling strength from victory. For the British, of course, the suction was in the Pacific. Thanks to "the splendid efforts of the British 8th Army" in Libya, Marshall said, Sicily looked attractive (which would have been a breakthrough had FDR not broken through already) but it must be part of a plan.

Brooke said a small invasion of France, which was all they could manage soon, would be unimportant. Marshall replied that a foothold in France would put the Germans in a box. An Allied bridgehead could be held and expanded if the enemy conceded air superiority, but to come out and fight in the sky he must pull planes from Russia. Brooke disagreed. The Germans had forty-four divisions in France, more than enough to "overwhelm us on the ground and perhaps hem us in with wire or concrete." We should make them defend the entire Mediterranean while we build up in England. An invasion of France would be "the final action of the war." Northern European railroads had too many routes to bomb, but Italian rail lines' closeness to the sea exposed them to raids and bombing.

The sea opened Admiral Pound's eyes. Sardinia's capture would not do much for shipping, he said, but Sicily's would. Brooke agreed. Portal challenged Marshall's thought that a bridgehead in France could be defended from the air, and whenever Portal spoke the Americans listened. Ian Jacob watched them "put their money on Portal" and "his unshakable honesty of thought and deed. They know he knows his stuff, and they trust him one hundred percent." Marshall found him the most approachable of the Brits and "the best mind of the lot." After the war, Churchill called him the ablest too, and more than up to a fight despite his gentility. "He berated me like a pickpocket" in front of the American ambassador.

Portal answered the American call for a war-winning plan. Specifics could not be planned very far in advance, he said. There were too many unknowns. The Germans would lose the war when they lost the means and the will to win it. Oil and aircraft were their scarcest means. Daylight bombing could disable their synthetic oil plants and immobilize their forces (music to Arnold's ears), and their aircraft would deplete over time. Their will to win turned on confidence in winning. If they kept losing battles as their means disappeared, they would start to see the hopelessness of their position. Bombing was the surest path to German despair. Every chance must be taken to destroy Germany's oil supply from the air, wreck her war industries, and produce "heavy casualties in her population and great misery by the destruction of their dwellings."

Relentless bombing and a series of Allied victories, however small, would make it "fairly certain that a point would be reached at which Germany would suddenly crack," but no one could know when or how.

King understood the British view, he said. Russia would make the main effort on land, supported by Allied diversions of German forces. After Allied troops cleared North Africa they could not be moved quickly to England from the Mediterranean. King then agreed that it therefore seemed "economical to use them in that area, if possible," a literal sea change for him that must have delighted the Brits. Sicily seemed "to offer a greater dividend" than Sardinia, though its price would be higher and Sardinia could be taken earlier. The dispositive questions were whether the Allies could afford the long delay before Sicily could be captured and satisfy the Russians without a second front.

After a full exchange on each Mediterranean option King spoke impressively again. Portal having identified the enemy's means and will as the keys to victory, King went entirely with means. The British Commonwealth had long since mobilized its military manpower, he said, but the United States had only reached about 60 percent of capacity. Russia, he guessed, had hit about 80 percent. China and India were "scarcely tapped." The greatest munitions production capacity was American. Britain's was next, but she could not fill her commonwealth's needs. The Russians were making more weapons than expected but not enough to arm themselves fully. "China and India were liabilities." Their manpower dwarfed their industries. Despite her industrial shortfall, Russia's geographic position and vast population made her Germany's worst enemy. China was similarly situated against Japan. We should therefore send Russia and China whatever they needed to throw more men into the fight, which led the Americans to "set great store" in Burma.

Arnold said the British view made a big cross-Channel invasion unlikely before the spring of 1944 (as if nothing else did) but decisions should be made now, not only for 1943 but also for 1944, given the war production lag. Brooke replied that "we should definitely count on reentering the Continent in 1944 on a large scale." Wedemeyer thought

Brooke "let the cat out of the bag" by pushing Roundup into 1944, but that cat had long since sprung. Portal said production "could never follow strategy precisely." Wars changed too quickly. Broad, hedged projections were the best one could do. Bomber production, for example, was a high priority because Europe was a fortress, and relentless bombing was required "to break into it."

Silent until now, Dill saw a chance to build an American bridge. There was "quite a possibility of beating Germany this year," he said, and they should "strain every nerve" to do it, for the sooner they did the sooner they could "turn on Japan. We must not let Japan consolidate her position for too long," but she could not be defeated this year, and Germany might be. King refused the bait. He doubted that Germany could be beaten before 1944 and only by blunt force then, not by failed morale. Was it "necessary to accept" that nothing could be done in northern France before April of 1944?

That depended on the German power to resist, Portal said. "If we concentrated everything we could on Germany this year" it was possible that she would crumble and a small force might deliver a coup de grâce, but unless the Germans broke down, "some 20 divisions would get us nowhere." Not to be forgotten was "the terrific latent power of the oppressed people" of Europe and Germany herself, which could only be unleashed when the crumbling began. It could start in the German interior and spread to the front, where the troops would be anxious for their families. Portal could not see them "fighting on and on, completely surrounded." A point would come when "the whole structure of Germany and the Nazi Party would collapse," quite possibly this year. In the meantime, the Allies must plan to open the cracks, which bombing alone could not do. Maximum pressure must be kept up on land.

After more discussion the planners were directed to examine the British plan for taking Sicily in Operation Husky and calculate its earliest launch. Wedemeyer saw the writing on the wall and soon sent a cable to his boss and fellow Channel crossing backer General Handy: "We still have our shirts but have lost a few buttons. Looks like Husky."

When the subject changed to supplying the Red Army and the cuts required elsewhere if the flow to Russia increased, Brooke wondered if the Russians were playing them. An "unsatisfactory feature of the whole business of supplying Russia" was "their refusal to put their cards on the table." One could not tell how stretched they really were. "It might well be that we were straining ourselves unduly and taking great risks when there was no real necessity to do so." The Russians had suffered *millions* of deaths in grinding up the German war machine and unspeakable Nazi savagery, but it was hard to make sacrifices for an ally that claimed distress and hid it.

Marshall asked for the British view on how to use the French in Tunisia. Their best-equipped formations should be better armed soon, but "political complications" were involved. Knowing London's political goals, Brooke said the French could be useful and an interim French government might "rekindle in them the desire to fight. Too many French were only waiting for the end of the war." Marshall wondered how Spain would react if the French patrolled Spanish Morocco's border with French Morocco. Brooke thought it wise to put Americans beside them to dispel any Spanish fears of aggressive French intent and deter Spain from crossing a border defended by troops "of inferior quality," a swipe at the French and a compliment to the Americans.

Kennedy thought Brooke did well. "We felt we were making some headway and that the Americans were beginning to see the situation more clearly. We were impressed by Marshall's friendliness and honesty of purpose." They could see he needed time to grasp their teaching, but "It was a relief to find that he was not obstinate or rigid in his strategic views." Ian Jacob thought George C. Marshall, nineteen years his senior, was "young for his age," unaccustomed to strategic thought, dependent on Dill as his "unobtrusive guide and leader." It had not been easy to convince him, Tedder wrote, "of the quite obvious fact" that the Allies lacked the wherewithal to invade France in *1942*. The British "had learned much in a hard school" but appreciated American "friendliness and willingness to learn" and Eisenhower's "outstanding ability as a coordinator and his determination to work most loyally with the British."

These were cordial postwar reminiscences, crediting the Americans with friendliness, honesty, loyalty, a capacity to be educated slowly, a willingness to learn, and a knack for coordination, all of which might have flattered a Border Collie. Churchill had told his War Cabinet after returning from Washington a year earlier that the Americans "were not above learning from us, provided that we did not set out to teach them."

Brooke told his diary he might be getting somewhere after three days of instruction, "dog tired" from the "slow tedious process, as all matters have to be carefully explained and reexplained before they can be absorbed." Even the American rebuttals betrayed a failure to understand, and the British had to start again. These were not the late-night thoughts of annoyance past its bedtime. Years later, Brooke told an interviewer that Marshall was one of the greatest gentlemen he ever met, a man of "extraordinary integrity. One could trust him with anything." The problem was, Brooke wrote for publication, "It was almost impossible to make him grasp the true concepts of a strategic situation." He lacked the ability to argue himself out of weak ideas and needed aides to rescue him. "Unfortunately, his assistants were not of the required caliber, and Cooke was of a very low category."

The Americans at large often drew British disdain, despite their superior power. The classically minded Macmillan had told Richard Crossman, a British psychological warfare expert, "We are like the Greeks in the later Roman Empire. They ran it, because they were so much cleverer than the Romans, but they never told the Romans this." Crossman later observed that "getting on with the Americans is frightfully easy, if only one will talk quite frankly and not give the appearance of being too clever."

It seems not to have crossed these British minds that the Yanks were not the only ones who sometimes failed to listen or absorb, that they grasped very well what the Brits were saying and questioned or rejected it for ample good cause, not least a two-and-a-half-year record of British defeat in battle and backtracking and conniving in conference. "Our people were always ready to find Albion perfidious," Marshall later said, an ancient French presumption of British treachery. "We were more suspicious of them than they were of us. They didn't think we knew enough or were smart enough to be treacherous."

Arnold met with his subordinate generals Eaker and Andrews to prepare their case for daylight bombing. Based near London in close cooperation with the RAF, the Texan Ira Eaker had demanded in writing that his officers treat them like brothers, invoking an RAF pilot who had flown in fast to save a wounded Flying Fortress from swarming German fighters. Mistaking him for an enemy, the Americans had greeted him with machine gun fire, which he took until it stopped when his Spitfire was recognized.

Eaker and his aide Captain Parton had moved into Le Paradou, the Harriman-Murphy-Macmillan villa. For two days at its dining room table, Parton pulled facts from his massive Eighth Air Force bombing report as Eaker condensed them for Churchill and tested the results on Parton while Murphy and Macmillan worked nearby on a proposal to de Gaulle and Giraud. Perhaps on his way to Harriman, Patton strode through the room with his ivory-handled pistols on his hips and his polished two-star helmet on his head. "Punctuating our labors," Parton told his diary, "were constant fascinating contacts with the mighty," by which he meant might at the top. "Generals are a dime a dozen."

Knowing Churchill valued brevity, clarity, and results, Eaker wrote "The Case for Day Bombing" in seven numbered points as simple as the first: "1. We can do a better job; day bombing is more accurate; small targets like individual factories can be found, seen, and hit." Puff-free evidence supported every point.

Roosevelt lunched on his veranda with his sons, Hopkins, and Army Reserve Captain George Durno, who had covered him as a reporter and accompanied him from Washington to write a narrative of the conference and handle the press when it ended. The sun had washed the grayness from FDR's cheeks, and Elliott was amazed by his new expertise on North Africa, including how to turn its deserts into Southern California.

The imperialists who pulled all the wealth from their colonies and put nothing back did not know what they were missing, he said. In everyone's interests, their colonized people's lives *must* improve after the war.

Churchill gave lunch to King, whose radar hummed when he realized he and Churchill were alone. The PM was wary too, but by King's rare admission the great man impressed him, enough to keep his hand on his watch. Churchill did most of the talking, "and what a smooth talker he was." At first King assumed he wanted something, but "he was just looking me over." He spoke of hitting the Germans in Europe's Mediterranean underbelly, a body part edged with water that attracted King more than Marshall. "Of course, he wanted first to clean up North Africa so that shipping would not have to go around the Cape of Good Hope, and in this all hands agreed."

Generals Arnold and Eaker and Arnold's subordinate Colonel Jacob E. Smart, flown in from Washington to help, exchanged airpower thoughts and information with Portal, Tedder, and Slessor. Hopkins and Harriman had told Arnold he had a rough time ahead of him, for Churchill had a solid case against daylight bombing and was ready to make it. Arnold ran into the prime minister on another stroll and poked at it as they walked.

The British liked their walks. Jack Dill had told Vivian Dykes that his Washington Secret Service agent had "a hell of a time following him on foot to the office in the mornings. No American is apparently capable of walking a mile." Brooke walked with Alexander that afternoon discussing everything from the Middle East to future operations. Walking on the beach, Churchill's physician Dr. Wilson found Dill and the British Chiefs of Staff at the crashing water's edge. On the long walk home, Brooke wrote, Portal, "who is full of odd scraps of information, which he usually keeps to himself, explained to Dill how the sap travels in a cactus plant." Wilson recorded "a great hunt for the P.M.," who had slipped away for a walk "without informing his keepers." He was hunted down on the beach, coat pockets bulging: "Interesting seashells in this part of the world."

It was not the first time. Having insisted on a late-night walk alone, Churchill had been stopped by a North Carolina farm boy who alerted the corporal of the guard by walkie-talkie: "I have a feller down here who claims he's the Prime Minister of Great Britain. I think he's a Goddamn liar." Churchill loved to tell the story.

Just before five, the American Chiefs of Staff and their advisors collected their notes and walked across the street to the White House to brief the president. Elliott bristled when they told his father that instead of planning "massive thrusts against the flanks of Europe" they were picking islands in the Mediterranean.

King said the British had "definite ideas" but no war-winning plan and seemed to rule out a Roundup invasion of France before April 1944. Marshall said the Americans would accept a Husky assault on Sicily but had not yet told the British. The question was whether France could also be invaded in 1943. The British would not commit to a date, but once the planners assessed Husky's needs, they would know what would be left for the Continent. Roosevelt repeated his idea to make several alternative plans and choose one later. Cooke replied obsequiously. No one else replied at all.

Averell Harriman was an Anglophilic fly on the wall: "Marshall is almost completely objective," he wrote. "King is crafty—always taking care of his war, namely the Pacific. Both always try to blame British for no Channel crossing. I got the feeling they understood the difficulties thoroughly but now and later will put the blame on the British for failure to act."

Marshall said the British were keen on knocking Italy out but not on her occupation, a big investment with a small return. FDR concurred and asked too many questions about Turkey. Churchill had been working him. After he complained that the Russians wanted American planes but not personnel, King said an American destroyer had been sunk and another damaged leading a convoy into Murmansk with no Russian escort. "We could help the Russians more if they would help us do so." Marshall

said as little as he could about Eisenhower's postponement of his drive on
Sfax: The British could not support it until March. If Roosevelt smelled
a rat, he did not ask to see it. He put several questions to Somervell,
who answered them neatly. Marshall valued Somervell highly, a logistical
magician who grabbed the bureaucracy and "shook the cobwebs out of
their pants," but Vivian Dykes had Somervell down as "a typical fascist."
Turning to the French, Roosevelt said Vichy had ordered its admiral in
Martinique to scuttle his ships if the Americans tried to take them, ending any chance to do so. Savvy Cooke observed that "the British were
becoming conscious of the fact that the United States was engaged in a
war in the Pacific." Their planners understood it, but their Chiefs of Staff
had not yet come around.

As FDR huddled with his high command, Churchill huddled with
his. Admiral Pound said the Americans had high ambitions for the
Pacific in 1943 and "seemed to expect that we would carry out a full-
scale invasion of Burma." Churchill felt confident of Roosevelt's support for Husky. He had reassured the president about Spain and that
Britain would fight Germany *and* Japan "to the bitter end." Definitive
agreements on individual operations would not be wise "until the whole
scene" was surveyed. He thought it likely that he and the president would
"intervene" within two days. In the meanwhile, "it would be best not to
bring matters to a head."

Five young American secretaries of the Women's Army Auxiliary Corps,
the first WAACs in a war zone, had been sent from London in December to work at Eisenhower's Algiers headquarters, Louise Anderson of
Denver, Colorado; Mattie Pinette of Fort Kent, Maine; Martha Rogers
of Jackson, Mississippi; Alene Drezmal of St. Paul, Minnesota; and Ruth
Briggs of Westerly, Rhode Island, captains all. A British troopship bound
for Algiers was thought to be safer transportation than a plane. At two
a.m. on December 21, a U-boat torpedoed the ship. The inadequate life-
boats were mismanaged and two of the WAACs were left aboard. They
"fully expected to die," Captain Anderson later said, "but we didn't want

to appear frightened in front of the men." The British captain threw "the maddest tea party" for the stranded survivors, but the ship was slowly sinking, and "all that gaiety was a coverup." After several life-threatening hours, the WAACs were literally tossed to a British destroyer. The three who had made it to a lifeboat spent the night at risk. They all reached Algiers with nothing but the clothes on their backs.

Two weeks later they were flown in to help at the Anfa Hotel, getting up at seven to take dictation, typing mimeograph stencils for the ultra-secret minutes, sometimes until three a.m., "honored at the confidence reposed in us." They shared a small villa with five secretaries of the Women's Royal Naval Service, the Wrens in one bedroom, the WAACs in the other, and slept on canvas cots before the Wrens brought them mattresses from HMS *Bulolo* in the harbor. Even in bedding the Brits were better prepared. Rubbing elbows with great names, Captain Pinette was impressed by Lord Mountbatten, and not because he was "one of the handsomest men I've ever seen." He "talks to people as if they're all alike, all on an equal footing."

Elliott Roosevelt had shown the shipwrecked WAACs great kindness in Algiers, and on the night of January 15 he and his brother brought them to the Villa Dar es Saada and introduced them to Harry Hopkins, "a drunken old S/B who thinks he is a lady's man," Captain Anderson told her diary. "The next day he had me called over to take a cable from him—purely a farce because his own staff always took care of that."

That afternoon, Franklin Jr. walked into the WAACs' office. "Dad wants you to come to dinner tonight," he said. Captain Anderson told her diary "We thought it was a gag to get us off work." Elliott and Franklin Jr. had "sworn they would do it somehow. So we went, with no expectations at all," and "there sat the President in the living room" with Hopkins and the former White House reporter Captain Durno, now presidential press handler in waiting. FDR put the women immediately at ease, and "we all sat around for a good hour drinking delicious martinis." Captain Pinette disliked Durno on sight. "He drank too much, and I thought he was disrespectful to the President."

Roosevelt praised the WAAC institution—proud to have started it all with Navy and Marine secretaries in World War I—kept everyone engaged, and seemed "almost like a sponge. He wanted to hear what other people said, no matter how inconsequential it was. He would cup his ear to listen to what you said." Mattie Pinette enjoyed their chat about Maine and his vacation home in Campobello. Much to her amusement, Elliott and Franklin Jr. "needled him" about politics. Louise Anderson found him "utterly charming, both his sons equally so and Frank completely wacky." They were all "delightful story tellers," and free conversation and free-flowing champagne improved an excellent dinner that reminded Alene Drezmal of a family party.

As if that were not enough, Hopkins excused himself for a few minutes and "in walks Averell Harriman," Winston Churchill, the notoriously charming General Alexander, several other British officers, and Harry in their wake. Captain Anderson felt Churchill take the room the moment he walked in. Captain Pinette enjoyed his competition with FDR. "One would tell something interesting and funny and the other one would feel that *he* had to do it." Captain Drezmal was struck by "a warm, personal feeling between them. You could feel it and see it."

Hopkins told the table he had not been able to get General Alexander to discuss the "inside strategy" that drove Rommel from El Alamein, but one of the women should ask. "He won't refuse a lady." One of them took the dare and proved Harry wrong. "Well," Alexander said, "we were faced with a brick wall, so we took a crowbar and broke a hole through it. Then we jiggled the crowbar around and widened the hole."

"So, you're not going to tell us the real strategy," Hopkins said. "No," Alexander said. "I believe not."

The WAACs described their encounter with the U-boat and its aftermath, including their flight from Algiers to Casablanca accompanied by six cases of Scotch for the Anfa Hotel. The major in charge "seemed more concerned about the scotch." One of the WAACs had written a gripping narrative of their harrowing experience at sea and lent it to Durno for his official conference narrative. He included it verbatim.

The celebrities signed the WAACs' short snorter dollar bills, Churchill stood up to toast "the woman's contribution to the war," Roosevelt toasted his torpedoed guests, Captain Drezmal toasted Roosevelt and Churchill, Elliott toasted his mother, and the toasting rolled into the night. The women went home at two, Captain Anderson's diary says, after an unforgettable evening "with the most important people in the world."

Marshall heard their story and sent an aide to let them know the Army would replace their possessions lost at sea. Informed on his return to Washington that torpedoed WAACs did not qualify, Marshall had the goods shipped personally and paid for them himself. Years later he told an interviewer he would have brought a WAAC to help him at Allied conferences "except King would have gone crazy if he had a woman on these things."

Patton gave dinner to Marshall, Pound, and Brooke, who discovered in his host a "real fire eater and a definite character" whose "swashbuckling personality exceeded my expectation." Admiration was not implied. "I did not form any high opinion of him," Brooke wrote after the war, "nor had I any reason to alter this view at a later date." Patton returned the compliment: "Brooke is nothing but a clerk" and "Pound slept most of the time. The more I see of the so-called great the less they impress me. I am better."

Churchill wired Eden a draft invitation to de Gaulle to meet Giraud in secret at Anfa, free of Anglo-American involvement unless they wanted it. Roosevelt was not mentioned, for security's sake. "It was to be hoped," a British diplomat wrote, that de Gaulle would understand "it was to his advantage to get his root in on the North African scene, which embraced the main riches of the French colonial empire." Murphy later said the Americans expected a de Gaulle–Giraud alliance to be "concluded with some pomp." Eisenhower was asked to invite Giraud when he returned to Algiers, headquarters to them both, and Roosevelt cabled Secretary of State Hull that the two French generals were expected: "I had hoped, as you know, to avoid political discussions here, but on arrival I find newspapers in London and at home have been making such a mountain out of a rather small hill that it would be bad for me to return without having settled the matter."

Throughout the conference, FDR received scores of code-broken enemy messages as a matter of course, as did Churchill, who also got a daily intelligence briefing from the Royal Navy's Captain R. P. Pim, who oversaw the prime minister's remarkable traveling map room, but Ian Jacob found that scarce war news produced Churchillian "bellows, as of a wounded buffalo." Late on Saturday night "a can of petrol was poured on the flames" in the form of a thin report on a British bombing raid on Berlin. After that, Churchill's furious cables produced a rushing "stream of stuff," largely unimportant "but sufficient to keep him quiet."

Nine

DAY FOUR:
SUNDAY, JANUARY 17

It was not a good day for France. Giraud's troops began to collapse in the ongoing fight for Tunisia and so did any great hopes for a de Gaulle–Giraud entente. The British did not do better. "A desperate day" at the bargaining table, Brooke called it. Arnold groused that Sunday was "No different than any other day" at Anfa Camp. It would not bring joy to his side either.

Hopkins had invited Eisenhower's aide Harry Butcher to breakfast and greeted him at half speed after the previous night's festivities. Hopkins said the president was driving everyone wild, demanding impossible trips to one dicey place or another, having fun making some of them up, but Ike had made a fine presentation to FDR, sharing the credit and taking the blame for the war in Tunisia. Butcher wondered how bad a beating Ike was taking at home on "the Darlan business." Hopkins said he had nothing to worry about. If he took Tunisia, he would be one of the world's great generals. Butcher asked what would happen if he failed and did not get a straight answer, not that he expected or needed one. When the conversation turned to the next battleground Butcher said Ike favored crossing the Channel. Hopkins was glad to hear it.

Hopkins let Butcher say hello to the president, breakfasting in bed and glad to see an old Washington friend. Given access to his commander in chief, the reserve lieutenant commander complained about a shortage of starch for his shirts. FDR called himself a "father confessor to all the boys," making light of the keener anxieties his generals and admirals brought him. Asked how long he would stay he said he was in no rush to leave and hoped to help Ike by bringing de Gaulle and Giraud together. He asked about de Gaulle's reputation in North Africa. Some civilians supported him, Butcher said, but his name was mud with the officers, who had been for Darlan and were now for Giraud. Some of the rest went over Butcher's head, like "a lot of this French stuff."

Eisenhower and Butcher returned to Algiers in a borrowed Flying Fortress. The worn-out engines that could have killed them had not yet been replaced on the general's own plane. Butcher told Ike what he already knew. His neck was in a noose. Roosevelt and Marshall had taken his work for granted, Eisenhower said, and had not been "effusive in praise." Surely Brooke had not. As the fight for Tunisia dragged on, Ike soon confided to his diary "a succession of disappointments," including the abandoned attack on Sfax that "I had so laboriously planned."

The American Chiefs of Staff opened their morning's business with good news from Arnold. Japanese aircraft losses were nearing an irreversible tailspin. The mixed news was Cooke's. The Combined Staff planners had agreed on a satisfactory Pacific strategy but not on Burma, where the British planners saw no path forward for nearly two years. King proposed to insist on an assault when the dry season started in November, repeating the importance of the Burma Road, but Marshall said Chiang Kai-shek was refusing to cooperate for lack of British naval support.

Somervell said Mountbatten was eager to recapture Britain's Channel Islands from the Germans as staging grounds for raids in France and for antisubmarine bases. In the end the little islands would remain in German hands until VE Day, Churchill letting 28,000 German troops continue their relatively benign occupation. They "can't get away," he said, and he did not wish to feed them.

"To our great surprise," General Kennedy later recalled, when the CCS reconvened "we found ourselves back where we had started" and "still poles apart." Brooke could scarcely contain himself. The British and American planners had produced dueling papers on Burma, and Marshall challenged the British view that Operation Anakim, the retaking of Burma, could not start this year. Brooke and Pound cited the scarcity of landing craft and naval support. King insisted that delay "would put us in a critical situation" and there was time before November to build ships. Mountbatten, who rarely spoke, accepted the need to reopen the Burma Road. The problem was finding the means.

King reassured the British that the Americans did "not envisage a complete defeat of Japan" before Germany, but they must be in ready positions when the time came. Brooke agreed, *unless* such "positions of readiness" would *delay* Germany's defeat, let alone jeopardize it, which seemed to provoke Marshall to the ultimate threat. Mere "readiness" to defeat Japan was not enough. If Anakim were dropped, "a situation might arise in the Pacific, at any time, that would necessitate the United States regretfully withdrawing from the commitments in the European theater."

Years later, Marshall confessed that he was bluffing, but the remark was incendiary and clearly made with feeling. American soldiers garrisoned many Pacific islands, he said, "Letting any of them down" was an "impossibility." The United States "could not stand for another Bataan," the appalling Japanese death march of captured U.S. troops in the Philippines. The United States Chiefs of Staff had accepted grave risks in the Pacific to sustain the war in Europe and lost Alaska's Aleutian Islands in the process. Attacking the Japanese in Burma would reduce those risks and free Americans to fight Germans. In his diary, Brooke called Marshall's angry speech a "long harangue."

King said he faced "enormous and continuous" demands in the Pacific, and Australia, "a Dominion of the British Commonwealth," accounted for many. Then Marshall struck again. The United States had 40,000 troops and three aircraft squadrons in Iceland, a key link in Britain's supply chain. He "was anxious to cut down these numbers." Pound was not fazed. A German invasion of Iceland was "quite out of the question." Even "a tip and run raid" was unlikely. The British had garrisoned Iceland with little more than half the relieving American force. King agreed and changed the subject to the Russians, perhaps to let Marshall cool down.

King said the Russians should be pressed to hit the German air forces in occupied Norway attacking Allied convoys to Russia. Pound agreed, but bombing Norwegian airfields had made very little difference before, and it was no use asking Russians to bomb ships. They were not trained for it, they would not even try when asked, even with British planes, and "it would be quite unsafe to rely on their promises." Portal called airfields "very unprofitable" targets. The British, Brooke said, had "most exhaustively" considered capturing the Norwegian airfields, without success, and the Tunisia campaign had forced the Germans to pull 250 planes from Norway, an example of the fruits of Mediterranean operations.

The CCS broke early, unable to make headway until the planners revisited Burma. Brooke had held his fire through most of the quarrel, reluctant to jump in before he saw his planners, which the British chiefs immediately did. To Brooke's astonishment, the planners reported that Cooke and Wedemeyer did not agree that Germany was the prime enemy "and were wishing to defeat Japan first!!!"

Brooke took a cleansing walk with Kennedy: "I found a new white heron, quite distinct from the egret." Macmillan liked to tease them when he caught them with binoculars. Now he understood why war plans took so long. "The birds leave no time for them."

Giraud accepted his invitation to Anfa the moment Ike presented it, and de Gaulle rejected Eden's. As a Foreign Office diplomat had it, "General de Gaulle started on a bad wicket." Eden met with him in London and cabled Churchill. Having "extracted a promise of absolute secrecy" he had told de Gaulle the prime minister was in North Africa for military talks with "important American personages." Not to be outdone, de Gaulle replied that *his* sources had told him such personages were in Accra (about 2,000 miles from Casablanca). When Eden delivered Churchill's invitation the general "expressed no pleasure." He had already offered Giraud a meeting, Giraud had declined, and he would not be glad to meet a fellow Frenchman under the auspices of foreigners who would pressure him to compromise, which he should not do.

Eden said the British had been loyal to de Gaulle (to the tune of some 70 million pounds), and his cooperation would benefit France, her allies, and de Gaulle, who replied that a compromise with Giraud and his Vichy men contrived by the British and the Americans—"les Anglo-Saxons" he liked to call them—might serve British interests but not France's or his. Giraud was a worthy candidate to join his National Committee and lead its army, subject to de Gaulle's control, but there were only two alternatives, Vichy or Fighting France, as his forces called themselves. Giraud, who was not too popular, had hopelessly tried to balance them. The British had "made a mistake in going into North Africa without de Gaulle." Now they asked him to come and help. Insulted that he had not been told of the conference in advance, it seemed to him self-evident that France was entitled to participate as an equal great power in the person of Charles de Gaulle.

Eden implied that Roosevelt was also at the conference, but why, de Gaulle asked, had Churchill not told him, and why had the president not invited him? If he agreed "to enter a race wearing the British colors while the Americans backed their own entry against me, the resulting comedy would be indecent, not to mention dangerous." Eden said de Gaulle would regret his refusal to help win the war. If Vichy elements won it, the general replied, "France would not have won much." Eden said he thought it inconceivable that de Gaulle should refuse a meeting arranged by the prime minister and the president of the United States. De Gaulle said no foreigner could invite him to meet *anyone* on French soil, but he would think about it.

Hours later he returned with a written refusal. He would meet Giraud in Chad, which he controlled, but not in "an exalted Allied forum." His assurance to Eden that his National Committee did not divorce France's interests from the fight against Hitler was not impressive. Eden pushed de Gaulle with every argument in his arsenal. "Nothing, however, would move him." De Gaulle sent Giraud a message. He was ready to confer on French African soil, one Frenchman with another, but not under Anglo-American wings. The Gaullist radio station in the French Congo called the Allies and the North African Vichyites "a basketful of angry crabs who would soon begin to devour each other."

General Auguste Charles Noguès came to Anfa from his magnificent governor's palace in Rabat, escorted to the White House by Patton, Murphy, McCrea, and Brigadier General William H. Wilbur, a hero of the landings at Casablanca and Noguès's fellow alumnus of the École Spéciale Militaire de Saint-Cyr. One American war correspondent called Noguès "a thin-lipped, blue-eyed" martinet "who would be imposing but for his slight stature." Another had him typed as one of many French officers who feared democracy more than Hitler. De Gaulle wanted him tried for treason, but Patton liked his influence over the sultan of Morocco and the Moroccan people and benefited from his acrobatic skill at pleasing whoever was winning.

Noguès had flipped from commanding French North Africa's forces in the war against Germany, to sending French partisans to Berlin for execution after France surrendered, to resisting the Torch landings, to fawning over Patton when they succeeded. Roosevelt would soon get a laugh at a press conference while dismissing the idea that the general was a friend of the Nazi Party: Noguès was loyal to one party, the president said, "a very definite partisan. He is for Noguès." He wanted to keep his position and his palace, and "he is no more pro-Hitler than I am. He is pro-Noguès—and the palace."

Roosevelt and Noguès exchanged pleasantries in French as FDR apologized for his. The president hoped Morocco had seen its last German for some time and Noguès cheerfully agreed. "Everyone was glad" when the sneering Germans left, he said, and the French were taking good care of the leftovers in concentration camps. They were not the only residents. Political prisoners of all stripes had joined them with American acquiescence. A *New York Times* reporter was appalled by "the sight of the American flag waving proudly in view of the poor devils in concentration camps established and kept full by Noguès." Patton had made an unlikely pal of Noguès, who had needlessly killed his troops only weeks before. Macmillan thought it "monstrous." For Patton it was useful. When Roosevelt asked Noguès how the local people's lives could be improved he replied with a vacant stare. Eisenhower called him "General No Way" for his position on reform. Murphy called him "General No-Guts" for self-explanatory reasons.

When Patton told the president that Noguès was providing "splendid cooperation" Roosevelt said the newspapers were selling nonexistent tensions. "The period for name calling" was over. Noguès replied that he was glad to help defeat "the enemy." When Roosevelt asked him if it would be appropriate to invite the sultan to dinner Noguès heartily approved, as did Patton. There was no higher compliment among the Arabs, Noguès said, than an invitation to share bread in one's home, the equivalent of killing enemies together.

Something about the French brought out the worst in FDR. Noguès said, when the subject came up, that the Jews had been released from concentration camps, "for the most part." Murphy said they wanted voting rights, but the president said the answer was simple, "there just weren't going to be any elections, so the Jews need not worry about the privilege of voting." Roosevelt had put many American Jews in positions of great power and had pressured Darlan to repeal the anti-Semitic laws, but what came next displayed his regrettable skill at telling people what they wanted to hear, a trait not unknown in politicians.

The Jews, Murphy said, were deeply disappointed that "the war for liberation" had not liberated them. "The whole Jewish problem," Roosevelt replied, should be carefully studied and plans made for progress, but Jews in the professions should be limited to their proportion of the population. When Noguès said "it would be a sad thing for the French to win the war" only to see the Jews control business and the professions, Roosevelt noted the "understandable complaints which the Germans bore toward the Jews in Germany" for comprising more than half of its professional class. Manipulative or not, had the remark been made public it would have screamed across a headline.

Macmillan urged Churchill to receive Noguès too. "Is he a good man?" Churchill asked. "Not very," Macmillan replied. "He is rather an equivocal character. 'No-Yes' we call him," another variation on the theme. "Why, then, should I see him?" Until he was removed, Macmillan said, "which I should like to see as soon as possible," he was the senior French official in Morocco. "It would be a courtesy to invite him."

Patton and Wilbur walked Noguès to the prime minister's villa on a warm afternoon that turned cold when Churchill confronted him in an often-used dialect of the PM's own making—French mixed with English spoken with a French accent when his Gallic vocabulary failed him, about which he was said to be "not the least bit self-conscious." The first thing he asked was whether Noguès would be phoning Vichy to report the location of the Allied high command. Macmillan watched Noguès squirm, "full of protestations," until Churchill, whom Noguès addressed as "Monsieur le Président," cut him off. The moon would be good for bombing that night, Churchill said, and whoever bombed Anfa Camp would be bombing Noguès too. According to Macmillan, "Poor General Noguès was thrown into great confusion." Macmillan assumed that messages had already passed between Noguès and Vichy, but the rest of the meeting "passed off agreeably enough."

Patton had not met Churchill before. "B-1 speaks the worst French I have ever heard," he told his diary, and "is not at all impressive." Patton was not surprised when Noguès told him later "he would much rather play with US, as B-1 wanted the whole world to run his way."

•　　•　　•

Over lunch at the White House, Churchill gushed to FDR, Elliott, and Hopkins about a sightseeing trip he had taken to the battered French battleship in the harbor. The president was as jealous as a child. "You got to see the *Jean Bart*? By gosh if you can get to see it then I can." Patton later heard that the Secret Service vetoed it, "a bunch of cheap detectives always smelling of drink."

On a more impactful subject Roosevelt aired the idea of announcing when the conference ended that the Allies would demand the unconditional surrender of the Axis powers. Hopkins liked it. Churchill frowned and rolled it over as he chewed. "Perfect!" he said. "And I can just see how Goebbels and the rest of 'em'll squeal!" Churchill closed the meal with a toast to unconditional surrender. Roosevelt said, "Of course it's just the thing for the Russians. They couldn't want anything better. Unconditional surrender. Uncle Joe might have made it up himself."

The Russians did want something better. Churchill sent Stalin a cable that day informing him of the RAF's first major bombing of Berlin, cold consolation for the missing second front.

Murphy and Clark met Giraud at the airport. Strikingly fit at sixty-four in gleaming cavalry boots and jodhpurs and an antique waxed mustache, Giraud was six feet two and straight as a bayonet, a "tall, fine figure of a man with a regal manner," Kennedy later called him. He brought three staff officers and General Mast, who had joined him in collaboration with the Americans in Torch as opposed to with the Germans in Vichy. Patton provided lunch and confided his thoughts to his diary: "I hate lunch. Giraud is an old type Gaul with blue eyes and limited brains."

Clark went from lunch to FDR and asked if he was ready for Giraud. Roosevelt wanted Clark's opinion of Giraud. He had heard he was difficult, the president said, and not very strong in North Africa. Clark cast his man as a spirited horse, cooperative when handled firmly, "a kind of symbol for France," head and shoulders above his competitors. Clark went to fetch Giraud and returned with him and Murphy.

Overconfident of his French, FDR waded into complexities and Giraud's confusion grew until an interpreter was found.

Giraud sat his chair as taut as a tuning fork. All that mattered, he said, was the future of France. Personal ambition was secondary, his own included. When asked about his administration in Algiers he said he opposed any changes. The president said it was quite correct to make no change until the people of France were free to choose a government. The king was sovereign in Britain, but the people were sovereign in the United States and France. He was focused, Roosevelt said, on two present needs, a well-equipped French army to help drive the enemy from North Africa and eventually from France, and no French political battles. Would it be possible to raise and support a 400,000-man French North African army?

Giraud said no. Moroccan troops were available, but the means to arm and equip them were not, and there were not enough "white officers and white non-commissioned officers" to lead them. Roosevelt said Noguès had told him that many such men were slipping through the Pyrenees into Spain and the challenge was to get them to North Africa. Giraud often said that generals got up early to do nothing all day while diplomats got up late for the same purpose, but he put his finger neatly on a diplomatic solution. Spain needed phosphates and should be glad to exchange shiploads of French veterans for shiploads of North African fertilizer. "Only give us the arms," he said theatrically, "the guns and the tanks and the planes. It is all we need."

Roosevelt promised every effort to get him arms, "not our old stuff, two, three and four years old," but the latest weapons "going to our own soldiers." Still, FDR seemed to doubt that a modern army could spring from almost nothing but French disarray. "It would be a very splendid thing" if Giraud and de Gaulle formed a committee to liberate France with Giraud in command of its armed forces, de Gaulle as his number two, and a respected civilian overseeing civil affairs. "Maybe we could get someone else out of France." Then he turned to Clark with a smile and recalled his pre-Torch rendezvous with the French: "Do you want to make another secret submarine trip, General?" Giraud was delighted, quite sure that he and General de Gaulle could agree on terms.

Regarding "the Jewish situation" Roosevelt repeated his remarks to Noguès, but Murphy watched Giraud's attention lag when the talk strayed from killing Germans. Murphy thought it clear that "this fighting general" would accept any arrangement that preserved France's empire and Giraud in military command. Giraud asked to be permitted to express his admiration for the Allied commitment to human rights and self-determination. Germany must be crushed once and for all and occupied after the war, as she should have been after the last one. Roosevelt agreed. It would be observed, Giraud went on, that he wore no decorations. He had sworn not to do so until he had marched through Berlin at the head of a French army. As the meeting wound down, FDR asked him to describe his escape from a German castle prison, a long since mastered tale.

The president was entertained but disappointed by Giraud and his phantom army and said so after he left. "I'm afraid we're leaning on a very slender reed." Then he threw up his hands with a laugh like a bark. "This is the man that Bob Murphy said the French would rally around! He's a dud as an administrator. He'll be a dud as a leader!"

According to Clark, Roosevelt had asked him to bring Giraud to Churchill and "stick around to see what the British thought," and Clark walked the Frenchman over, but Churchill's staff "took Giraud in tow and politely showed me to the door," as the president had expected. Giraud's designated translator, Major Charles Codman, a blue-blooded Boston reservist, remembered it differently. The meeting had been previously arranged, Codman wrote, and it was he who led Giraud to Churchill, who responded to their ring at his garden gate personally "and hurried down the path at a trot." Codman wondered why a great man "invariably seems smaller than one had imagined him." Churchill was "very affable, and full of steam," Codman thought. He had met Giraud before the war and told him he had not changed. Giraud returned the compliment. "I'm strong," the prime minister replied, "and yet it's hard. But whisky is the water of life. Will you have a whisky?"

On Churchill's inquiry, Giraud said he had not heard from de Gaulle. Churchill said nor had he. "It's astonishing. He ought to be here. I gave him all the means to come. He's being pig-headed, naturally. A tough customer, your friend de Gaulle." Did Giraud know him? De Gaulle had served under him, Giraud replied, and their relationship was not bad. "Quite a character," Churchill said, but he would never forget that de Gaulle was the first foreigner who did not give up on England in June 1940. In the interest of France, in their common interest, he would like to see Giraud in agreement with de Gaulle. Ideally de Gaulle would leave London "and settle in Algiers with you." Of course, Giraud replied. Churchill said de Gaulle must come to Anfa first, which he would do anytime now, no doubt. In the meantime, Giraud could settle his military problems with the Allied general staff. Now "Come and see my maps."

The British directors of plans met with their Chiefs of Staff to review the combined planners' report on operations against Japan. Some of its introductory assumptions were "unsatisfactory," the minutes say, which sounds like a Brooke explosion over its failure to call Asia and the Pacific secondary theaters. The planners explained that Admiral Cooke had "definitely refused" the Germany First policy. Knowing Cooke to be more Kinglike than King, the British chiefs reassured themselves that even King endorsed that dogma, and went on to set the stage for future backsliding: According to the British minutes, the report's sole object was to estimate the minimum forces required in Asia and the Pacific in 1943; "it did not follow that all the forces which might be recommended would necessarily be a first charge on our combined resources in 1943." After all, even the leaders of Japan understood that after Germany's defeat "she herself would be finished."

The Americans were determined nonetheless to keep her bleeding and finish her when the time came with the smallest loss of American lives. There was no inconsistency in beating Germany while pressuring Japan, and no inability to do so.

Eisenhower cabled Hopkins from Algiers. How valuable it had been to see the president and the CCS, especially Marshall. Much good would come from the conference. A note to FDR was attached. Their visit had been "an uplifting experience," the general wrote, a half-truth at best, and would improve his operations. "I cannot tell you how much I appreciated the kind words you had to say about our efforts in the past." The last three words were telling.

Joined by Hopkins and Harriman, Roosevelt gave dinner to Churchill, Leathers, Cunningham, Somervell, and King, a cast attuned to the shipping shortage. They grappled with logistics until one a.m. King pummeled the prime minister with demands for a hot Pacific war, an often poor choice of tactics in the case of Winston Churchill, who pummeled back. In the presence of King's commander in chief, Churchill accused the admiral of withholding information about his Pacific dispositions and landing craft production and "putting the cart before the horse," Japan before Hitler. But Churchill respected men who hit back. King told his fellow Americans the next day he had "tried to explain to the Prime Minister" the importance of China and Burma and had gotten his support to build a stronger air force in China and start retaking Burma in November, contingent on Chinese help. No doubt in return, implicitly or otherwise, King told Churchill that if Sicily turned out to be next, he would find the naval escorts.

Churchill cabled his War Cabinet. The dinner had been productive. "Admiral King, of course, considers the Pacific the first charge on all resources," and Marshall was very keen on Burma and accelerating Bolero's buildup in the U.K. at the Mediterranean's expense. "On the other hand, I am satisfied the president is strongly in favor of the Mediterranean being given prime place." Nothing definite had been settled but they were clearly of one mind. Fond of calling the Mediterranean Europe's "soft underbelly," Churchill said the president seemed sold on Husky, "which he suggested to me last night should be called 'Belly,'" a bit of joviality it seems. Churchill had countered with Bellona, the Roman Goddess of War.

Ten

DAY FIVE: MONDAY, JANUARY 18

O n "a lovely cool morning with a strong sea and strong wind," Kennedy joined Brooke for a shoreline bird walk as Cooke and Wedemeyer discussed their planning room tactics at the Americans' morning huddle. Cooke was blocking a British planners' push to get landing craft to England "badly needed in the Pacific," without telling them much. They "have rightly kept us in the dark" on some of *their* operations in *their* strategic spheres, he said, "and should accord us the same privilege" in ours. But despite what the British planners had told their chiefs, Cooke and Wedemeyer had not dropped Germany for Japan. The order of their enemies' defeat was less important than keeping them *all* under pressure. Cooke posed a reasonable question. "Shall we defeat Germany first" or "bring the war to a successful conclusion expeditiously" everywhere?

The British Chiefs of Staff's conception of Germany First, Cooke wrote later, came to starving the Pacific war "until all the needs and demands of the European theater had been fulfilled," which was not far from true. Many senior American officers felt the British were unnerved in both theaters, "insufferable not only in their arrogance but in their timidity about striking the enemy." They were surely more experienced at modern war than the Americans. They were also more experienced at losing. But for the Battle of Britain, they had lost every campaign they had fought against the Germans until two months before the conference. Churchill had struggled since 1940 against his military's fear of failure, which in 1942 had become habitual and arguably paralyzing. "You must remember that our army had met the Germans at their height," Portal said years later, "and after they had been pushed around, they began to feel in their heart that they weren't the equal of the Germans." El Alamein and Torch had bucked them up, but they had grown so accustomed to shortage and defeat that they expected them. The Yanks having never lost a war, hubris pushed them the other way.

On the very day of the Torch landings, Cooke had sent King a cogent memo that argued for keeping Germany *and* Japan "under continuous and increasing pressure" and jeered the British for proposing that "we hold Germany while we hold Japan." Before the Americans left for Casablanca one of King's senior staff had advised him that Japan "is more of a threat to our national position than is Germany" though "Germany is unquestionably the British primary enemy. With two such dangerous military powers pitted against us I do not believe it desirable to designate a 'primary' one." Cooke agreed in emphatic type: "Terming GERMANY our primary enemy and speaking of an offensive in the ATLANTIC and defensive in the PACIFIC are both out of date and should be definitely and completely discarded."

Wedemeyer told the American Chiefs of Staff that the British planners preferred to take Sardinia over Sicily, but he supported neither if the minutes of yesterday's CCS meeting were correct and Pound was about to move ships from the Pacific to the Mediterranean. It was necessary to open the Med, King replied. Sicily was the place to do it. If Sardinia were taken first the British would want Sicily later, and the only realistic alternative, sending the troops in North Africa to England, would accomplish nothing, for a Channel crossing was still far off.

King reported Churchill's dinner party commitment to retake Burma and support an expanded American bomber force in China but rankled at the PM's fretting over the U.S. Navy's Pacific dispositions. The Allies,

King said, could do everything the British were willing to do in Sicily or the Brest peninsula without diverting forces from the Pacific.

When the CCS reconvened, the British had massed a dozen officers for battle, Jack Slessor included. At times, Slessor wrote, the meeting "became uncomfortably warm," stirred by British evasions and American resentments.

Churchill having made a dinner table pledge to retake Burma, Brooke could only ask if landing craft would be left for the rest of the world. King assured him that new U.S. production would supply all they needed, a mouth-shutting show of American wealth. The Yanks took their vast industrial capacity for granted, a British general wrote, while the Brits found it "hard to overcome a lifetime of niggling, cheese-paring parsimony." No longer in a position to resist, Brooke tried this: Operation Anakim "is now definitely on the books, is being planned, and should be put to the front." King saw the vagueness and pushed for a black-and-white date but the British pushed back and the minutes came out in a pale shade of gray: "all plans and necessary preparations should be made" for Anakim, whose "actual mounting" would be assessed in the summer, and "if" it came off in 1943, the Americans would help with naval vessels and shipping "by diversion from the Pacific Theater."

What followed was a testy discussion of conflicting papers on the right mix of effort to bring against Germany and Japan, the fundamental issue that could still leave the Allies divided. The British paper was fixed on the Germans, of course, keeping only enough pressure on Japan to "hinder" her consolidations and protect vital Allied interests. The American paper called for winning the war as quickly as possible by destroying the strength of "all our adversaries" faster than they could replace it. The "major portion" of force should be thrown against Germany, "the most powerful and pressing enemy," but not enough to delay *Japan's* defeat. The Allies were stretched along 12,000 miles of the Pacific from Singapore to Alaska while the enemy was "strongly established" around Japan, from which he could strike where he chose. The Allies must wear him down by attacking points of *their* choosing important enough to draw a response they could defeat. If they could not hit the Germans hard in 1943, they could smash the Japanese. Rather disingenuously, the British paper accepted this in principle, "provided always" that any action against Japan "does not prejudice the earliest possible defeat of Germany," the ritual incantation.

The Americans proposed to retake the western Aleutians in 1943 and capture a vast sweep of Southwest Pacific islands—the Solomons, the Gilberts, the Marshalls, New Ireland, eastern New Guinea, the Carolines "up to and including" the fortified Japanese anchorage at Truk, New Britain, and its stronghold at Rabaul. Operations should start now in Burma. To accomplish all this, 250,000 more men must be allocated to the war on Japan, 500 more planes, the greater part of new warship construction, and 1,250,000 tons of new shipping.

The British paper countered with less of all these things, dismayed that even that might postpone Germany's defeat. The simultaneous taking of Truk and Burma would surely prolong the war in Europe, though one of the two might be possible without a flagrant violation of Germany First, "our agreed strategy," to which King's inner circle had *not* agreed.

Brooke protested the American failure to confirm that Germany came first. Marshall replied that the British seemed to want an active Mediterranean war and merely enough force kept "dormant" in Britain to take advantage of a future German crack. Some of that force could be used elsewhere. The Americans could use it in the Pacific. Manpower was not the shortage. Landing craft and shipping were. Should we let them sit idle in England or do something with them in the Pacific?

"Tempers were getting a little frayed," Slessor wrote later, "or anyway Alan Brooke's was." Brooke had a less than endearing habit of shaking his head energetically before a colleague finished talking then cutting him off "like a Gatling gun," which he may have done now. Slessor never forgot how Brooke "hammered" Marshall on the need to beat Germany first. To defeat both enemies simultaneously was impossible. They had to choose one or the other, and Brooke could not have been more emphatic on the consequence of error. If they tried to beat Japan first, "we shall lose the war."

Given the long-agreed necessity to put *Germany* first, Brooke said, the question was whether to invade northern France or "exploit our successes in North Africa." The Mediterranean was the place to attack, and to pull the most Germans from Russia "it must be all-out." The British understood the situation in the Pacific and would do all they could to help, but unless the Germans were constantly pressed, they would recover from their Russian and African losses "and thus prolong the war."

Churchill had long since measured Marshall: In his "quiet, unprovocative way he means business," and if the British were "too obstinate" they might regret it. They came close to regretting it now. Marshall said the United States Chiefs of Staff had "no idea that we should not concentrate first on defeating Germany," but the war should be won as quickly as possible, by which he meant the whole war. He favored invading Northern Europe but opposed tying up a big force in Britain "awaiting an uncertain prospect" when it might be used elsewhere. The war against Japan was being fought "on a shoestring" and the means must be supplied to defeat her.

Brooke corrected Marshall like a tutor whose pupil had not done his reading. The British did not propose to tie forces up in Europe doing nothing, he said, but a certain concentration of strength must be reached before an attack can begin, a principle too elementary to recite without insulting every American at the table. As for Japan, the British would support a Pacific offensive that did not delay Germany's earliest possible defeat, a phrase he repeated endlessly. King replied fairly that *any* move in the Pacific could be read as delaying Germany's defeat and leave the Pacific "totally inactive."

With the figurative scent of cordite in the air, Portal tried to calm the room, which was not a job for Brooke. Typically frank to a fault, Brooke was not good at voicing respect for an adversary's arguments. For him it was a form of deceit, and Brooke was incapable of deceit except against the enemy. Churchill's close friend Dr. Wilson had watched Brooke hurl facts "like hand grenades," treating experts like fools. "In his opinion it was all just common sense; he had thought it all out. Not for a moment did it occur to him that there might be another point of view." Portal, on the other hand, was a conciliator, respecting the other chap's position without retreating from his own. When an issue could not be resolved in the planning field, he later said, he saw no way to test it but the battle-field, unless a respectful debate left "everybody having their say and being persuaded, in the end, to agree."

Now Portal said the British Chiefs of Staff had always accepted the need to pressure Japan. "They had perhaps misunderstood the U.S. Chiefs of Staff and thought the point at issue was whether the main ef-fort should be in the Pacific or in the United Kingdom." In "the British view" the Mediterranean was the better prospect than northern France for "getting at Germany" quicker. In the meantime, heavy bombing, the bomber pilot said, could damage the Germans continuously. For now, it was the only way of attacking them directly at all.

With his mind made up for Sicily, Marshall began to tease it out. He was "most anxious" to avoid a commitment to "interminable" Mediter-ranean operations. He had always thought the main effort against Ger-many should start in northern France. Portal said it was impossible to know "exactly where we should stop in the Mediterranean," since the British hoped "to knock Italy out altogether," which would help the Rus-sians most by pulling German troops into Italy and might "open the door to an invasion of France."

Marshall was not soothed. Combined with the buildup in the U.K., major Mediterranean operations might prevent retaking Burma, and he was "not at all in favor of this," an understatement corrected by King. They had often been close to *disaster* in the war on the Japanese, King said. The United States wanted only to keep the initiative and move into *position* for "the final offensive against Japan." He felt "very strongly" that the Pacific war's details should be left to the Americans charged with winning it. The operations they envisioned "would have no effect on what could be done in the Mediterranean *or* from the United Kingdom."

There would be "plenty of forces" in Europe for the "necessary" Mediterranean operations, "and it was now determined that such operations should be undertaken." With that it had finally been said.

Portal replied that the British Chiefs of Staff "would be satisfied if they could be assured of this point," but Marshall was not yet ready. Inadequate resources to throw against Japan had jeopardized Germany First in 1942, he said. Bombers earmarked for Britain had been flown to the Pacific to avoid a catastrophe and "a huge diversion of U.S effort" from Europe. The Americans had nearly been forced to cancel Torch until King made "a most courageous decision" to pull strength from the Pacific. "A hand-to-mouth policy" in the war on Japan was a false economy. Burma's recapture would make a tremendous contribution to Japan's defeat and produce a great economy of forces.

Brooke said the British thought it sufficient to stop at taking Burma and Rabaul. Taking Truk would require too much force and shipping. King replied that the same American forces would take all three in succession, not sit idle in between. In fact, "It might well be that Truk would, after all," be impossible to capture this year. Marshall suggested a consensus might be forming on the "need" to take Rabaul and the "desirability" of taking Burma. Could it not be agreed that the forces that took Rabaul should push on to Truk if possible?

No, the British said, and started sliding back on Anakim. Even if Burma could be taken with the same forces that took Rabaul, Portal said, he would not like to commit to it without considering whether "some other operation more profitable to the war as a whole might not be desirable." What if fading German strength produced a chance for "breaking into France? Should they turn their backs on it because they were committed to Anakim?" Marshall said surely not. A meeting might be needed next summer to decide these things. But Brooke would not leave well enough alone. For now "we should limit our outlook in the Pacific to Rabaul, which should certainly be undertaken," prepare for Anakim, decide whether to launch it later, and defer Truk.

Marshall agreed that Truk and Anakim could wait. The American planners had merely proposed operations that "might" be carried out in 1943 "with the means available." Perhaps upset by too much conciliation, King took a shot at the Brits. What they wanted, he said, were strict constraints in the Pacific and unlimited action in Europe. It was beyond impracticable to move Pacific forces to Europe, it was logistically impossible. Burma was not an *alternative* to Europe but a separate undertaking thousands of miles away. Marshall, however, took another step toward compromise. He would agree to limit the assault on the American list of islands to forces already in the Pacific, draining nothing from Europe, a trial balloon that floated past Brooke but stuck in the mind of Sir John Cotesworth Slessor, who was listening intently.

Now Cooke jumped into the mix, which would have provoked the Brits even before he said his piece. Cooke was "so repellant," Jacob wrote, "that our people found it hard to get along with him at all." His predecessor had been "an uncouth customer, but he was gaiety and bonhomie itself compared with Cooke." Cooke made his case, no doubt scowling all the way, that a very large part of America's Pacific shipping merely kept the fleet maintained 7,000 miles from home. Soon the United States would produce fifteen oceangoing LST landing craft a month, which could not be ready in time for the Mediterranean by the summer but *would* be ready for Burma in November. Underlying Brooke's view of this was his unexpressed observation that for King and his crew, "The European war was just a great nuisance that kept him from waging his Pacific war undisturbed."

As the meeting broke for lunch, Brooke saw it breaking altogether. "I was in despair and in the depths of gloom." Dill asked Slessor if he thought it was as hopeless as it looked. Slessor was sure it was not. Dill could see it too, but Brooke confessed dejection as he walked Dill up to the restaurant. "It is no use. We shall never get agreement with them." "On the contrary," Dill said. "You have already got agreement to most of the points, and it only remains to settle the rest. Let's come to your room after lunch and discuss it."

•   •   •

Slessor later recalled that "we found ourselves faced with a virtually complete impasse," and the odds of closing the gap "looked somewhat remote—to put it mildly." But Slessor's senior staff role assigned him "the pleasant position of a somewhat detached observer" with a broad field of vision and a narrow scope of responsibility. Steeped in all the issues, free from junior "donkey work" and the Chiefs of Staff's burdens, he was able to see the woods as clearly as the trees. "Not being embroiled in the heat of the discussion myself," he could "watch the trend of the argument" without getting burned "and perhaps form a better idea of what each side was getting at than the protagonists themselves," by "discerning trends of opinion" and "noticing any special attitudes of mind or reactions among the participants."

After three months in Washington in 1941 and four days at Anfa, Slessor knew the minds of both tribes' chiefs better than they did. They were closer to agreement than they thought, "based partly on a misunderstanding of words—some of which have faintly different shades of meaning in English and American." But that was easily fixed. "The real trouble" was a vision-blurring cloud of suspicion, an American belief that the British "didn't care a damn about Japan" and a British perception that the Yanks were bent on a Pacific rampage that would cripple the war in Europe. Slessor knew neither was true, for "our interests and honour were deeply involved" in defeating Japan, with as many "scores to pay off" as the Americans, who understood that Germany threatened both their countries' lives as Japan did not.

Clearing the air of literal and figurative smoke, Slessor grabbed a quick lunch at the Restaurant Panoramique, took a "scruffy little notebook" to its roof garden, sat in the sun watching the surf roll down the beach, and "scratched out" a rough agreement that "looked rather good to me when I read it through." Portal thought so too and gave it a few tweaks. Perhaps the Americans would buy it. "Let's try it on them." Five minutes before the meeting reconvened, an RAF staff officer risen from the ranks as a clerk finished typing it with carbon copies.

Where Brooke had seen nowhere to go, Slessor's rooftop draft found the deal hidden under the logjam. Without a needless word, it made tacit agreements explicit, deferred unavoidable differences, gave the British nearly every big thing they wanted, left the Americans enough to please them, and saved face all around, a mediator's tour de force. Slessor told the story "not to show what a clever chap I was," for anyone properly trained and experienced could have done it, but to illustrate how "a detached observer can sometimes find a solution to a situation that, to the actual participants, looks uncommonly like an impasse." His modesty did him credit, but Slessor was a clever chap indeed.

In final form, his section headed "Operations in the European Theater" began with "the object of defeating Germany in 1943 with the maximum forces that can be brought to bear upon her" in "five main lines of offensive action": (1) capturing Sicily and thereby making Mediterranean traffic more secure, relieving German pressure on Russia, and increasing pressure on Italy; (2) an expectation of other "limited offensive operations as may be practicable with the forces available"; (3) an attempt to make Turkey "an active ally"; (4) "the heaviest possible bomber offensive against Germany"; and (5) the assembly in Britain of "the strongest possible force" prepared to invade the Continent "as soon as German resistance is weakened to the required extent."

What the draft did not say was as important as what it did. The pivotal words "practicable," "strongest possible," and "required extent" were not defined, which made them acceptable. Everyone knew that, absent an unlikely German collapse, Marshall's invasion of France would not come in 1943, but the possibility was left open and a vigorous Bolero buildup was endorsed. Nothing explicit was said about what came after Sicily, and the allusion to future offensives included no other Mediterranean commitments, which the Americans would have refused. Nine months later, as a cross-Channel force was building, Marshall exploded at Churchill when he spoke of taking Rhodes: "Not one American soldier is going to die on that goddamned beach."

Slessor's section headed "Operations in the Pacific and Far East" consisted of hedged commitments and deferred disputes: (1) Asian and

Pacific operations would "continue with the forces allocated [Marshall's thought of minutes earlier], with the object of pressuring Japan, retaining the initiative and attaining a position of readiness for the full scale offensive against Japan *by the United Nations* [emphasis added] as soon as Germany is defeated"; (2) "These operations must be kept within such limits as will not, in the opinion of the Combined Chiefs of Staff, prejudice the capacity of the United Nations to take advantage of any favorable opportunity that may present itself for the decisive defeat of Germany in 1943"; (3) Subject to "the above reservation," preparations to take Burma and Rabaul would proceed, followed by the Marshall and Caroline Islands "if time and resources allow," without "prejudicing" Anakim. Every base was touched, heavy with ambiguities, letting events shape the future.

While Slessor was drafting on the roof, Brooke was sitting with Dill on the edge of Brooke's bed, "I must confess without much hope," Brooke wrote later, as Dill reviewed every settled point and "those where we were stuck." Knowing with whom he dealt, Dill asked how far Brooke would move. Not an inch, he said. "Oh yes you will," Dill replied. "You know that you must come to some agreement with the Americans" or Roosevelt and Churchill would decide the whole thing, and "You know as well as I do what a mess they would make of it." Nothing could have moved Brooke faster. Minutes before the meeting resumed Dill asked his leave to discuss the open issues with Marshall, and Brooke "had such implicit trust in his ability and integrity that I agreed."

At just that point, Portal knocked on Brooke's door and handed Slessor's draft to him and Dill. It did not give Brooke all he wanted, but it met his needs. It pained him to accept the American position on the war against Japan, but the caveat saved it: "provided always that its application does not prejudice the earliest possible defeat of Germany." Seeing its simplicity, how neatly it squared the circle and overlapped Dill's ideas, Brooke decided to accept this "bridge for our difficulties."

While Slessor's compromise was working its way to Brooke, Patton had Marshall and Giraud to lunch. Marshall and the Frenchman exchanged salutes and the American asked in translation, "Are you, by any chance, the Major Giraud whom I knew in 1918?" Giraud was delighted. "Why, of course, you are Captain Marshall!" Together they had planned an attack on a German position. Now they were brothers in arms.

After Eden's report that de Gaulle had spurned his invitation to Anfa arrived at midday, Churchill sent for Macmillan, furious at de Gaulle for undermining the war and Churchill's standing with the Americans, the French Resistance, and the British people. Number one on the PM's list of options was to "depose" him and elevate a follower. Option two was to embrace Giraud. Churchill and Macmillan chose option three. Eden must swallow the humiliation and go back to de Gaulle. Options one or two would cost too much in British and French opinion. De Gaulle must be persuaded that to see Giraud would be advantageous to him.

Unaware of it all, Somervell went to Giraud's villa to discuss his weapons wish list. Their translator Major Codman found Somervell "an impressive figure. If he weren't a general, he would be a big business tycoon." He shook Giraud's hand and turned to Codman: "I want you to begin by telling this Frog that Uncle Sam is no Santa Claus." Codman considered leading with Père Noël but took a chance on Somervell's French. It might be wise, he advised Giraud, to start slow and ramp up. It soon occurred to both generals that they liked each other, and Somervell left converted to Giraud.

Hosting lunch with Hopkins, Roosevelt laughed when Churchill broke the news that de Gaulle was not coming, the first of many such laughs at the prime minister's expense. Macmillan judged them "not altogether to his liking." Apart from the chance to rib Churchill, the politics were important to the war and to FDR personally. Captain McCrea was surprised to hear him tell Churchill "rather sternly" it was up to him to get his man to Anfa. "Above all," as Jacob wrote, it was "essential that the French in North Africa should not gain the impression that the American and British governments are at cross-purposes."

Macmillan was grimly amused. "Here was our great hero, the winning horse we had bred and trained in our stable; and when the great day came it refused to run at all." Murphy and Macmillan worked through the afternoon on the first of many pitches to de Gaulle. Murphy told his friend that de Gaulle was a "creature of chance" created by the British, "a Frankenstein monster" escaped from their control. His French support was exaggerated, and the British should welcome the opportunity to discard him. Macmillan advised Churchill that it might be best for *Giraud* to invite de Gaulle if national pride was the barrier. Anglo-Americans should not direct French affairs. Churchill was in no mood and would not have cheered up when Roosevelt cabled Eden: "I have got the bridegroom. Where is the bride?"

By the time FDR wired Cordell Hull his snicker had become a narrative: "We delivered our bridegroom, General Giraud, who was most cooperative on the impending marriage," but "our friends could not produce the bride, the temperamental lady de Gaulle. She has got quite snooty about the whole idea and does not want to see either of us and is showing no intention of getting into bed with Giraud." By the time he got back to Washington Roosevelt had perfected his lines: The bride had not shown up, but "I had the bridegroom there, gardenia in his buttonhole, his striped trousers creased and the ring in his waistcoat pocket."

Regrettably timed for the jilted groom and the missing bride, Eisenhower told his diary that the ongoing fight for Tunisia exposed "the inability of French troops" to hold Germans. Mostly Arab or Berber, they were legendary fighters with hand-me-down rifles, no technical skills, and no chance against the German army. Thinking they were up to it, Eisenhower wrote, the Allies had given them antitank and antiaircraft weapons and asked them to defend key mountain passes. "We made a bad error." The Germans kept driving them back, one small attack at a time.

When the Combined Chiefs of Staff reconvened, Slessor's compromise and its carbon copies passed around the table. "I can still see Marshall and King poring over it," Slessor wrote years later, "exchanging a few words in undertones, Marshall making some notes on it in pencil. After about five minutes, Marshall and King merely whispering rather than withdrawing to confer." When the Americans looked up Marshall said they would accept it with "minor amendments," the U-boat menace to be given first priority and a sentence to be added on European operations: "In order to ensure that these operations and preparations are not prejudiced by the necessity to divert forces to retrieve an adverse situation elsewhere, adequate forces shall be allocated to the Pacific and Far Eastern Theaters." What was adequate promised future quarrels, but King had enough to satisfy him.

No important draft agreement ever slid untouched through a roomful of powerful men, and the Combined Chiefs of Staff started picking at this one before Dill shut the picking down. Perhaps, he said, Ismay, Slessor, and Somervell (two level British heads and a sensible American) might withdraw to make the changes and clean up the draft for the president and the prime minister. As Dill well knew, a deal is not a deal until it is a deal, but the longer the parties thought they had one the more they would want to keep it. Kennedy thought they should have compromised on day one, but "it has done good to blow off steam and probably the process was necessary." Brooke "could hardly believe our luck."

Luck had nothing to do with it, but for the presence of Slessor and Dill. Simple as it seemed, Slessor's ingenious draft was enduringly flexible, gave both sides what they needed, forced no pills they could not swallow, managed their five-star egos, and kept the United Nations united. Even so, Brooke thought the settlement reached "on this memorable day was for the greater part due to Dill," for Brooke could not have moved Marshall without him. Since December 1941, Dill had managed the war at Marshall's side for nearly as long as his earlier stretch at Brooke's, and their three-way trust was crucial. Had it not been for Dill, neither Marshall nor Brooke may have given a little.

Marshall raised the underground resistance to the barbaric occupation of Poland and whether free Polish forces in exile could help. Brooke described their service in Britain and the Middle East and General

Władysław Sikorski's hopes to get some of them into Poland to stiffen its "secret army" of all but unarmed men. Sikorski could trigger sabotage and revolt on the cusp of liberation, but a premature rising would be slaughter. Marshall said the Germans were uprooting a Polish region's people with "great brutality" and asked how the British had answered Sikorski's plea to disrupt it from the air. The Poles had been told it was impracticable to do so, Portal said, but Polish airmen had participated in the two recent raids on Berlin, which let them be cast in part as reprisals, "a great encouragement to the Russians as well as the Poles."

Admiral Cunningham joined the meeting and briefed the Royal Navy's war in the Mediterranean. Marshall had worked with Cunningham in Washington and later called him "a splendid man, a real fighter," and an honest negotiator. "I was fond of him and admired him greatly." King, on the other hand, had thought it constructive to let Cunningham know that the British had run the world for three centuries but "the United States Navy now has something to say about the war at sea, and that fact should be faced, whether palatable or not." Cunningham appreciated King's "immense capacity and ability" more than his sometimes "rude and overbearing" style.

If the Germans took southern Spain, Cunningham said now, their artillery could threaten the Strait of Gibraltar, but effective counter-measures were available. A fellow English sailor was not so sure. Pound said German gunnery on the French side of the Strait of Dover had not sunk a single ship, but the gate to the Mediterranean was less than half as wide.

Unlike Marshall, Cunningham did not think many ships would be lost taking Sicily, but the assault "would be a very expensive operation." As Wedemeyer had predicted, the Royal Navy admiral contradicted the British claim that Sicily's capture would make Mediterranean shipping much safer. North African air and naval bases would protect about 85 percent of that traffic, he said. Sicilian bases would make it 90 percent. The British had always formed a solid shield wall until now, and Portal plugged the gap. From the air "the possession of Sicily would make a very considerable difference," he said. Stripped of Sicilian bases, enemy planes would be hard-pressed to hit Southern Mediterranean shipping at all.

A little later, Mountbatten told Hopkins and Harriman "at length," Harriman wrote, why he and all the junior British staff officers favored Sardinia over Sicily. Bombing from Sardinia could threaten the "heart of Italy's life and transport." The capture of Sardinia in Operation Brimstone was "dead now" but Mountbatten—persistent to the end, even after the end—still hoped for its resurrection.

Patton was taking a walk to a guard-changing ceremony just outside the wire when Elliott Roosevelt hailed him from a jeep and invited him to ride with the president. Patton climbed in and found A-1 in his blue Navy cloak enjoying his first trip off campus. B-1 went too, and Jacob was glad to see them leave the military conferees "in comparative peace." Machine guns, mortars, and antiaircraft guns were laid out for their inspection. Two infantry platoons performed parade ground drills and marched behind a band. A 275-pound musician tickling a flute amused FDR.

Soon after the ceremonials closed, the Combined Chiefs of Staff, joined by Churchill, Ismay, and Dill, brought their newborn war plan to Roosevelt in the Moroccan Modern White House dining room for the conference's first official plenary session. With the doors and windows closed and the heat on, Churchill prised open a window as the others found their seats—white-leather chairs with glossy black arms and legs at a matching oval table with white splayed legs and a glossy black top. A Moroccan rug filled the room.

The session began with a courtesy that might have been gamesmanship had it not come from Marshall. Roosevelt asked who chaired the military meetings, and Brooke said General Marshall was "invited by us to perform that function," but when Roosevelt asked Marshall to start, he deferred to Brooke, as a gentleman might, putting Brooke on the spot with no preparation. The Americans had just accepted what amounted to a British plan. Some indiscreet remark might blow it up, and Brooke's specialties included neither tact nor subtlety, but he summed the plan up brilliantly with a tactful presentation and a subtly British line.

"After seven days of argument," he said (actually five that felt like seven), the Combined Chiefs of Staff had made "definite progress." They had reaffirmed their agreement to concentrate on Germany's defeat and relieve the Russians, and there might be a chance to win the war in Europe this year. They would build on Torch's success with visible preparations for an amphibious assault that threatened the entire Mediterranean, forcing the enemy to disperse his forces and pull strength from Russia, but the blow would fall on Sicily.

"We might hope" to so weaken the Germans that an invasion of the Continent would be possible in 1943. Massive bombing would cripple the enemy and depress his morale while the Allies gathered strength for "a thrust across the Channel." Vigorous efforts would be made to induce Turkey into the war to acquire its airfields in range of Romanian oil. A campaign to capture Rabaul and eastern New Guinea would proceed in the Pacific while plans were made to take the Marshalls and Truk "if the situation permits." Burmese bridgeheads and airfields "might" be seized in December and the Burma Road reopened before the May monsoon "if" landing craft could be shifted from the Pacific after Rabaul was taken.

Marshall challenged not a word, added support for Chiang Kai-shek, and gave the floor back to Roosevelt, who deferred to Churchill as Marshall had to Brooke. Churchill went straight to what Dill had told him troubled the Americans most. He wished to make it clear that "if and when Hitler breaks down" and "Germany has been brought to her knees" Britain would turn all out against Japan with her honor and her interests at stake. Churchill's government would sign a treaty if the president thought it necessary to reassure the American people. Roosevelt waved the gesture off. Churchill's word was good. He was confident, the president said, that everyone in the room was of one mind. But the Allies should solicit the same pledge from the Russians.

Not yet done reassuring the Yanks and filling the Combined Chiefs of Staff's big plates with more than they thought they could chew,

Churchill put "a sharper point" on Brooke's thrust across the Channel and proposed to set a date and name a commander. In 1942, he said, he had not supported Sledgehammer's limited invasion of France, but now it was their duty "to engage the enemy on as wide a front and as continuously as possible." Everything should be done to make a significant Channel crossing possible this summer "with all available forces" if the Germans started buckling. Roosevelt agreed and proposed to accelerate Bolero's buildup in the U.K. Always striking in every direction, Churchill thought they might "work into the general scheme" an assault on Rhodes, the Dodecanese islands, or both. Even if they could not be launched, feints could help conceal Sicily as the target. Knowing Roosevelt saw China as a badly neglected child, Churchill added that General Chennault's "Flying Tigers" based in Kunming should expand.

Roosevelt endorsed giving prospects for a 1943 Sledgehammer operation "a more real existence" as opposed to "something which might be done with spare resources" and touted his support for Chiang Kai-shek. Even a small boost in aid would jolt Chinese morale, and so would invading Burma. Chiang should be told that 200 to 250 more bombers were coming soon, some to be based in India and refueled in China on their way to and from Japan. In planning a bombing campaign, it should not be forgotten that "the Japanese people panic easily."

The president raised the need for "every possible precaution" to conceal their Mediterranean plans and deceive the enemy. "Even in our thoughts it would be inadvisable to specify our objective." Perhaps resuming his code name jovialities, FDR said the Allies had been fortunate to pull Torch off by surprise, and he worried about Berlin finding out Sicily was next. Its code name should be changed to something like Underbelly to keep them guessing. King missed the joke if such it was. Deception, he said, could be achieved by diversions.

Roosevelt asked his Chiefs of Staff to comment on what "Sir Alan Brooke" had outlined. King said the CCS had gone "a long way toward establishing a policy of how we are to win the war." He was confident that "the right policy" would emerge from these "proposals." He would have preferred "a complete concept for concluding the war" but was "well pleased with it as it is," as sunny a remark as he ever made. And sunny it should have been with his Pacific offensives preserved, Burma in the crosshairs, and the U-boat written up as the first charge on Allied resources. A meeting of men who worked 3,000 miles apart was "a valuable means of attuning thought," King said, and many misunderstandings had been dispelled.

Marshall said he had arrived preferring a full-scale Roundup invasion of France in 1943, but the decision had been made to take Sicily, and he laid out Husky's wisdom graciously. He had changed his mind, he said, based in part on the damage Husky would do to Italy and indirectly Germany, but primarily because it would open Mediterranean shipping. Maritime tonnage was "in all things the governing factor." He believed that "Sir Charles Portal" agreed, though Admiral Cunningham "had not attached much value to Sicily."

The British were prepared for this too. There "might have been a misunderstanding," Portal said. Admiral Cunningham certainly expected a major reduction in lost shipping if Sicily were taken after Tunisia. With Sicily in enemy hands, the Allies would lose about fifteen ships out of a hundred crossing the Mediterranean. If Sicily fell they would lose about ten, a 50 percent improvement in numbers of lost ships, not the 5 percent Cunningham had mentioned. Cunningham was known to be fearless on a battleship's bridge and tongue-tied with Churchill, and he may have misspoken to the CCS, but a four-star admiral in command of the Mediterranean might have been expected to be better at assessing its security, let alone at arithmetic. Something was off, including *Portal's* math, but no one pressed the point.

With Husky on the books, Marshall said, Roundup was out for 1943. If German troops "held firmly, we should probably not be able to do it this year even if the German people began to crumble." The British kept a spearhead of about 20,000 men ready to cross the Channel and their number could expand, but barring "a complete crack in German morale," a 1943 invasion of northwest France could only be limited. It would take three months to refit landing craft used in Sicily and get them to England. The weather would turn before then, but if German troops were "folding fast" or withdrawn in large numbers, the Channel should be crossed with any means available.

Roosevelt proposed to send civilian ships and ferries to England, "in case Germany cracks." Mountbatten said five Great Lakes steamers had already been sent. FDR asked King to see what more could be done. Marshall thought "it would be poetic justice if the withdrawal from Dunkirk in small ships could be reversed." Brooke made no recorded comment.

Marshall gave the Asian-Pacific strategy a satisfactory grade. It included "effective measures" that he hoped would prevent another flood of crises. General Chennault's air force in China would expand, but the burden of supplying it by air would be huge, and planes were in demand elsewhere. When the Combined Chiefs of Staff met again at some other place and time, they should "make the necessary adjustments" to the strategy against Japan, guided by events.

Marshall touched on issues not yet decided, including his proposed new system for command and control of British-based bombing: The CCS should set goals and priorities, British commanders should choose targets and timing, but American techniques should be left to American discretion, an unspoken reference to daylight bombing. No objection was heard. Churchill held his fire.

Another "vital question," Marshall said, was how to keep the Russians fighting at the highest pitch, but his commitment to supply them was plainly finite and distasteful. It was not yet clear how many ships the Allies could keep losing in convoys bringing arms and sustenance to the Russians through the Persian Gulf and the Barents Sea. The convoys might be sharply reduced. It was "entirely within the power of Germany" to stop them altogether. None would proceed while Husky was under way, and Stalin must be notified. Marshall did "not believe it necessary to take excessive punishment in running these convoys simply to keep Mr. Stalin placated."

Churchill changed the subject to Turkey. In the last war, when Turkey was a German ally, Churchill's campaign to take her Gallipoli peninsula, a costly failure, had caused his resignation as First Lord of the Admiralty. Macmillan believed it made Turkey personal for him. The Turks, Churchill said, should be tempted into the war with gifts of modern weapons and thoughts of postwar power, but "since Turkish troops do not handle machinery particularly well" the Allies should send specialists. Crowning his work with FDR, Churchill proposed that the British "be allowed to play the Turkish hand" as the Americans did with China and French North Africa.

Roosevelt not only concurred but also volunteered that if a full-scale Roundup invasion of France were undertaken later it should be under British command. Brooke aspired to that command and so did Marshall, who could not have been pleased. Neither said a word. Churchill proposed to defer the choice, but it would be wise to appoint a British officer to oversee planning now for, generally speaking, an officer of the nation that contributed the most forces to a given operation (as the British would in 1943) should command it.

The prime minister went on to say it would not be long before Montgomery's Eighth Army would move from Libya into Tunisia, where Churchill assumed it would come under Eisenhower's supreme command, but he thought it wise for Alexander to be Eisenhower's deputy. Roosevelt and Marshall agreed on the spot. Marshall told Churchill later the proposal had astonished him. When the Eighth Army reached Tunisia British strength would predominate there, and Marshall had assumed the British would expect one of their own to be in command. Churchill replied that it had never crossed his mind. But everything crossed his mind.

Roosevelt paid tribute to "Sir John Dill," Washington and London's "indispensable link." Dill merely said he was satisfied with the conference's progress, a modest man's modest reply. Marshall applauded Admiral Cunningham's contributions to Torch. Churchill, who loved the *beau geste*, directed that Marshall's praise be included in the minutes for the prime minister's presentation to his War Cabinet.

Churchill proposed to send the conferees' agreement to Stalin. "The Soviet is entitled to know what we intend to do," so long as intentions, not promises, were conveyed. He was also inclined toward a closing public statement "that the United Nations are resolved to pursue the war to the bitter end, neither party relaxing in its efforts until the unconditional surrender of Germany and Japan has been achieved." But first he would consult his War Cabinet. Roosevelt seems not to have mentioned that the idea was his, but Churchill had said before that a negotiated peace would only delay "a final spring of the tiger."

Dill asked the president if he had any information about de Gaulle's intentions, a peculiar question, given Churchill's role as de Gaulle's handler and FDR's calculated distance from the man. Roosevelt said he had arranged to have General Giraud come to Anfa, but "so far the Prime Minister had not been able to effect such arrangements with General de Gaulle," a jovial shot to the ribs, perhaps, typical of FDR. It would not have entertained the prime minister. Churchill fairly described the essence of de Gaulle's snit and said he had advised him that if he declined their invitation the president and himself would have to "consider whether or not he was a leader who merited their support."

Roosevelt said Giraud would like to be relieved of some civil responsibilities and claimed to have enough officers and noncommissioned officers to lead an army of 250,000 men. He should be "instructed" to raise one. Churchill matched Roosevelt's tone. The Allied governments, he said, should have a hand in North Africa's administration, and Eisenhower should "present his demands" through civilian agents, except when "he wished to exercise his prerogatives as military commander of an occupied country." (Churchill had lately reminded FDR, "We were not invited" to North Africa "but fought our way on shore with the loss of 2,000 men.") Murphy and Macmillan should have a veto over French North African affairs and Eisenhower "must be supreme in all matters military and civil" until French sovereignty was restored postwar.

Brooke described the heavy weapons the French had and what the British would give them. Marshall called for the best available, for "if we are to equip the French, we must make good units of them." Roosevelt suggested including some such units in the attack on Sicily, "even if only as a reserve." Churchill hoped the United States would still send three more divisions to North Africa as planned, despite the success expected in Libya and Tunisia, an apparent implication of Mediterranean operations beyond Sicily. Marshall avoided the issue. The troop movement schedule had not changed, he said, but the planning for Husky would include its review.

After the session broke up Ismay drafted a message for Churchill to his War Cabinet. It had been "a most satisfactory meeting" with everyone in agreement. Marshall's compliment to Admiral Cunningham was included, as was FDR's "warm tribute to Field Marshal Sir John Dill."

Kennedy spent the evening with British and American staff "and translated the generalities of the agreed statement into a definite programme." The result was a draft rendition of the "tentative" plan for 1943 and a suggested agenda for the rest of the conference—a critical examination of each anticipated operation to determine its requirements, how to fill them, and target dates "where practicable." The British, of course, had exquisite memoranda already in the bag on every point but one. The Pacific they left to the Americans.

A bewildered young combat photographer on the Tunisian front had been flown to Casablanca with his cameras and equipment and ordered to report to the Army's downtown headquarters, where Patton chewed him out for coming into his presence in a uniform half British and half American. And then, Patton wrote, "I sent him to see his pa." Driven down to Anfa, not knowing why, Corporal Robert Hopkins showed his pass at checkpoints on the way, marveled at Anfa Camp, and was directed at its gate to the Villa Dar es Saada.

Ike's aide Harry Butcher had arranged it all and tipped the corporal's father, who feigned surprise. "And then I hear this roar of laughter," Robert recalled later. "It was the President," who knew him well and invited him to lunch: "Tell me about the war."

•   •   •

Giraud had Brooke to dinner at the villa the Americans had assigned him. They talked in the living room about the nightmare May of 1940 they had endured in the same part of France, a lunch Giraud had enjoyed with the king, and his dime store novel escape from the Boche. When they moved into the dining room, there sat Harriman, Macmillan, Murphy, and two French officers, an eccentric bit of staging. The warm conversation in French improved a casual meal.

Brooke knew Giraud was not the man for the hour, but which French general was? "Poor Giraud," Brooke wrote later, "an attractive personality of great charm, but the very wildest" military ideas. "Politically he was no match for de Gaulle, whom I think he inwardly despised. He was one of those queer personalities that fortune occasionally throws forward into positions of responsibility which they are totally unfitted for." What a sorry French hand the Allies had been dealt, "Darlan who had ability but no integrity, Giraud who had charm but no ability, and de Gaulle who had the mentality of a dictator combined with a most objectionable personality."

Churchill cabled Eden a message for de Gaulle. If he refused to come to Anfa "in his fantasy of egotism," British support for his Free French leadership would have to be reviewed. "For his own sake, you ought to knock him about pretty hard" and tell him the president was inviting him too. "The man must be mad" to jeopardize his relationship with the United States of America.

FDR enjoyed a quiet family dinner before his sons slipped away, escorted to the infamous casbah by a Navy shore patrol detail. They returned very late to find their father chuckling in bed over a 25-cent copy of *The Man Who Came to Dinner* with *The New Yorker* at his side. The casbah had been dull, Elliott wrote later. Dull until two a.m.?

Patton hosted dinner for Marshall, Hopkins, and Churchill, who brought his aide Commander Thompson, Cunningham, and two Scotland Yard detectives who had asked Patton's leave to guard the house. Patton graded Hopkins clever and intuitive, "a pilot fish for a shark," and he "smoked my last three good cigars." Hopkins asked Patton, apparently in earnest, if he would like to be an ambassador. Having shown great diplomatic ability, he was needed in that role. This was an odd bit of casting. If appointed, Patton replied, he would resign and go fishing. "General Marshall made me talk to the P.M.," Patton wrote that night, "and we got on well," as one would think they would. "He strikes me as cunning rather than brilliant but with great tenacity." Always attuned to the flaws of other men, great men in particular, Patton spotted one of Churchill's. "He is easily flattered—all of them are."

Eleven

DAY SIX: TUESDAY, JANUARY 19

Churchill sent Clement Attlee a less than thrilled review of the war plan. There was not much to it "compared with the mighty resources of Britain and the United States and still more with the gigantic efforts of Russia. I am inclined to think that the President shares this view, as Hopkins spoke to me on the subject yesterday, saying in effect, 'It is all right, but it is not enough.'" Despite "our tremendous efforts on the sea and in the air, I still feel this most strongly, and during the remaining days of our conference we must bend ourselves to the task of weighting our blows more heavily."

Arnold told Hopkins over breakfast that he was not thrilled either. The treatment of the Southwest Pacific was too vague. Nothing should be tied up there based on assumptions of future success. He could supply all the aircraft the plan demanded, but King wanted planes sent to islands with no airfields. Arnold doubted that the Burma Road would be reopened, his own high priority. It was crucial to strengthen General Chennault and start bombing Japan from China. Hopkins then ran into Dr. Wilson, who asked him why he considered these conferences worthwhile, implying that he should not. Harry said the president "loves the drama of a journey like this." Wilson thought Roosevelt and Churchill shared an "instinct to escape, to take a long break. Besides, neither of them, in a way, has ever grown up."

With scant revisions the Americans accepted at their morning meeting the global strategy now called "Conduct of the War in 1943" as Ismay, Slessor, and Somervell had tweaked it. Marshall said the president would be interested in its Russian aid provisions and should be told his Chiefs of Staff were not in favor of "destroying ourselves" getting convoys to the Russians. The point clearly troubled Marshall, who had made it several times. Everyone knew the war could not be won without the Russians, but no one was obliged to like them. News of the loss of four of eighteen ships in a convoy to Murmansk prompted Churchill to telegraph Eden: "This will make our position with the Bear even worse than it is now."

King said the British would insist on controlling their own aircraft in French West Africa, for they did not trust the French with them, but it was necessary that they do so. Marshall agreed; the French must be trusted completely or not at all. Aware of the worth of commanding the sea, King said he would not object to even more Mediterranean operations, so long as they ran on assets already there, as the war plan anticipated.

Wedemeyer updated his message to his boss, General Handy, that the Americans had been losing their shirt as they bargained for an invasion of France: "The shirt is gone. I don't give a damn. It was dirty anyway. Husky is next." Even Wedemeyer had been convinced that the Americans had come to Anfa with muddy plans.

After "Pictures and more pictures," Arnold told his diary, the CCS reconvened at ten. "Rather to our surprise," Kennedy wrote, the Americans accepted the edited war plan "with only a few trifling amendments." Slessor's draft had called for "The heaviest possible bomber offensive against Germany." Now the bombing objective was "the German war effort," which encompassed targets in occupied France and Holland. The original mandate to assemble "the strongest possible force to invade the Continent" was buttressed by a commitment to keep it "in constant readiness." The British, Kennedy wrote, "did not conceal from ourselves that the agreement was short-term, but it was enough for the moment." The Americans had performed an "about face" thanks to Dill's quiet influence with their delegation and his "profound friendship" with Marshall.

Smooth and brief, the morning session focused on the French. King wanted them introduced to post-1940 warplanes. The question was whether to treat them "as full allies" or keep some degree of control. Portal lined up with King and favored training French pilots in England on modern British aircraft, then handing the planes over. It was agreed to put the French West African coast under British command, except for a French aviation zone when French training and equipment allowed. Marshall supported arming a quarter of a million North African troops under French command even at the cost of "our own forces."

Roosevelt and Churchill having ordered a public communiqué on the conference's results and a written report to Stalin, three British officers and three Americans were chosen for the drafting, including Slessor, who had earned it.

Franklin Jr. returned to his destroyer and Hopkins told Harriman and Murphy that Giraud's aide Count André Poniatowski, whose royal Polish family had emigrated to France in the nineteenth century, had asked to see him. Harriman said the count was his former brother-in-law (Harriman's was a small world) and Hopkins asked him to join them. Roosevelt did not want Poniatowski to be told that de Gaulle was stiffing them. That was "British business." It was up to the British to tell Giraud.

Poniatowski told Harriman and Hopkins that Giraud must take the lead in any coalition with de Gaulle, who could be his number two. The Americans did not disagree.

Giraud came to Roosevelt at noon. Hopkins and Murphy were there. Whenever an official visitor arrived, FDR would give Captain McCrea a look if he wanted him to stay and take notes. Roosevelt was charm itself as he welcomed Giraud and a dashing young French officer, and he gave McCrea the look. His Groton French improved with use, and Murphy had little to do but to buff up a nuance when asked. Hopkins was impressed by Giraud's energetic confidence, his eagerness to follow Roosevelt's lead, and his warlike disposition: "I know he is a Royalist," Harry wrote, "but I have a feeling that he is willing to fight."

Roosevelt told Giraud he was thinking of "suggesting" a committee for the liberation of France composed of Giraud, de Gaulle, and a French civilian. The important thing was to choose a pristine figure. He did not wish to "appear to be suggesting anyone," but he had heard good things about two such men. Giraud objected to neither and mentioned a third. "Of course," FDR said, Giraud would be "the senior member," de Gaulle would be his chief of staff "or some such convenient title," and the civilian would relieve him of the burdens of administration to let him run his army. "No distractions should be permitted to interfere with the conduct of the war," which Giraud was delighted to hear.

A whiff of friction drifted in when Giraud insisted on also heading *civil* affairs, in which he had shown no interest. Plainly he had been coached. FDR was equally plain. Giraud was France's representative in North Africa "at the moment," not the embodiment of France. Giraud did not speak for her, and nothing would be settled about the rest of her empire's leadership until he worked things out with de Gaulle, with whom he must share power. Giraud confined his sullenness to silence. When FDR disapproved of political prisoners, Giraud said "practically all" had been freed and the rest were charged with "other crimes."

Hopkins thought FDR gave a masterful presentation on French resistance to the Germans, "emphasizing the fighting." He was pleased to tell Giraud that the Combined Chiefs of Staff were discussing how to arm a French North African Army and General Marshall was intent on getting them the latest weapons. Giraud was joy personified. Roosevelt led him to the veranda to be photographed with him and beckoned Giraud's aide to join them with Hopkins and McCrea, a typically thoughtful gesture. Hopkins watched the president warming to Giraud.

Elliott and Hopkins got a harbor tour from Patton, shopped for rugs, and had several sent up to the president to take his pick. The other wares on offer did not impress Hopkins, but a look at how "the Navy knocked the hell out of the *Jean Bart*" did.

Having been told that London had been bombed the night before, the first raid in quite some time, Churchill had a message sent under his Anfa code name to his Downing Street staff, fretting as any decent head of household would: "Air Commodore Frankland wishes you to ensure that Mrs. Frankland and the servants go down to the shelter" at the first sound of sirens.

Over lunch with Churchill, Arnold tried again to sell him on daylight bombing "and why we figured that the Germans could not stop us." Experience proved, the American said, that U.S. bombers, soon to be protected by "long-legged" fighters with releasable auxiliary fuel tanks, could get to their targets and back before dark. Like Ebenezer Scrooge, Churchill agreed to be visited by Arnold's three high-ranking messengers in turn, Lieutenant General Andrews, Major General Eaker, and Major General Carl A. Spaatz, in command of all U.S. Army Air Forces in the European Theater. Arnold did not claim to know, he later wrote, whether the RAF doubted daylight bombing's effectiveness, or feared unacceptable losses, or that "we would do something they could not," but he "talked long and hard" and got the sense that Churchill would go along but had to tell the RAF he had put up a fight.

Arnold got it backward. As Portal had made plain at two CCS sessions, it was not the RAF who resisted the American policy. Arnold's and Eisenhower's memoirs say basic differences in British and American bombing doctrine clashed at Anfa Camp. "This was not really so," Slessor wrote in his. The RAF's leaders understood the value of bombing day and night and declined to tell the Americans how to choose their own tactics though they flew from British soil. Portal later said, "I did my utmost to persuade our ministers, particularly Mr. Churchill, to encourage them to go on." It was Churchill who had dug himself into an anti-daylight hole.

Briefed and befriended by Arnold and his subordinates, Slessor had studied their methods and liked what he saw. It was plain to him and Portal that pressing the Yanks to abandon their "almost passionate belief" in daylight bombing or accept the lesser role of bombing ships at sea, both of which Churchill wanted them to do, would be keenly resented and "vigorously resisted" and push them toward the Pacific. "Moreover," Slessor wrote later, "we really thought they would be proved to be right in their fixed determination."

General Spaatz had been called down from Algiers as Eaker and Andrews had been summoned from London and Cairo. Churchill sat down with all three, one after the other. Years later he recalled most vividly his talk with Ira Eaker.

Described by his aide Captain Parton as a constant cigar smoker, "short, stocky, balding, square-jawed, and eagle-eyed," not unlike the prime minister, Eaker and his staff had arrived in 1942 at the commandeered Wycombe Abbey School for Girls, where plaques in the officers' dormitories still read "Ring Bell for Mistress." The local lord mayor gave a dinner in their honor, eloquent in his robes, and urged Eaker to speak. The Texan won his hosts with three sentences: "We won't do much talking until we've done more fighting. After we've gone, we hope you'll be glad we came. Thank you."

Eaker long remembered Churchill coming down the Villa Mirador's stairs in his RAF uniform "with the sun shining through the windows" overlooking an orange grove. The uniform might have had a comic effect had Eaker not heard that when Churchill met with senior officers he sometimes matched their dress, as did King George VI. Eaker took it as a good omen. He had half an hour.

"Young man," Churchill said—Eaker was forty-six—"I am half American. My mother was a U.S. citizen. The tragic loss of so many of your gallant crews tears my heart." Daylight bombing in France and Holland made their losses far worse than the RAF's at night, and they "had never thrown a bomb on Germany." Eaker, of course, was familiar with this view, which seemed to trouble him deeply. Churchill watched and

listened as he rebutted it "with powerful earnestness," skillfully and te-
naciously, including a reminder that over 600 American planes had been
pulled from Britain for Torch and his bomber command was only approaching full strength. Then he handed the prime minister "The Case
for Day Bombing." Churchill motioned him to a couch, sat beside him,
and read it, sometimes muttering it half aloud.

Eaker's memo praised the RAF, wisely and accurately, but the British were trained for night flying, it said, and the Americans were not.
Flame-dampening engines hid the RAF in the dark while the Americans' were "flaming torches" at night, "cold meat for the enemy fighter."
British pilots had been flying in fog and rain since flight school, but
"our people are not equal to English weather at night." Many would
lose their lives getting used to it. The recent rate of British losses nearly
doubled the American. Armored U.S. bombers with .50 caliber machine
guns pointed in all directions flew in twenty-plane box formations of
two or three boxes each and confronted German fighters with thousands
of rounds a minute, which typically backed them off when they did not
bring them down. Captain Parton had reported in October that Flying
Fortresses absorbed staggering punishment. One made it home with over
2,000 bullet holes, two engines dead, the other two hit, four men badly
wounded, "and all control wires, etc. shot up."

It was not that it was better to bomb by day, Eaker's paper said.
Bombing day *and* night gave the enemy no rest and kept him in action
or on alert "around the clock, 24 hours of the day." As Churchill read
that line aloud, "he rolled the words off his tongue as though they were
tasty morsels." When the Americans set a factory afire in the afternoon,
the memo said, they marked it for the RAF that night. "It helps a lot,
this joint business." The Americans would soon hit Germany, and the
more the German people and their troops looked up at sixty daylight
bombers "with U.S. under their wings" they would realize "the mag-
nitude of the effort against them and the inevitability of their doom."
Let daytime bombing "combine and conspire with the admirable night
bombing of the RAF to wreck German industry, transportation and

morale." Together they would "soften the Hun" and set him up for the kill.

Having mumbled the memo through, Churchill handed it back. "Young man," he said, "you have not convinced me that you are right, but you have persuaded me that you should have further opportunity to prove your contention. How fortuitous it would be if we could, as you say, bomb the devils around the clock." When he next saw the president, Churchill said, he would recommend that day bombing continue "for a time." Eaker was deeply relieved, having feared his commander in chief was softening on a point that could lose the war.

Later that day, Churchill told Arnold he would give daylight bombing a trial and say no more about it. "We had won a major victory," Arnold wrote. The CCS never debated the issue, the only major point resolved at Anfa informally.

Reconvening after tea, the CCS considered Germany's oil shortage and how to make it worse. Portal hoped the Americans could disable her synthetic oil plants in daylight bombing, but Somervell said new intelligence suggested enemy oil was not as scarce as the British thought. Even if Romania's oil fields were knocked out, new Hungarian sources would replace them, but destroying only two tetraethyl lead plants would cripple aviation fuel production. Portal said the return on oil must be balanced against the assault on Sicily, which depended on air superiority, one of many such dilemmas. This one was assigned to the Combined Intelligence Committee, the senior officers who coordinated, exchanged, and assessed Allied intelligence.

Marshall agreed with Brooke that Turkish airbases could play "a determining part" in the war but questioned the British bid to play the Turkish hand. Somervell said an Anglo-American agreement on arming Turkey had just been reached in Washington, but Brooke called it "not acceptable in London," for the president's commitment to the prime minister at yesterday's plenary session to let the British handle Turkey superseded it. Marshall said he was confused about their intentions. Brooke was not confused and invoked a British defense treaty with Turkey, previously unknown to the Americans. It seems that no offense was taken.

The Dodecanese islands had just come up when Giraud walked in at Marshall's invitation, escorted by his American translator Major Codman, who was not surprised when "every star-studded personage in the room rose instinctively" for Giraud. Slessor was impressed despite himself by this "tall, erect, somehow rather Edwardian figure," so naive and out of touch with modern war that Macmillan had been reminded of the White Knight in *Alice in Wonderland*, which his grandfather had published, for Giraud seemed to live in the clouds. Allied officers struggled with his rigidity, limited intellect, and museum-quality ego, but no one could deny the presence of Henri Giraud. "He gives one the impression of a knight of the days of chivalry," Kennedy wrote, "much the same type as de Gaulle, rather temperamental and difficult but inspired." An American journalist thought him "born out of his time," an arrow-straight "startling figure" from the Age of Louis XIV.

Harriman thought Giraud never put a foot wrong at Anfa, and this was no exception. Marshall introduced him, seated him at the center of the table, told him that the Combined Chiefs of Staff were honored by his presence, and hoped he would share his views on whatever he wished to discuss, particularly his armed forces and how quickly they could expand. No one was very interested in anything else he might say, and neither was he. Lord Mountbatten intervened at one point to correct Major Codman's translation, and Kennedy felt sorry for the American, "but he was all square a few minutes later" when he disputed another lordly intervention's accuracy and Giraud declared him right and Mountbatten wrong.

Giraud said he was proud to participate in the conference and solemnly declared the French army's reentry into the war. As proof of its will to win and its ability to do so he cited yesterday's action in Tunisia, which had demonstrated the quality of his troops and their worthiness to bear modern arms, the same engagement that had demonstrated their incompetence to Eisenhower. His army, Giraud said, could muster three armored divisions and ten mobile infantry divisions, if suitably armed, and French pilots could man a thousand-plane air force of British and American aircraft, if they had them. In the past six days they had shot down five enemy planes and lost one. Confident that France would make a great contribution to the war, Giraud shared some strategic thoughts and predicted that Tunisia, Sicily, Sardinia, and Corsica would be taken within two months. It was impossible to take them all in four, but Slessor admired his spirit: "Giraud was a gallant old gentleman, but perhaps not very up to date in the realities of modern warfare." King put it bluntly later: "he had no good ideas at that time."

Marshall declared himself grateful for General Giraud's views and told him Admiral King and Generals Arnold and Somervell were looking closely at how quickly his troops could be armed. Brooke expressed great pleasure with Giraud's report and assured him that the British would promote an important French military role. Portal had "the clearest recollection from two wars" of the skillful French air forces and hoped they would soon join their allies in Europe. Pound welcomed French naval forces, having seen their contributions when the war began. King said arrangements were under way to rehabilitate French warships without mentioning that his navy had shelled them.

After Giraud replied formally to each officer in turn Marshall asked Dill if he would like to say something. With a few poignant words Dill transformed Giraud from an old prig to an old friend. General Giraud's very presence inspired him, Dill said. Knowing how much he had suffered for France, Dill was immensely pleased to have the general back at his side leading French forces to victory. As Kennedy looked on, "Giraud lit up at once" and remembered "Sir John Dill" fondly as a distinguished corps commander of the BEF, for "he and I lived in true military brotherhood." And then, Arnold wrote that night, "General Giraud gave quite a talk."

In September 1940, he said, when France was in defeat, he had told the German generals who came to him in prison that they had lost the war. Their chance to invade England before autumn closed the Channel was gone, and sooner or later the United States would come to her aid. How long the war would last he could not tell, but Germany could not win. They had asked him to sign a paper giving his word not to try to escape, as he had in 1915, on his daily escorted walks through the castle prison's grounds. He had solemnly refused and advised them for good measure that he would never sign anything. When they asked if he was *thinking* about escaping, he replied that his thoughts were his own affair. "You are my jailers. I am your prisoner. It is your duty to guard me. It is my duty to escape. Let us see who can carry out his duty best." It had taken him a year, he told the Chiefs of Staff, "but now I am here amongst you once more," leading a new French army.

"At the conclusion of this little speech," Kennedy wrote, every man in the room burst into applause as "General Giraud got up and with great courtesy took his leave."

Dill took a walk with Kennedy, one of his many protégés, then they sat by the shore with sea birds cruising the evening sky. Dill recalled his time as Chief of the Imperial General Staff, when Britain had been near death and Dill "had to fight Winston" constantly. And yet, he said, "we had not made many mistakes."

Churchill dropped by the White House for cocktails and brought his only son. Blessed with his father's confidence and his mother's looks, elected to Parliament unopposed at twenty-nine in September 1940, which was not that impressive under the circumstances, Randolph Churchill was a captain of British commandos. Mountbatten had ordered him in from Algiers, yet another gift to fathers in high places. From that moment on, Jacob wrote, Randolph "became attached to our party as a kind of fungus, his only function being to annoy everyone, constantly interrupt business, be present when the P.M. was talking on important subjects with Hopkins, Harriman, etc., and to play bezique when the P.M. should have been working or resting."

Churchill's secretary Jock Colville wrote that Randolph could "make one shudder. He talks of world domination as the greatest ideal and says he admires the Germans for desiring it. He wants it to be our main aim." Elliott had been eager to get to know his British counterpart until Randolph started bloviating for nearly an hour on the need to protect British hegemony in the Mediterranean at the cost of prolonging the war, schooled his father and the president on handling the French, and deplored the war plan's mistakes, a spectacular feat of boorishness that FDR met with "amused detachment."

In the afterglow of Randolph's performance, Churchill came to Brooke at the hotel, still lusting after Marrakech. Macmillan thought Hopkins had encouraged him by mentioning a local ruler there who had beheaded three prime ministers in succession some years earlier. Here was "a man of imagination," Churchill had said. "I simply must go to Marrakech and meet him." The PM told Brooke he planned to go on Saturday with the president, see him off for home on Sunday morning, and stay two days to rest and paint, a pleasure he had set aside when Hitler invaded Poland. Then he would fly to Cairo for military consultations and on to Ankara to coax the Turks into belligerency. He was looking forward to Marrakech and wanted Brooke to join him. Another Liberator tour with Churchill did not excite Brooke, but orders were orders, and he relished a two-day rest. He arranged a hunt with a Marrakech sheik and a tour of the Atlas Mountains.

Churchill had Harry and Robert Hopkins, Harriman, and Alexander to dinner with Randolph. The PM told Harry he was anxious for the president not to tell Giraud that de Gaulle was not coming. De Gaulle might yet change his mind. Alexander kept the room in his hand chasing Rommel through the desert, but Randolph kept interrupting until the lowly Corporal Hopkins told him to knock it off. Remarkably enough, he did. Not long before, Randolph had bragged to Harriman about an affair with a colleague's wife and had since discovered Harriman's affair with his, which may have put a chill on the evening.

Eden had received Churchill's pointed draft of a second message to de Gaulle, which the PM had authorized him to soften. Eden cut its best line. Churchill had written that the Allies were about to rearrange North Africa's leadership and would like to consult de Gaulle. Should he choose to reject this opportunity, "we shall endeavor to get on as well as we can without you." After Eden was done with the message it threatened nothing wittier than extreme consequences. Eden phoned de Gaulle and asked him to come to the Foreign Office to receive it. He said he was otherwise engaged. Within the hour, one of his subordinates told one of Eden's that de Gaulle assumed Churchill's message was provocative and wished to avoid a scene. Eden had it delivered. De Gaulle later wrote that "after many such experiences" its threats rolled off his back.

Murphy sent Eisenhower a message using Clark's favored acronym for French generals: "The YBSOB from the north thus far refuses to come and play with us." The first two letters stood for yellow bellied.

Patton gave a dinner for the president, invited some of his senior officers, and led a tour of Villa Maas like a boy showing off a treehouse. Apart from its carved wooden ceilings, dubiously sumptuous furnishings, and a colored glass inlaid wall that conjured sunsets at the touch of a switch, the tour featured racks of Wehrmacht uniforms abandoned in the basement, long-winded German titles on several doors, and the evicted Nazi potentate's office left intact, portraits of Hitler included.

Patton's officers backed his dinner table pitch to their commander in chief that tanks did the fighting that mattered. Infantry held the ground that armor had taken. "I imagine," Elliott wrote later, "it was I who put in a word about aircraft." Patton allowed that airpower had its place in support of armor, and FDR enjoyed the whole thing, grist for teasing Elliott.

Patton called for his staff car and took the president back to the White House, where Churchill was waiting in his zip-up rompers, having just left the Anfa Hotel's Le Bar Américain with Ismay and Randolph, whose gin-soaked barroom blather had annoyed the young New Yorker Captain Parton. The prime minister looked older than Parton had expected, "a gentle, old woman's face." Roosevelt and Patton talked in the car and *kept* Churchill waiting, a distinction Patton was proud to record. The president was "a great statesman," Patton wrote, a thought he shared with FDR, who predictably told Elliott later that Patton was "a delightful man."

After Patton went home, well past eleven, FDR was wheeled into the White House, where Churchill started talking for two hours. Roosevelt asked if de Gaulle could not be pushed to see Giraud. Churchill sighed and lifted his eyebrows. "De Gaulle," he said. He was "on his high horse. Refuses to come down here. Refuses point-blank. Jeanne d'Arc complex." He began to say sadly that de Gaulle had been incensed when Ike picked Giraud as Darlan's successor then bent his head and shook it. The president was not impressed: "You've got to get your problem child down here." Churchill said he simply could not move him. De Gaulle was all for combining his organization with Giraud's but insisted on choosing its members. "Of course, this won't do." Roosevelt called for a harder push and Churchill nodded. "Of course," he said, "I can't answer at the moment for what he will do." The PM wondered casually whether control of some temporary authority might be better left to de Gaulle after all, which Roosevelt dismissed almost rudely.

After Churchill left, Roosevelt stayed up in bed talking and smoking with Elliott, who learned that his father's petulance had been calculated. Perfectly jaunty now, he had been playing the prime minister. He suspected that Churchill could summon de Gaulle whenever he chose, for Churchill's was the hand that fed him and their interests overlapped. Had Roosevelt known de Gaulle he would have known better. According to Elliott (not considered history's most reliable source), FDR told him Churchill and de Gaulle meant to keep their colonies after the war, but colonialism had to go, or its rivalries and exploitations would cause another war. "Winnie is a great man for the status quo. He even *looks* like the status quo." He would not be easily moved when the war was won. "The look that Churchill gets on his face when you mention India!"

Whether FDR said any of this or not, he meant every word.

Twelve

DAY SEVEN:
WEDNESDAY, JANUARY 20

atton ran into Dill at breakfast with Hull and Wedemeyer, who said they were scrambling for more staff. Patton thought there were too many now. Slessor captured Patton's view: "Stand back and let the dog see the rabbit—what the hell's all this goddamn 'planning'—where's the enemy?—why don't we get going?" In Patton's presence Mountbatten pinned a medal on a rare American participant in August's Anglo-Canadian attack on the Channel port of Dieppe, Lord Louis's wayward brainchild, designed to gather intelligence, lift morale, and destroy German coastal defenses. Over half of the 6,000 raiders had been killed, wounded, or captured.

Churchill sent a message to his War Cabinet. What did they think of an Allied declaration that the war would go on until Germany and Japan surrendered unconditionally, with Italy excepted to encourage her defection? The president liked the idea "and it would stimulate our friends in every country."

In a cable to Attlee and Eden, Churchill proposed to stop at Marrakech and Cairo after the conference and fly on to Ankara. In reply, thinking him unlikely to cajole the Turks into the war, they reminded

him of broken Turkish promises and urged him not to "run these flying risks except in cases of absolute necessity." Entirely unpersuaded,
Churchill shared his plans with Ismay and granted his request to stop
in Algiers to confer with Eisenhower on his way back to London but
told him not to "loll about" there. "I assured him," Ismay later recalled,
that "since my association with him I had lost the habit of 'lolling about'
anywhere."

Guided by Somervell and Leathers, the CCS discussed the shipping
shortage at their morning meeting, chewed on the burden of supplying the ungrateful Russians, and swallowed it only to the point of "prohibitive cost." It was not a question of placating Stalin, King said, but of
keeping the Red Army fighting, for "our main reliance in Europe" was
on them. "No effort should be spared to place in Russian hands every
possible tool of war." With this the British agreed. As a senior British diplomat wrote, the British Chiefs of Staff hoped the Russians would bleed
the Germans halfway into 1944 before the Anglo-Americans attacked
"the exhausted animal."

The CCS consigned Turkey to the Brits and approved a British paper
on the war in the air. A bomber offensive would help clear the enemy
from North Africa, followed in order of priority by depleting his Mediterranean air and naval forces in preparation for taking Sicily, air support once Husky was under way, and attacking Romanian oil refineries.
Bombing that might drive Italy from the war was also favored.

Noting that Montgomery's Eighth Army in Libya would enter Eisenhower's theater when it chased Rommel into Tunisia, Brooke officially
nominated Alexander as Ike's hands-on deputy. Overall command of
Husky, Brooke said, "or whatever operation in the Mediterranean might
be decided upon"—a perhaps unnoticed tell of British division over Sicily versus Sardinia—must soon be assigned, and Eisenhower would likely
be the man. If so, Alexander could relieve him of that burden too.

The British had wrestled with their choice for commander in chief

of the European Theater. An American was desirable with U.S. power on
the upswing, and Eisenhower was a talented executive, blind to nationality, but he had never seen a German with a weapon in his hands. Brooke
had his doubts about Alexander's flaws but none about Ike's. Making
Alex his deputy, Brooke later wrote, subordinating a British warrior to a
manager from Kansas, would flatter the Americans, who did not "fully
appreciate the underlying intentions. We were pushing Eisenhower up
to the stratosphere whilst we inserted under him one of our own commanders." It was Churchill's idea, Ismay wrote, "grasping the substance"
of command and "letting go the shadow." The Americans took the bait,
subject to the concurrence of Eisenhower, who spotted the chicanery
and did not take it lying down; "burning inside" he sent a hot message
to Marshall insisting on his ultimate authority. "While the situation was
accepted," Tedder later wrote, "the Americans did not want it rubbed in."

Murphy came to the White House to revisit the French with FDR and
Hopkins. The British, they all agreed, must be persuaded to deny de
Gaulle control of French North Africa. Churchill, Macmillan, and Elliott
joined them for lunch in the garden. With the British at the table, the
discussion turned from clipping de Gaulle's wings to coaxing him to fly.
What concessions might get him to Anfa? Was everyone sure Giraud was
a necessary player? Was it sheer French pique that prevented a marriage
of convenience? Elliott's memoir recites the questions, not the answers,
for no one had a good one. Someone had told Roosevelt that de Gaulle
refused to come to Anfa under duress, especially from him.

Sometime that day, probably now, FDR asked Churchill with a
gleam in his eye who paid de Gaulle's salary. "Good idea," the PM said.
"No come no pay."

Husky was the subject of the afternoon's CCS meeting, which went better than Brooke had hoped. He laid out two alternatives for the British
role in taking Sicily. Option one was to launch their assault from England and follow up from their eastern Mediterranean bases, giving the

invaders an earlier start but exposing them to heavy fire from the air as they steamed through the mined Sicilian narrows. The British had chosen option two, to mount their main attack from the eastern Mediterranean.

If the major part of the assault came from North Africa, Brooke said, "training would be the bottleneck." Mountbatten projected three weeks training for brigades with no amphibious experience. A simple brushing up might take ten days. Two weeks of rehearsal were essential either way. Much of what Brooke's diary says of Mountbatten has to do with "half-baked thoughts," but he agreed with him for once. Training could not be rushed. That said, British readiness had been projected for the end of September, and that was unacceptable. Various devices were being considered to make the end of August possible. Wedemeyer foresaw "no difficulties" in assembling the American forces by July or early August. Savvy Cooke was still more aggressive: "I would not accept anything later than July" and "thought it could be done in June." The minutes do not include the word smug.

Portal suggested that the British and Americans should plan separately, then determine the earliest date when both would be ready, which might be too late to be acceptable. Brimstone was the unspoken easier alternative, and Portal had his eye on those Sardinian airfields. True to form, Marshall said Sicily had been chosen "and we ought not to be diverted from it by the apparent difficulties of the undertaking." Also in character, Brooke called for "every possible permutation" to make Husky go in July. In any case, its benefits would start long before its launch, for the Germans must pull troops from Russia as soon as they realized the next assault would come in the Mediterranean. The combined planners were instructed to consider "all possible expedients" to accelerate Husky, and Brooke proposed to expedite the rest of the conference, eager, perhaps, to close the casino while he was ahead.

Three bird debuts thrilled Brooke on his walk with Kennedy, a long-beaked wimbrel among them, but his relief from the weight of the world was brief. After a drink with Kennedy, he was on his way to his room and his bath when a British diplomat working with Macmillan "dumped Giraud down on top of me." Giraud took Brooke's time and tried his patience, both of which were scarce: "I could not escape for half an hour and had to listen to all sorts of short cuts towards winning this war," none of which made sense.

Near the end of a walk on the beach, Churchill passed some U.S. sailors singing on the sand with a guitar. He got into a trailing sedan on the adjoining road and started the driver home then asked him to drive back. Pulling up beside the Americans he rolled a window down, made a request for "You Are My Sunshine," and got it with an encore, to everyone's delight.

Giraud and his aide Count Poniatowski called on Roosevelt. Hot on their heels came His Majesty's Prime Minister, who finally broke the news to Giraud. According to Giraud, Churchill "threw his hat on the sofa and grumbled that de Gaulle was making a fuss about coming." It was simply unacceptable. If de Gaulle refused a final summons, the British would cut him loose. Roosevelt heartily approved.

Churchill hosted a festive dinner for Roosevelt, Elliott, Harriman, Hopkins senior and junior, Alexander, and Dr. Wilson. The PM's excruciating son was there, his aide Commander Thompson, and his two secretaries. The American Army Engineers had built ramps for FDR. Shoptalk was off limits and Churchill showed off his impressive traveling map room, installed by shipwrights and electricians brought over on HMS *Bulolo*, contrived and overseen by the Royal Navy's Captain Pim. On wall-mounted maps of every theater, a round-the-clock staff tracked with shaped, colored pins the position, composition, direction, and speed of every Allied convoy at sea; all pertinent naval and air forces, hostile and friendly; and enemy warships about to leave port, prompting warnings sent to Allied ships. Elliott stood riveted to the life-or-death game on the North Atlantic chart, where gray destroyers protected red cargo ships from Luftwaffe squadrons of menacing black T's and U-boat wolf packs, "sinister little coffin-shaped ebony pins."

Churchill wrote Clementine that "Harry Hopkins produced five

Negro soldiers who sang most melodiously to us." Unprepared for "You Are My Sunshine," they harmonized a spiritual and its chorus, "Ain't gonna study war no more." FDR nodded. "Those are my sentiments too." Captain Pim noticed how a "Danny Boy" solo "touched the Prime Minister deeply." Churchill's next message to Eden said the president was "in great form and we have never been so close."

Generals Marshall, Clark, and Andrews were Patton's guests for dinner, which produced what he called a two-hour Marshall monologue. "My guest book," Patton wrote his wife, "had I kept one, would be an envy to all lion hunters." Brooke wrote home too: "I have seldom had a harder week or one with a heavier strain."

Churchill cabled Eden late that night: "I must really have an answer about JOAN OF ARC." Unless he arrived soon, events would pass him by. Earlier that day, unbeknownst to Churchill, de Gaulle had let his National Committee persuade him to come. He told Eden he would have refused had Roosevelt not seconded the invitation. Then he handed him a grievance-laden acceptance citing many insults. The haughty bride would join the wedding party and might be coaxed to the altar. As de Gaulle recalled later, "I made no particular haste to begin my trip."

Sammy Schulman, "a round, cheery-faced" wire service photographer who had followed FDR for years and had been in Casablanca for weeks, unaware of the cast at Anfa, was sitting at a downtown bar with a reporter when three Secret Service men wandered in. Sammy knew them all. They advised him that he was the only man in Casablanca who did, and "if so much as a whisper of this gets out" he would be prosecuted. The reporter they threatened with everything but death, but the president liked and trusted Sammy, who was soon employed as an Anfa Camp photographer.

"The back of the work here is broken," Brooke told his diary, "and thank God for it!" It was one of the hardest things he had ever done. The arguments with the Americans had been heated at times, "yet our relations have never been strained. I hope we shall leave here with a more closely united outlook on the war." He had gotten almost everything he had hoped for, and the Americans were "friendliness itself," but difficult to work with, each in his own unfortunate way. Marshall was good at assembling strength but had no idea how to use it. He had come to Casablanca "without a single real strategic concept" and contributed little more than a "somewhat clumsy criticism of the plans we put forward." King was "a shrewd and somewhat swollen-headed individual" with blinders fixed on Japan. Arnold was barely worth mentioning.

Thirteen

DAY EIGHT:
THURSDAY, JANUARY 21

The British were not popular at the American morning meeting. King suspected that "the late date" they anticipated for Husky meant Churchill wanted a Brimstone assault on Sardinia first, just "for the sake of doing something." Husky would surely follow and delay a Channel crossing. Cooke said the British planners had studied Brimstone exhaustively and wanted to see it executed. They "admitted" to having 400 unique new landing craft well suited to Sardinian beaches "and probably have more. We have none" and should request some for Husky. Arnold complained that the British resisted bombing factories that made U-boat parts merely because they were hard to hit.

King was in an ugly mood. On top of equipping the Russians, the Chinese, and the French, now there was talk of the Turks. If the Americans sent them arms, they must be told where they came from, that the British were not their benefactors, that weapons were for use. Marshall was unhappy too, still nursing Churchill's remarks about taking Rhodes and the Dodecanese islands. There were not enough landing craft to go island hopping in the Mediterranean. Marshall feared that new production earmarked for the Channel would never get there.

If King was wary of the Turks and Marshall of the Mediterranean, Somervell was looking hard at the convoys to Russia. They "should not be sacrosanct," as Marshall had said the day before and the day before that. King disagreed. The Russians were the mainspring of the European war, he said again, and "no effort should be spared" to supply them, so long as it was not prohibitively dangerous.

At the British chiefs' morning meeting Admiral Pound protested that the crucial war on U-boats was being curtailed by bombers diverted elsewhere and new campaigns in the Mediterranean and Southwest Pacific. This, the minutes say, was a view he had "often expressed before."

Captain McCrea's easy morning began with an hour's ride up the coast from the White House to the sultan of Morocco's palace in medieval Rabat with Brigadier General Wilbur, the only senior American officer at Anfa who was fluent in French and knew something about North Africa. Patton had provided the car, the driver, and Wilbur and alerted the palace that the sultan and his grand vizier would be invited to dine with the president. Roosevelt was eager to meet this native monarch, said to be deep in General Noguès's pocket, and explore his postwar ambitions.

Several days earlier Patton had invited the sultan and his thirteen-year-old prince imperial to an inspection of combat vehicles and found that "the mention of God with the Sultan is a one-hundred-per-cent hit." Patton liked the bright young sultan and took his fascinated son under his wing. He chatted with them in French and identified every tank and armored car they passed, but when they came to a less impressive vehicle he could not recall its French name. The sultan replied in English. "You mean laundry truck."

It occurred to McCrea as he and Wilbur crossed the sultan's grounds that Hollywood could not have set such a magnificent scene. The Americans passed through ancient white walls to a blare of trumpets, entered a courtyard of raked white sand, and approached the exquisite palace gleaming white in the morning sun. A Moroccan cavalry troop in exotic red dress saluted them, mounted on magnificent white Arabians with red saddle blankets.

The Americans were escorted to the colonnaded throne room where the sultan's ranking courtiers were seated. Curtains parted to another trumpet fanfare as the sultan appeared in magnificent white silk robes and took his gilded throne. His visitors were announced in Arabic, French, and English, and the president's handwritten invitation was read in all three. The sultan spoke only to his *chef de protocole*, who accepted the invitation and asked if the prince might come. McCrea said the president would be pleased if he did. Everyone stood as the sultan retired, and McCrea was informed on his way out that the prince was a great admirer of General Patton.

Ten miles up the coast, a strong wind was blowing chill in from the sea as Roosevelt made his way to General Clark's Fifth Army in an olive drab, Daimler-armored sedan with Patton, Hopkins, Harriman, and Murphy. The president's physician Admiral McIntire was a prudent addition. On the road they gawked at fuel dumps, bomb racks, Arab cavalry, veiled women, and horse and camel teams pulling plows. No self-respecting camels would pull together. In something like a small-town parade, military police led the way on motorcycles, followed by a jeep, a reconnaissance car, the president's sedan surrounded by jeeps manned by Secret Service men with tommy guns, two truckloads of heavily armed troops, two more reconnaissance cars, and a second motorcycle unit. MPs and sentries commanded every crossroads. Fighter planes followed overhead. Patton rode with Hopkins, surprised to find him "quite war-like" and "in favor of discipline."

When the motorcade sped up as it passed through villages Mike Reilly stood in his jeep pointing wildly at the sky as other Secret Service men craned their necks. When the villagers brought their eyes down the president was past them. Orders that no one without a need to know would be told he was coming were clear but not foolproof. An inquiry had been made to an officer in charge of a band. Did they know how to play "Hail to the Chief"?

The motorcade stopped just short of its destination, the first presidential inspection of troops on foreign soil. Behind a privacy screen, Roosevelt was carried to a jeep with a sweater under his suitcoat and a fedora on his head, and Clark got in beside him. He "started out asking questions," Clark wrote, and never stopped. As the jeep approached the head of Clark's army, its "division and battalion flags massed with the Stars and Stripes," Roosevelt brought his hat to his chest and a high wind snapped the flags. Driven slowly and formally down the highway, FDR passed hundreds of tanks and howitzers and their crews and 130,000 helmeted troops at shoulder arms, three or more deep and a mile long, expecting no one better paid than Clark. On the president's face was the heartfelt sign of their country's admiration and support. Some of them dropped their jaws before he was past. "Jee-zuss," he heard one say.

Clark might have been amused, he thought, had he not been in fear of some lone unbalanced man. The troops' shouldered arms were empty, or supposed to be, but the Secret Service insisted on training tommy guns on them as they passed. Harriman noticed dryly that some of the officers inferred "a lack of confidence in their men," but their "thrilled reaction to the President was to me very moving," and Roosevelt's sight of so many brave, high-spirited young Americans, "well equipped and ready to fight," was "a tonic for his soul." As they approached a "Negro unit," Roosevelt had his driver pass slowly between their ranks.

Afterward the president was carried to a chair, having learned that "once in a jeep is enough to last quite a time," and shook the hands of fifty young men decorated for valor in the landings, some of them lightly wounded. At first, Harriman wrote, they could not believe it was he, "and then it was thrilling to see their faces light up and hear their cheers." Hopkins observed something different about "the set of the mouth" of bemedaled men. Patton had known it since 1918. He was surprised that Hopkins did.

Seated at a folding table beside a field kitchen, flanked by Secret Service men with their backs turned to their charges, Roosevelt, Hopkins, Patton, and Clark lunched with ordinary troops on boiled ham, sweet potatoes, string beans, bread and butter, and fruit salad served in mess kits, "al fresco," Patton wrote. A spirited Army band played "Deep in the Heart of Texas," "Chattanooga Choo Choo," and other popular tunes as the president tucked into his meal, admitting he had hoped for a hot dog. Just before he left, he asked to take his mess kit home, but when Clark ducked into the kitchen tent, he was told it had been washed with a hundred others and grabbed the nearest one. "I'll have them put it in the Smithsonian," Roosevelt said.

Driven down the road in his Daimler sedan, FDR was lifted into another jeep, and the 9th Infantry Division's smiling young Americans marched past him visibly thrilled. He held back tears when he was told they would soon be in combat. The motorcade's last stop was a fresh dug cemetery enclosed by a white picket fence overlooking the sea and the battleground at Port Lyautey. American men and boys were buried in one section, French in the other, under identical white crosses. The president removed his hat as wreaths were laid in both sections.

Patton rode back with FDR, who spoke of history and antique armor, "about which he knows a lot." Only two men were fit to succeed him, he said, Hopkins or Vice President Henry Wallace, and neither had a personality. He spoke of Churchill "to his disadvantage," Patton wrote, omitting the specifics. Germany and Japan "must be destroyed." He worried about the postwar influence of the reactionary American Legion, as Patton thought he should.

On his visit to his troops, Signal Corps photographers had "buzzed around" the president "like flies around a horse's ears," an appalled British officer wrote. "I wanted to kick them." Patton shared that shortsighted view. "Millions of pictures" had been taken, he wrote that night, "and none for the glory of the troops, all for the glory of F.D.R. and for Clark when he could get a chance. It was very disgusting." The Secret Service had somehow crossed Patton too: "Must remember to get Flat Foot Riley."

Patton was wrong about glory. The commander in chief's heartfelt tribute to his troops had boosted their morale and his, and the photographs and newsreels would give their country comfort. A junior officer from Oklahoma City wrote his mother three months later that the president's "wordless speech" as he rode past his countrymen at arms had touched and inspired them. "I could see it in every one of my men. It was the most impressive thing I have or expect to witness in my lifetime." Having led them since in combat, "it still gives me a thrill every time I think about it." Many family members sent the president their thanks. "My son is in Africa, I believe," Mrs. Myrtle Milliken wrote from Buzzards Bay, Massachusetts. "I have been all tightened up inside with worry and heartbreak—and then the news that YOU had been to Africa yourself. I am not good at self-expression; but I can say that all the tension left me and I could cry with relief. . . . If you can go where you send the boys, it somehow makes me feel he is nearer and safer."

Once home from Morocco, Roosevelt ordered and signed letters to the parents and wives whose loved ones had driven his jeep, or manned the Villa Dar es Saada, or guarded its doors, or lay in Port Lyautey's cemetery, with a picture of its neat white crosses enclosed. Many of them replied.* "It is difficult to express just how much it meant to be certain my son, Oran Lass, was safe and well," his mother wrote from Kansas City, "but having sons in the service yourself, I know you understand." Mrs. June Long of Temple, Pennsylvania, was grateful to the president for "telling me that you saw my husband and that he is well and safe. Gosh! That made me feel swell to hear you say that. You see sir I am not married so very long, and I am like thousands of other women. I worry about him all the time." Mr. Edwin G. Miller wrote from West Bend, Wisconsin: "My wife and I are the happiest people on earth today. . . . His mother and I will never forget that our son, just a country boy, had the honor of serving the President of the United States. We pray that the Good Lord will guide you through this conflict so it will soon be over and all of our boys will be home again." Mrs. Ella M. Duane of West Newton, Massachusetts, took comfort in the thought "that my son is buried in a hallowed grave in a cemetery, and not in an unknown unmarked spot."

• • •

---

* Some original punctuation has been corrected to promote clarity and avoid distraction.

Gen. Sir Alan Brooke, October 1942. Brilliant but obstinate,
he led the British military delegation.

Gen. George C. Marshall, 1945. Admirable but cold,
he headed the American military delegation.

The Anfa Hotel, site of the Casablanca Conference.

The Villa Dar es Saada, FDR's Anfa Camp White House.

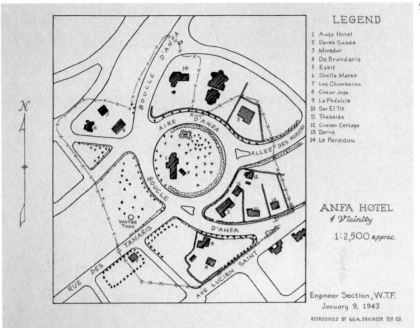

The Anfa Camp site plan. The hotel is in the center, FDR's villa (No. 2) is across the rotary at five o'clock, Churchill's (No. 3) is at two o'clock. Other participants shared other villas.

The senior American team on FDR's veranda. Standing left to right, Hopkins, Arnold, Somervell, and Harriman. Seated, Marshall, FDR, and King.

The military conferees at the negotiating table. Left to right, King, Marshall, Arnold, Deane, Dykes, Wedemeyer, Ismay, Mountbatten, Pound, Brooke, Portal, and Dill.

The Secret Service detail with FDR's armored Daimler sedan. Mike Reilly is in the middle. Macmillan can be forgiven for thinking they looked like gangsters.

Before or after a plenary conference in Roosevelt's dining room at the Villa Dar es Saada. Standing left to right, Jacob, Ismay, Mountbatten, Deane, Dill, Portal, and Hopkins. Seated, Arnold, King, Churchill, Roosevelt, Brooke, Pound, and Marshall.

Hopkins, FDR, and Patton at their field kitchen lunch.

FDR inspects the troops. General Clark salutes the flag in the middle of the jeep's backseat.

The guests at FDR's dinner party for the Sultan of Morocco. Standing left to right, Patton, Murphy, Hopkins, the Prince Imperial, Noguès, the Sultan's Grand Vizier, the Sultan's *chef de protocole*, Elliott Roosevelt, and McCrea. Seated, the Sultan, FDR, and Churchill.

Generals Giraud (left) and de Gaulle touch
hands in front of FDR and Churchill.

Sir John Cotesworth Slessor. Lamed by childhood polio, he
rests his right arm on his cane. He crafted the draft agreement
that both sides accepted with minor amendments.

Roosevelt and Churchill meet the press. In the center, Capt. Louise Anderson records the proceedings with her stenotype machine.

Captain Anderson with her stenotype machine and a friend after the press conference. "We're practically buddies by now."

The CCS had begun their morning session with the smallest fleet of escorts that could sink or ward off enough U-boats to keep the Atlantic open. A recent American report had summed the problem up. The Allies' weapons production capacity exceeded their shipping capacity, which exceeded their escort capacity. Pound protested, as he had at the British meeting, that the CCS had made the war on U-boats the first charge on Allied resources, then endorsed operations that would deplete it, and they should record their reasons.

The U-boat regained its primacy in the ensuing review of instructions to commanders choosing bombing targets. Based on Slessor's work, the document came to be known as the Casablanca Directive. "Your primary object," it said, "will be the progressive destruction and dislocation of the German military, industrial, and economic system and the undermining of the morale of the German people to a point where their capacity for armed resistance is fatally weakened." Subject to adjustment, the priority targets were U-boat construction yards, aircraft factories, transportation systems, oil plants, and other war industries. Additional targets included U-boat bases, if attacking them proved successful; Berlin, when "especially valuable results" would damage German morale or motivate the Russians; and Italian targets hit in support of Mediterranean operations. Important ships caught in port and other targets "of great but fleeting importance," an elegant British phrase, should be opportunistically bombed.

Bomber group commanders were instructed to "take every opportunity to attack Germany by day," hitting targets "unsuitable for night attack," to "sustain continuous pressure on German morale," deplete enemy fighter planes, and draw aircraft from Russia and the Mediterranean, the next amphibious target. Any invasion of the Continent would have maximum air support. In bombing occupied countries, British and American commanders would conform to any orders His Majesty's Government might issue "for political reasons." Arnold had won his battle for daylight bombing without fighting it in the long room. Every other point in the bombing directive was controversial.

Marshall demanded to know the "precise implications" of British politics driving bombing decisions. Portal said political considerations often took excellent targets off the board when there was no time for CCS review. The Americans, for instance, drew "considerable criticism" in Britain for never bombing Germany. If the entire weight of their bombs fell on French U-boat bases, killing French citizens, destroying French homes, "there would be very serious criticism indeed." Marshall acknowledged the difficulty. No one mentioned the incineration of German or Italian children or their grandparents.

In a rare British split, Brooke and Portal parted company with Pound. King backed his fellow admiral, and the sailors won. The U-boat had been at the top of their bombing list, but Portal did not consider U-boats a mortal danger. New construction, "particularly in America," could replace sunken ships. Brooke too put the highest value on bombing the Reich itself, the only present way to hit Germany directly, but Pound said now was the time to level her U-boat bases in four French ports on the Bay of Biscay. Sporadic attacks did nothing. "If the Germans had gone on bombing Plymouth, Liverpool and Glasgow instead of stopping when they did, we should have been placed in a very difficult position indeed." Now the Germans must be put in that position.

King complained that the recent British raids on Berlin had dropped twice the bombload that fell on the U-boat base at Lorient. Portal said all four bases should be destroyed if possible, and a far greater bomb weight had fallen on Lorient than Berlin in relation to area. Brooke said the war could not be won by defeating the U-boat alone. Bombing U-boat targets was a defensive strategy, less important than the offensive. Bombs dropped on Germany destroyed her power directly. Depleting U-boats made "only an indirect contribution." No one drew an ironic analogy to the American view that the Germans must be beaten in Germany, not in "periphery pecking."

Marshall said the eventual invasion of France would require air attacks on German defenses and military formations. Portal assured him that industrial targets would yield to close air support when the invasion was ready. Arnold stood up for Ira Eaker's Eighth Bomber Command.

No one was more eager to bomb Germany than they, he said. U-boat targets had been hit in support of Torch, and hundreds of American bombers would soon be in England "where we were now thinking in tens." Marshall stressed again that British officers would pick the targets for bombing missions launched from Britain but Americans would choose their own tactics.

Next came the draft report to Stalin. Some changes were suggested and accepted, as was Portal's bid to strengthen the reference to bombing. The British heavy bomber fleet in England would soon expand from 600 to 1,000, the American from 200 to 900, "a fact that Mr. Stalin should be glad to learn."

A British paper on Bolero was not ready, and Marshall asked for an update. Brooke said the British could absorb 120,000 American troops a month. "The immediate necessity" was to appoint a supreme commander for a continental invasion and a staff to start the planning. King called it urgent. Neither Marshall's nor Brooke's ambition for the job was mentioned. Two plans were needed, Brooke said, one for a limited Sledgehammer attack in 1943, the other for a decisive Roundup invasion in 1944. Marshall saw no difficulty in training, equipping, and transporting the biggest invasion force in history. The troops shipped to North Africa in November had been trained on the fly. Preparations to cross the Channel should be deliberate. Every American unit would be trained before it left the United States.

Brooke repeated, apparently for the slower learners, that any cross-Channel attack in 1943 must be small and an all-out invasion deferred, but however small a Sledgehammer operation might be, it should be planned as a step toward Roundup. Somervell said troops could be shipped directly from America to captured French ports, and Marshall suggested separate operations to capture them from the sea. Brooke explained that it would be easier to take a bridgehead and "widen it out" to the ports. Marshall then raised the thought of flank attacks through Denmark or Holland. Pound ruled them out. Denmark lacked the required ports, air cover would be difficult, and the Germans could fight in

Holland behind canals. All of this supported Brooke's view that Marshall was no strategist.

In a prize-worthy work dump, the Combined Chiefs of Staff closed the meeting with instructions to the planners to write up nothing less than "the command, organization, planning and training" required to invade France in 1943 and, in the alternative, 1944. It was due the next day. The floating British nerve center HMS *Bulolo* was armed and ready with experts and files.

Churchill convened the British Chiefs of Staff at noon and pushed them to make the war go faster. He had "heard September mentioned" for Husky, which "of course would be quite unacceptable," unlike May. "It surely could not be necessary to train every single man," and insufficient "ingenuity was being displayed in overcoming obstacles." It would be most unfortunate if the British were not ready when the Americans were.

Brimstone was exhumed when Dill raised the thought of attacking Sardinia in May and Sicily in August or September, as King had foretold. Portal thought it "well worth considering," but Brooke said it had been studied and rejected, and Pound called it "very difficult, if not impossible," though Cunningham had given Kennedy the opposite impression. Mountbatten doubted that troops could be trained for both missions "in quick succession," and Churchill killed the idea. Sardinia might entail a long campaign, prevent us "from securing the richer prize of Sicily," and suspend Russian convoys too long. To Kennedy it seemed "a thousand pities" that they could not do both.

Kennedy watched the weather turn rough at Anfa. "It blew a gale outside," and Churchill raised a storm at Villa Mirador. As if the British planners had not enough to do, he called them in at two and beat them up for an earlier Husky launch until four, the only time he challenged the military at Anfa. Roosevelt never did. Eisenhower had learned in London what the PM could do "when he turns the sun lamp on." Savvy Cooke had heard that "Churchill blew up" when his Chiefs of Staff told him Husky could not be ready by June, and they "fell back on their planners." When the planners stuck to their story "Churchill blew up the planners." He did not enjoy excuses, and planners were unpopular with him. The "machinery of negation" he called them, tired of their conclusions that his wildest ideas were wild. He demanded a way to strike Sicily by "the June moon." Kennedy noticed that Churchill's bluster did not change the math.

Much to his mortification, Brooke collided with his own side too, rehashing into the night with the other British Chiefs of Staff and their planners the pivotal decision for Husky, which they had debated in London for weeks and had already sold to the skeptical Americans. Stubbornly leading the charge for Brimstone, Mountbatten reported a rumor that the Americans would not be ready for Husky until September. Portal still liked Brimstone too, as the planners always had. Ismay was wobbling, and Pound, Brooke wrote, "was, as usual, asleep and with no views either way!" Frustrated beyond words, Brooke watched the room firm up against him. Once an attack succeeded, he later wrote, everything looked easy, but refusing to abandon a careful plan that seemed flawed "for a thousand good reasons" was "a superhuman job!"

Churchill was not present but had staked himself out for Husky. Whatever was done in 1943 "must look big to Stalin." Brimstone was "that piddling operation." In the courage of his convictions, even Brooke's director of plans Brigadier General Guy Stewart pressed hard for Brimstone. Brooke fought "a hammer and tongs battle" with his friends and may have snapped a pencil. "I told them that I flatly refused to go back to the American Chiefs of Staff and tell them that we did not know our own minds and that instead of Sicily we now wanted to invade Sardinia!" It would "irrevocably shake their confidence in our judgment." They might even go back to rejecting the Mediterranean entirely. Brooke had bound his team to Husky and would not let them go. "Being a very obstinate man," Jacob wrote, "further argument only annoyed him" and incited him "more rabidly."

In the end Brooke agreed to suggest to the CCS that Brimstone be raised from the dead only if it seemed by March 1 that Husky could not be launched by August, a seemingly irreproachable idea.

•   •   •

Churchill sent Attlee and Eden an American draft of a combined press release, bland with one exception: "General de Gaulle was invited to come from London but declined. General Giraud will proceed with the organization of a French army." If de Gaulle stood him up, Churchill wrote, "the President will make an arrangement very favorable for General Giraud which I shall not easily be able to resist. Giraud has made an excellent impression here, military and political alike." Harriman could see that Roosevelt and Churchill had come to like Giraud: "Confidence in him grew and is now on a solid foundation with both great men."

Roosevelt had returned to his villa after his trip to his troops. "Couldn't have been a better change," he told Elliott. A little bustle in the hall and Churchill came bouncing in "just for a second" with news from London. "And good for once. De Gaulle. It begins to look as though we'll be successful in persuading him to come." Churchill was beaming but Roosevelt merely said, "Good. Congratulations, Winston. I always knew you'd be able to swing it," and wheeled himself to his room.

Attlee and Eden cabled Churchill that the War Cabinet endorsed a demand for the unconditional surrender of Germany and Japan but rejected exempting Italy, which would not play well in Turkey or the Balkans. "Knowledge of all rough stuff coming to them is surely more likely to have desired effect on Italian morale." Churchill's plan to fly to Cairo and Turkey was rebuffed. The former was too dangerous, the latter fraught with failure. Attlee and Eden urged him to come home and report to Parliament when the conference ended. Churchill balked, as they surely knew he would. Eden sent him a personal message asking him to back down, to which he did not reply.

Before the day was out Churchill sent Hopkins a note. Assuming "the bride arrives tomorrow morning" and Giraud and de Gaulle come to terms on the wedding, would it not be wise to have them both to lunch? After that would come dinner at the White House with the sultan. "Dry, alas!" as Churchill had been told, in deference to the Muslim faith. "After dinner, recovery from the effects of the above."

Fourteen

DAY NINE: FRIDAY, JANUARY 22

Dozens of war correspondents long since working in American or British Commonwealth officers' uniforms, depending on their nationality, were flown to Casablanca in three transports from Algiers without explanation. One pilot mistook a Spanish Moroccan airfield for his destination, and a Spanish antiaircraft crew fired on the approaching plane, killing a young Canadian reporter. At their downtown Casablanca hotel, a "grave-faced" American general bound the others to the strictest secrecy and told them to remove their press insignia, lie low, and say nothing to anyone. A chambermaid greeted Drew Middleton, the *New York Times* correspondent: "So you have come to see that great man, the President Roosevelt?" Stalin and Franco were said to be with him.

FDR was ready to wrap things up, but Hopkins advised him to postpone the press conference set for noon. The CCS had not yet agreed on much of what the reporters would want to know, the headline news should be a total meeting of Anglo-American minds, and "the de Gaulle thing might be in the bag in another 24 hours." Roosevelt reluctantly agreed. The men responsible for his safety were eager to see "the super brass hats" on their way, Arnold wrote, but "Everyone seems to like it here" and "be satisfied with life."

Murphy sent Hopkins a note: de Gaulle was expected today. Giraud would host him for lunch. They would then be "shut in a room." After they came out, Churchill should receive de Gaulle and walk him to the president.

Hopkins found Churchill in bed in a pink robe enjoying wine with breakfast, which Harry could not help noticing. Safe whole milk was unavailable, the PM said, and having "a profound distaste on the one hand for skimmed milk and no deep-rooted prejudice about wine, he had reconciled the conflict in favor of the latter." He seemed relieved to hear that the press conference had been postponed to the following day, and satisfied with the military conference, but Hopkins was disappointed that Husky, not Roundup, had been chosen for the next operation. It seemed like "a pretty feeble effort for two great countries," and the brass might decide they could do more when the president "put the heat on." Churchill said nothing memorable enough for Hopkins to preserve, except for a complaint about a photo session set for noon. He did not look his best so early in the day, he said, but he could put on a warlike face whenever he liked.

The British Chiefs of Staff met at nine for a "preliminary run over the course" and a heated exchange between Portal and Pound about bombing French U-boat bases. Portal was afraid that, given a green light, the Americans would attack those bases whenever they could, at the expense of bombing Germany.

The combative mood spilled into the long room. The Combined Chiefs of Staff approved for Roosevelt's and Churchill's review a draft report to Stalin that stressed what he would want to hear, made no promises, and omitted what they chose not to share with the Kremlin. The fireworks began when they turned to Husky. Brooke said the British planners had squeezed their launch date down to August 15, unless Tunisia fell sooner than expected, but the August 22 moon would be better. Marshall deplored the delay. August 1 would work for the Americans, he said, perhaps earlier, deflating the false British rumor of unreadiness.

It galled Brooke to resurrect Brimstone. Some "unforeseen and insurmountable difficulties" might delay Husky too long to be acceptable, he said, and they ought to be ready with an alternative. Marshall said he understood that Brimstone was the only Mediterranean alternative, and he would like a frank discussion. Revisiting its disadvantages, Brooke said Sardinia's capture would not help clear the Mediterranean and "not be as great a blow to Italy" as Sicily's, but it would put something important on the board for 1943 if Husky could not be mounted in time to keep the enemy on the back foot.

The American response turned Brooke into a prophet. Several days earlier, Eaker's aide Captain Parton had spotted Marshall looking haggard. Countless burdens had fallen on him since. On this ninth day of pressure, Sardinia was behind him, and there he meant to keep it. An invasion of France or Sicily would produce "great results," he said. Brimstone was "a minor operation" and would jeopardize both. It would only postpone Husky, not replace it, and the United States Chiefs of Staff cared more about getting ships through the Mediterranean and relieving the Russians with a big operation than bombing Italy from Sardinia. To set Husky aside for Brimstone was to "seek the softest spot before turning to the harder spot" and make it harder, anathema to Marshall. With King's and Arnold's support he put it simply: "the United States Chiefs of Staff are very much opposed to the Operation Brimstone."

Brooke agreed emphatically on going "all out for Sicily," but an alternative should be ready "in case of absolute necessity." The discussion flipped between Sicily and Sardinia yet again. King said the best time to attack Sicily would be just as the Germans lost Tunisia, and the longer Husky's delay the stronger Sicily's defenses would be. Mountbatten said the same was true of Sardinia and pushed hard for Brimstone. Portal spoke as logically as ever. Italy's collapse would help the Russians more than anything else and Brimstone might do it. To strive for the best and prepare for the worst, Husky should be set for July and Brimstone energetically planned in case Husky's preparation proved intolerably long. Husky would help the Russians very little in late summer. "Brimstone in June would be better than Husky in September."

As Brooke had foretold, Marshall's patience for British backtracking had expired. He had never been angrier at this table, and his anger was a palpable thing. He had gone to London in July pressing to invade France and was "put off with North Africa." Now they had settled on Husky, and "there should be no looseness in our determination." Brooke and Portal endorsed determination, and if Portal tried to calm the storm he failed. Marshall rejected Portal's claim that knocking Italy out was crucial. "We must be determined to do the hard thing and proceed to do it." In Sardinia the Allies "might be shot at from three directions" and neutralized for a year. If Husky fell through, and he had to accept some lesser operation, someone else would have to be found to sit in his chair. So disturbing was this threat that the minutes excised it. Kennedy's diary preserved it.

Brooke replied that taking Sardinia would not be easy and "we should go bald-headed for Sicily," but if it were clear by March that Husky could not start by August, they must either have an alternative or accept a year of idleness and give the Germans time to lick their wounds. A recent British paper had warned that even an unsuccessful invasion of France "against unbroken German forces" would do more to help the Russians than anything else but it was not "a practicable operation of war" and its failure "would be a disaster." On the other hand, "If Germany is allowed breathing space to recuperate for a year or more, she may well become unbeatable."

Whatever was said of Sardinia after Marshall's threat to resign, the minutes do not record it. Ironically, Brooke's unwilling pitch for a Brimstone fallback was his only decisive loss at Anfa. Husky was confirmed with a July 25 target date, chosen for its favorable moon. Eisenhower would have supreme command, Alexander would be his deputy for the ground war, Cunningham for the sea, Tedder for the air, leaving not much for Ike to do but grapple with the French while the British ran the war against the Germans.

As the conference wound down, the Americans had renewed their support for Germany First, grudgingly in the case of the Navy; acquiesced in the British push for the Mediterranean, to Marshall's disappointment; endorsed several other British-hatched plans; and handed the Brits control of the war in Europe in 1943. "This was really the culmination of all my efforts," Brooke wrote that night. With his goals achieved and his fears dispelled it was "an untold relief that this meeting is drawing to a close." The Americans had fallen into line with most of his ideas, and so had the Brimstone dissidents who had challenged Sir Alan Brooke.

Wedemeyer sent his boss General Handy a synopsis: "We came, we listened, and we were conquered." Marshall had done a magnificent job, almost on his own, for his aides were overwhelmed by British staff who "swarmed down upon us like locusts." Handy later said that "relays of well-informed British planners" had simply "snowed them under." The Brits were good enough not only to plan American operations but German operations too. They could tell you how many enemy divisions could attack a certain place in so many days "and they were right!" When the Brits came at the Yanks, they "never forgot what they were after. You head them off here, they'd come at you another way." There was nothing rude about it. "The British planners were just smarter than hell."

Just before noon FDR lifted his arms and two Secret Service men carried him to one of two white-leather dining room chairs on his back garden lawn in lovely cool weather. Churchill took the other chair as Sammy Schulman, Corporal Hopkins, and other Signal Corps photographers stood the Combined Chiefs of Staff behind them. The warlords laughed as Hopkins questioned who the top brass *were* for photographic purposes. It seemed to him there were two or three around the edges "who didn't belong there." A decision was made for inclusion, and Somervell, Ismay, and Mountbatten joined the team picture as Churchill donned his warlike face.

General Kennedy was introduced to FDR. "I was greatly taken with him," he wrote, struck by his natural, friendly charm and his "fine head and face." Nonetheless, after what seemed like "a fortnight of continuous conference," Kennedy was not alone in thinking he had reached "the limit of what is bearable. We could not have done it in less time. But it is a good thing it is nearly over for we should all be getting on each other's nerves if we should stay here much longer."

General Wilbur took a knee before Roosevelt's chair as the president draped the Medal of Honor around his neck in the presence of the great and near great. When the invasion force landed at Casablanca in November, Wilbur, one of Patton's staff, had volunteered to deliver a surrender demand in a jeep, returned in the dark through sixteen miles of intermittent fire, and taken command of a tank platoon to capture a French artillery battery shelling an American position, a brave but not legendary performance. Wilbur was the war's first Medal of Honor winner "and that," Hopkins wrote, "was ground out" for the public, who were thought to need a hero. When Ismay congratulated Patton on his subordinate's achievement Patton's eyes filled with tears: "I'd love to get that medal posthumously."

Hopkins and Harriman had an interesting lunch with Mountbatten, who swore them to secrecy about his undying infatuation with Sardinia, which Hopkins wrote down as soon as he had the chance. Lord Louis was proud of his picked team of bright young officers and men charged with contriving "unorthodox operations" and exotic gear, some of which worked and was used. Many British officers scoffed at the "long-haired scientists" Mountbatten led in pursuit of the irregular. To King it seemed that "all the available 'cranks' got a hearing under the command of Mountbatten." Among the schemes he shared with Hopkins and Harriman was a plan to stuff a worn-out submarine with explosives, ram it against a cliff, and blow a road into France, followed by his commandos. "He says he gets no more interest in this," Hopkins wrote, than in ships made of ice.

Mountbatten's head genius Geoffrey Pyke was an unwashed eccentric who had wasted an hour of Vivian Dykes's time with a plan to tunnel into Norwegian glaciers to carve out guerrilla strongholds. "The abominable snowman," Dumbie called him. Mountbatten touted "Pykrete" at

Anfa. One of Pyke's more intriguing ideas, Pykrete was simple sawdust mixed with water to be frozen in molded blocks from which vast unsinkable aircraft carriers would be built. Any holes blasted out by bombs or torpedoes would be filled with liquid Pykrete and frozen in place in seconds by an onboard refrigeration plant. Experiments proved the concept viable, a protype was built, and serious men took it seriously. Cost and complications eventually ruled it out.

Kennedy's Anfa diary calls Mountbatten "a curious character, full of charm and never abashed," and a very fine officer, "but it is a great pity he has been pushed by Winston into positions for which he has not the wisdom or experience." Hopkins sized him up as "a courageous, resourceful man" pushed around by tired superiors.

As Marshall and FDR conferred over lunch Elliott eavesdropped on the stairs like a six-year-old. Once the Americans committed to the Mediterranean, Marshall said (which Roosevelt had casually done on day two), they had found it hard to push an invasion of France in 1943. According to Elliott's postwar account, Marshall reported a CCS agreement that any future attack on the Italian boot should be carefully limited. The minutes contain no such agreement. Not even a discussion.

Marshall made a case for Eisenhower's fourth star. With his army stuck in Tunisian mud, showing scant success in combat, the timing was problematic, but a promotion would only bring him even with some of his deputies. Roosevelt was not having it. Promotions should go to men who had done some fighting. Ike was doing a good job, but he had not yet taken Tunisia and would not be promoted until there was "some damn good reason for doing it." Marshall said Eisenhower was cutting "overhead" to prepare for serious battle, and the French should be armed as quickly as possible to relieve Americans from lesser duties. Marshall complained that the British had insisted on striking Europe from the south instead of the northwest and implied that he acquiesced for solidarity's sake. He worried about Stalin's reaction.

• • •

De Gaulle arrived at noon like the Queen of Sheba. "With his fine sense of drama," Macmillan wrote, his nick-of-time entrance just before the conference closed focused everything on him. Unknown on the political stage before 1940, he snatched the featured role from Franklin Roosevelt and Winston Churchill.

Le Grand Charles emerged from an RAF plane in a simple uniform and an operatic snit with a four-officer entourage and asked if a certain Vichy official was there. He was not. If he *had* been, the great man said, he would have refused to see him. His welcome was unsatisfactory. Neither Roosevelt, nor Churchill, nor an honor guard paid him homage. General Wilbur, his classmate at the École Supérieure de Guerre, greeted him in Roosevelt's name, Churchill sent a representative, and Giraud sent a colonel who invited de Gaulle to lunch with his rival. Insufficient deference all around. From the mud-smeared windows of the car that awaited him, de Gaulle deduced that the Allies wished "to conceal the presence of General de Gaulle and his colleagues." Wilbur assured him that Roosevelt, Churchill, and "all the really important ones" had been protected in the same way.

His lovely white villa inflamed him. Giraud's, which adjoined it, was pink but otherwise nearly identical, "to suggest equality," Murphy thought, a status to which de Gaulle did not aspire. He measured the villas' distances from the Villa Dar es Saada with his eyes and concluded that Giraud's was closer. "It is inadmissible," a hissing aide explained, that "General de Gaulle should accept lodgings that are inferior to those occupied by some casual French officer." He had to be convinced that de Gaulle's villa was a few meters nearer the center of power than Giraud's. No French troops arrived to salute or guard France personified, who took offense from the barbed wire encircling Anfa Camp, which "no one was permitted to enter or leave," and the American soldiers who protected, cooked, and kept house for him as they did at the other villas. "In short it was captivity." He did not object to Les Anglo-Saxons inflicting it on themselves, "but the fact that they were applying it to me, and furthermore on territory under French sovereignty, seemed to me a flagrant insult."

De Gaulle brought his courtiers to lunch at chez Giraud and greeted his host: "Bonjour, mon Général. I see that the Americans are treating you well." And that was just the beginning. "'What's this?' I said to him." He had asked Giraud repeatedly for an interview, and now they had to meet encaged by foreign barbed wire, an affront to France herself. Giraud said he had not been free to do otherwise. De Gaulle said he was not surprised, given the position in which Giraud let the Americans put him. Having dressed the older man down, he declined to have lunch until French soldiers relieved the Americans guarding his villa, after which the two of them spoke of old times at Giraud's table. De Gaulle asked Giraud to recount his escape from his German captors' prison, a sure way to his heart. When had Giraud been invited to Anfa? de Gaulle asked. On Saturday afternoon, Giraud said, and he had arrived on Sunday morning. "On Sunday afternoon," de Gaulle replied, "General de Gaulle said that he would not come."

After they left the table the ball rolled downhill fast. Giraud insisted that politics did not interest him; he spent his time on the war and never read a paper or turned on a radio, but despite his zeal for killing Germans, which de Gaulle much admired, he had nothing against Vichy or its governors. As Macmillan had it from a witness, de Gaulle replied with "a violent diatribe against Darlan and his successors, and poor Giraud was under the impression that he was being blamed for all their faults." Giraud thought it wise to avoid an argument and let de Gaulle do most of the talking but contributed the unhelpful thought that the underground French Resistance's reddish tint was "incomprehensible if not reprehensible." As de Gaulle got up to leave, having never even raised the subject of an agreement, Giraud asked what his plans were. He had none, he said. He would see the president that afternoon and then decide.

The British had put politics away "in a desperate conflict with Germany," Macmillan wrote, and de Gaulle's self-promotion repulsed them. But Roosevelt had decreed the necessity of a marriage, "even if it was a shotgun wedding," and "Murphy and I were responsible for the arrangements." No one envied them.

Macmillan and Harold Mack, a British diplomat not to be confused with Harold Macmillan, kicked the matchmaking off with a call at de Gaulle's villa, where the general later wrote he had been waiting "with calculated reserve." De Gaulle looked worn and edgy but spoke very calmly, aired many grievances, and deplored the indignity of meeting on French soil under American guns. Giraud's administration could not swallow Fighting France, he said, and declared that the French people rejected Vichy's authority in Africa. In France's unfortunate position she required a "mystique," either Vichy's or de Gaulle's, and now that all France was occupied, every Frenchman stood with de Gaulle. He and he alone could save France from communism.

Macmillan said he and Murphy were working on a unity plan that Roosevelt and Churchill could propose and de Gaulle and Giraud could accept. So here, de Gaulle wrote later, "was the expected intervention." De Gaulle said Giraud was an honest man who had not kept up with the times and had chosen to combine with Vichy because he had no other support. Their dealings were a French affair, to be settled on de Gaulle's terms, the first of which was no unification with Vichy's most repugnant men in Africa. At Macmillan's emphatic urging, de Gaulle agreed to see the prime minister that evening. Once de Gaulle came to Anfa, Mack wrote at the time, they could not let him and Giraud depart "without announcing an agreement of some kind."

Later that afternoon, one of de Gaulle's entourage gave Mack his terms: (1) Giraud would command a unified French authority's armed forces; (2) de Gaulle would be its political leader; (3) all French African Vichy laws would be abolished, all Vichy men disempowered. Giraud liked part one but would take no orders from de Gaulle and would not betray his friends. Murphy and Macmillan briefed FDR, who told them he would see de Gaulle that night. The president was as cheerful as a puppy. After all, he said, they had twenty-four hours before he left for home.

The Americans had produced a convincing outline of the Asian-Pacific war in short-staffed haste, and when the CCS reconvened King drove it home with a map, starting with the stunning sweep of Japanese conquests, including all of China's seaports and much of its interior, all of Manchuria, Indochina, Korea, Malaysia, Thailand, the Philippines, and the Dutch East Indies, all but a sliver of Burma, and many strategic island chains. Turning next to every major threat and opportunity, King said the Americans meant to work their way toward positions from which to bomb Japan. The taking of her home islands, still "remote" in time, would be accomplished by the same means that could threaten the British Isles—blockade, bombing, and, if need be, amphibious assault. The minutes say only that King's report was noted, which suggests that the British wished not to prolong it.

In contrast to the plain American outline on the Japanese war, the elegant British planners' report on "Continental Operations in 1943" was a work of narrative art unencumbered by a needless word, a clumsy phrase, or a debatable punctuation mark. Wedemeyer had wired Washington that British preparation, staffing, and analysis had been the conference's decisive factor and here was an example.

Three kinds of Channel crossings might succeed in 1943, it said— raids designed to draw and deplete the Luftwaffe; the taking of a French bridgehead; and a major invasion in the event of "a German disintegration." The enemy would keep improving his strong defenses, but the quality of his troops was likely to decline. The airpower and reserves he could throw at the point of attack were crucial. The establishment on the Cherbourg peninsula of a short, easily defended line with English-based air support was the only possible objective for a force meant to take and hold a bridgehead, which could not succeed before the enemy's reserves were much drawn down, but by August they might be. The key factors were his ability to concentrate those reserves and his troops' morale. If their will to win collapsed, a landing in France might be merely "an administrative problem," but even negligible resistance would slow the assault down for lack of landing craft capable of putting vehicles on the beach. An August 1 launch should be prepared, but the decision would depend on the level to which those reserves had to sink before the attack had a reasonable chance, which ought to be studied now.

Brooke stressed that any Channel crossing that summer would require American airborne troops, for Husky would consume all of Britain's. Mountbatten stressed the need to turn the beach defenses, a "quite impracticable" task without the required infantry and armor.

A *combined* planners note declared "no chance" for a large-scale invasion of France in 1943 "against unbroken opposition" but backed a limited version if conditions made it practicable. Subject to other commitments, the strongest force the Allies could assemble should be constantly ready to cross the Channel as soon as the enemy's means to resist sufficiently decayed. A recovery of the Channel Islands should be planned, along with seizing "critical political and military centers in Germany" after a "sudden and unexpected collapse of German resistance." The uncertainties demanded flexible preparations. A supreme commander should be named forthwith, supported by an Anglo-American staff and land, sea, and air commanders. Brooke and Marshall agreed it was too soon to name a supreme commander—neither man mentioned himself or the other—but a staff should be assembled now.

Mountbatten handed out drawings of his long-haired scientists' new amphibious support vessel and joined King, Cooke, and Somervell in a detailed presentation on what an invasion of France required, including lessons learned from his failure at Dieppe.

Marshall, Arnold, and Patton walked two miles together, British style. Arnold had heard a false rumor that de Gaulle had refused to see the president but agreed to reconsider. "What a bunch these Frenchmen are." Patton toured HMS *Bulolo* in the harbor and found it interesting but too complicated.

Late that afternoon de Gaulle met with Churchill alone and even came to him instead of the other way around. "The P.M. is a bad hater," Dr. Wilson wrote, "but in these days, when he is stretched taut, certain people seem to get on his nerves; de Gaulle is one of them." Frenchmen "do not find it easy to accept any foreigner as a superior being and Winston does not like that kind of agnosticism." Churchill began by "venting two loads of steam, as if to get it over with." De Gaulle followed suit, perhaps for old times' sake. "I would never have come," he said, "had I known I was to be surrounded, on French territory, by American bayonets." Churchill shouted, "This is an occupied country!" And then they got down to business.

The British had lately settled on what Harriman's notes call "a dual-headed regency" led by Giraud and de Gaulle, which did not impress the New Yorker: "I always considered it cock-eyed." The best it could achieve was a tawdry veneer of unity, sure to dissolve in time, for the two competing factions had nursed "personal hatreds" since France fell in 1940. No immediate marriage was "possible or wise."

Churchill told de Gaulle he had to settle with Giraud. Churchill would back him "on a basis of equality" but "no personality" could block a French entente without being removed. As de Gaulle told the tale, Churchill informed him that the president of the United States and His Majesty's Prime Minister had solved the French Empire's leadership problem. De Gaulle and Giraud would head a governing committee and Vichy's governors would not only stay in power but also populate this committee as their equals, for the Americans accepted these traitors and wished them to be trusted. Giraud would command the French African army because the Americans demanded it.

De Gaulle told Churchill this arrangement "might appear adequate at the quite respectable level of an American sergeant, but I did not dream that he himself could take it seriously." De Gaulle thought very highly of the prime minister and the president, he said, but not of their attempt to dictate French affairs. "Without me, no, *against* me," the Allies had installed a system in Algiers, and now, having found it unsatisfactory, they wished to pull Fighting France into it. Fighting France would not play their game. If it had to disappear "it preferred to do so honorably."

"Look here," Churchill said. Having fought *British* appeasers for years, *he* had brought several into his government. "Well, they followed along so well that today you can't tell them from the rest." Any Frenchman who found himself an obstacle to French unity or "the two great allies" was duty-bound to efface his ambitions. No one would be allowed to obstruct the path to victory, and "I should not hesitate to speak in public about these matters," much as he would regret to identify de Gaulle as an obstacle. De Gaulle replied that Churchill had lost sight of what had happened to France. Unlike the prime minister, de Gaulle was not a politician trying to make up a government and attract a parliamentary majority. Churchill asked him to reconsider. He understood that de Gaulle would confer that night with the president of the United States. He would find him resolute. If de Gaulle continued to obstruct the British government, it would not hesitate to break with him.

De Gaulle "was very formal," Churchill later recalled, "and stalked out of the villa and down the little garden with his head high in the air." Churchill walked him to the gate, where a British marine presented arms. "Please observe," the PM said, "that if there are American sentries here, there are also British soldiers side by side." De Gaulle strode away like Charlemagne, and Churchill walked back to the house with "a whimsical smile." Dr. Wilson stood at the door. "His country has given up fighting," Churchill said, "he himself is a refugee, and if we turn him down he is finished. Well, just look at him! Look at him! He might be Stalin, with two hundred divisions behind his words. I was pretty rough with him. I made it quite plain that if he could not be more helpful, we were done with him."

And how did he like that? Wilson asked.

"Oh, he hardly seemed interested."

Tears filled Churchill's eyes when Wilson repeated something Hopkins had said, that Roosevelt mocked de Gaulle for anointing himself Joan of Arc's heir. "France without an army is not France," Churchill said. "De Gaulle is the spirit of that army, perhaps the last survivor of a warrior race." For him "England's grievous offense" was helping France up from her knees. "He cannot bear to think that she needed help."

The British got their hopes up when one of de Gaulle's men told Mack that the general had returned from Churchill with an attitude "of very mild approval."

Hopkins put on his dinner jacket and fortified himself for the alcohol-free dinner in honor of Sultan Sidi Mohammed ben Youssef, Mohammed V. Patton was fond of the sultan, "a very handsome young man, extremely fragile, and with a highly sensitive face." Patton's liking for such a man does credit to them both.

The eel-like General Noguès had been invited, keen to keep an eye on the sultan in foreign company. Patton took him to a house just outside the wire to gather the sultan and his three-person retinue, all of them dressed in white silk robes and brocaded white cloaks. The sultan's grand vizier, whose house it was (the wire jogged to exclude it) was said to be "bright as a button" in his nineties with gleaming gold teeth that proclaimed his place in life. The sultan's *chef de protocole* was not as colorful. The prince imperial, a smart, appealing boy, spent the evening in a red fez. Thrilled to see Patton again, the prince had let him know that when he became sultan Patton would be his grand vizier "and we will go everywhere in a tank." McCrea had drawn a seating chart with Churchill at the president's left, the sultan at his right, and Noguès several seats away, disadvantaged as an eavesdropper, monitored by Hopkins and Murphy. Elliott Roosevelt was there but Randolph Churchill was not, a good deal for the Americans.

Mohammed V, a descendant of the Prophet, was the Muslim world's religious leader and, theoretically, Morocco's absolute ruler under an eighth-century sultanate. An American reporter thought the French gave him "little more freedom than a boarding school girl," but Murphy knew better. Apart from the medieval deference of Morocco's subordinate pashas, the sultan had religious authority, popular sway, and considerable independence. The French had enthroned him on his father's death despite his inferior status as the youngest of three brothers, thinking him more docile than the rest. With access to the ear of the president of the

United States his docility proved exaggerated. It was not the first occasion. Before the Allies landed, he had blocked the deportation of 250,000 Moroccan Jews to Nazi death camps and protected them from Vichy persecution as best he could.

Before Churchill arrived the sultan and his grand vizier asked to see Roosevelt alone. They told him they distrusted both de Gaulle and Giraud and urged him to promote a postwar Moroccan plebiscite on independence. His support sent them thrilled into dinner. Before Corporal Hopkins left the room he took pictures of the guests, which entertained the prince.

The president took the head of his glossy oval table. At its foot sat Harry Hopkins, whose notes mention Noguès nervously beside him, "the bird that de Gaulle wants pitched out of here," stripped of his Moroccan sinecure. "He obviously likes it, because he lives in a big palace and is the big shot in this part of the world. I wouldn't trust him as far as I could spit." Nor would Macmillan. "It seemed to me a monstrous thing," he wrote, "that General Patton should be so easily impressed by the gay hunting parties and the lavish entertainments which Noguès gave in his honour," having needlessly cost the lives of hundreds of his men and hobnobbed with Nazis only weeks before. Kenneth Pendar, the American diplomat in Marrakech, was appalled by this "Vichyite character" whose saber-armed guards and trumpet fanfares left Patton and his tough subordinates as "dazed and dazzled" as boys. "These Americans are easy to handle," a French-speaking reporter had overheard Noguès say. "I can make them do anything I want."

Soon after everyone was seated, a snappy British marine brought a dispatch to the prime minister, who excused himself and returned in twenty minutes, not as steady on his feet as before. Hopkins retrieved the dispatch after dinner and found it inconsequential. Churchill "was never the worse for drink in my experience," Ian Jacob wrote years later. "It is not for me to explain this phenomenon."

Hopkins thought Noguès looked uncomfortable, as if the president might relieve him of his burdens at any moment, but Roosevelt's proximity to the sultan was the cause of his unease. Everyone else was enjoying himself but for Churchill, who was rude on orange juice and water, watching Roosevelt chat with the sultan "volubly in bad French," Patton wrote that night, "really doing his stuff" on His Majesty about sharing Moroccan wealth with the Moroccans.

The sultan should not let foreign interests drain his country, Roosevelt said. Churchill tried to change the subject and failed. The sultan asked for the president's thoughts about France's future in Morocco. The postwar scene, he replied, would of course be sharply different. Churchill coughed, spoke of something else, and was ignored. "Different how," the sultan asked. French and British financiers, FDR said, made fortunes "dredging riches out of the colonies" that ought to be improving their people's lives. Oil might be under Morocco. The question was how to get it out. Elliott watched the sultan "pounce." He would love to see Moroccans do it, but they lacked the technical skills. FDR said universities could educate them, "let's say in the United States." The sultan might engage the right firms, American firms, to advance his country's development. A sovereign Moroccan government could control it, share its revenues, and eventually take it over. "Ten years from now your country will be independent." Churchill was apoplectic, and so it went from there.

Presents were exchanged after dinner. Roosevelt gave the sultan an inscribed photograph of himself in a heavy silver frame, which may have seemed light when the sultan presented a sultan's gifts, an exquisite Moroccan dagger for FDR, trimmed in gold in a golden scabbard, nestled in an inlaid teakwood box, and a pair of golden bracelets and a fabulous gold tiara riddled with gems to bring home to the first lady. The president caught Elliott's eye, glanced at the tiara, and winked. To Hopkins it looked like "the kind the gals wear in the circus, riding on white horses. I can just see Mrs. Roosevelt when she takes a look at this."

The dinner broke up with the sultan aglow in the light of "a new future for my country," Noguès visibly upset, and Churchill fleeing the scene, "biting at his cigar." The sultan and the president had impressed each other, and it all whipped through Morocco overnight. More than two decades later, Macmillan called Roosevelt's performance "a curious and impolitic maneuver" aimed at a native ruler under French "protection," embarrassing to the British as much as the French. Churchill considered it a conscious provocation, which it clearly was, and an insult to de Gaulle, who promptly heard all about it and was not a hard man to offend. Roosevelt's physician Admiral McIntire understood that Noguès was "quite agitated at the thought of a New Deal in Morocco."

Patton brought the sultan and his entourage home. "Truly your President is a very great man," the sultan said, "and a true friend of myself and my people. He shines by comparison with the other one," perhaps the only time Churchill was so described. It had been the happiest day of his life, the sultan told Patton later, and "I shall be very worried until I hear that the President is safely home."

Churchill returned to the White House minutes later, swallowed the outrage of Roosevelt treating the sultan like a sultan, briefed the president, Hopkins, and Murphy on his afternoon bout with de Gaulle, and asked FDR to receive de Gaulle in the morning. Hopkins advised Roosevelt to see him now if he felt up to it. Perhaps Harry thought it wise for them to meet before de Gaulle heard about the sultan. Murphy went to fetch de Gaulle, and Churchill went home.

Murphy the diplomat broke the ice diplomatically with de Gaulle. "We are all happy that you are here," he said in fluent French. "It must be good to be back again among your own people." De Gaulle said he never would have stayed in this house, caged by American wire, had he not been told it was owned by a Dane as opposed to a Frenchman. Murphy said he would not presume to advise the general about French politics, but it would help if he joined forces with Giraud without preconditions. Within three months he would control North African politics, for Giraud had no political ambitions. "Political ambitions can develop rapidly," de Gaulle said. "For example, look at me!"

The self-effacing humor was unexpected and encouraging. Murphy replied that President Roosevelt would only deal with Frenchmen "on a local basis" until the people of France could choose their leaders. He had maintained relations with Vichy to support the spirit of France, and an understanding with Giraud would make a crucial contribution. De Gaulle played a classic card: He was here as a prisoner of his colleagues. He would discuss whatever the president liked but he could make no decisions without his National Committee. When Murphy reported this later Roosevelt called it nonsense.

Murphy walked de Gaulle and an aide to the White House, and Mike Reilly led them in. Reilly thought they were "a serious lot" and de Gaulle had chips on both shoulders. Elliott's metaphor was Homeric: De Gaulle "arrived with black clouds swirling around his high head." Hopkins found him cold and austere. Murphy introduced him and left.

With Hopkins at his side, Roosevelt met de Gaulle's hauteur with bonhomie. Pleasantries were exchanged, lovely on the president's part, formal on de Gaulle's. The general later wrote that he knew Franklin Roosevelt and his "messianic" country, having never set eyes on either. The president had historic aspirations. The peace he meant to win must be his, built as he would have it, including France's recognition of FDR "as its savior and its arbiter." Its premature revival would frustrate these ambitions and Roosevelt was wary of de Gaulle, for "like any star performer he was touchy as to the roles that fell to other actors." No one knew that touchiness better than de Gaulle, who had all of this right.

It was 10:15 when the general sat down, a very tall man awkward in a too-small chair. De Gaulle noticed drapes moving in the corners and shadows flitting in the minstrel's gallery: "Because of these indistinct presences, the atmosphere of our first discussion was a strange one." It slowly dawned on Hopkins that most of the Secret Service detail was lurking behind curtains and half-open doors like extras in a Marx Brothers movie, "and I glimpsed a Tommy gun." Hopkins left the room and asked the other agents what *that* was all about. They could not take chances, they said. "None of this hocus pocus had gone on when Giraud saw the President," but de Gaulle had a certain notoriety. Hopkins thought "nothing in Gilbert and Sullivan could have beaten it" and guessed wrong that de

Gaulle had missed it. Topping off the mood of a bedroom farce, Elliott cocked an ear on the staircase and McCrea took notes behind a door ajar, getting Roosevelt's side of the conversation.

De Gaulle later recalled that "we vied in good manners" and preserved "a certain vagueness" about France. Roosevelt acknowledged in hit-or-miss French the diversity of French political views, which almost matched the number of Frenchmen, but as far as he could tell, none that could not be reconciled. He assured de Gaulle that the United States would help his great country restore her destiny. In reply the general grunted. Roosevelt added that it would be an honor. "It is nice of you to say so," the Frenchman said. FDR struck de Gaulle as eager for a deal, but behind his charm and "beneath his patrician mask of courtesy," he "regarded me without benevolence."

As de Gaulle had the poetry to describe it, Roosevelt sketched with a lighter hand the same dictatorial terms that Churchill had struck with a hammer, "gently permitting me to understand" that they would be accepted because Roosevelt had so decreed. The president said there could be no government of France until its people could choose one, and no one had elected de Gaulle. The general replied that France had chosen him already. Joan of Arc had earned legitimacy leading France against its invaders and so had he. He and he alone must choose the members of a merged French authority, he said, naming Vichyites who had to go. Roosevelt said personalities must not stand in the way of unity. Why worry about Noguès, for example? Let him keep his palace. De Gaulle invoked a Fighting French colleague imprisoned at hard labor. Roosevelt said it was something, at least, that Vichy had not shot him or dispatched him to Devil's Island.

According to de Gaulle, they avoided confrontation, realizing that neither of them would benefit and amity might help them both, though de Gaulle had hardly been allowed to complete a sentence. Roosevelt was fixed on his own view of French affairs and cordially uninterested in his guest's. He had traveled a long way, he said, and the one thing he wanted to bring back was an agreement between Frenchmen for the war's prosecution and the liberation of France through a shared provisional authority, not a government, mind you, provisional or otherwise. The president supposed that General Eisenhower's arrangement with Admiral Darlan "had been the source of some wonderment" to de Gaulle, but *he* had always thought the North African problem was military, the politics incidental. He had thoroughly approved of Eisenhower's decision to accept Darlan as an ally, and progress had been made before the admiral's untimely death, for Darlan had been willing to pressure the enemy.

Behind his crack in the door, McCrea thought de Gaulle said something about French sovereignty, which the president brushed away. "The occupied territory's" sovereignty was "not under consideration." None of the current contenders for power embodied French sovereignty, which rested with the people, as it did in America. Unfortunately, they could not exercise it now. After the North African landings, General Eisenhower had been obliged to take the political situation as he found it and work with the men in authority, so long as they assisted him.

Mike Reilly's Secret Service qualifications did not include French but, peeking through drapes slightly parted, he knew what de Gaulle meant by *ma dignité*. FDR spoke with quiet earnestness, de Gaulle with a sullen edge as Roosevelt's "Dutch chin" jutted closer to de Gaulle's French nose and "the '*ma dignités*' poured forth." McCrea heard Roosevelt say that because the French people were temporarily disenfranchised it was necessary to resort to the concept of trusteeship. The Allies fighting for France in North Africa held her political reins as trustees, for France was like a helpless child. Had McCrea seen de Gaulle's face he would have had more to tell.

Roosevelt said he had spoken with General Giraud, who "was very definite on the one point that mattered, namely to 'get on with the war.' " Politics would not divert him from driving the enemy from French soil. Americans had been divided after their civil war, but they subdued their pride and prejudice for the national good and reunited. France's leaders should follow their example. Regrettably, de Gaulle was not caught on film. The only course that would save France, the president said, "was for all of her loyal sons to unite to defeat the enemy." When the war was won, victorious France could again assert her sovereignty at home and in her empire, and her people would settle the politics.

De Gaulle made a graceful withdrawal, having seen more to like in FDR than he let on. Hopkins thought Roosevelt had a hypnotic effect on him, a perhaps overwrought impression, but de Gaulle told his aide as they walked away, "I have met a great statesman today. I think we got along and understood each other well." The president had a gift for making skeptics like him despite themselves, and the general had impressed him too, which enhanced his fear that de Gaulle was a budding dictator.

Churchill, Macmillan, Mack, and Murphy returned when it was over, relieved to hear the president say he had gotten on nicely with de Gaulle. He had never met a man of de Gaulle's type before, he said, quite impractical, with a disturbingly spiritual light in his eye. Roosevelt sketched his preferred French arrangement—de Gaulle, Giraud, and some civilian heading a colonial governors committee in which de Gaulle would have a majority. Churchill countered with *"deux grands chefs"* equally empowered. FDR said he would accept a committee of two or three as the French might agree.

Macmillan and Mack thought de Gaulle and Giraud wanted a deal. Giraud's men preferred an agreement in principle, the specifics to be worked out in Algiers, and Giraud planned to see de Gaulle again tomorrow. Macmillan, Mack, and Murphy were instructed to keep working and inform the two Frenchmen that the president and the prime minister would see them late tomorrow to discuss the agreement they had made. Churchill cabled his War Cabinet. Roosevelt had been "much more kindly and paternal" with de Gaulle than he. "They parted on almost affectionate terms. We shall see what will come of the dual treatment."

Fifteen

DAY TEN:
SATURDAY, JANUARY 23

The sultan's admiration for Patton did not offend him. Soon after the general took Casablanca, Mohammed V had draped around his neck the Order of the Grand Cross of Ouissam Alaouite, Morocco's highest honor. A personal tribute accompanied Patton's medal: "*Les lions dans leurs tanières tremblant à son approche.*" This too went over well. On Saturday morning at Anfa Camp, Patton bestowed the medal on Marshall, King, and Arnold "in my capacity as a grand cross," which he understood to be "a sort of apostolic succession." King soon told Patton, "I trust that when you appear, the lions continue to tremble in their dens."

Roosevelt slept late and Hopkins fielded drop-ins like the sultan's grand vizier. Assured of the strictest secrecy, the old man spoke ill of the French. The sultan had welcomed the Americans with joy, he said, "but will the joy continue?" The sultan was ready "to throw himself into the arms of Mr. Roosevelt" and hold a plebiscite, certain that his people would put their future in his hands, but after America won the war, how would it treat Morocco? Hopkins said the occupation would end, and the Americans would leave empty-handed. The president felt that many peoples "have not had their rightful share of the good things of the world." They should have them after victory was won. The president had "become a warm friend of the Sultan and his country" and hoped for closer ties, "profoundly impressed" with Morocco, its people, and the sultan, who had stood up to the Germans and proved himself a great man.

Elliott discovered a French biography of his father in the Villa Dar es Saada's library and showed it to him at breakfast. FDR inscribed in French a profuse note of gratitude to the house's evicted owner. "Now stick it back on the shelf," he said, wishing he could watch her open it, warning Elliott with a wink not to sell it.

Giraud met with de Gaulle's respected colleague General Georges Catroux, a former governor of Indochina purged by Vichy, and proposed to head a governing *Comité de Guerre* with de Gaulle as his number two, titled high commissioner, administering the colonies already under his wing. A third man they would choose together would oversee the rest. Catroux and other Gaullists would play key roles. Giraud found Catroux as reasonable as he had hoped, and Murphy sent Hopkins a note: The proposal made sense. Two equal rivals could not run a taut French war. De Gaulle might mistake the French people's hatred of the Germans for their love of him, but Giraud "wants to play ball with de Gaulle and to respect his sensibilities." They would have lunch today and "a long tête-a-tête."

Giraud convinced Macmillan he could not serve under de Gaulle. He wore five stars to de Gaulle's two and had earned them when de Gaulle was a colonel. De Gaulle had been his student, twelve years younger than he, de Gaulle had served under Giraud's command, and Giraud was no second-place man. Regrettably, nor was de Gaulle. Macmillan later recalled how "Murphy and I hurried from one imperial villa to another" drafting and tweaking compromises "without much hope." Giraud accepted every one "without a murmur." De Gaulle rejected them all. He proposed some of his own but never budged a *centimètre* from his core proposition: Giraud could lead the army; de Gaulle would have control. Macmillan found himself "in the embarrassing position of continually trying to persuade Churchill and Roosevelt to give de Gaulle another chance, which he seemed always unwilling to grasp."

With their arguments behind them, the CCS absorbed a few new papers and tweaked a final report to the president and the prime minister. It occurred to Ian Jacob, who had drafted it, that had he jotted down in London what the British might achieve "I would never have written anything so sweeping, so comprehensive, and so favorable to our ideas," which had "prevailed almost throughout." The British had fielded a stronger team, united on almost every issue but Husky versus Brimstone, backed by a shipload of human and material resources. The Americans had come poorly prepared and outmanned. "Divided, they naturally fell to our combined front," which Jacob saw as a victory for both sides.

The Americans, in fact, had not been swept from the field. To begin with the improbable, King was a happy man. The British had committed to retake Burma and attack the Japanese after Germany's defeat, abandoned their case for a defensive Pacific war, and given the U.S. Navy a reasonably free hand. Arnold put it plainly: "No change was made in our Pacific policy." King understood sea power, to say the least. He and his staff had favored the Mediterranean over the Channel when the choice was discussed in Washington and had merely gone along with Marshall. He thought Husky over Roundup was wise.

The U.S. Army too had done reasonably well. Arnold's daylight bombing had been saved, Sicilian airfields would be taken, and devastating bombing would start. Marshall was disappointed that Roundup had been pushed into 1944 but knew it had to be. It "would have been preferable to close immediately" with the Germans in Western Europe had it been possible, he later told the secretary of war. "It was not." Nonetheless, he had stood firm for Husky once chosen, quashed the Brimstone rebellion, and achieved his paramount goals. Bolero would proceed and the Channel would be crossed. Soon named to lead the invasion's planning, Major General Sir Frederick Edgeworth Morgan later wrote that the British Chiefs of Staff "were not pleased at having been made to commit themselves to the cross-Channel adventure more than a year in advance." They had lost their Asian empire to Japan, fought Hitler alone for a year and a half, won their first offensive victories near the end of 1942, and "the skin of our teeth was wearing a bit thin."

"It has been a wonderfully good conference in the end," Kennedy wrote. "Brooke's personality and drive have accomplished great things. Both sides are really convinced now that we are on the right lines and we can now drive ahead with the war on a coordinated plan." Discarding his first impression, Hopkins sent Dill a note after reading the final report: "Jack: I think this is a *very* good paper and damn good plan—so I am feeling much better." Churchill cabled Attlee and Eden: "It now remains to add speed and weight to all our actions."

Giraud brought his staff to lunch with de Gaulle and refined the proposal he had put to Catroux, which de Gaulle correctly identified as Roosevelt and Churchill's child. Giraud would be in charge. De Gaulle would be general of the army. Noguès and other loathsome Vichy men would keep their governors' mansions. Paranormal skills were not required to predict de Gaulle's response: Giraud must know that the people of France, once freed, would condemn the Vichy regime from which his powers sprang. What Giraud proposed was a dictatorship with window dressing, a consulate at the mercy of foreigners in which Giraud would seize Napoleonic powers "under Roosevelt's protection" without being up to them. A nearly unanimous plebiscite had made Bonaparte first consul, de Gaulle told Giraud, noting that Giraud had none. Bonaparte had showered the people with victories and conquests. De Gaulle hoped Giraud would too, but where were his laurels at the moment? Bonaparte had brilliant governing skills. Did Giraud think he could match them?

Giraud held his own in the ensuing repartee, starting with the thought that these were political points in which he had no interest. He only wished to build an army with confidence in "our American allies" who would arm as many divisions as he could produce. He would raise half a dozen in six months. "Will you have half as many? And who will give you weapons for them?" De Gaulle said France's armies belonged to France, not Giraud, as he would soon discover if they could not come to terms. Once unity was achieved there would be no military difficulty. Vichy was an illusion soon to vanish. Fighting France *embodied* France and had earned a mystique that made any other governing French entity inconceivable. Giraud said mystique would not trump his divisions.

De Gaulle said Fighting France alone had kept the idea of France alive since 1940, which gave it a higher status than "late-comers" should expect. If de Gaulle took second place to Vichy's man his troops would not understand. Many Frenchmen admired Giraud as a military leader, an asset that de Gaulle would hate to lose. The sensible solution was plain. Giraud should "rally to Fighting France." De Gaulle would form a wartime government in Algiers and Giraud would lead its army, much along the lines of Georges Clemenceau, France's great World War I premier, and Ferdinand Foch, his military subordinate. This new administration would personify France, condemn Vichy, and declare the 1940 armistice null and void from its inception. In time it would become the French Republic's government (exactly as FDR feared).

Refusing to accept an underling's role disguised as a division of labor, Giraud tried the British approach. He and de Gaulle might be subordinate to a committee led by a neutral civilian, which de Gaulle dismissed out of hand. Giraud refused to purge his Vichy friends and de Gaulle refused second place. Hoping that the weight of things to come would eventually move Giraud, de Gaulle proposed to send him a liaison headed by Catroux. Giraud agreed but there was little to cheer in that. A gloomy luncheon followed. According to Giraud, "We separated correctly if not coldly."

Minutes later, Murphy came to de Gaulle, who asked how Murphy thought the French North African public would react when they heard there was no agreement. Murphy said many would be satisfied, even relieved to see de Gaulle sidelined, and less than 10 percent of French North Africans supported him.

•   •   •

General Wilbur came to de Gaulle, who unburdened himself in French. Marshal Pétain had been his mentor. Now the real Pétain was dead and the new one had "the spirit and attitude of a grandfather." Until the Americans landed, the only forces fighting for France had been de Gaulle's. Giraud was an able general but did not represent the true France, for he owed his position to Vichy. If he somehow got back to France, the people would rise against him and the communists would win. Giraud should join de Gaulle, not the other way around. The Anglo-Americans might cut de Gaulle off, and then he would have to fold up. He preferred defeat to dishonor.

Calling himself a friend of France, Wilbur advised his classmate that the French must settle their differences now, before the Allies invaded France, or she would hold a weak hand at the peace table. One unified French command could reach her suffering people faster than two, and many Gaullists came to Wilbur seeking unity. De Gaulle replied that if others came, he should tell them that de Gaulle had seen Giraud and they had not resolved their differences, but he was sending a liaison. Wilbur hoped de Gaulle would urge his followers to support the American forces. This he agreed to do and asked for Wilbur's address, for he wished to stay in touch.

"In the evening came Mr. Harold Macmillan," de Gaulle remembered later, "to confront me with a tirade of concern as to the future of Fighting France." Then Wilbur returned with French officers' messages and a warning that the conference would be over in twenty-four hours. De Gaulle replied with a message for Wilbur's superiors. How strange it was that in the midst of the battle for Tunisia in which French forces, including his, were heavily engaged, no Allied general thought it useful to tell him a thing or ask him a question.

There were reasons for this. Brooke had recorded his assessment of de Gaulle in 1941—"a most unattractive specimen. We made a horrid mistake when we decided to make use of him!" Six months later he feared that "Eden's support of de Gaulle will go near losing the war for us if we do not watch it." Marshall later said no sons of Iowa farmers would fight in France to raise statues of de Gaulle.

In a late-night talk with Murphy and Macmillan, de Gaulle made his final offer. He and Giraud would rotate in a governing committee's chair. All Vichyites would be excluded, all ties to Pétain repudiated. If that was not acceptable it would be best to work separately, exchange liaisons, agree not to snipe at each other, and let something more come in time. Macmillan could see that de Gaulle liked option one. Murphy pushed for option two. Macmillan and the British diplomat Harold Mack recommended option one to Churchill, who accepted it, absent "unreasonable conditions," and sent the two Brits to Hopkins. The president, Hopkins said, "had been very anti–de Gaulle during the day and was ready to destroy him" in American public opinion. Unless he accepted some agreement, FDR would announce a collaboration with Giraud and publicly declare de Gaulle unwilling to help the Allies win.

On a "phenomenally lovely" afternoon, the Combined Chiefs of Staff and their advisors walked over to the White House to discuss their final report with Hopkins, the prime minister, and the president in his sleek Moroccan dining room. The event was a debate, not a blessing, and the issues were carried by the better argument, not by the higher rank. The chiefs gave no quarter to Roosevelt or Churchill and Hopkins gave none to the chiefs, who respectfully exposed Roosevelt's amateurism and rebuffed Churchill's obstinacy. Any German or Russian general who made such remarks to Hitler or Stalin would have risked his command if not his longevity.

As far as he knew, Churchill began, this was the first time in history that allied military leaders had met for so long a time, free from political pressure, to form a common strategy. The part about pressure was a stretch, Churchill having blown up his planners and cajoled their American peers. Arnold's planner Colonel Smart liked the "friendly tutorial fashion" in which the PM had addressed them, but "we were being measured." Roosevelt honored the Combined Chiefs of Staff's historic achievement and proposed to consider their report in detail.

The discussion began with their approach to securing the Atlantic, where the gravest threats were U-boats, as Churchill wanted them always to be called, "rather than dignifying them by calling them submarines." Sufficient escorts to protect every convoy could not be produced before August, and it would likely be 1944 before they could sink more U-boats than the Germans could build. Convoys to Russia would continue, "subject to the proviso" that they would not survive "prohibitive cost." Roosevelt asked Hopkins what he thought of that. Harry said the existing Russian protocol had a similar clause, which could not be invoked without "violent objections from Premier Stalin." Churchill stood with Stalin, for "no investment could pay a better military dividend. The United Nations cannot let Russia down."

King said the convoys might stop in June if their escorts were pulled into Husky. Hopkins said the Allies had been prone to see the convoys as a "political expediency," not a military necessity, and should consider stopping them permanently. The Russians could be compensated with something unexpected, planes perhaps, and munitions might be sent through Alaska, Persia, or both. Churchill thought not. It would be "a great thing" if the convoys could continue through Husky, though the Allies had never promised to *bring* munitions to Russia, only to make them available at Allied ports. Echoing Churchill, Roosevelt called support for the Russians "a paying investment." To cut it off this summer would hobble them when they were fighting hardest.

Marshall bristled at Harry's reference to "political expediency." Support for the Russians was a military necessity second only to defeating the U-boat, though it must not put Husky at risk. Pound declared flatly that if the convoys continued through the summer "the Royal Navy could not play its part in Operation Husky." Churchill said "We must tell Mr. Stalin the facts." The convoys would probably not expand, and Husky might suspend them. Mr. Stalin should also be reminded that the Allies were not obliged to continue them at all. Roosevelt agreed. The Russians must be told, "in justice to them."

Harriman knew that Roosevelt and Churchill were pleased with the conference's results, "but for the slowness of the new military moves," and the Husky discussion began with Churchill pushing for June over the report's expectation of July. Marshall stood his ground. If they set · an unachievable date, then shifted to a practical one, they would throw every other schedule off. The issue had been studied exhaustively. Even July would be a challenge. Roosevelt asked if the timing might accelerate if Tunisia were taken in March instead of April. It would help, Marshall said, but the bottlenecks were landing craft, crews trained to run them, and soldiers trained to attack from them. Husky would be delayed if Tunisia were taken later than expected but sooner would not advance it. As Slessor later wrote, wonderful maps in American magazines with huge colored arrows "sweeping in massive pincer movements" across hostile ground were "all very well for the chap who draws the arrows."

Roosevelt asked if Mediterranean weather would not make Husky's landings easier than landings in Morocco from the Atlantic. Mountbatten said the difficulty was not the climate but the defenses. Marshall pulled it back to training. Some of the Torch landings had been made in the wrong places, as much as eighteen miles away. Roosevelt suspected poor navigation. Marshall repeated that the landing craft must be built and the training done. There was no way around it. Churchill suggested "combing the navy" for navigators, which Pound rejected. His navy needed its navigators.

Churchill abhorred the thought of the Allies standing idle through June, and Roosevelt was with him. Brooke said the timing had been studied meticulously and sharpened his point with a barb. September had been proposed, then rolled back to August before the Combined Chiefs of Staff put "the same kind of pressure" on the planners "that the President and the Prime Minister were now applying." The launch had then been stretched to July, but August was more likely. To set too early a date would prejudice the operation. Marshall was right that training alone could be cut, a potentially "disastrous" economy.

Churchill surrendered nothing. "All these points must be rigorously examined before the July date can be accepted," he said; "intense efforts" might even hasten the loading. Roosevelt said it was all based on estimates, like the state of Italian morale, which seemed to be slipping. The Italian people might revolt, and then we must be ready to strike, if not in Sicily, then in Sardinia or on the Italian mainland. He would like to set Husky for June, understanding it could be July. Marshall said no. To set an early date at the cost of preparation would not make it easier to react to such a breakthrough. The troops would be moved into place early, ready to seize an opportunity. Brooke backed Marshall again. If an Italian collapse seemed imminent, the Allies would be ready to give it a push with a smaller force.

The prime minister was unmoved. General Marshall's arguments were "most convincing," and he was right to preserve Husky's integrity, but Churchill was not persuaded that integrity was incompatible with June. Some quicker method might be found to move troops. This too had been examined, Marshall said. King soon wrote himself a note that "Churchill was rather stubborn about his own ideas."

Returning once again to the hard thing, Marshall said Husky would be a bigger operation than the Allies had planned for France before they fought the Germans in Tunisia. They must expect the same ferocity in Sicily but be ready to improvise if the enemy weakened suddenly. King said one of the "innumerable items" to consider was the need for armored landing craft, which he and Lord Mountbatten considered essential. None were yet available for American use in Sicily. To catch the Germans on the run as they fled from Tunis would be ideal, but July was the best the Allied forces could do.

The military repulsed the politicians in the end, and July withstood June. In what might have been mistaken for a poke at his commander in chief, Marshall recalled the election-driven "incentive" to hasten Torch's launch, which had not proved possible. Churchill said that when the election was not permitted to influence Torch "much admiration in England" had followed.

"Cover plans" came next, feints and minor operations designed to divert attention from Sicily. Churchill suggested a feint toward Norway, one of his cherished impractical targets, but the northern convoy route to Russia ran along the Norwegian coast, and Brooke did not conceal his scorn. "It might be awkward for the Russian convoys if we gave the Germans cause for reinforcing Norway." Spreading Husky's preparations across the North African shore would be "much the best cover," disguising the objective and scattering the enemy. FDR contributed the improbable thought that the creation of General Giraud's French army might make the Germans think southern France was the target.

Churchill called the Americans "very generous and broad minded" in the Mediterranean command arrangements. He did not say they had been conned. Not without some cause, Wedemeyer later wrote that the British were rife with ulterior motives and "subtle deals" while the country boys only wanted to win the war and go home. "We were just that naïve."

Regarding the coming air offensive against Italy from North Africa, the prime minister proposed that bombing Rome should be an option but not carried out without discussion. FDR agreed. Churchill had told an aide in 1940 that a few more bricks knocked off the Colosseum would do it no harm.

Churchill lent support to the fastest possible Channel crossing. It was very disappointing that only four fully equipped American divisions would be in Britain by mid-August. Could not "the Queens" (the converted liners *Queen Mary* and *Queen Elizabeth*) deliver troops more quickly? Somervell said they were fully employed. Cargo ships were the limiting factor. Churchill again was not put off easily. Could the equipment list not be cut, "fighting men for the beaches" being "the prime essential"? Somervell said it had all been considered, everything possible would be done, and it would help if the British lent Husky more cargo ships. Churchill promised every effort and suggested that the word "vigorously" be added to the plan to seize a bridgehead in northwest France if the Germans crumbled.

Roosevelt wondered if "sufficient drive" could be achieved if they merely appointed the decisive invasion's chief of staff now and a commander later. Marshall said it was a question of whether the right man was available. For now, Brooke said, a chief of staff "with the right qualities" could do what needed doing. Again neither Brooke nor Marshall jockeyed for the commander's role, even indirectly.

The discussion closed with Japan and the report's identification of shipping as her crucial weakness. Japan had begun the war with six million tons of it. A million were sunk in the first year. Once another million were gone the Japanese could not hold the islands they controlled from Burma to New Guinea and must pull in their lines. The best anti-shipping weapon was the submarine, but aircraft based in China could play a major role. Roosevelt was disturbed to find nothing in the report on bombing Japan from China; nor was he pleased with an island hopping approach in the Pacific, a costly, deadly, time-consuming business compared to bombing. But the Americans were not yet close enough for meaningful bombing except, perhaps, from China. In something like a huff, Arnold said he was aware of the need to build airpower in China. More planes were about to arrive, and he would leave Casablanca for India to consider ways to bomb Japan from China. Marshall called it vital to support China's war.

Churchill urged the CCS to amend their report to reflect the afternoon's discussion. As revised, it would "fittingly embody the results of a remarkable period of sustained work." Roosevelt congratulated them. China would get a full paragraph in the edited report. King had the last word, expressing full accord "with Sir Alan Brooke as to the great value of the basic strategic plan which has been worked out at this conference. In my view this has been the biggest step forward to the winning of the war." Had it been their venue, the British might have counted the silver.

Hopkins took Churchill aside and told him his request for more information about tube alloys would be granted. One of the underpinnings of Germany First—"the priority of Hitler's extinction," Churchill called it—was a well-grounded fear that German science and engineering could produce a war-winning superweapon even on the brink of defeat. Brooke thought it might "snatch victory from under our noses." A month and a half had passed since anxious scientists produced the first chain reaction at the University of Chicago, and Churchill had been pressing for more details on this "very secret matter" of tube alloys, British code for atom bombs.

The Combined Chiefs of Staff gathered one last time to secure loose ends and admire each other. Marshall paid gracious tribute to the British Eighth Army and its capture of Tripoli, the news of which was just in. Portal thanked the Americans for their hospitality and applauded Patton's arrangements. Marshall thanked the British for their spirit of cooperation and their readiness to understand the American point of view and thanked "Sir John Dill" for his invaluable work, the only man he singled out to commend. Brooke thanked Marshall in return and gave his own special praise to Dill.

For once unreservedly pleased, Brooke wrote General Archibald Wavell, who commanded British forces in India, that prospects for retaking Burma had improved, an essential part of the war against Japan, more profitable than what the Americans had proposed for the Pacific. He did not add that the Americans had insisted on Burma. The conference, Brooke told his diary, had achieved something more than the right strategy. "It has brought us all much closer together and helped us to understand each other's difficulties in a way which we could never have done at a distance."

As Marshall and Jacob had feared, Churchill made Roosevelt a tourist before the war came back at them both. "You cannot go all this way to North Africa without seeing Marrakech," Churchill told him. "Let us spend two days there. I must be with you when you see the sunset on the snows of the Atlas Mountains." Marrakech was a perfect place to relax and refresh their friendship, which had taken some wear at Anfa. The Paris of the Sahara, Churchill called it, where the Berbers had been fleecing caravans coming up from Central Africa for centuries, not to mention their proprietorship of "the most elaborately organized brothels in the African continent," the PM later wrote. "All these institutions were of long and ancient repute." The diplomat Kenneth Pendar's stunning Marrakech house had come to the PM's attention, perhaps through Dill, its recent visitor. It would accommodate them both, he said, with "plenty of outside room for our entourages." He had no trouble dispelling Marshall's advice to shun Marrakech, having "worked on Harry Hopkins." They would motor there after the next day's press conference.

Roosevelt and Hopkins enjoyed a quiet dinner with their sons until Murphy and Macmillan came by, soon joined by Churchill and Randolph, who was anything but quiet. Together they worked for hours past midnight on the courtship of Charles de Gaulle. Murphy said de Gaulle had lost his chance and should be dropped. FDR was inclined to agree, but Churchill, Macmillan, and Hopkins were not. The PM apologized to his bodyguard: "Sorry to keep you out so late, Thompson, but we have to marry these two somehow!" Murphy and Macmillan started working on the trick of a wedding announcement somehow palatable to both generals. Macmillan would present it to de Gaulle in the morning, Murphy to Giraud.

Roosevelt worked on a report to Chiang Kai-shek on the military conference and dictated notes to a Navy yeoman for the next day's press conference. Working with Hopkins, Elliott, and Randolph, FDR and Churchill drafted a public communiqué to be embargoed for three days, giving everyone time to escape. Back on liberty from his destroyer, Franklin Jr. rolled in drunk, slapped an admiral on the back, and called him an old SOB. Hopkins counseled the admiral to put him in arrest and confinement, presumably in jest.

Just before he left at half past two, the last man out the door, Churchill lifted a glass to unconditional surrender.

Sixteen

THE DENOUEMENT

Ian Jacob watched the British delegation dissolve on Sunday morning "exactly like breaking up at the end of term." Summoned to Churchill's room, Jacob found him with the windows closed and the heat on, "dictating and having breakfast by turns," revising the American draft of the press release. Churchill asked Jacob to check the conferees' titles and bring Hopkins his changes.

Captain McCrea later wrote that he and FDR's physician Admiral McIntire had enjoyed the pleasant villa whose owners had been "unceremoniously moved out," and the eviction "weighed a bit" on them. They left thank-you notes and two bottles of excellent brandy on the living room table. "Was this enough? Perhaps not. We left our names and addresses, but neither of us ever heard from the enforced hosts."

Churchill wrote Clementine that Anfa had improved him. His indigestion had faded, his "house-maid's elbow" was disappearing "of its own accord," and after "ten days of very hard work for the Staffs and a good deal for me and the President" the results were "in every respect as I wished and proposed." Comic relief had been supplied by "the attempt to bring de Gaulle to the altar where Giraud has been waiting impatiently," making a far better impression than anyone had expected. De Gaulle was casting himself as Clemençeau, "having dropped Joan of Arc for the time being," and Giraud as Foch, a highly respected general disposable at the great man's pleasure. "Many of these Frenchmen" hated each other more than the Germans. Not one cared about liberating his people as much as feathering his nest and grooming his plumage. "When a country undergoes so frightful a catastrophe as France, every other evil swarms down upon her like carrion crows."

When Jacob walked into the White House at ten, Murphy was working on a joint communiqué to sell to Giraud and de Gaulle, and Hopkins was working in bed in his robe and pajamas with a bowl of cigarette butts on the floor. His room looked like a crime scene. Sitting on the "tumbled" bed, Jacob reviewed Churchill's work with Harry, who made "some very sensible alterations."

Macmillan and Mack took the draft communiqué to de Gaulle and Murphy to Giraud, "the messengers" de Gaulle called them later. Its tone was brighter than the facts allowed and its content was artful, but it might just be bland enough for de Gaulle. In three days of "friendly conference," it said, Giraud and de Gaulle had reached "a complete understanding." They would jointly chair a committee for the liberation of France and combine their forces, equipped by the Anglo-Americans, led by French officers. French Africa's governors would continue in their duties, subject to the committee (a vaguery de Gaulle might accept), but there would be no government of France until its liberated people chose one. The agreement, "made by Frenchmen, with Frenchmen," had the full support of the president and the prime minister.

Giraud endorsed the draft in principle and de Gaulle turned it down. This "Anglo-American text which was now to become French," he told the messengers, was impermissibly vague and irredeemably soiled. It was dictated by the Allies, implied that de Gaulle had renounced any role but a colonial administrator's, and told a false tale that an agreement had been made. No foreign power, whether or not it was friendly, high, or low, could dictate French authority over French affairs. The only acceptable merger would make de Gaulle Clemençeau and Giraud Foch.

De Gaulle would issue his own communiqué. As a courtesy, he would tell General Giraud what it would say. General Giraud would no doubt reciprocate. De Gaulle said he regretted that military matters had been settled at Anfa without including France, French forces in action notwithstanding. If he had been invited to the military conference, he would have come immediately. He "harangued about Vichy," Mack wrote at the time, demanded again the dismissal of all French African officials tainted by Pétain, and classified Fighting France and Vichy as "La France Combattante and the traitors."

Murphy told Hopkins in Harry's storm-tossed room that Giraud would work with de Gaulle but not under him. Macmillan came in moments later and announced that de Gaulle was demanding just that. The president would not stand for Clemençeau and Foch, Hopkins said, but he might be okay with Giraud running French Africa "and de Gaulle the rest of the show." Hopkins went to FDR, who was sitting up in bed and "none too happy" with the news. "Yesterday he wanted to be Joan of Arc," the president said. Now he was Clemençeau. Hopkins advised against discarding him. De Gaulle and Giraud were searching for a solution. De Gaulle might sign some helpful statement and be photographed with Giraud. One last shot at pacifying him might work. Beating him up would not. "If there is any beating to be done, let Churchill do it." Having held Roosevelt at bay, Hopkins told Macmillan that Churchill *must* deliver de Gaulle, and Macmillan went back to the PM, who agreed to see both opera stars again.

As Macmillan stood by, Murphy handed two documents to Hopkins, who was not impressed. "I don't think the President would be well-advised to sign anything like this."

After several rounds of failed negotiations, Giraud strode into the White House in his calvary boots and jodhpurs, stiff as a varnished oar, accompanied by an aide. Hopkins and Murphy were there. Speaking French well enough to incite him, Roosevelt asked Giraud to see de Gaulle again and drew a sharp reply.

"That man! He is a self-seeker."

"If I told you that I share some of your misgivings, and that this is precisely why I urge that you . . ."

"And a bad general."

But Giraud played the hand he was dealt. "It is understood, Monsieur le Président. It is understood." He repeated his willingness to work with de Gaulle and sign a communiqué and asked to read a memo aloud. Jacques Lemairge Dubreuil, the right-wing French industrialist who had first put Murphy in touch with Giraud, had written it, having flown to Casablanca after meeting in Washington with de Gaulle's nemesis Cordell Hull, who told him he would find a surprise in North Africa. Lemairge Dubreuil's request to join Giraud in his meetings with FDR had been denied but Murphy handed Roosevelt a translation of what Lemairge Dubreuil had written, interjecting when Giraud lost the president in French. The press conference would start at noon, only minutes away, leaving no time for reflection, let alone consultation.

After patriotic recitations, including a mysterious claim that Torch had come at "the demand of the French," the lengthy memorandum said in essence that France had no government. Until its people chose one, the American and British governments recognized Giraud as France's commander in chief with the "the right and duty of preserving all French interests under the military, economic, financial, and moral plane"—the political plane was omitted—and bound themselves to his aid. Eisenhower, Murphy, and Giraud, the memo said, would work out the specifics. Much of the document clashed with the Darlan agreement, and it claimed to bind the British, who had not seen it, much less approved it. Roosevelt endorsed it all.

Giraud also brought a paper purporting to record agreements made with him at Anfa. First, the Americans would arm his troops with the most modern arms available. FDR wrote "*Oui*" in the margin. Second, 65,000 tons of civilian supplies would be shipped to Giraud each month and 165,000 tons of French shipping would be transferred to the Allied pool. Eleven French divisions would be armed and a thousand planes delivered within six months. Next to this the president wrote, "*Oui en principe.*" Third, Giraud and the American and British governments agreed that all French forces fighting Germany should unite in one authority with "every facility" provided to Giraud. Roosevelt wrote "*Oui,*" endorsed a specified pro-French currency exchange, and agreed *en principe* to French control of propaganda radioed into France with Allied consultation.

Giraud left elated and de Gaulle was left in the cold, but the United States government considered none of this binding, least of all FDR. The Combined Chiefs of Staff, like Churchill and the British diplomats, had not so much as seen it. Marshall later told the president neither he nor Somervell had made *any* specific commitments to Giraud. When Roosevelt returned to Washington, Secretary of War Stimson told him Cordell Hull was sure the exchange rate had been changed over a drink. Roosevelt laughed "and virtually admitted that the other covenants in the paper might have been accomplished in the same way."

Negligence is not a likely explanation for scrawling "*oui*" on a French declaration of American foreign, military, and monetary policy as if it were a charity ball subscription. Macmillan later wrote that Murphy was concerned about the "rather slapdash methods of doing business" that the president enjoyed at Anfa, let alone his contempt for French North Africa's Imperial Council. But Roosevelt meant to do what he liked in the region and did not much care what these French papers said.

As Roosevelt met with Giraud, Macmillan brought de Gaulle and his staff to Churchill. De Gaulle recalled it later as their ugliest confrontation of the war, which was no small achievement. De Gaulle could not accept Giraud's proposals, he said, and had come to say farewell, which triggered "a furious scene." Churchill "showered me with bitter reproaches" and promised to condemn him to Parliament and the people of France unless he reconsidered. At the very least he must sign some conciliatory public statement. Serene as the Maid of Orleans, de Gaulle invoked his friendship with Churchill, their alliance, and the prime minister's poor judgment. Churchill's demand to satisfy the Americans at any cost was rejected by France and not to the advantage of England or Europe.

The participants' accounts of just what happened next are irreconcilable, but Churchill's bodyguard left a vivid and credible recollection: The prime minister suddenly gathered his papers and walked de Gaulle and his staff to the White House. Halfway there they saw Murphy and Giraud coming out together and de Gaulle began to turn away, but Churchill urged him forward and stopped for a word with Giraud as de Gaulle and his aides walked in. One way or another, depending on the narrator, Macmillan wound up inside with Roosevelt, de Gaulle, Hopkins, Murphy, and Elliot. Churchill and Giraud remained outside.

Hopkins found de Gaulle "calm and confident. I liked him." Whether de Gaulle liked Roosevelt or not he admired his tradecraft as the president received him in French with "kind and sorrowful" skill. Roosevelt said he was disappointed in himself, having failed to persuade the general even to accept a benign communiqué. De Gaulle said he would not sign a meaningless paper or take orders from Giraud. Roosevelt made a last-ditch plea to help win the war and liberate France. The world should not see her divided. Her leaders should come together. "In human affairs the public must be offered a drama," he said, misusing the word *drame*, which implies tragedy and may have amused de Gaulle. The news that de Gaulle and Giraud had met in secret with Churchill and Roosevelt, the president said, and signed an encouraging communiqué, however thin, would provide the *drame* they needed.

As the president worked on de Gaulle, a Secret Service man beckoned Hopkins aside and told him Churchill was saying goodbye to Giraud on the front lawn. Churchill walked in a moment later, and Harry went after Giraud. De Gaulle, for once, looked surprised and confused when Hopkins returned with Giraud. Churchill merely grunted, but Roosevelt caught the ball in stride and turned his charm on the French prima donnas. The clock had struck noon, the hour set for the press conference, and the back lawn was full of buzzing war correspondents wondering why they were there.

De Gaulle said he and Giraud had agreed to do their best to work something out in the future, and paused before he said "together," begrudging the word. The president asked if France's liberation was not their common goal. Giraud agreed energetically. De Gaulle thought a moment and concurred. FDR relaxed a bit. Had they not already agreed to establish a liaison? Should they not also agree to declare their intent to accomplish these things and settle the details later? If they wrote twenty words and signed them, the public would be satisfied. De Gaulle shook his head.

"I return home a very disappointed man," the president said. "It is with what amounts to a broken heart that I must go back to America and Prime Minister Churchill must go back to England to tell the public that de Gaulle of the Free French would not put his name to a simple statement that the liberation of France was paramount to all other issues." De Gaulle seemed deep in thought. Then he suddenly said, "I will do it!" He would give Giraud a draft after Roosevelt and Churchill left for home. FDR beamed and urged the generals to shake hands. To Elliott they seemed to circle each other like wary dogs before they grabbed and dropped the quickest handshake in history. It was not enough for the prime minister. Murphy was taken aback by the sight and sound of Churchill "in a white fury," shouting ungrammatically in denture-clicking hodgepodge French with a finger in the face of Clemençeau reborn: "General, you cannot obstruct the war!"

De Gaulle was the soul of composure. It was he who had been obstructed, he said. French Africa supported him, and he should not have been excluded from the November landings. As de Gaulle described the scene, Churchill attacked him flamboyantly, to ingratiate himself to FDR, but Roosevelt paid no attention and kindly made a last request. Would de Gaulle agree to be photographed with him, the prime minister, and General Giraud? De Gaulle was quick to agree, for Giraud was a "great soldier." Before he could think again, Murphy and Macmillan all but shoved him and Giraud out the door and onto the veranda.

• • •

In perfect weather, three dozen uniformed war correspondents had been standing on the lawn before a microphone and two white-leather dining room chairs when Elliott brought out two more. Captain Louise Anderson, the only woman there, was sitting at a table with her stenotype machine. Helmeted sentries with fixed bayonets paced the purple-and-scarlet-flowered trellises. Generals and admirals were spotted around the rim. A British correspondent felt "a very noticeable amount of goodwill." Fighter planes circled overhead. Scanning the crowd through a window, Hopkins spotted Sammy Schulman and mentioned it to the president, who asked him to put a thought in Sammy's ear.

Moments later, Roosevelt, Churchill, de Gaulle, and Giraud electrified the crowd. Hopkins wondered whether de Gaulle or the press were more surprised when the four of them walked out "or rather the three of them because the President was carried to his chair." Hopkins had a word with Sammy as Roosevelt waved the newsmen closer and gave them the dubious privilege of sitting on the damp grass. Churchill was in game day form with a dove gray homburg and a big cigar. On his left lapel was a V for victory pin and the American Distinguished Service Order bar that Pershing had awarded him in 1918. "The citation says it's for gallantry in the presence of the enemy," Churchill told a reporter, "but they jumped that bit in my case." As if to keep the peace, Roosevelt sat between de Gaulle and Giraud, neither of whom knew where to look, certainly not at each other. "Don't you want a hat," Churchill asked the president? Confident, tanned, and relaxed, Roosevelt said, "I was born without a hat." No one knew better than he how to swim in a sea of cameras.

As a dozen flashbulbs popped, Sammy Schulman called out, as if it were his idea, "Oh, Mr. President, can we have a picture of the two generals shaking hands?" The president put his fingers under the two French arms on either side of him and urged them up. With no alternative but a scene, the generals stood and touched hands as far from each other as the laws of physics allowed and sat down in record time. Sammy cried out, "I didn't get it, Mr. President," so they stood up and did it again,

barely close to smiles as Roosevelt and Churchill beamed. Ten days of
high-level toil had produced less than a minute of faux *esprit de corps* but
Roosevelt had his dash of *drame*. "This is an historic moment," he said,
for the benefit of any reporters who needed guidance. He shouted "bon
voyage" to the French as they withdrew, having played their parts on the
stage. Macmillan and Murphy trailed behind them, the *New York Times*
correspondent Drew Middleton later wrote, "exactly as nursemaids follow wandering children."

It is hard to believe that anyone was fooled—a British correspondent
found it "all rather embarrassing, like the first rehearsal of an amateur
play"—but the photos and celebratory captions ran in all the papers. De
Gaulle had it right: All four performers smiled, the scripted moves were
staged, and the scene was played as FDR directed. When he spoke to
the Washington press off the record a few weeks later he was downright
brazen: "If you run into a copy of the picture, look at the expression on
de Gaulle's face!"

Roosevelt had typewritten notes in his lap and followed them closely
for the cross-legged scribes on his lawn. Middleton thought him at his
best, "the quick mind, the resonant voice, the impatient gestures. His
warmth and vitality filled the little garden." He had the empathetic presence of mind, or someone on his staff did, to begin his remarks to the
press with regrets for their colleague's loss to a Spanish antiaircraft gun
on his way to Casablanca. A historic conference had been called, he said,
to plan the next phase of the war, sustain the United Nations' initiative,
pool their resources, and deploy them across the globe. The Combined
Chiefs of Staff had lived and worked together for ten days, befriending
their opposite numbers, and the scope of their work was "unprecedented
in history." The only specifics he mentioned were support for Russia and
China, and then only broadly. A report had been sent to Mr. Stalin, he
said, whose absence he regretted and explained.

And then came the headline news, but for the conference itself and
the brief French farce. No spur-of-the-moment whim, it was in the president's notes. Purporting to speak for himself and the prime minister, he

announced that world peace required the total elimination of "Jap and German war power"—cleaned up in the official transcript as "German, Japanese, and Italian war power"—and the unconditional surrender of Germany, Italy, and Japan. This did not mean the destruction of their populations. It did mean the end of their conquests and subjugations of other nations. The president suggested a headline: This had been "the Unconditional Surrender meeting."

Churchill's head had snapped around at "unconditional surrender." The *policy* was no surprise to him, of course, having toasted it the night before after seeking and obtaining his War Cabinet's approval of it. But its declaration had been excised from the first draft of the public communiqué, and Churchill had not expected Roosevelt to announce it, surely not without discussing it with him. FDR said little more, having said quite enough, and left the microphone to the prime minister.

In a letter to Clementine dictated earlier that day, Churchill, once a war correspondent himself, had not looked forward to this event "to which all the journalists in North Africa have been bidden. They are in an exceedingly bad temper and have been doing their best to work up political sensations out of the squalid tangles of French North African politics." But he added a marginal note after the fact: "We charmed them all right." And so they did. Roosevelt had followed a script, but Churchill spoke impromptu with all the wit and color expected of him. Ambushed by unconditional surrender, he embraced it before he could gather his thoughts: "I agree with everything that the President has said." He could hardly do otherwise.

"This agreeable spot" had been the scene of the most intense, important, thorough, successful war conference he had ever seen. Anfa had become "the active center of the war." He wished the other leaders of the United Nations could have come. "Free conversation is one of the sinews of war." But some were leading the fight on their own soil and "geography is a stubborn thing." One thing he could confidently say. Nothing in this war would ever come between him and the president.

He sympathized with the war correspondents' lot and asked them to remember that not everything can be organized "when you throw yourself ashore," press arrangements included, and "a trial is imposed upon you," but he asked them to rise to the occasion and not let censorship and other "minor annoyances" darken their reporting. For Churchill, objective wartime journalism was an oxymoron. The press should be a cheerleading team. "To keep your sense of proportion," he said, "is a patriotic duty." He hoped they had "a good and encouraging" story to tell "our people" about their military leaders' unity, thoroughness, and integrity. "Give them that picture and make them feel that there is some reason behind all that is being done."

The president had organized the North African invasion, Churchill said, giving him too much credit, and had changed the course of the war with Churchill "his active, ardent lieutenant." (After reading that line in the Allied press, Goebbels wrote that "no such humiliation has probably been seen in British history," but the epic failure of German intelligence to detect the ten-day stay within Luftwaffe range of Roosevelt, Churchill, and their high command caused true humiliation in Berlin.) Hitler had called them idiots and drunkards, Churchill said, a laugh line guaranteed, and now "he has been hoodwinked, fooled, and out-maneuvered by the great enterprise which was launched on these shores." As for Rommel, "the fugitive of Egypt and Libya," the British Eighth Army had chased him fifteen hundred miles, and he was "still flying before them. But I can give you this assurance—everywhere that Mary went the lamb is sure to go."

Having absorbed FDR's unforeseen rejection of any thought of a negotiated peace, Churchill closed in Churchillian style. The United Nations' unconquerable will to persevere must be sustained "until we have procured the unconditional surrender of the criminal forces who plunged the world into storm and ruin."

With that he deferred to FDR, who praised some military stars and left others out, the price of naming names. Roosevelt did the best he could with Giraud and de Gaulle. But for the shotgun handshake, the unsettled French rift could only be ignored, and he could not have ignored it more deftly. He and the prime minister had felt that "here we were in French North Africa," a good place and time for a Frenchman-to-Frenchman talk. De Gaulle and Giraud's discussions had stressed "one common purpose," the liberation of France. "They are at work on that. They are in accord on that." There was reason now to hope that France's fighting men would participate in her deliverance, and no more than that should be said at this time.

Folksy touches followed. He had visited American troops "up the line," the president said, and "lunched with them in the field, and it was a darn good lunch." He wished the people back home could see how well they were armed and their excellent health and spirits. "I want to say to their families, through you people, that I am mighty proud of them."

He wished to say a word about the brave men they had fought in North Africa. The moment the fighting stopped, the French army, navy, and local population had given "wholehearted assistance in carrying out the common objective that brings us to these parts." This he identified not as winning the war but improving people's lives. For the past two years, much of French North Africa's wealth had gone to the German army. "That time is ended, and we are going to do all we can for the population." He had given "one very delightful party" for the sultan and his son, and "We got on extremely well." The sultan was committed to his people's welfare and he, like them, gave the Allies his full support.

Roosevelt closed after Churchill whispered in his ear. "Oh yes," he said. He and the prime minister would like to shake the correspondents' hands and get to know them. The reporters and photographers filed past them and gave them their names and hands. The president intoned "Glad to know you!" "Glad to know you!" Churchill gave every man a manly stare as he grasped his hand. "What's your paper, eh?"

As the correspondents milled about, Hopkins chatted with some he knew, and no doubt gave Sammy Schulman an extra squeeze of his hand. Harry's friends assured him that Roosevelt's and Churchill's appearance had been a surprise. Captain Anderson told her diary they "both greeted me very cordially. We're practically buddies by now." Someone snapped her picture with her stenotype under her arm and Churchill at her side. Delight was on her face, the hint of a smile on his.

As Roosevelt and Churchill met the press on the back lawn Patton brought General Noguès through the front door with Vice Admiral François Michelier, who had come to pay their respects before the president left Morocco. Patton spotted Britain's minister to Algiers, who "hung around the door" until Captain McCrea "pushed him out." Roosevelt was making "very frank" remarks about de Gaulle when Churchill came in, lingered without good cause, started to leave, and thought better of it. Patton detected a "laughable" anxiety to leave FDR alone with the French, who spotted their British minders. "I hope A-1 did too." Before he left for Marrakech, Roosevelt was presented with a Moroccan leather portfolio of all his callers' autographs.

As the American planners gathered their papers, Colonel Smart recalled later, an officer came in and told them FDR had demanded unconditional surrender. "You could have heard a pin drop." Only later did the policy strike King as a mistake. Marshall was too busy to give it deep thought. Slessor thought it made no impact on the other Chiefs of Staff, none of whom had been consulted. Nor had Allied experts on psychological warfare or internal Axis affairs, nor the State Department, nor Stalin. Drew Middleton followed Roosevelt's suggestion in his lead paragraph in *The New York Times* and called the Casablanca Conference "the 'unconditional surrender' meeting," which matched the two-inch headline.

The Combined Chiefs of Staff and their senior officers dispersed across the globe to London, Washington, Algiers, Malta, Persia, India, and China. General Eaker and Captain Parton made a bomber flight to Marrakech for a few days' rest and returned to England with a bomb bay full of oranges, "judiciously distributed." Some of the staff stayed at Anfa to close up shop. Three days passed before *Bulolo* steamed for home, escorted by two destroyers. After working hours, Louise Anderson told her diary, British and American officers threw parties at some of the best villas, "so it was still impossible to get any sleep."

De Gaulle wrote three sentences and submitted them to Giraud as their joint communiqué. They had met, they had talked, they had agreed that the fight for the liberation of France and the enemy's defeat was the goal of "all Frenchmen," united with their allies toward that end. Giraud's sole revision struck a blow against democracy. He crossed out a commitment to the triumph of "democratic principles" and substituted "human liberties." A British Foreign Office official gave credit where it was due. "That something was saved from the wreck must be attributed in large measure to the helpful attitude of Mr. Harry Hopkins, who throughout maintained a scrupulously fair attitude which showed the fullest comprehension of the Prime Minister's difficulties." De Gaulle's staff put his name ahead of Giraud's on the joint communiqué. Giraud said, "Let him have this little pleasure." Mack asked Giraud how he felt about it all. Nothing more could be expected from a first meeting, he said. It was "necessary to proceed by degrees and pursue the tactics of the parrot climbing the sides of his cage."

Seventeen

MARRAKECH

Roosevelt, Churchill, and their inner circles made a five-hour motorcade run down to Marrakech on a straight desert road, passing caravans on the way. Brooke and Jacob flew ahead of them in Churchill's Liberator with his staff. Churchill had the president to himself in FDR's bulletproof sedan and they talked a lot of shop, led and followed by machine-gun-mounted half-tracks and self-propelled artillery. American troops and armored cars were posted every 150 yards, antiaircraft guns at intervals. Spotter planes searched for the Luftwaffe. Ian Jacob observed that "the Americans don't believe in half measures." The convoy stopped at three for baskets of sandwiches, boiled eggs, and mincemeat tarts, a British operation involving Scotch.

If Casablanca was a modern city and Anfa a luxurious playground, Marrakech was a red-walled tale from the Arabian Nights, an exotic mix of Arab and Berber culture, ancient mosques, multicolored stucco homes, fragrant citrus groves and honeysuckle. Its Sinners' Concourse had hosted assorted sins since the Middle Ages. Vivian Dykes had loved Marrakech when Marshall's party passed through on the way to Casablanca: "I wanted to wear a turban and those big oriental trousers. I felt like an *Esquire* cartoon." Brooke found the scenery "astonishing," the

medieval town in the foreground, snowcapped pink and purple mountains in the distance, stunning flowers everywhere. To FDR "Marrakech
seemed far from wars and rumors of war."

As Marshall's party had, the statesmen and their intimates shared Kenneth Pendar's extravagant home. The Taylor Villa it was called, named
for the rich American whose widow leased it to the State Department, an
"amazing" house in FDR's description, an "extraordinary" mansion of magnificent "Moorish design" and "exquisite details" in Harriman's, "a fairyland
villa" in Churchill's. Two interior courtyard gardens with pools of colored
fish delighted the PM. Harriman thought they "might have been lifted
bodily from a Maxfield Parrish painting." Navy Chief Petty Officer Arthur
Prettyman, the president's Black valet, slept on a couch in the library as he
had at the Villa Dar es Saada. Corporal Hopkins roomed with his father. It
is doubtful that anyone roomed with Randolph. Brooke and Jacob and a
junior officer got by in the famously luxurious La Mamounia Hotel.

Churchill insisted on leading Roosevelt up the sixty winding stairs
of the Taylor Villa's stone-built tower for its dazzling sunset view. There
was only one way up for FDR, who called for "my horses" with a laugh.
With his arms around their necks, two Secret Service men linked hands
and lifted him. He teased them all the way up, perhaps ill at ease with his
underscored disability as Churchill belted out a spontaneous ditty: "Oh
there ain't no war, there ain't no war, there ain't no war today." Roosevelt
was seated in a wicker chair on the low-walled open platform at the top
and the great men sat in silence in an iridescent world of changing colors.
As the evening chill set in Churchill called for the president's blue Navy
cloak and draped it around his shoulders.

Later they sipped tea on the veranda with their host. "Well, Pendar,"
Churchill said, "I must say your soldiers get the beauty prize." He had
never seen "such a magnificent lot of men" as the troops who lined the
road from Anfa. Roosevelt was taken to his room and Churchill walked
the gardens with Dr. Wilson. "I love these Americans," he said. "They
have behaved so generously."

Harriman, Randolph, McCrea, and the Hopkinses toured the huge

Marrakech bazaar, "a big fair" Harry called it. Harriman called it extraordinary, a fantastic array of magicians, Berber dancers, Arab storytellers, flute players charming cobras from baskets, local acrobats on winter break from the Ringling Bros. and Barnum & Bailey Circus. On the way to the bazaar and back, Hopkins, the former social worker in a New York City slum, was shocked by a depth of poverty he had never seen.

Marrakech was "a lovely change" for Brooke, relaxing after ten grueling days and nights: "It did me the world of good, as I felt a sort of flat feeling as a reaction after the strain." He spent the afternoon in the hotel's gorgeous garden with desert oasis birds distinct from the seaside tribes just half a day's drive away, intrigued by European breeds with Moroccan variations, charmed by the blue-gray head of a finch whose crest should be reddish brown. Jacob thought Brooke had managed the conference well. "He certainly put his back into it and was exhausted by the finish." For better or worse—and no one could really know which—he had changed the course of the war and saved countless lives at the cost of countless others. Had it not been for the birds, he wrote, "and the company they provided, I could almost have sobbed with the loneliness."

Kenneth Pendar was a charming young man of delicate voice and manner, polished at Saint Paul's School and Harvard, an expert on Byzantine art, an intelligence agent more than a diplomat. His guests enjoyed his company, but surely not as much as he enjoyed theirs. Having flown up to Casablanca several times to discuss the French with Murphy, he delighted in hosting great men "when the top hats are off and the photographers have gone home, and statesmen sit around the dinner table." Just before dinner he found Roosevelt alone in the salon, reclining on a sofa, drenched in Moroccan luxury. The president held out his wrist: "I am the Pasha. You may kiss my hand."

Churchill enjoyed "a very jolly dinner" in his zip-up rompers and black-velvet slippers monogrammed in gold. American soldiers hastily trained as waiters relieved the French staff, serving lobster and filet mignon. For dessert came a three-foot nougat replica of Marrakech's twelfth-century tower, candlelit from within. Churchill turned to FDR: "How on earth does one attack a thing like that?" Easy, Roosevelt said, lopping off its top with his knife and tipping it onto his plate.

"We all sang songs," the prime minister later recalled, "and the President joined in the choruses." Harriman preserved a fragment of a Churchill solo: "There's nothing to do but die; nothing to eat but food, etc." Churchill was at his best, Roosevelt showing signs of fatigue. Dr. Wilson was touched by the "affectionate little speeches" they made to each other. Harriman watched the PM crane his neck in search of a private talk with FDR but the seating, "to Churchill's great annoyance, made a tête-a-tête impossible." Harriman could see that "Roosevelt rather liked the idea," perhaps out of patience with Churchill's lobbying. "It never bothered him much when other people were unhappy."

Pendar was impressed by Roosevelt's newborn knowledge of Morocco. They talked about promoting its independence, improving its people's lives, and weaning them off what FDR called "Koran teaching." The French barely educated them, Pendar said. Roosevelt said every Moroccan child should have a compulsory education. Pendar explained why a local New Deal would take generations, if then, to penetrate the culture, though Moroccans "are realistic and materialistic and go away from the Koran," accepting medicine for their children from missionaries. Churchill "interjected a pessimistic and realistic note occasionally," Harriman wrote. "He doesn't like the new ideas but accepts them as inevitable."

Pendar told the president that news of his talk with the sultan had flashed down to Marrakech overnight, thrilling the Moroccans with a new experience, a powerful foreign leader respecting their country and its people. FDR voiced admiration for the sultan, the French, and their marvelous civilization, and concern for their future. There was talk of rebuilding their army, not only to fight, but also to restore their self-respect and France's status as a cornerstone of the Atlantic democracy. Pendar asked Churchill for his thoughts about de Gaulle. "Oh, let's don't speak of him," Churchill said. "We call him Jeanne d'Arc and we're looking for some bishops to burn him."

Charming though Roosevelt was, Pendar found Churchill wittier, but FDR commanded the room, not only with the aura of the president of the United States but also with "his spiritual quality." When Hopkins teased them both about how little they had worked at Anfa, Churchill replied that Harry had missed his vocation. He should have been a general. Roosevelt seized the honor of proposing the first toast. "To the King," he said, and every man rose but he.

When the party moved into the salon, Churchill spoke with Harriman over too many hands of bezique, "in high dudgeon" over Roosevelt springing unconditional surrender on him. He made it clear "he did not like the manner of it. I had seen him unhappy with Roosevelt more than once, but this time he was more deeply offended than before. I also had the impression that he feared it might make the Germans fight all the harder." And yet he had not told the president on their ride down from Anfa or he would have told Harriman he had. He surely knew Averell would tell him. Churchill was not known for avoiding conflict, but conflict with FDR he did not need.

Roosevelt and Churchill might have gotten their homework done before dinner instead of after midnight, a ponderous meal, and self-indulgent beverages. Now they had to tackle the draft reports to Stalin and Chiang and instruct the CCS on the war plan's execution, having sensed that their critique at yesterday's plenary session may not have stuck. Working through much of the night was recreation for Churchill but not for FDR, who disliked "Winston hours." Brooke had warned Kennedy about Churchill's midnight shift: "It is very hard to stick to important principles late at night." In the morning you wake up and ask yourself, "Now what *did* I do last night? Was I too weak?"

Pendar's salon, the diplomat wrote later, was "not meant for work." Two tables were pushed together, a lamp was stuck in the middle, and the aging leaders of the Western world toiled past three a.m. like negligent freshmen in the throes of exam week. Hopkins drafted, Harriman edited, Roosevelt and Churchill revised, and Churchill's secretaries Leslie Rowan and John Martin typed in the library. Their report to Stalin informed him that the choice of Sicily over a second front was good news for him. The Germans would be pressured, and arms shipped to Russia through the Persian Gulf would come faster. No one knew better than Churchill that Stalin would be furious, as he duly turned out to be. Limited as it was, Stalin's briefing was more informative than Chiang's, who had no need to know about Europe.

Roosevelt and Churchill's directive to the CCS "cordially approving" their report reminded them that their civilian superiors wanted four things "steadily pressed": (1) keep the Russian convoys going; (2) expand Chennault's air force in China; (3) invade Sicily in June, not July or August; and (4) be ready to cross the Channel by September if the Germans started folding.

No one was surprised that Churchill sipped his way through the exercise. Roosevelt's physician Admiral McIntire watched the two of them work, pleased "that our man seemed the fresher of the two at the finish, and that without stimulants." Churchill's valet did not distinguish himself. Jacob wrote that "Sawyers always has a dog's life on these journeys," jumping night and day to the PM's whims, but not that night. Hearing odd noises in the courtyard, Pendar went out for a look and discovered that Sawyers "had misjudged the strength of Moroccan wine but was still full of cockney dignity." When their work was done, Roosevelt and Churchill seemed relieved to have the conference behind them, a working vacation though it had been for them both. As a diplomatic obligation, they shared a closing drink. "Now Winston," the president said, "don't get up in the morning to see me off. I'll be wheeled into your room to kiss you goodbye." Churchill would not hear of it. He could get into his rompers in no time.

"Both men had a catching quality of optimism," Pendar thought, but Churchill seemed fixed on the now, Roosevelt on the yet to be. Helping when he could, Pendar had watched FDR work late into the night finding just the right words to keep Stalin mollified, China fighting Japan, and the Combined Chiefs of Staff fixed on his priorities at the lowest cost of lives. Sometimes he stopped and gazed into space with a look not quite sad but "of someone who comprehended sadness."

Eighteen

HOMEWARD BOUND

On his way back to the war Corporal Hopkins hitched a ride with Harriman on a Liberator flight to Algiers. His father diaried their poignant parting without an extra word: "Drove to the field with Robert and saw him fly off to the front again."

Roosevelt had been roused from a few hours' sleep to be driven to the airport when Harriman told him Churchill resented his unconditional surrender surprise. It did not upset him. Nothing much did. As the Secret Service lifted him into the car, Churchill came out in the predawn chill in his rompers, black-velvet monogrammed slippers, Chinese red, green, and gold silk dressing gown with dragons rampant, and RAF officer's hat, as nonchalant as a duke dressed for dinner. He asked for the privilege of seeing the president off, and Roosevelt said he would be honored. Churchill called for his stick and his morning cigar and got into the car with the president, Pendar, and others. Brooke had always thought the dragon gown alone "was worth going miles to see, and only Winston would have thought of wearing it," which he often did, presiding in bed over councils of war "rather like some Chinese mandarin."

American infantry encircled the airport in the mist and Roosevelt was wheeled up a ramp to the same Pan Am Clipper that had brought him. Churchill followed him in like a worried mother and saw him "comfortably settled down, greatly admiring his courage under all his physical disabilities and feeling very anxious about the hazards he had to undertake." Roosevelt grasped his hand and thanked him. "God bless you Mr. President," Churchill said. "Safe home. I trust we shall meet sometime this summer."

Leaving the plane in what Pendar called "this very original costume," Churchill spotted Roosevelt's Navy photographer and menaced him with his stick. As Captain McCrea recalled, the PM "let out a roar. It was really a roar." "Don't you dare, young man! You with that camera—don't you dare!" McCrea waved the petty officer away and FDR "had a good laugh about it." Churchill had recovered his poise when a gaggle of photographers approached: "You simply cannot do this to me." They let him drop the hat and the cigar and smile as the flashbulbs popped.

Churchill took a last stroll on the tarmac with Hopkins, pleased about the conference and confident of victory, but reminding Harry of hard times to come, as if to stiffen his resolve. When he got back in the car, he put a hand on Pendar's arm. "Don't tell me when they take off. It makes me far too nervous. If anything happened to that man, I couldn't stand it. He is the truest friend. He has the farthest vision. He is the greatest man I have ever known."

They rode back in silence until Churchill spoke, having ruminated about American public opinion. "Pendar, don't you think your countrymen will be thrilled when they hear that their president has flown here with the courage of an eagle" and seen his troops "in the theatre of battle?" Pendar had to agree, but we Americans, he said, are "an unpredictable people." As they approached the Taylor Villa, a French officer in Pendar's social circle rode by on horseback in civilian dress. Churchill all but spat at him. "Look at that little yellow Frenchman. Why isn't he fighting?" Pendar defended his friend but the PM lost interest when two Arabs passed by on one mule. He flashed them his famous two-fingered V, mischievous as a teenager, buoyed by their thrill and his celebrity.

At breakfast with Dr. Wilson, who often attacked his smoking,

Churchill tossed his head and rolled a big Havana in his mouth. "There is one nice thing, Sir Charles, about getting up early in the morning. You can get in an extra cigar."

Churchill summoned Brooke just as he and Jacob were leaving for the mountains. Pendar showed them in. Minutes later "a terrific commotion" arose from Churchill's lavish room. He was "storming around the blue-green-and-silver bed like a furious cherub," Eden and Attlee having vetoed his flight to Turkey yet again. He had read the offending telegram as he lay in the magnificent bed, "looking at the Atlas Mountains, over which I longed to leap in the 'Commando' airplane which awaited me so patient and contented on the airfield." He fired back a reply: The War Cabinet's objections had convinced neither him nor the president, who had authorized him to urge the Turks to receive him "as soon as your decision has been made," as if it had not been made twice already.

Brooke had often seen Churchill holding court in bed but nothing like his performance in Mrs. Taylor's fantastic room, tiled from floor to ceiling in Moroccan mosaics, the head of the fabulous bed in a softly lit Moorish alcove, its powder blue silk bedspread trimmed in six inches of lace. "And there in the bed was Winston" in his Chinese dressing gown, smoking a big cigar, what was left of his hair standing up in religious light. "It was all I could do to remain serious." Brooke would have given anything to take "a colored photograph."

Churchill told him they were flying out at six p.m. Mourning his brief vacation, Brooke said he was under the impression that the prime minister had been longing to paint Marrakech for years. Surely he could not do it justice by then. Churchill simply said he was leaving at six and dropped the plural pronoun. "All right," Brooke said, "if we are off at six p.m. where are we going?" He had not decided, Churchill said. He was waiting for the War Cabinet's wishes. Tomorrow he would either be in the House of Commons or in Cairo on his way to the Turks, reducing Brooke's holiday to a matter of hours after ten days of constant pressure. He had just enough time to glance at the birds in the foothills.

As Brooke and his friends left the Taylor Villa, grimmer than when they arrived, Churchill shouted across the house to his valet: "Sawyers, my painting things! Please put them out on the tower!" A talented painter who called his amateur art "a joyride in a paint box," he worked on the view from Mrs. Taylor's minaret "in towering good spirits," produced his only painting of the war, and had it sent to Roosevelt.

Later that afternoon, Attlee and Eden gave up and blessed Churchill's trip to Egypt and Turkey, which inspired a message to them both as he flew with Brooke to sunny Cairo instead of gloomy Parliament: "We are just off over the Atlas Mountains, which are gleaming with their sunlit snows. You can imagine how much I wish I were going to be with you tomorrow on the Bench, but duty calls."

De Gaulle rejected an American Liberator for his flight back to London, insisting that "American pilots had no idea of navigation, and he had no desire to land in France." He asked the British to fly him to Libya where some of his troops were fighting and was denied. He was sure that they invented excuses, which they probably did. After he reached Gibraltar, briefly tailed by two Luftwaffe fighters, Kennedy dined with him there and found him depressed. He said he could not combine with Giraud, who was tainted by Vichy. It would be hard to form a postwar government and he feared a civil war. The Germans had just shot 250 "subversives" in Marseilles, 180 men and 70 women.

Patton gave dinner to Marshall and three other officers lingering at Anfa and wrote to a friend back home: "You will probably have read in the papers and seen on the movie screen that for the last ten days we have been very busy entertaining the leading lights of the world. It was very amusing but was not war. Personally, I wish I could get out and kill someone."

Pug Ismay wrote a note to "my dear Ike" in gratitude for "the princely hospitality of Anfa Camp." A formal letter expressing the British delegation's thanks was on its way, to be shared with "all the good fellows on your staff who have been so helpful to us," but "like all formal letters, it is impersonal and somewhat pompous and I am therefore adding this private line to assure you that we mean every word of it."

• • •

After one of two Lancaster bombers returning several British officers and Harriman to England weighed in a bit heavy before takeoff, two suitcases chosen at random were moved to the other plane with their owners, Brigadier Generals Guy Stewart, Brooke's director of plans, and Vivian Dykes, who had not been home to his wife and children for thirteen months. The bomber carrying Harriman and Ismay had just landed at an RAF airfield when the second was attacked by a Junkers 88 that seemed to come out of nowhere. The Lancaster lost an engine and part of a wing and cartwheeled into the runway, killing Dykes and Stewart and another officer.

Stewart was deeply mourned, and FDR awarded Dykes America's Distinguished Service Medal for his work in Washington, the first British officer so honored. "We have had some bad knocks in the last three and a half years," Ismay wrote, "but it is no exaggeration to say that no single event has cast such gloom over this office as Vivian's death. I miss him all the time, and I shall always miss him. . . . He was a grand man in a tight place—never flustered, always courageous, absolutely dependable."

Roosevelt had begun his trek to Washington with an eight-hour flight from Marrakech to Bathurst, where his return to the USS *Memphis* felt like coming home. Arrangements had been made for a tour of the Gambia River on HMS *Aimwell*, a Michigan-built Lend-Lease tug, and Roosevelt invited Lord Swinton, resident minister of British West Africa. As they steamed partway up the river and back, FDR gave his lordship an earful on the Gambians' shameful condition.

Roosevelt flew on to Liberia, one of Africa's few independent countries, founded in 1822 as a refuge for freed American slaves and free-born Black people escaping bigotry, a vital Allied source of wartime rubber defended by the United States in return for bases. FDR had insisted on the trip to dignify Liberia, which received American economic aid, a model, he thought, for liberated colonies of the future. Roosevelt hosted lunch at the U.S. Army officers' club for President Edwin Barclay and joined him in reviewing 450 American Black troops. Captain McCrea admired the terrific regimental band's rendition of the national anthem. "They certainly put swing into it," Roosevelt said, "but I think I'm a purist when it comes to 'The Star-Spangled Banner.'" Most of them were veterans of Cab Calloway's Harlem band.

Next came a tour of the Firestone rubber plantation and what the presidential log called a "picturesque African village" whose residents came out "in various forms of dress and undress." As shameless as any colonial grandee, Firestone paid them eighteen cents a day and extracted two dollars a year for the privilege of their mud-built, straw-roofed huts. All their needs were filled, the log implied. Thinly clothed in a hot climate, they had shelter provided by their employer and picked their food in the jungle. "The white man's conception of laziness therefore abounds."

Flown back to Bathurst, Roosevelt stopped his car to watch Gambian troops march to their barracks in song. The log recorded the "wild, primitive strain" of their voices, "straight from primeval hearts, for these black men had not long known the ways of the white man." The British encouraged their false belief that if the Allies won the war they could emigrate to America. Remarkably enough, FDR left behind on the *Memphis* his copy of the minutes of the closing plenary conference, marked "U.S. Secret British Most Secret." A steward turned it over to the captain, who sent it to McCrea unread.

After crossing the Atlantic to Brazil, FDR dined with its president, who led his country into the war before the week was out. Roosevelt's party flew on to Trinidad and picked up Admiral Leahy, recovered from bronchitis. The president celebrated his sixty-first birthday in flight and touched down off Miami having flown a route of more than 14,000 miles, start to finish, most of it over hazardous land or water, some of it in reach of the enemy. His hollow-eyed party reached Washington in four inches of snow after a twenty-four-hour train ride.

On the following day Roosevelt briefed Vice President Henry Wallace, Speaker of the House Sam Rayburn, the Senate Foreign Affairs

Committee, and other congressional leaders at the White House. On the day after that he reviewed it all again with Marshall, King, and Leahy. It was fortunate for the British and de Gaulle that Leahy had been in Trinidad instead of Casablanca. He was flatly against a Mediterranean campaign and surmised that little had been achieved at Anfa but the British Pacific sign-off and small progress uniting Giraud, "who was fighting in North Africa, and de Gaulle, who was talking in England."

Brooke and Alexander helped Churchill explain to Turkey's president, Ismet Inönü, why he should slap the Wehrmacht in the face, which he took under advisement, and informed him of "the great concentration of forces we have decided to make in the Central Mediterranean." Turks having fought Italians for centuries, Churchill told them the Allies meant "to destroy Italy, shatter her entirely; beat her out of the war."

Churchill and Brooke stopped in captured Tripoli on their way home and were moved by the victorious 51st (Highland) Division on parade. They had seen the desert-browned Scots six months earlier, Brooke wrote, "raw pink and white," before they took 2,000 casualties driving Rommel from El Alamein. Moved by their warlike pride and "the wild music of the pipes," Brooke felt like a winner for the first time in the war. "It was only after having stared utter perdition in the face that one could sense the fathomless depth of relief, caused by a realization that victory had now become a practical proposition. I felt no shame that tears should have betrayed my feelings, only a deep relief." Churchill cried too.

Back in London, Churchill told the House of Commons "there has never been, in all of the inter-allied conferences I have known, anything like the prolonged professional examination of the whole scene of the world war" as the Casablanca Conference, whose "dominating aim" was to hit the enemy "on the largest possible scale and at the earliest possible moment" and make him "burn and bleed." Great Britain and the United States had been peaceful countries. Now they were "warrior nations," heavily armed, "with an increasingly clear view of their salvation."

Among many other blows, he said, the Americans would bomb the Germans by day while the RAF hit them at night. Together they would hammer them "round-the-clock, and the devils will get no rest." Raising his eyes to the gallery, Churchill gave Ira Eaker a look that thanked his muse.

AFTERMATH

S oon after he returned from Morocco, FDR spoke off the record to the American Society of Newspaper Editors. "You can't leave things to the military," he said, "otherwise nothing gets done. Now that's a dreadful thing to say," but when generals and admirals hammer out a strategy "they spend a month or two" at it. On the other hand, "if you get certain laymen to stick pins into them all the time—prod them, if you like—and say you have got to have an answer to this, that and the other thing within so many days you get an answer." After November's North African landings, he and Churchill had asked the generals and admirals for new plans. In January, they said it would be months before they had any. "So we decided that we would have them meet. I am afraid we met so that we could stick the pins in."

Prodded from Tokyo and Berlin more painfully than from London and Washington, the Combined Chiefs of Staff brought clashing national interests to the Anfa Hotel, deep strategic differences, aggressive personalities, and cultural and personal resentments. Naturally enough, debates turned into battles and threatened to divide them. Hitler was counting on it. They had known going in that they had to find a plan. Bristling with pins they did.

It is sometimes said that the Russians won the war in Europe and the Anglo-Americans helped, but neither could have won without the other, and Anfa's war plan set the Allies on a winning course. Some have called the results of the Casablanca Conference a tentative outline for 1943, but the American historian Rick Atkinson has called it "part of the American coming of age, a hinge on which world history would swing for the next half century," diverting "nothing less than the future of civilization." The course the Allies set at Anfa wobbled on the way to victory but never lost its fix on true north—a British-conceived Mediterranean campaign to knock Italy out of the war, drain German strength from Russia and Northwest Europe, and enable the American push to invade France, and relentless American pressure on Japan. As Portal reminded King, specific long-range plans are impossible in war, but in six ensuing conferences, the Allies kept their Anfa plan on the beam, wrestling like brothers all the way.

TRIDENT

After the British outclassed the Americans at Anfa "we got organized," General Handy later recalled, "and got so we could kind of hold a candle to them." Determined never again to let the mother country roll them, they set up and staffed at the brand-new Pentagon a planning system based on London's and the radical innovation of Army-Navy cooperation. Marshall reminded his peers in April 1943 how the British had embarrassed them in January. The next time they would "be together and ahead of them."

They hosted a two-week conference in Washington in May code-named Trident, focused on what would come after Husky, preceded by a sharp intramural dissection of every Mediterranean target the British might suggest, not only for what it might cost and contribute but also for its impact on Roundup. Far from weakening their defenses in France, the Germans had strengthened them after Torch, and some U.S. Army planners and Eisenhower himself were starting to believe that another

Mediterranean strike might predestine a stronger invasion of France, as Brooke had been preaching like a brassbound Calvinist minister. Marshall remained a doubter with an open mind.

A hundred Britons crossed the Atlantic on the *Queen Mary* and met their match in a formidable team of Americans united on their home court. They gathered in the magnificent Directors Room at the Federal Reserve Building on Constitution Avenue with at least twenty staff officers backing both sets of chiefs as Roosevelt, Hopkins, and Churchill huddled in the White House. Eisenhower's tail was no longer between his legs and four stars were on his shoulders when the news arrived on day two that General Arnim and some 250,000 Axis troops had surrendered in Tunisia. North Africa was secure, six months after Torch instead of the predicted two weeks.

Rommel had attacked the Americans through the Kasserine Pass in February and driven them fifty miles back, but Allied armor and infantry and Tedder's combined air forces had recovered their ground in days. It took three more months for Patton, Montgomery, Anderson, Tedder, the French, a New Zealand corps, and Cunningham's fleet to break the enemy's Tunisian defenses and force Rommel back to Berlin, another painful lesson on fortified German strength. From start to finish over 350,000 Axis troops had been captured or killed in Tunisia, fulfilling Churchill's prophecy that the Allies would have more in the bag after the enemy came to them instead of the other way around. Combined with his casualties in Russia, Hitler had lost nearly half a million men and a staggering toll of planes and heavy weapons since the CCS flew to Casablanca four months earlier.

As the Trident Conference convened, Roosevelt backed Marshall's full push for Roundup, out of patience with British stalling. Hopkins thought it safe at last to leave him alone with Churchill. Backed by fast growing military-industrial strength, the Americans spoke with one voice, demanded an invasion of northwest France in the spring of 1944, and resisted a British plan to invade the toe of Italy after Sicily, followed by a push into the Balkans. Consensus seemed out of reach as it had at

Anfa until Marshall cleared the conference room of everyone but the CCS and angrily promised again to go full speed against Japan unless the Channel got top priority.

The compromise they hatched looked far more American than British. A May 1, 1944, target date was set to invade France with twenty-nine divisions, three to five more a month to follow. Roundup was now "a first charge" on Allied resources, preceded by a bomber offensive laid out in "the Eaker Plan." Four American and three British divisions would be shipped from the Mediterranean to the U.K. by November 1, 1943. Air superiority over northwest France would be achieved by April 1944. In lieu of a commitment to invade Italy, the British agreed that Eisenhower's Anglo-American staff would plan and the CCS would judge the most efficient Mediterranean operations that could force Italy's surrender. Coming close to Churchill's demand at Anfa to launch Husky in June, Ike confirmed a July 10, 1943, date. Marshall refused to send aircraft from the Pacific to the Mediterranean, where any further buildup would be limited. The Japanese would not be held but attacked. Building on Anfa's generalities, the CCS approved a step-by-step offensive.

The only clear-cut British victory was a pullback from Anfa's expectations of a major assault on Burma in the fall, the Brits having made their case that Operation Anakim would drain too much power. A heavier airlift across the Hump to China would take precedence over opening the Burma Road.

SUMMER OF 1943

Sicily was attacked on July 9 with nearly equal numbers of American and British Commonwealth troops and a French contingent. Patton, Alexander, and Montgomery led the fighting on the ground, Tedder in the air, Cunningham at sea, all under Eisenhower's command. Two weeks into Husky, Mussolini was deposed. The fighting took four more weeks.

U-boats had done such damage in the Atlantic in February and March that the very existence of convoys, transatlantic troopships, and a continental invasion were at risk. In the last days of March, following the priority set at Anfa, Liberators based in Iceland and Newfoundland and Royal Navy ships with improved detection gear had begun to turn the tables with pilots and crews trained as teams. As commander in chief of Coastal Command, Slessor sent bombers over the Bay of Biscay in June with deadly results. Not a single ship was lost to a U-boat in June or July. Though the U-boat fleet was never eliminated, it was crippled and the Battle of the Atlantic won.

In 1943 and beyond the Allies produced many thousands of new and improved warplanes, and the Combined Bomber Offensive authorized at Anfa and refined at Trident devasted Axis warpower in Europe, pulled Luftwaffe fighters from Russia, and inflicted unsustainable losses. Much of German industry and the better part of Berlin, Hamburg, Dresden, Nuremburg, Würzburg, and other German cities were destroyed, leaving countless civilian men, women, and children in the hundreds of thousands shattered, crushed, or burned to death.

QUADRANT

Three months after Trident, the Quadrant Conference convened in August 1943 at Quebec's Frontenac Hotel. Family tensions ran high, and the British came by sea, reminiscent of lanterns and Paul Revere. After meeting with FDR, Churchill gave Brooke the personally crushing news that Marshall would command the invasion of France, now called Overlord, another sign of American ascendancy. Within minutes Brooke endured "a most painful meeting" of the CCS. The Mediterranean suction pump had caused U.S. Army planners grave doubts about whether Overlord could or should be launched in mid-1944 if at all, echoed by Savvy Cooke, but Marshall stood fast for the Channel. With FDR's support, he denied a British plea to be released from their pledge to move seven divisions from the Mediterranean to the U.K., refused to trim the plan for invading France to support an Italian campaign, and threatened yet again to turn his back on Europe. Brooke blasted him in his diary, also yet again, for a maddening incapacity to grasp British strategy as opposed to rejecting it, which for Brooke was the same thing. Even Dill found Marshall "unmanageable and irreconcilable" and threatening to resign.

On the edge of boiling over, the CCS again went off the record and cleared the staff, an incredible sixty-odd officers. Brooke told his British and American peers that "the root of the matter" was a lack of trust. The Americans mistrusted the British intent to cross the Channel and the British were inflamed by recurring American demands, regardless of changed conditions, to execute plans that the British had endorsed. "Lawyers' agreements" Brooke called them in his diary and perhaps at the table. It was not a term of endearment. "I then had to go over our whole Mediterranean strategy" again, he wrote, to prove Overlord's dependence on it. Husky's mission was accomplished on the following day when Patton took Messina on August 17, two miles from the toe of Italy. That alone, it has been said, made Italy choose itself as the next target.

A second room-clearing argument came on August 19, "another poisonous day" for Brooke, which began with Churchill shaking a fist in his face over a senseless idea and ended with a Brooke-Marshall rematch that exhausted them both and led to another compromise produced by Dill as marriage counselor. Within the Mediterranean force limits set at Trident, Southern Italy would be attacked in Operation Avalanche. Overlord was confirmed as "the primary US-British ground and air effort against the Axis in Europe" and its May 1, 1944, target date stood. Coinciding with Overlord, landings in the South of France, Operation Anvil, would draw Germans from the main event and take Toulon and Marseilles as ports of resupply and reinforcement. Plans would be drawn to defeat Japan within a year of Germany's fall, but Rabaul would be neutralized instead of taken, a step back from Anfa's expectations.

With the room still free of staff, Mountbatten staged a Pykrete demonstration against Brooke's better judgment. A block of ice was set beside a block of Pykrete and Mountbatten pulled a pistol from his pocket, inducing the rest of the high command to rise and move behind him. The first bullet shattered the ice. The second bounced off the Pykrete, barely missed Portal, and clipped a leg of King's pants. To the best of the British marine Sir Leslie Hollis's memory, Brooke and "I both emerged from under the table at the same moment." A British messenger in the hall ran into an office assigned to Hollis and breathlessly told his secretary, "The Chiefs have started shooting each other!"

AUTUMN OF 1943

Italy's post-Mussolini government surrendered on September 3 and Germans poured in. When Clark's mixed American and British Fifth Army landed at Salerno six days later the Germans had fourteen divisions in Italy and threw in nine more by the end of October, drawn equally from Russia and Northwest Europe as if on Brooke's command. In the interim, a fierce German counterattack nearly pushed the Allies back into the sea only days after they landed, lending still more weight to the hypothesis that Roundup would have failed in 1943.

Later in September Churchill asked Roosevelt to send Marshall to meet him in Tunis and was denied, another sign of expanding American dominion. Admiral Pound resigned as First Sea Lord after suffering a stroke, replaced by Cunningham, and died in October of a brain tumor, which unbeknownst to him and his British and American friends had caused his recurring somnolence. His loss was deeply mourned.

After Stalin agreed to meet Roosevelt and Churchill in November, Churchill wired FDR almost pleading to meet separately first, for their current plans, he said, were grossly defective. Again he questioned Overlord and talked up the Mediterranean, again he tried to renege on his agreement to send seven Mediterranean-based divisions to England by November 1, and again he was held to a lawyers' agreement.

SEXTANT

On their way to meet Stalin in Tehran, Roosevelt, his Chiefs of Staff, and Secretary of War Stimson met the British and Chiang Kai-shek for a preliminary match in Cairo code-named Sextant. With them came Eisenhower, the American China Burma India Theater commanders Generals "Vinegar Joe" Stilwell and Claire Chennault, nearly a hundred other American officers, thirty warrant officers and enlisted men, and uncounted diplomats, political staff, and support personnel, enough to catch whatever the Brits might throw.

Brooke dreaded another conference. "The stink of the last one is not yet out of my nostrils." Had the Americans let the Allies take Crete and Rhodes, he told his diary, they could have had the Balkans "ablaze by now" and might have won the war in 1943. Brooke was still choking on shipping those seven divisions to England from the Mediterranean to prepare for a "nebulous" second front, but every Mediterranean goal set at Anfa, Washington, and Quebec had been met. Sicily had been taken, the Med had been reopened, Southern Italy's strategic airfields had been captured, and forty-five German divisions had been drawn from France and Russia to the Mediterranean and the Balkans. But the British had started to fade. Having overtaken them in military-industrial production, troops, ships, planes, and nearly every other measure of power, the Americans brought lopsided strength to the battlefield and the bargaining table.

Apart from near contempt for Chiang Kai-shek and his Chinese army, the British brought five goals to Cairo—to drive further up the Italian boot, boost supplies to Balkan partisans, help them expel the Germans, pull Turkey into the war, and postpone Overlord. They achieved the first two only. Roosevelt and Churchill, never well cast as the second lead, had begun to draw apart as the Yanks took the reins. At FDR's direction, they went to Cairo determined to dominate the Brits, veto a Balkan invasion, and refuse to let Overlord slip, and this they proceeded to do. On their first day together, Churchill had a good talk with Roosevelt, then nothing much ran smooth. One session ran white-hot. King and Brooke traded insults, Stilwell told his diary, and King "almost climbed over the table at Brooke. God he was mad. I wish he had socked him."

Chiang had nothing to say about defeating Germany, of course, and according to Brooke "uncommonly little" about defeating Japan. Chinese generals met with the CCS twice. According to Brooke, he welcomed them politely and could not get them to speak. According to Stilwell, he insulted and cross-examined them and barely *let* them speak, prompting Stilwell to come to their hot defense and suggest a British "inability or unwillingness to fight." When Marshall called for a major assault on Burma with British, Indian, and Chinese forces, Brooke implied an American intent to fight to the last of anyone else's men.

More suspicious of Churchill's ambitions than Stalin's, Roosevelt stalled at Cairo, anticipating the Big Three's meeting in Tehran. Hopkins warned Dr. Wilson, "You will find us lining up with the Russians." Roosevelt told Churchill he had 400 years of "acquisitive instinct" in his blood, which left him unable to see why any country would not take another's land when it could: "A new period has opened in the world's history, and you will have to adjust yourself to it."

Brooke and Marshall closed the Cairo meetings with what Brooke called "the father and mother of a row," which produced another settlement inspired by what might be called the Dill Rule: If Brooke and Marshall could not settle things, Churchill and Roosevelt would. The Americans agreed that the British Mediterranean command would be free from Eisenhower's control, now confined to Overlord; the British positions on the Mediterranean would be a basis for future discussion (a tepid concession); and Overlord's May 1, 1944, date would be open to adjustment for cause. The Americans refused to postpone an attack on islands south of Burma.

TEHRAN

Both delegations flew from Cairo to Tehran for a conference called Eureka, where the British found the Americans and the Russians as closely aligned as if they had planned it. Overlord was all that mattered, Stalin said, Italy a diversion. Nothing should be wasted on secondary operations or flirtations with the Turks, who would not join the war. The

Anglo-Saxons argued in the Red Czar's presence, making Brooke feel less like negotiating than "entering a lunatic asylum or a nursing home." Churchill's interpreter thought Stalin "seemed puzzled at the open display of disunity between the Americans and the British." And then he smiled.

It was Marshall's considered opinion that Stalin was "a rough SOB who made his way by murder and everything else and should be talked to that way," but Roosevelt was in charge. Having never met Stalin, he meant to charm him from suspicion into friendship, which had worked for him in politics since 1910, not least with Churchill. Getting nowhere aligning with Stalin on military strategy, FDR tried sarcastic jabs at Churchill's very Englishness. Stalin cracked a grin at the first tease then let himself go with belly laughs, surprised and thrilled by the capitalist rift. He laughed again and shook Roosevelt's hand when the president took a chance and called him Uncle Joe. The cozying up to Stalin at Churchill's expense rocked the prime minister.

Roosevelt rocked him again with anticolonialism. Soon after Casablanca, FDR had told Eden to expect no advance commitments from him to return British colonies seized from Japan and approved a State Department plan for United Nations trusteeships to aid and protect colonized peoples not yet prepared for statehood while their colonizers helped the others to self-government and independence. Eden balked at independence. Roosevelt pressed the point again at Cairo and Tehran, advanced it with Stalin out of Churchill's presence, advised him not to discuss India with the prime minister, and laid the groundwork for a postwar anticolonial front with Stalin and Chiang against France and Britain. Citing horrors seen in Bathurst, FDR told the Washington press he had made it clear to Churchill that "we will let all the world know" if London refused to "toe the mark" and free its colonies. "Well, the Prime Minister doesn't like that idea."

The Tehran conferees' report called Overlord and Anvil—the twin invasions of France from two directions—"the supreme operations for 1944," to be carried out in May with no impediments allowed. Stalin promised a Russian offensive once Overlord was under way, to keep the Germans from moving forces from Russia to France, a striking role reversal, and pledged to declare war on Japan after Germany's defeat.

Roosevelt, Churchill, and the CCS returned to Cairo for three more days, debating whether to use landing craft to take those Burma-adjacent islands or assign them to a second Italian landing set for January at Anzio. Roosevelt supported Brooke over Marshall, yielded Burma's place to Italy, and told Marshall he could not rest easy without having him in Washington. To Marshall's disappointment Eisenhower would command Overlord, not he.

A third of the Luftwaffe was destroyed in the Mediterranean in 1943. By the end of that year the Germans had moved another twenty divisions into Yugoslavia, Greece, and the Aegean, further draining their strength in Russia and Northwest Europe, further vindicating Churchill and Brooke.

ITALY AND FRANCE

On January 22, 1944, supported by Italian troops, Allied forces met light German resistance at Anzio but could not break out of the bridgehead and fought off brutal counterattacks for months as Clark pushed slowly north to their relief. As the British had foretold, Hitler pulled still more Germans from Russia and France. Fifteen percent of his army would be drawn into Italy in 1944, taking 536,000 casualties.

Churchill tried to postpone the invasion of France almost to the end. On April 19 he told his Foreign Office that Overlord "has been forced upon us by the Russians and the United States military authorities." On June 4, two days before the Normandy landings, Clark took Rome, which the Germans had declared an open city. Marshall wanted to end the Italian campaign and focus on "the great venture." The British wanted to fight their way to the Balkans and abandon Anvil. Roosevelt backed Marshall on France, but the fight for Italy went on.

Hitler had moved four more divisions from Northern Europe to Italy only weeks before D-Day. Just before the landings Churchill signed on as an observer on a British cruiser, stopped only by the pleas of his sovereign, whose secretary suggested that "His Majesty's anxieties would be increased if he heard his Prime Minister was at the bottom of the English Channel." Air superiority enabled the invasion. On June 6, 1944, a total of three Luftwaffe fighters attacked the beach. A few days later Churchill and Brooke observed a naval bombardment from a warship. Hoping to be shot at in return, Churchill was disappointed, Brooke wrote, when "the Boche refused to take any notice of the rounds we fired."

Decades later the American General Handy speculated that Roundup might have succeeded in 1943 but for Torch, Husky, and the invasion of Italy, overlooking his own experience on Omaha Beach: "It was God-awful . . . it was nip and tuck. . . . Afterwards you lose sight of how close it is if it's a success." It would not have been close before massive bombing day and night, the depletion of the Luftwaffe, the opening of the Mediterranean, the clearing of the Atlantic, and huge German losses in Russia, North Africa, Sicily, and Italy made nip and tuck a possibility. Throughout the war, usually outnumbered, the Germans outfought the Allies, man for man, almost every time, attacking or defending, in control of the air or not, whether winning or losing the battle.

The Americans soon had more divisions in the field than the British. As the predominantly American invasion of the Continent pushed on with Patton racing Montgomery to the Rhine, the balance of Allied power shifted still more to Washington from London and never went back. When the ratio of troops reached three to one, his secretary wrote, Churchill knew "his role was now to counsel rather than control."

Renamed Dragoon, Anvil fell on the French Riviera on August 15. Nearly 80,000 American troops and a French contingent captured Toulon and Marseilles, liberated southern France, and took 100,000 German prisoners, all of which heightened French morale but had little effect on the battles to the north.

QUEBEC AGAIN

With the end in sight the Americans met the British in Quebec again in September 1944 for the Octagon Conference with a cast of 125. Churchill told Roosevelt he now led the earth's strongest power and observed by way of balance that if Britain had not held on in 1940–41 and Hitler had seized the French and British fleets "nothing would have saved this continent." Roosevelt was inclined to agree. They were cordial again as FDR grew prematurely frail at sixty-two under the weight of his wartime burdens. Victory over Germany and Japan now seemed a matter of when and how. In his opening remarks, Churchill said the British Empire had reached its peak, while American power and influence were "ever-increasing."

Churchill offered in plenary session to explicitly commit the Royal Navy, post-Hitler, to fight beside King's in the Pacific, which King no longer wanted, having no further need to share its victory. When he sidestepped the offer Roosevelt accepted it, to King's displeasure. The irony deepened the next day when King offered the British a minor role. As Arnold described it "All Hell broke loose!" King called the mighty Royal Navy a liability, implied that Churchill was in no position to command the CCS, and "nearly had words" with *Marshall*. After the cooling down the British accepted a vaguely "balanced and self-supporting" Pacific role, meaning no support from King, which could not have startled them.

All the while the Americans had been taking ground from the Japanese, closing in on their home islands. The United States Army Air Forces had started bombing Japan and Japanese-occupied Manchuria from Chinese bases in the fall of 1943. By the spring of 1945 the Americans would fight their way to the Marianas, close enough to bomb Tokyo and other wood-and-paper Japanese cities and factories from island bases. Bombing, blockade, and lost ships and battles had all but destroyed Japan's means to resist defeat, except by a suicidal defense against a hand-to-hand invasion of Japan, when Hiroshima and Nagasaki were obliterated in August of 1945. Her surrender came too soon after Germany's for Britannia to rule her waves. A British carrier task force took part in the final rounds.

SIR JOHN DILL

Brooke pressed Churchill repeatedly to arrange a peerage for Dill, which he agreed to do and never did. For his crucial role in keeping the Anglo-Americans united Brooke called Dill the single most valuable officer of the war. "I shall never be able to forgive Winston for his attitude towards Dill."

On November 4, 1944, Dill died in Washington at sixty-two of aplastic anemia. In his last illness, King had traveled miles, almost every evening, to visit him at Walter Reed Hospital. Marshall read scripture at the funeral in the National Cathedral. Thousands of troops lined Wisconsin Avenue as the Union Jack–covered coffin rolled on a gun carriage to Arlington Cemetery. Dill was the first soldier buried there who was not an American. Marshall, King, and Arnold were honorary pallbearers. "I have never seen so many men so visibly shaken by sadness," a mourner wrote. "Marshall's face was truly stricken." Marshall wrote to Churchill in response to his faint praise of Dill. "To be very frank and personal, I doubt if you or your Cabinet associates fully realize the loss you have suffered."

YALTA

After Overlord's success, the Allied armies had pushed the Germans east across France, Belgium, and Holland as the Red Army pushed them west. In January 1945, less than twenty miles from the German border, the Wehrmacht lost the Battle of the Bulge in Belgium, Hitler's last throw of the dice. In February, the CCS met in Malta on their way to meet Stalin in the Crimea. With Dill in his grave they collided. Marshall laid into Brooke and Churchill for pressuring Eisenhower on how best to conquer

Germany and disparaged Montgomery in absentia. Brooke defended his protégé and disrespected Marshall's, also absent, refusing to endorse Ike's plan for the final push. Years later, Marshall called the session a "terrible" thing, but "we always came to a harmonious conclusion."

With Hitler sure to be broken soon, the Yalta Conference, code-named Argonaut, focused on the postwar world and just a few military points. Stalin pledged to join the war against Japan three months after Germany's defeat, a prescient calculation. Physically and mentally debilitated two months before his death, Roosevelt was again rude to Churchill and deferential to Stalin. Churchill leapt from his seat when their foreign ministers reported an agreement for trusteeships in liberated colonies. "While there is life in my body no transfer of British sovereignty will be permissible!" Assured that only prewar Japanese colonies were at stake he sat down.

Roosevelt soon told the Washington press that "Dear old Winston" would never shed his "mid-Victorian" views. "This is, of course, off the record." Roosevelt also declared that Stalin "will work for a world of democracy and peace" and offered Poland's exiled leader comfort: "Of one thing I am certain. Stalin is not an imperialist." Russian assurances of benign intent snookered Churchill too.

DE GAULLE AND GIRAUD

The French had made trouble all the way. Confident of his powers to charm and persuade, FDR had left Casablanca convinced that he had "managed" de Gaulle. In this he was mistaken. The bogus handshake at the Villa Dar es Saada had done Giraud no good and de Gaulle no harm. Murphy later called de Gaulle's defiance at Anfa an "unproclaimed victory."

After they returned to Algiers from the Casablanca Conference, Murphy handed Macmillan a copy of Giraud's ghostwritten memoranda giving him primacy in North Africa and everything else he wanted, which Roosevelt had blessed with a "*oui*" and an "*en principe*" and not a word to the British. In London, Macmillan wrote, "they naturally caused emotion and even anger." On his way back from Turkey, Churchill took Murphy in hand in Algiers, resulting in FDR's agreement to adjust his political commitments to Giraud, rendering harmless what could otherwise have been explosive. The British objected as well to massive arms shipments to the French at the expense of Allied needs. When the Americans cited Roosevelt's agreement with Giraud the British rightly said they were strangers to it. The CCS agreed at Trident to arm the French when resources allowed, behind British and American needs, perhaps with captured German weapons. The Americans eventually trained and equipped eleven French divisions, nineteen aircraft squadrons, and much of the French navy.

In a talk with the Algiers press a few days after leaving Anfa, Giraud could not have been more flattering to de Gaulle: "I don't want trouble. The only trouble I want is trouble for the Boche." Roosevelt wired Churchill soon thereafter: "I take it that your bride and my bridegroom have not yet started throwing the crockery. I trust the marriage will be consummated." No wedding gifts were broken, but nor were there conjugal relations.

In June 1943 de Gaulle signed an agreement with Giraud, brokered by Macmillan, that nearly matched what he had rejected at Anfa, a joint chairmanship of a Committee of National Liberation. Giraud's joy was brief. A few days later he signed papers he did not understand and may not have read that gave de Gaulle supremacy. A French civilian advising Giraud had warned Murphy and Macmillan, "When the general looks at you with those eyes of a porcelain cat, he comprehends nothing!" De Gaulle soon relieved him of his military command. In a series of humiliations, Murphy wrote, "courageous old General Giraud was deprived of one honor and position after another." By D-Day he was isolated in an Algerian country house and out of the army altogether. As the Germans were driven from Tunisia, they had seized Giraud's daughter and grandchildren and shipped them to a concentration camp where his daughter died. Three months after the invasion a deranged Arab sentry shot him in the neck and miraculously failed to kill him. He died in Dijon in 1949.

In November 1944 de Gaulle rode with Churchill in an open car through the Arc de Triomphe and a sea of Parisians convulsed with liberation. Eden told a friend that they shouted Churchill's name as no British crowd had, and "not for one moment did Winston stop crying."

De Gaulle was elected president of France in 1958 and served until 1969, overlapping for two years with Macmillan as prime minister and Eisenhower as president. He infuriated them both and tormented their successors. It was Churchill's successors Attlee, Eden, and Macmillan who presided over the dissolution of the British Empire, which Churchill had sworn not to do, and France that fought losing wars to keep Algeria and Vietnam under French control.

UNCONDITIONAL SURRENDER

Roosevelt's demand for unconditional surrender has been questioned since he delivered it. As Churchill had foreseen, Goebbels squealed and tried to use it to incite last-ditch resistance, but the facts bear it out as a reasonable choice. A master politician, FDR had compelling reasons not only to declare it at Anfa but also to suggest it as a headline. Churchill and his War Cabinet, no fools or beginners they, had excellent cause to endorse it before and after it was announced.

First, the negotiated deal with Darlan leaving Nazi collaborationists in power in North Africa had only recently roiled the press, soured British, French, and American public opinion, eroded Allied unity, and may have left Stalin wondering what was next, a second front in Europe or a second deal with fascists. Unconditional surrender took deals off the table.

One of Roosevelt's principal speech writers put his second reason simply: "He wanted to ensure that when the war was won it would stay won." No "soft peace" would leave room for a fascist revival or limit military or political penalties imposed on the aggressors. In the same breath that demanded unconditional surrender and several times thereafter, FDR assured the German, Italian, and Japanese people that they had nothing to fear, and Churchill did the same. To announce the demand in advance showed confidence in the war plan and boosted Allied morale. The very idea of winning the war and leaving Nazis in power in Germany, fascists in control of Italy, or warlords leading Japan was absurd. Churchill had publicly called for Germany's utter defeat since 1940. "Negotiation with Hitler was impossible," he wrote later. "He was a maniac with supreme power to play his hand out to the end, which he did; and so did we." The resolve of Axis war criminals who expected the end of a rope or a cyanide capsule however they lost the war was not stiffened by the prospect of unconditional surrender.

Critics have argued that the policy may have deterred a German coup. In July of 1944 senior German officers guiltless of atrocity risked horrifying deaths in an attempt on Hitler's life, which cost them their own and many more. Unconditional surrender was not what frightened them.

Finally, the thought of ordinary Axis combatants fighting harder for fear of unconditional surrender more than death or mutilation in battle may be doubted, excepting many thousands of Japanese who preferred suicidal resistance at every stage of the war.

Roosevelt's declaration was attacked nonetheless, soon and long after he made it, particularly though not exclusively by predictable critics, the Germanophile General Wedemeyer included. Wedemeyer's memoirs say he told Marshall on their way to a photo shoot at Anfa that he hoped he had not offended the American Chiefs of Staff by condemning so strongly at their morning meeting any thought of demanding unconditional surrender, which would stiffen German resolve. As Wedemeyer had it, Marshall stopped him in his tracks and told him never to suppress his candid views. The trouble is, none of the minutes mention unconditional surrender, let alone Wedemeyer's opinion. Marshall, the American note-taker General Deane, and others recalled that it never came up. Perhaps no one remembered Wedemeyer's passionate speech. Conceivably it was purged from the minutes, Marshall's demand for candor notwithstanding. It is also conceivable that, consciously or otherwise, Wedemeyer wrote his memoirs while wracking his brain to record and report what his readers might think he ought to have thought.

WHAT IF?

Some historians think the war would have been shorter had different choices been made at Anfa. Given the endless variables, this is specula-tion at its height, and different minds, well informed or otherwise, have speculated differently. When asked long after the war what would have happened if Marshall had commanded the invasion of France, Brooke replied correctly: "That's a very difficult question to answer. There are so many ifs. . . . You get led on from one if to another, and I don't think one gets very far with them."

There is less speculation in the thought that the post-Anfa landings in Sicily and the precarious bridgeheads at Salerno and Anzio not only taught the Allies lessons but also suggest what the Germans would have done at Omaha Beach or elsewhere in France before the Allies learned them, built their strength, and eroded and diverted the enemy's. The British historian Lord Andrew Roberts is convinced for good cause that "A different quartet from Roosevelt, Churchill, Marshall and Brooke might have taken different decisions, but it is unlikely that any would have significantly shortened the Second World War."

The Americans, as Roberts says, were probably wrong to think Roundup could have succeeded in 1943 and right to demand Overlord in 1944, for the Germans could be "harried" from the Mediterranean but could only be "killed" by the loss of Berlin and the Ruhr. The Brit-ish, he goes on, were right about taking North Africa, Sicily, and Italy as far north as Naples and wrong to insist on fighting further up the boot through fortified mountain terrain against ferocious German resistance "with fewer returns than the great effort and loss of life strategically jus-tified, especially after the fall of Rome." Fixed on the Mediterranean, Churchill and Brooke overplayed a winning hand.

Naval specialists debate the wisdom of this or that move in the Pacific, but Japan lost the war at Midway if not at Pearl Harbor. The rest was a brutal slog that ended in Nagasaki. It will never be known if it could have been easier, but no less a critic of American strategy than Brooke told a BBC audience in 1958 that while the CCS were arguing about Europe, the United States Navy and Marines did "the most astonishing things" to defeat Japan. "Their march through the Pacific was really a marvel." Mountbatten oversaw vicious fighting in Burma in 1944 and its recapture in 1945.

None of it could have worked so well without remarkable Anglo-American cooperation, all the quarrels and suspicions notwithstanding. A few weeks before VE Day, May 8, 1945, Churchill congratulated Marshall on the "magnificent" performance of Eisenhower's armies and Marshall's historic achievement as the "organizer of victory." The American replied that their greatest success had been to achieve "the impossible, Allied military unity of action."

MOROCCO

Whatever might have happened had the Allies invaded France in 1943, Anfa once taken was held. Months after the conferees dispersed, Americans still occupied Anfa Hill. "The Ice Cream Front," they called it, manned by "the chair-borne infantry." The Anfa Hotel was demolished years later and replaced by luxury apartments. Roosevelt's Villa Dar es Saada remains in private hands. Casablanca's American consul general resides in Churchill's Villa Mirador.

After Roosevelt's North African journey was disclosed, the gilded Mrs. Taylor was furious to learn he had spent a night in Marrakech at her gorgeous Taylor Villa. She despised him as a traitor to his class, threatened to sue, and had to be convinced that a jury might not share her outrage over the commander in chief's overnight rest in her rented-out mansion on his perilous trip home from a war zone.

Sultan Mohammad V demanded Moroccan independence in 1947

with American support and threw in with militant nationalists. The French deposed and arrested him in 1953 and exiled him and his family. Permitted to return in 1955, he negotiated Morocco's independence with General Catroux, took the European title King of Morocco, endorsed its first congress, established trade unions, and died young at fifty-one in 1961. His thirty-one-year-old son, Patton's boyhood admirer, succeeded him as Hassan II, aligned Morocco with the United States, and helped write its constitution in 1962. He suspended it three years later in the face of riots fueled by popular discontent, suppressed human rights, consigned his opposition to jail or worse, and survived two violent coup attempts. He died in 1999, succeeded by his son Mohammed VI, Morocco's current king, a staunch Western ally.

ROOSEVELT AND CHURCHILL

Roosevelt died on April 12, 1945, less than three months after his fourth inauguration, eighteen days before Hitler's suicide. Churchill was moved to tears as if by "a physical blow." The president's push for decolonization survived him and bore fruit, but Churchill lost his bet on the Turks, who joined the war on fatally wounded Germany not long before it ended and never fired a shot.

After the Germans surrendered unconditionally, Churchill was driven to the House of Commons. "No engine power was necessary," his bodyguard Thompson wrote. "The car was literally forced along by the crowd." A Tory he remained, but he knew the war had changed things. Britain's upper-class boys had been brave, he said, but middle-class boys had saved it and earned "the right to rule it." This they proved less than two months after VE Day when the British people turned the Conservatives out and Churchill with them, succeeded by Clement Attlee, whom Churchill had called a sheep in sheep's clothing. At Churchill's first post-election meeting with his Chiefs of Staff, Brooke said next to nothing "for fear of breaking down" and admired how Churchill stood the blow. De Gaulle was not surprised by "this disgrace inflicted by the British

Nation upon the great man who had so gloriously led her to salvation," for the likes of Winston Churchill "had become inadequate in this era of mediocrity."

Still a ringing voice in world affairs, Churchill invoked in Fulton, Missouri, in 1946 a "special relationship" between the United States and the British Commonwealth and declared that the Soviet Union had dropped "an iron curtain" across Europe. He was eighty-one when the Conservatives returned to power in 1951 and restored him as prime minister. He mentored the young Queen Elizabeth and resigned in declining health in 1955, succeeded by Eden. In 1963 Congress made him the first honorary U.S. citizen in history at President John F. Kennedy's request. He died in 1965 at ninety, casting doubt on the risks of wine and cigars at breakfast. With his active consultation, the planning of his state funeral, Operation Hope Not, had begun a dozen years earlier. Britain's dockworkers had been among his ardent critics. As his body was borne up the Thames, the dockworkers lowered their cranes.

Nearly eighty years after Churchill painted a lovely view of Marrakech from the Taylor Villa's tower, the movie star Angelina Jolie sold it at auction, a gift from her ex-husband Brad Pitt, for $11,500,000.

MARSHALL

As President Harry Truman's secretary of state, Marshall presided over Europe's postwar recovery, overseeing what Truman insisted on calling the Marshall Plan, not the Truman Plan, for which Marshall earned a Nobel Peace Prize. In retirement he rejected a million-dollar offer in 1950s money for the rights to his memoirs, gave his papers to the George C. Marshall Research Foundation, and assigned it all the profits from his authorized biography. Slessor's memoir called Marshall "a great man, head and shoulders above any other American officer I have known, and there were not many in the British Service to hold a candle to him." When he walked into his country club's dining room, everyone stood up. He died in 1959 at seventy-eight.

BROOKE

Brooke carried on to victory as Chief of the Imperial General Staff and earned the ultimate rank of field marshal. At his initiative, Churchill arranged for Marshall, King, and Arnold to be honored by the king as Knights Grand Cross of the Order of the Bath on the Fourth of July 1945. At the behest of Attlee's government, the king made barons of Portal and Brooke, who chose the simple title Alanbrooke. Influential opinion pushed them up a notch to viscounts.

Churchill's memoirs gave Brooke scant praise, but when Brooke's abridged diary was published in 1957 Churchill was deeply hurt even with its sharpest barbs excised. Brooke sent a copy "to Winston from Brookie" with "unbounded admiration, profound respect, and deep affection," and several more lines of praise. Churchill wrote a thank you note that mentioned only in passing his restrained opinion of the wisdom of publishing diaries, but his secretary Jock Colville wrote that "Brooke was the only man on whom I ever saw him deliberately and ostentatiously turn his back."

Brooke retired in 1946 but could not educate his children on half-pay. He had hoped to be named governor general of Canada, but the post went to Alexander with his warm congratulations. Having saved his country's life at Dunkirk and played a crucial part in its victory, he sold his most valuable bird books, gave up his country house in Hampshire, and moved his family into the gardener's cottage, where he died a month short of eighty in 1963, a leader of the Royal Society for the Protection of Birds. Erected in 1993, half a century after the Casablanca Conference, his statue stands in Whitehall today.

After the war was won, Montgomery called Brooke the greatest soldier, sailor, or airman any country had produced on either side. The posthumous tribute of a leading member of Parliament and a veteran of the war might have pleased Brooke even more had he heard it: "Viscount Alanbrooke, I am quite sure, would prefer to be remembered as an ornithologist than as a soldier."

Acknowledgments

My first thanks must go to the men and women who planned and won the war, saved our civilization, and left it to us to elevate or squander. Next in line for gratitude are the diarists, note takers, letter and memo writers, masters of the minutes, journalists, photographers, memoirists, interviewers, historians, biographers, and archivists, amateur and professional, who made and preserved the record on which this book was built.

Bob Bender, its consummate editor, improved the book immeasurably with a perceptive eye, an incisive mind, a gentle hand, and the mastery of his art. Its copy editor, Fred Chase, sharpened it throughout. Phil Metcalf, associate director of copyediting, brought the book across the finish line. It was a pleasure to work with associate editor Johanna Li, a true professional. I cannot thank the entire Simon & Schuster team enough.

I am grateful to many archivists and librarians, including Catherine Williams at the Liddell Hart Centre for Military Archives at King's College in London; Jessica Collins, Katherine Thomson, and Chris Knowles at the Churchill Archives Centre, Churchill College, Cambridge; Geoffrey Henson of the Air Force Historical Research Agency, who found among its records General Eaker's memorandum "The Case for Daylight Bombing" and the minutes of the American Chiefs of Staff's separate meetings at Anfa; Michelle Kopfer at the Dwight D. Eisenhower Presidential Library & Museum; Justine Melone at the U.S. Army Heritage and Education Center, Carlisle, Pennsylvania; Michelle Krowl and Mike Klein at the Library of Congress; Patrick Fahey, Virginia Lewick, and

Christian Belena at the Franklin D. Roosevelt Presidential Library and Museum; Janice D. Jorgensen at the United States Naval Institute; and Mary Warnement, Carolle Morini, Carly Stevens, and Rebecca Giver Johnston at my fabulous second home, the Boston Athenaeum. The historical researcher Andrew Lewis's help in finding unpublished records at the Liddell Hart Centre and the National Archives in London was invaluable. Karen Needles discovered the book's previously unpublished cover photo and some of its forgotten illustrations at the American National Archives. Captain Louise Anderson Locke's stepdaughter Patricia Gardetto was the principal source of the previously unpublished material on the WAACs' dinner at the Villa Dar es Saada, which would not have been preserved without her.

I am indebted to the Trustees of Field Marshal Viscount Alanbrooke for permission to quote extensively from his diaries and postwar commentary on their contents. I know of no book about World War II that better captures the day to day pressures, burdens, and rewards of high command than *War Diaries, 1939–1945: Field Marshal Lord Alanbrooke*, which is referenced in the bibliography and highly recommended. I thank Benita Stoney, Alanbrooke's granddaughter, for helping me reach the Trustees, Allen Packwood, director of the Churchill Archives Centre, for permission to quote at length from Lieutenant General Ian Jacob's narrative of the Casablanca Conference, and James Parton III, Esq., for insights about his father, Captain James Parton.

Many thanks to Don Hawkins, mapmaker extraordinaire, who designed and created the book's maps of the European and Pacific theaters of the war and cheerfully put up with my nitpicks and revisions. Among the illustrations, David Richardson sharpened Anfa's site plan visually without making any other changes.

No thanks can sufficiently recognize Alice Martell of The Martell Agency, simply the best, most supportive, hardest-working literary agent in New York. Alice has made all of my published work possible from the start.

My son and daughter, Erin and Scott Conroy, and my daughter-in-law,

Jo Ling Kent, helped pick the book's title and encouraged the whole endeavor when I was not sure whether to pursue it. I again thank my parents for inspiring my love of history that began at age five or six. My father crossed the Channel on D-Day in an LST landing craft as a seventeen-year-old Navy medic, awed by the massive sea power that surrounded him, grateful that the waves of warplanes overhead were "all ours." I thank him for that too.

My precious wife, Lynn Fitzgerald Conroy, is the fulcrum of my life, without whom none of my books would have been written. Her patience and support for my two and a half years of continuous work on this one was nothing less than saintly. I do not know how to thank her for all that.

Abbreviations and Short Titles Used in the Notes and Bibliography

AFHRA	Air Force Historical Research Agency, Maxwell Air Force Base
AIR	The National Archives (British) designation of documents generated by the British government's Air Ministry
ANDERSON PAPERS	Papers of Louise Anderson Locke
BUTCHER'S DIARY	Papers of Harry C. Butcher, "Diary—Butcher (January 8, 1943–May 5, 1943) (1)" (Eisenhower Library)
CAB	The National Archives (British) designation of documents generated by the British government's Cabinet Office
CHAR	The Churchill Archives designation of some documents in its files
CHURCHILL ARCHIVES	Churchill Archives Centre, Churchill College, UK
DIXON'S CASABLANCA DIARY	FO 660/86, Pierson Dixon, "Anfa Camp, Casablanca Diary of Events de Gaulle–Giraud Negotiations"
DURNO	George E. Durno, "Flight to Africa: A Chronicle of the Casablanca Conference Between President Roosevelt and Prime Minister Churchill," FDRL, OF 200_2_U, "Casa Blanca Conference Jan 9–31, 1943; Durno's Chronicle."
EISENHOWER LIBRARY	Dwight D. Eisenhower Presidential Library and Museum, Abilene, KS

FDRL	Franklin D. Roosevelt Presidential Library and Museum, Hyde Park, NY
FO	The National Archives (British) designation of documents generated by the British government's Foreign Office
HANDY INTERVIEW	Interview with Thomas T. Handy for Dwight D. Eisenhower Library
HARRIMAN NOTES	Harriman papers, Box 163, "Chron File Jan 1–19 1943," notes transcription
HOUGHTON LIBRARY	Houghton Library, Harvard University, Cambridge, MA
IMPRESSIONS OF ANFA CONFERENCE	FO 660/88, Pierson Dixon, "Impressions of ANFA Conference: French Question"
JACB 1/20	Operation "Symbol," Brigadier E. I. C. Jacob, Churchill Archives, JACB 1/20
KENNEDY'S DIARY	Papers of General Sir John Noble Kennedy, Sections 4/24 and 4/25 (Liddell Hart Centre for Military Archives, King's College, London)
KING'S FLIGHT LOG BOOK	King papers, Box 34, "Flight Log Book 1942–43" (LOC)
LIBBY ORAL HISTORY	Oral History of Admiral Ruthven E. Libby (United States Naval Institute, Annapolis, MD)
LOC	Library of Congress, Washington, DC
LOG OF THE TRIP	"Log of the Trip of the President to the Casablanca Conference—9–31 January 1943" (FDRL)
MACK'S ACCOUNT	FO 660/85, Harold Mack to William Strang, 1/28/43, followed by Mack's account of negotiations with de Gaulle and Giraud at Anfa
PARTON, MEMOIR	"Lt. Gen. Ira C. Eaker, USAF (Ret.): An Aide's Memoir." *Aerospace Historian* 34, no. 4 (Winter/December 1987): 226–35.
PARTON'S DIARY	Papers of James Parton, diary (Houghton Library, Harvard)

PATTON'S DIARY

PORTAL ORAL HISTORY

SLESSOR MEMORANDUM

WEDEMEYER INTERVIEWS

The diary of General George S. Patton, Jr. (LOC)

"Reminiscences of Charles Frederick Algernon Portal" (Columbia University Oral History Research Office, New York, NY)

AIR 75/11, Slessor Memorandum, "Casablanca Conference: Conduct of the War in 1943," 18 January 1943

Albert C. Wedemeyer Papers, Interviews with General Albert C. Wedemeyer, U.S. Army Heritage and Education Center, Carlisle, Pa.

Notes

PRELUDE

1   *moonlit:* www.timeanddate.com.

1   *Brooke's Channel crossing:* Brooke, p. 3; Bryant, pp. 33–34.

1   *"Colonel Shrapnel":* Dykes, p. 13.

1   *last war's stars:* Fraser, pp. 59–81.

1   *"Fighting Brookes":* Bryant, p. 6; Fraser, pp. 36–39.

1   *"evening talk":* Brooke, p. 30.

1   *"awful futility"* . . . *"ghastly":* Brooke, p. 3.

2   *Brooke in France and Belgium through Dunkirk:* Fraser, pp. 131–71.

2   *Brooke's origins:* Brooke, p. xiv; Fraser, pp. 39–45.

2   *decay . . . "efficiency":* Brooke, pp. 4, 7, 10–16, 35, 62–63; Fraser, pp. 137–38.

2   *"dog's breakfast":* Montgomery, p. 54.

2   *Profile of Dill:* Brooke, p. 4; Danchev, "Field Marshal Sir John Dill," pp. 28–29, 37; Pogue, vol. 2, p. 143; Kennedy, p. 161; Colville, p. 182.

2   *Gort conference:* Brooke, pp. 8, 10–11, 16.

2   *subject of disaster:* Danchev, "Field Marshal Sir John Dill," pp. 34–35; Fraser, pp. 59–81.

3   *haunting feeling:* Brooke, p. 17.

3   *led a ceremony:* Brooke, p. 15.

3   *judgment of General Montgomery:* Brooke, pp. 18–19; Montgomery, pp. 55–56.

3   *birds . . . nature . . . "anemones":* Brooke, e.g., pp. 36, 52–54, 160; Fraser, p. 538.

3   *charming drawings . . . illustrated letters:* Fraser, pp. 41–46, 53, 85, 225.

3   *flipped their car:* Fraser, pp. 92–93.

3   *burst appendix . . . "fighting chance":* Brooke, pp. 56–59.

4 *after dawn on May 10:* Brooke, p. 59.

4 *moved north into Belgium . . . punched through . . . no word of him:* Brooke, pp. 59–64.

5 *Churchill and the French:* Churchill, *Finest Hour*, pp. 42–49; Wingate, pp. 1–7; Kersaudy, pp. 41–46.

5 *withdrawal . . . "dolls" . . . "blur" . . . "paradise":* Brooke, pp. 64–67.

6 *"fight on to the end" . . . "surviving inhabitants":* Finest Hour, pp. 56–57.

6 *colonel named Charles de Gaulle:* Kersaudy, p. 45.

6 *"Nothing but a miracle":* Brooke, p. 67.

6 *called the Germans the Boche:* e.g., Brooke, pp. 72, 90, 347.

6 *"wonderful soldiers":* Brooke, p. 68.

6 *Nervous breakdowns:* Brooke, pp. 64–69; Lord, p. 18.

7 *"like a long hairpin":* Bryant, p. 91.

7 *May 24–25 . . . plan . . . "windowpane":* Brooke, pp. 68–70; Bryant, pp. 96–118; Lord, pp. 22–24; Collier, p. 39.

7 *calm command . . . "wasps" . . . "silly":* Bryant, p. 102; Brooke, pp. 64–75. And see Brooke, p. 93.

7 *Atrocities:* Lord, p. 64; www.bbc.co.UK/wwtwo/dunkirk_audio.

8 *"greatest menace":* Danchev, " 'Dilly-Dally,' " p. 24.

8 *De Gaulle's counterattack:* Kersaudy, p. 42.

8 *Brooke began to lead . . . "shot that chap":* Brooke, pp. 70–72.

8 *Montgomery's movement:* Brooke, pp. 70–72; Montgomery, p. 57; Bryant, pp. 106–11; Lord, pp. 96–104.

9 *"in the balance" . . . "fight on":* Finest Hour, p. 100.

9 *Brooke on the beach:* Brooke, pp. 72–74; Montgomery, p. 58; Hamilton, *Monty*, pp. 383–84.

9 *Captain Albany Kennett Charlesworth:* www.chch.ox.acuk/fallen-alumni.

10 *safely evacuated:* Brooke, p. 63.

10 *Brooke comes home and is sent back:* Brooke, pp. 74–75; Finest Hour, p. 191–94.

10 *Charles de Gaulle:* Kersaudy, p. 51; *Finest Hour*, p. 159; Spears, vol. 2, p. 274; Wilson, p. 87.

11 *Churchill in France again:* Finest Hour, pp. 152–58.

11 *Energized by the thought:* See Ismay, p. 147.

11 *"You and I will be dead" . . . "final hypothesis":* Sherwood papers, Box 40, interview with Ismay, 7/11/46, pp. 1–2; Box 6, Ismay to Sherwood, 7/23/46.

12 *Brooke returns to France:* Brooke, pp. 79–82; Fraser, pp. 167–71.

13 *"shaking himself":* Kennedy, p. 208.

13   *second miracle:* Brooke, pp. 82–85; *Finest Hour*, pp. 192–94.

13   *on a wretched trawler:* Brooke, pp. 85–88.

14   *British loss of life and equipment and evacuation figures: Finest Hour*, pp. 141, 144–45; Lord, p. 274.

14   *defending southern England . . . "wracked with doubts":* Brooke, p. 93.

14   *lunch at Downing Street:* Brooke, p. 94.

14   *"true colors":* Brooke, p. 451.

ONE: SIBLING RIVALS

15   *Stark's memorandum:* Steven T. Ross, ed., *U.S. War Plans: 1938–1945* (Boulder, CO: Lynne Rienner Publishers, 2002), pp. 55–66.

16   *"swift, overwhelming blow" . . . "fall by the way": Finest Hour*, p. 495.

16   *Profile of Hopkins:* Adams, passim, p. 160 ("bright young man"); O'Sullivan, p. 16; Leahy, p. 138.

17   *Roosevelt had met Churchill:* Meacham, pp. 4–5.

17   *"no liberty" . . . "arsenal of democracy":* Roosevelt, *Public Papers*, vol. 12, p. 639.

17   *Hopkins in London:* Sherwood, pp. 234–62; Churchill, *Grand Alliance*, pp. 22–24; Lash, Joseph P. *Roosevelt and Churchill 1939–1941* (New York: W. W. Norton & Company, 1976), pp. 273–85; Meacham, pp. 83–97; Adams, pp. 200–212.

18   *"Never absent from British minds":* Matloff and Snell, *1941–1942*, p. 30.

19   *The ABC talks:* Matloff and Snell, *1941–1942*, pp. 33–48; Fraser, pp. 227–28.

19   *British and American strategy:* See Ehrman, Howard, *Grand Strategy*, Jones, passim.

20   Marshall's biographical sketch is drawn from Pogue, *Education*; Roll; Cray; and Katherine Marshall, p. 283.

21   *"ambition had set in":* Pogue, *Education*, p. 57.

21   *"gave everybody hell":* Roll, pp. 20–21; *Marshall Interviews*, p. 197.

22   *"magnificent body of men":* Roberts, pp. 9–10.

22   *"seldom smiling" eyes:* Pogue, *Education*, pp. 285–86.

23   *"Don't you think so, George?":* Pogue, *Education*, p. 323.

23   *Was that all right?:* Pogue, *Education*, p. 330.

23   *"Never got too friendly":* *Marshall Interviews*, p. 620.

24   *"practice of arms":* Pogue, *Education*, p. 347.

24   *"He could laugh . . . familiarity":* Wedemeyer, pp. 121–22.

24   *"in the machine":* Marshall, *The Papers*, vol. 2, p. 134.

24   *phoned the wives:* Handy Interview, pp. 169–70.

24   *No one bragged:* Wedemeyer Interviews, Section 4, pp. 13, 42.

25   *"outside himself":* Cray, p. 277.

25   *"magnificent looking":* Slessor, p. 362.

25   *"Episcopalian":* Roll, p. 5.

25   *"striking and communicated force":* Dean Acheson. *Present at the Creation: My Years in the State Department* (New York: W. W. Norton, 1969), p. 140.

25   King's biographical sketch is drawn from Buell, Whitehill and King, and Love.

25   *"shoot King":* *Eisenhower Diaries*, pp. 50–51.

26   *"one outstanding weakness":* McCrea, pp. 188–91.

26   *nothing was named:* Buell, pp. xix–xx.

26   *Brooks Brothers uniform:* Buell, pp. 10, 48.

26   *Dykes and Dykes on King:* Dykes, pp. 4, 81, 195–96.

26   *"always sore":* Roberts, p. 251.

26   *"time of day":* Roberts, p. 97, citing U.S. Army Heritage and Education Center, Carlisle, PA, General Paul Caraway Interview, Section 6, pp. 50–51.

26   *"born with the idea":* Whitehill papers, Box 69, unlabeled notebook.

27   *Mattie Egerton:* Buell, pp. 12, 28, 36–37.

27   *"under hatches":* Buell, pp. 21–25, 30, 36; Whitehill papers, Box 69, unlabeled notebook, pages headed "Black Marks."

27   *"too smart":* Buell, p. 31.

28   *"imperious disdain":* Buell, p. 87.

28   *cuckolded:* Love, p. 140; Buell, pp. 89, 302–8; Roberts, p. 98, quoting Sir William Jackson and Lord Bramall, *The Chiefs: The Story of the United Kingdom Chiefs of Staff* (London: Brassey's, 1992), p. 226.

28   *thesis:* King papers, Box 23, "Naval War College Thesis."

29   *"knew enough":* Buell, p. 105.

29   *"physical wreck":* Kennedy, p. 155.

29   *"lonely bay":* *Grand Alliance*, p. 427.

30   *"cherished friendship":* Meacham, p. 347.

30   *"expecting rabbits":* Danchev, *On Specialness*, p. 80.

30   *"British production":* *Grand Alliance*, p. 434.

30   *"soon to die":* *Grand Alliance*, p. 432.

31   *"stinkers":* Danchev, " 'Dilly-Dally,' " p. 37.

31   *"essence of straightforwardness":* Brooke, p. 192.

31   *Brooke's elevation to CIGS:* Brooke, pp. 199–201.

31   *"infected":* Kennedy, p. 181.

31 *"gobble"*: Patrick Howarth, *Intelligence Chief Extraordinary: The Life of the Ninth Duke of Portland* (London: Bodley Head, 1986), pp. 164–65, quoted in Roberts, p. 108.

31 *"flatly disagree"*: Brooke, p. xv.

32 *"No, no, sir"*: Bryant, p. 11.

32 *"I cannot hear"*: Leasor, pp. 168–69.

32 *"these Brookes"* . . . *"Dear Brookie"*: Fraser, pp. 202, 502.

32 *King soon described Dill:* King papers, Box 34, "Flight Log Book 1942–43" ("King's Flight Log Book"), p. 4.

32 *"tremendous problems"*: *Grand Alliance*, p. 626.

33 *"nothing but ruin"*: Churchill, *Hinge of Fate*, p. 324.

33 *"I wheeled him"*: *Grand Alliance*, p. 663.

33 *"Mr. President" and "Winston"*: Pendar, p. 153.

33 *hope of rescue:* Winston Churchill, *Winston S. Churchill: His Complete Speeches, 1897–1963* (London: Chelsea House, 1974).

34 *"knew their stuff"*: McCrea, p. 136; Buell, pp. 162–63.

34 *"on the beam"*: Buell, p. 172

34 *"Lord Root of the Matter"*: Leahy, p. 138.

34 *his team understood: The War Reports*, p. 157.

35 *"grow wearisome"* . . . *"dilatory"*: *Eisenhower Diaries*, pp. 40, 42.

35 *125,000 troops and 200,000 reservists:* Murphy, p. 110.

35 *In the end: Foreign Relations of the United States* ("*FRUS*"), pp. 210–17.

36 *"long history"*: Dykes, p. 69.

36 *the Navy "us" and the Army "them": Marshall Interviews*, p. 611.

36 *"Light relief"*: Dykes, p. 90.

36 *The British and American systems:* Matloff, *1943–1944*, pp. 6–7; Brooke, p. 247; Fraser, pp. 30, 206–8; Wedemeyer, pp. 179–81; Roberts, pp. 107–8; Buell, pp. 242, 267.

36 *"administratively impossible"*: Slessor, p. 400.

37 *"drug store strategists"*: Wedemeyer, p. 180.

37 *Cordell Hull: The Memoirs of Cordell Hull* (New York: Macmillan, 1948), vol. 2, p. 1111.

37 *"I was fortunate"*: Brooke, p. 247.

37 *"greatly liked"*: Kennedy, p. 161.

38 *"I had done nothing like it": Marshall Interviews*, p. 590.

38 *"freshman innocence": Marshall Interviews*, p. 608.

38 *"with a whole gang of people"*: Roberts, p. 71.

38 *"This country has not"*: Bryant, p. 234.

39 *Marshall's CCS design:* Roberts, p. 74; Buell, pp. 168–69.

39 *"show the President how to run the war"* . . . *"hell of a row":* Wilson, p. 21.

39 *"most complete unification":* The War Reports, p. 153.

39 *"might have lost it":* O'Sullivan, p. 1.

39 *"half-baked":* Brooke, p. 215.

40 *"no substitute":* Wilson, p. 21.

40 *"Trust me":* Hastings, p. 192.

40 *"tremendously favorable":* Matloff and Snell, *1941–1942*, p. 108.

40 *"stiff-necked":* Eisenhower Diaries, pp. 44–45, 47, 50.

40 *Marshall and Dill's friendship:* Marshall Interviews, pp. 622–23; Danchev, *Very Special Relationship*, passim; Danchev, "A Special Relationship," passim; Danchev, " 'Dilly-Dally,' " pp. 33–36; Danchev in Keegan, pp. 60–68; Dykes, p. 71; Fraser, p. 229, Wilson, p. 767; Franklin D. Roosevelt Presidential Library and Museum ("FDRL"), Map Room Papers, "FDR to Churchill, January–March 1943," Dill and Marshall exchanges, pp. 574, 576, 579.

41 *"Dumbiedykes":* Dykes, pp. 1–3; Leasor, p. 97; Roberts, p. 94.

41 *"non-white races":* Buell, Appendix V.

41 *On March 7, a telegram:* Roberts, pp. 122–23.

42 *unprecedented concentration:* Buell, pp. 178–79.

42 *"And that's the size":* Eisenhower Diaries, p. 51.

42 *"one or two pretty mean fights"* . . . *unwritten understanding:* Pogue, vol. 2, pp. 372–73.

TWO: THE ROAD TO CASABLANCA

43 *"the tremendous importance":* Matloff and Snell, *1941–1942*, p. 182.

43 *"cigarette holder gesture":* Pogue, *Ordeal*, p. 306.

43 *"dispersion debauch":* Stimson, pp. 416–17.

43 *broad-brush strategy:* J. M. A. Gwyer and J. R. M. Butler, *History of the Second World War*, vol. 3, *Grand Strategy: June 1941–August 1942* (London: Her Majesty's Stationery Office, 1964), Appendix III.

44 *"heart and <u>mind</u>":* Hinge of Fate, p. 314.

44 *"fundamental difficulty":* Kennedy's diary, quoted in Roberts, p. 132.

44 *Marshall's and Brooke's impressions of each other:* Brooke, pp. 246–49; Pogue, *Ordeal*, p. 308; Sherwood, p. 523.

45 *Profile of Wedemeyer:* Wedemeyer, pp. 10–12, 14, 31, 34–38, 53–55, 80, 370; Wedemeyer Interviews, Session 3, pp. 30–42; Session 4, pp. 1-11, 16; Session 5, pp. 6–11; Dykes, pp. 125, 205–7.

45 *"full fury":* The War Reports, p. 8.

46 *Hollis on the American plan:* Leasor, pp. 19, 14, 184, 188–89.

46 *"castles in the air":* Brooke, pp. 246, 249; Kennedy papers, Sections 4/2/4 and 4/2/5 ("Kennedy's Diary"), 12/20/42.

46 *"polite suggestions"...* "almost unimpeded": Wedemeyer, p. 105.

47 *"fighting the dead":* Roll, p. 249.

47 *"masterly document":* Hinge of Fate, p. 283.

48 *"misgivings":* Wedemeyer, p. 113.

48 *"further dispersions":* Pogue, *Ordeal,* p. 318.

48 *Ismay on crossing the Channel:* Ismay, p. 250; Wingate, pp. 1–45; Pogue, *Ordeal,* p. 310; *Marshall Interviews,* p. 621.

49 *"so many battles":* Fraser, p. 255.

49 *"faced now":* Leighton and Coakley, p. 383.

49 *"only right":* Dykes, p. 141.

49 *On May 28:* Matloff and Snell, *1941–1942,* p. 234.

49 *FDR promised Stalin's foreign minister:* Sainsbury, p. 52.

49 *Mountbatten:* Matloff and Snell, *1941–1942,* p. 235; Brooke, pp. xliv–xlv; Colville, p. 193; Wedemeyer, pp. 108, 136–39.

50 *"Tack Hammer":* Atkinson, p. 12.

50 *"time and energy":* Kennedy, p. 245.

50 *Marshall told FDR:* Matloff and Snell, *1941–1942,* pp. 235–36.

51 *anxious to a man:* Brooke, p. 267; *Marshall Interviews,* p. 590.

51 *"careful study":* Hinge of Fate, p. 433.

51 *"virtuoso":* Wedemeyer, p. 170.

51 *five times as many Germans:* Danchev, *On Specialness,* p. 32.

51 *a division averaged 15,000 men:* Wedemeyer, p. 66.

51 *no responsible:* Hinge of Fate, p. 434.

51 *CCS met...* "achieve nothing"... "explosion"... bagpipe band: The War Reports, p. 154; Wedemeyer, pp. 158–59; Brooke, p. 267; Dykes, pp. 158–59; Fraser, pp. 257–59.

52 *wrath...peevish...moved:* Brooke, p. 268.

52 *standing by...deepest thoughts:* Brooke, p. 269.

53 *"turning our backs"...indecisive:* Wedemeyer, pp. 158–59; Matloff and Snell, *1941–1942,* pp. 238–44; Dykes, p. 128; Brooke, pp. 272–73; Buell, pp. 215–17.

53 *"attractive personality":* Brooke, pp. 268.

53 *"ancestor Marlborough!":* Brooke, p. 273

53 *"explosive greetings"...* "strong enough": Colville, p. 134; *Eisenhower Diaries,* p. 70.

54   *"commanding idea" . . . "war baby"*: *Hinge of Fate*, p. 434.

54   *"decisively against Japan"*: Matloff and Snell, *1941–1942*, pp. 268–69.

54   *Marshall was bluffing*: Pogue, *Ordeal*, pp. 340–41.

54   *"My first impression"*: Buell, p. 208.

55   *"Defeat of Germany means the defeat of Japan"*: FDRL, Secretary's File, Box 3, "Hopkins, Harry," FDR to Marshall, King, and Hopkins, 7/15/42.

55   *"queer party"*: Brooke, p. 280.

55   *"pummeling each other"*: *Hinge of Fate*, pp. 439–40.

55   *"Sphinx"*: Brooke, p. 283.

55   *"defensive, encircling"*: Matloff and Snell, *1941–1942*, p. 280.

55   *"blackest day"*: Butcher, p. 24.

56   *"only thing" . . . "completely ready"*: *Marshall Interviews*, pp. 594, 622.

57   *"our top men"*: Wedemeyer, p. 165.

57   *lack of enthusiasm . . . recorder*: Wedemeyer, pp. 164–65.

57   *"too much to hope"*: Dykes, p. 198.

57   *"intelligible"*: Dykes, p. 206.

58   *"falling market"*: Dykes, p. 213.

58   *"the dictating power"*: Dykes, p. 208.

58   *"The defeated"*: Hastings, p. 55.

59   *"brand of soap"*: Hastings, p. 55.

59   "Moi, je suis la France!": Tedder, p. 129.

60   *"subject to the invader" . . . "judge freely"*: Funk, *De Gaulle*, p. 11.

60   *"Not at all"*: Jackson, *De Gaulle*, vol. 2, p. 17.

60   *"A great man?"*: Kersaudy, p. 138.

60   *"Tennessee denunciation"*: Stimson, p. 546.

60   *"almost in desperation"*: Murphy, pp. 115–17.

60   *Giraud's escapes*: Price, pp. 19–27, 40–53; Crawford, pp. 60–62; Brooke, p. 362; discussion with Hopkins in Wilson papers, unmarked page.

61   *"feelings of defeat"*: Murphy, p. 111.

61   *"the Great General Giraud"*: FDRL, Map Room Papers, "Casablanca Conference—27 Nov. 1942–14 Jan. 1943," untitled 19-page report, p. 15.

61   *"Contraband"*: Atkinson, p. 43; Funk, *de Gaulle*, p. 35.

62   *"suggestion" . . . "acceptable formula" . . . "as soon as possible"*: FDRL Map Room Papers, Box 165, "Casablanca Conference" folder, "Translation of Letters Sent by Mr. Murphy to General Giraud," November 2, 1942.

62   *how to bear it*: Brooke, p. 333.

62   *"the gallant French"*: *Patton Papers*, p. 102.

63   *"before Election Day"*: Roll, p. 257.

63 *Democratic National Committee:* Harriman, p. 172.

63 *"the incarnation":* Butcher's Diary, p. A-148.

64 *"reinforce failure":* Hastings, p. 279.

64 *Kingpin:* Dykes, p. 235.

64 *"no excuse": Hinge of Fate,* pp. 649–50.

65 *"solemn obligations . . . prima donnas":* Kimball, vol. 1, pp. 667–69.

65 *novice Tunisian campaign:* Atkinson, pp. 167–250; Clark, p. 139; Price, p. 216.

65 *"unfitted and unprepared" . . . "our Italians":* Atkinson, pp. 258–59.

65 *"workmanlike divisions": Marshall Interviews,* pp. 587, 619.

65 *"Since 1776" . . . "the Almighty":* W. S. Churchill, *Secret Session Speeches* (London: Cassell, 1946), pp. 76–96.

THREE: THE BIRTH OF THE CASABLANCA CONFERENCE

67 *"no time for exultation":* Roosevelt, *Public Papers,* p. 485.

68 *"indecision and divided":* Harriman, p. 176.

68 *"solemnly undertaken": Hinge of Fate,* pp. 650–51.

68 *sent Stalin a message:* FRUS, p. 489, n. 1.

68 *"measureless disaster": Hinge of Fate,* pp. 561–62.

68 *"glorious news":* FRUS, p. 493.

69 *Stalin's reply:* FRUS, pp. 493–94.

69 *his short-term ambitions:* Matloff and Snell, *1941–1942,* p. 363; Leighton and Coakley, p. 664.

69 *"no ringers":* Harriman, pp. 177–78; Harriman papers, Box 163, "Chron file Jan 1–19, 1943."

69 *"cookie-pushers":* Sherwood papers, Box 38, "Torch" folder.

70 *"if possible with Harry":* FRUS, p. 491.

70 *"mosquitoes":* FRUS, p. 491.

70 *"about twenty-five":* FRUS, p. 496.

70 *"typically British":* Harriman, pp. 177–78.

70 *"queer the pitch":* FRUS, pp. 495–96.

70 *"at the earliest possible moment": Hinge of Fate,* p. 665.

70 *One minute . . . move him:* Brooke, pp. 344–48; Matloff and Snell, *1941–1942,* pp. 377–78; Leighton and Coakley, p. 66.

71 *unable to frame:* Matloff and Snell, *1941–1942,* p. 378.

71 *preferred Sardinia . . . "easy prey":* JACB 1/20, pp. 67–72; Tedder, p. 391.

71 *"'sardines'" . . . "we did not promise":* Brooke, p. 346.

71 *"desperately trying":* Brooke, p. 345.

72 *"nice fellow":* Dykes, p. 90.

72 *McCrea and Mike Reilly:* McCrea, pp. 125–26; Reilly, pp. 136–38.

72 *"beaten up":* FRUS, p. 497.

72 *"plans satisfactory":* FRUS, pp. 496–97.

72 *On December 10:* Matloff and Snell, *1941–1942*, p. 363; Buell, p. 236.

73 *"an insight":* Brooke, pp. 347–48.

73 *Roosevelt cabled Churchill:* FRUS, pp. 498–500.

73 *That same day:* Leighton and Coakley, p. 662.

73 *On December 15:* Brooke, pp. 348–49; Kennedy, p. 277.

74 *"a crystallization" . . . "is defeated":* Kennedy's Diary, 1/1/43.

74 *"Life is not easy":* Kennedy, p. 278.

74 *a safe place to meet:* FRUS, p. 500.

74 *cab driver:* Reilly, pp. 139–41; McCrea, p. 130, tells a slightly different version.

75 *Baghdad to Siberia:* Sherwood, p. 668.

75 *"tsetse fly country":* McCrea, p. 129.

75 *Three events . . . "his surprise":* Kenneth Davis, p. 74; Brooke, p. 350; *Hinge of Fate*, pp. 643–44.

75 *one word . . . "Unfortunate":* McCrea, p. 127.

75 *"to my advantage":* De Gaulle, vol. 2, p. 78.

75 *Giraud . . . succeeded Darlan:* Funk, *de Gaulle*, pp. 41–42, 50, 57; Kersaudy, p. 231.

76 *Churchill endorsed:* *Hinge of Fate*, pp. 644–45.

76 *three potential paths:* Matloff and Snell, *1941–1942*, p. 365.

76 *De Gaulle's invitation to Giraud:* Funk, *de Gaulle*, pp. 61–62; de Gaulle, vol. 2, pp. 79, 82.

76 *Ian Jacob:* Richardson, passim.

76 *"Iron Pants":* Colville, pp. 166–67.

77 *"excellent accommodation":* JACB 1/20, p. 15.

77 *Patton had commandeered:* Murphy, p. 152.

77 *"no place in Casablanca was really safe":* Murphy, p. 165.

77 *thought it tasteless:* Codman, p. 75.

77 *"ostentatiously magnificent":* Patton Papers, p. 129.

77 *"understands French?":* Butcher, p. 239.

77 *"certainly is a magnificent looking man":* JACB 1/20, p. 16.

78 *Eisenhower's headquarters:* JACB 1/20, pp. 19–30.

78 *"honest, simple-minded chap":* JACB 1/20, pp. 104–5.

78 *"obviously still hankering":* JACB 1/20, p. 37.

78 *Casablanca bombed:* "Ack-Ack Fire at Casablanca," *Life* magazine, 3/15/43, pp. 33–36; Patton's Diary; Patton, *War*, pp. 27–28.

79 *Humphrey Bogart and Ingrid Bergman:* Sherwood, p. 665.

79 *"Does the Boss"... "delighted":* FRUS, p. 503; Harriman, p. 178.

79 *HMS* Bulolo ... *"exactly as if"*... *British herd:* FRUS, p. 501; Murphy, pp. 167–68; JACB 1/20, pp. 38–40.

79 *All told:* CAB 1/20/75, "Composition of British Delegation" and "Administrative Arrangements (2nd Revise).

80 *"full bag of clubs":* JACB 1/20, p. 39.

80 *leather folders ... binders:* Atkinson, p. 269; Cline, pp. 215–16.

80 *"aliases":* FRUS, pp. 504–5; Churchill and Churchill, *Speaking for Themselves*, p. 473.

80 *"Basic Strategic Plan for 1943":* FRUS, pp. 735–38.

80 *The British sent two papers:* FRUS, pp. 738–52.

81 *"The next thing was to convince":* Kennedy, p. 277.

81 *key word was "adamant":* Matloff and Snell, *1941–1942*, p. 378; Leighton and Coakley, p. 664.

81 *De Gaulle, Giraud, and Roosevelt:* De Gaulle, vol. 2, pp. 79–82; Murphy, p. 145; Funk, *de Gaulle*, p. 62.

81 *State of the Union:* McCrea, pp. 130–32; Harriman papers, Box 163, "Chron File Jan 1–19, 1943."

82 *FDR's meeting with the Joint Chiefs; unconditional surrender:* FRUS, pp. 505–14; Pogue, *Organizer*, pp. 32–33; Gilbert, p. 300, n. 1; Matloff and Snell, *1941–1942*, pp. 131–32.

82 *Churchill and his high command had been gearing up:* Brooke, pp. 341–46, 349–50, 356.

83 *over by four ... serenity:* Roosevelt Day by Day, 1/7/43, www.fdrlibrary.marist .edu; www.Artofthe print.com/artistpages/woolf_Samuel_johnson_franklin roosevelt.

83 *"Ask Wedemeyer":* Wedemeyer, p. 171.

83 *"difficult time":* Brooke, pp. 356–57.

FOUR: THE GATHERING OF THE TRIBES

84 *"wanted to make a trip":* Harry Hopkins, vol. 2, p. 667.

84 *"feels he must go":* Suckley, p. 194.

84 *private train:* FDR Day by Day, 1/9/43; McCrea, pp. 129–34; Sherwood, pp. 668–69; Suckley, p. 189; Harriman, pp. 180–81.

85 *Skymasters:* Arnold, *American Airpower*, vol. 1, p. 458; Ismay, p. 285; Dykes, p. 220; Pogue, *Organizer*, pp. 17–18, 613, n. 27.

85 *Marshall's guests Dill and Dykes:* FRUS, p. 721 n; Danchev, *Very Special*, p. 114.

85 *"blasted protocol"*: King's Flight Log Book, 1/9/43; Leonard Mosley, *Marshall, Hero for Our Times* (New York: Hearst Books, 1982), p. 227.

85 *"born that way"*: Whitehill papers, Box 69, unlabeled notebook, p. 9.

85 *"passenger list"* . . . *American base:* Arnold, *Global Mission*, pp. 389–91.

86 *Arnold's background:* Arnold, *Global Mission*, pp. 1–124.

86 *"commit suicide"*: Arnold, *Global Mission*, p. 4.

86 *dominant personality:* Parton, "Aide's Memoir" ("Parton, Memoir"), pp. 114–15.

86 *Arnold's treatment in England:* Arnold, *American Airpower*, vol. 1, pp. 132–66.

87 *"deep appreciation"*: Arnold, *American Airpower*, vol. 1, p. 182.

87 *"really dumb"*: Arnold, *American Airpower*, pp. 1, 60.

87 *"Arnold's paramount interest"*: Ismay, p. 286.

87 *lived on King's yacht:* Cooke papers, Box 11, "Speeches, Writings and Interviews," "Casablanca Conference," p. 1.

87 *Dykes and Dill on Cooke:* Dykes, pp. 202, 225, 235, n. 27.

87 *"Briefly and succinctly"*: Whitehill papers, Box 69, "Libby" folder, Libby to McDowell, 9/26/42.

87 *King had tried:* Arnold, *Global Mission*, p. 463; Buell, p. 274.

87 *King discussed with Cooke and Wedemeyer:* Wedemeyer, pp. 174–75.

88 *"not practicable"* . . . *"British point of view"*: Cooke papers, Box 11, "Speeches, Writings and Interviews," "Casablanca Conference," pp. 4–5; "Strategical Policy of the United States for the Conduct of the War," paragraph 6 (j), and "Memorandum for Admiral Cooke," 1/6/43.

88 *star flare:* Arnold, *American Airpower*, vol. 1, p. 460.

88 *Bathurst:* Pogue, *Organizer*, p. 18; Arnold, *American Airpower*, vol. 1, p. 461; Elliott Roosevelt, p. 75.

89 *Pendar's observations:* Pendar, pp. 136–39.

89 *"Yesterday seems so far away"*: Suckley, p. 196.

89 Dixie Clipper: Log of the Trip, pp. 3–4; Matthew Costello, "The Wings of Franklin Roosevelt: The Dixie Clipper and Sacred Cow," www.whitehousehistory.org/the-wings-of-franklin-roosevelt-1; Brooke, p. 266.

90 *Roosevelt in flight:* Suckley, p. 196; Log of the Trip, pp. 3–4; Sherwood, pp. 669–71; Grace Tully, *F.D.R. My Boss* (New York: Charles Scribner's Sons, 1949), p. 210; King, p. 415.

90 *Flying risks in 1943:* Sherwood, p. 669; McCrea, pp. 133–34; *Hinge of Fate*, p. 376; Normanbrook, pp. 211–12; Brooke, pp. 430, 653–54.

90 *"we are off to decide"*: Sherwood, pp. 671–72.

91 *Patton wrote his wife: Patton Papers*, pp. 153–54.

91 *Lieutenant Colonel Elliott Roosevelt:* Elliott Roosevelt, p. 60.

91 *"I sneaked away":* Ismay, pp. 284–85.

91 *would continue to show:* CAB 80/39, C.O.S. (43) 32, January 27, 1943, "War Cabinet Chiefs of Staff Committee 'Symbol' Note by Secretary."

91 *ins and outs . . . "exception":* Ismay, pp. 284–85; Kennedy, p. 279.

91 *Engraved cards:* JACB 1/20, card pasted into p. 41.

92 *Brooke brought General Kennedy:* Mackesy, p. 43; Roberts, p. xxxix.

92 *Queen Victoria:* Brooke, p. xxvii, n. 12.

92 *"migrants from Europe":* Kennedy, p. 281.

92 Profile of *Slessor:* Vincent Orange, *Bomber Champion: The Life of Marshal of the RAF Sir John Cotesworth Slessor, GCB, DSO, MC* (London: Grub Street, 2006), passim; Max Hastings, "Slessor, Sir John Cotesworth," *Oxford Dictionary of National Biography* (Oxford, UK: Oxford University Press, 2004); Overy, *The Bombers and the Bombed*, p. 74.

92 *"crudely converted" Liberator:* Slessor, p. 443.

92 *trussed . . . pretend to sleep:* JACB 1/20, pp. 43–45.

93 *"grim and squalid business":* Dykes, p. 182.

93 *"Sleep was out of the question":* Ismay, p. 285.

93 *"bed companion":* Brooke, pp. 357–58.

93 *"elaborate plans" . . . the press:* Harriman papers, Box 163, "Chron File Jan 1–19 1943," notes transcription ("Harriman notes"), p. 2; Harriman, p. 180; JACB 1/20, pp. 41–42.

93 *American pilot hosted: New York Times*, 1/27/43, p. 4, col. 8.

94 *"rather an unpleasant moment":* Wilson, pp. 85–86; *Hinge of Fate*, pp. 674–75.

FIVE: ANFA CAMP

95 *General Kennedy woke up:* Kennedy, pp. 279–80; Kennedy's Diary, 1/14/43.

95 *haggling was rare:* Reilly, p. 148.

95 *Churchill on the tarmac:* Parton papers, diary ("Parton's Diary"), 1/14/43; Kennedy's Diary, 1/14/43; Kennedy, pp. 279–80; Ismay, p. 285; Roberts, p. 316; Pendar, p. 140; Hastings, p. 285.

96 *"peas in drums":* JACB 20/1, p. 46.

96 *enjoyed it like toddlers:* Pendar, p. 140.

96 *The Anfa Hotel:* Macmillan, *Blast of War*, p. 192, Macmillan, *War Diaries*, p. 7; JACB 20/1, pp. 10–11, 14, 48–53; Murphy, p. 151; Churchill and Churchill, *Speaking for Themselves*, pp. 471–72; Tedder, pp. 389–90; Elliott Roosevelt, p. 63; Brooke, p. 358; Arnold, *American Airpower*, vol. 1, p. 463;

United States Naval Institute's Oral History of Vice Admiral Ruthven E. Libby ("Libby Oral History"), p. 69.

96 *Anfa Camp:* FDRL, Secret Service Records, Box 20, "Trips of the President, 1934–1943" (annotated chart of Anfa Camp); Murphy, pp. 152, 165; JACB 20/1, pp. 46–54; Log of the Trip, p. 11; *FRUS*, p. 522; CAB 120/75, "Anfa Conference Security"; FDR Library, "OF 200-2-P-OF 200-2-U Trips of the President," Box 62, and Kennedy papers ("Kennedy, JN: 4/7"), military directory for the Anfa Hotel titled "Notes on Anfa Camp"; Churchill Archives, GBR/014/KNNA 1/1; "Additional Notes on Anfa Camp"; Libby Oral History, p. 69; Brooke, p. 358; Macmillan, *Blast of War*, pp. 192–93; Macmillan, *War Diaries*, p. 7; Thompson, pp. 109–9; Slessor, p. 443; Reilly, pp. 148–51; Parton's Diary, 1/14/43; Arnold, *Global Mission*, pp. 218–19; Tedder, p. 390; Suckley, p. 198; Churchill and Churchill, *Speaking for Themselves*, pp. 472–73; Clark, p. 147.

97 *"many local rumors":* Butcher papers, "Anfa Cables (Outgoing) [January 14–26, 1943] (1)"; Durno, p. 67; Roosevelt, *Public Papers*, vol. 12, p. 57; Wilson papers, unmarked page; Codman, p. 71; MacVane, pp. 176–77; Pendar, p. 140.

97 *Washington by radio:* King's Flight Log Book, p. 15.

97 *Brits spoke with London:* JACB 20/1, pp. 40–41.

98 *Marshall's orderly:* Katherine Marshall, p. 135.

98 *elevator, mosquito nets:* Hall papers, "Interview—Mattie on Casablanca," p. 61.

98 *"elastic":* JACB 20/1, p. 50.

98 *"decidedly doubtful books":* JACB 20/1, p. 52; Moorhead, p. 149.

98 *Roosevelt's villa:* FRUS, p. 522; Hotel Directory, "Notes on Anfa Camp"; Macmillan, *Blast of War*, pp. 193–94; Macmillan, *War Diaries*, p. 8; Murphy, p. 165; Reilly, pp. 148, 152; JACB 1/20, pp. 12–13, 51–52; Pendar, p. 136; Elliott Roosevelt, pp. 65–66; Sherwood, pp. 673–74; Churchill and Churchill, *Speaking for Themselves*, p. 473; McCrea, p. 137; Slessor, p. 443; FDRL, OF 200-2-u "Casablanca Conference Jan. 9–31, 1943."

99 *"sardine can":* Parton's Diary, 12/28/42.

99 *Churchill's villa:* Macmillan, *Blast of War*, p. 193; Macmillan, *War Diaries*, p. 8; Elliott Roosevelt, pp. 66, 104; Sherwood, p. 673; Churchill and Churchill, *Speaking for Themselves*, p. 473; JACB 20/1, pp. 12, 51; Wilson, p. 88; Pendar, pp. 136, 155–56; Harriman, p. 181; FDRL, Box 62, OF 2200-2-P-OF 200-2-U Trips of the President, "Casablanca Conference" folder, "Personnel in Villa # 2."

99 *"have been cleaned out":* Kennedy's Diary, 1/13/43.

99 *"Conditions most agreeable":* Churchill Archives, CHAR 20/127, Stratagem 7.

99 *"roaring up": Hinge of Fate*, p. 675.

100 *the table talk's drift:* Harriman notes, pp. 2–3.

100 *At a glance, he wrote Clementine:* Churchill and Churchill, *Speaking for Themselves*, p. 473.

100 *the casbah:* FDRL, "Cuneo Papers," Box 110, "Churchill at Casablanca" folder.

101 Years of Endurance: Marshall, *The Papers*, vol. 3, pp. 530–31; Pogue, *Organizer*, p. 36; Churchill and Churchill, *Speaking for Themselves*, p. 473; Arthur Bryant, *The Years of Endurance, 1793–1802* (London: Collins, 1942), p. ix.

101 *Minutes of the American meeting:* Air Force Historical Research Agency ("AFHRA"), Doc. No. 119.151-1, "Joint Chiefs of Staff, January 1943," pp. 1–7.

101 *"Copper":* FDRL, Box 15, "Casablanca Conference Trip File," "Plan of Signal Communication," p. 3.

101 *The American meeting:* FDRL, Map Room Papers, Box 15, "Casablanca Conference" folder, "Plan of Signal Communication," p. 3; Arnold, *Global Mission*, p. 393; Wedemeyer, p. 174; Buell, p. 270; King, p. 416; Cooke papers, Box 24, "U-S-British Strategy," p. 1.

101 *a "Most Secret" memorandum:* AIR 9/168, "Unparaphrased Version of a Secret Cypher Telegram Not One Time Table," 12/31/42.

102 *Fifteen percent . . . "the greater power" versus European strength:* Matloff, *1943–1944*, p. 15; Atkinson, p. 285; Hastings, p. 289.

104 *"didn't quite see how" . . . "dark hole":* JACB 20/1, p. 63.

104 *"shooting off the cuff":* Marshall, *The Papers*, vol. 3, pp. 634–35.

105 *"No rigid view":* Marshall Interviews, p. 613.

105 *"bluff and hearty":* Parton's Diary, 1/14/43.

105 *German bombs killed 30,000:* Overy, *The Bombers and the Bombed*, pp. 41–42, 62.

105 *Harris on bombing:* Grayling, p. 103.

105 *"a graveyard": Time,* 2/15/43.

105 *a more humane approach:* Holland, pp. 15–16.

106 *"bearing down":* Arnold, *Global Mission*, p. 393.

106 *"pestiferous hole":* Suckley, p. 197.

106 *"incredibly squalid" . . . barges:* Durno, pp. 39–40.

107 *"how to tackle" . . . vicious circle:* JACB 20/1, pp. 55.

107 *Dill's briefing:* JACB 1/20, pp. 54–57; CAB 120/76, Stratagem 13; Danchev,

Very Special, pp. 65, 120, 177, n. 31; Kennedy, p. 280; Kennedy's Diary, 1/13/43; Pogue, *Organizer*, p. 189; Fraser, p. 316.

108 *"still convinced"*: Kennedy, p. 280.

108 *The British chiefs' meeting with Churchill:* CAB 99/24, pp. 98–99; JACB 20/1, p. 57; Kennedy's Diary, 1/13/43; Brooke, p. 358; Normanbrook, pp. 198–99.

109 *Churchill hosted a sailor's supper . . . "I suspected":* JACB 1/20, p. 58; Cooke papers, Box 11, "Speeches, Writings and Interviews," "Casablanca Conference," pp. 2–3.

109 *Profile of Mountbatten:* Pogue, *Organizer*, p. 312; Wedemeyer Interviews, Session 6, p. 19; Pendar, p. 138; *Marshall Interviews*, p. 584; Brooke, e.g., pp. 167, 282, 356–57, 388; the film *In Which We Serve*; Libby Oral History, pp. 243–44; JACB 1/20, p. 69.

110 *Brooke and Portal broke the ice:* Arnold, *Global Mission*, p. 393.

110 *Patton and the British on Clark: Eisenhower Diaries*, pp. 84, 94; Brooke, pp. 322, 333–34; Patton's Diary, 1/10/43; JACB 1/20; 22–23; CAB 120/76, Stratagem 13.

110 *General Ira Eaker:* Eaker papers, Corresp. Box I:9, "1 Jan–March 1943"; Parton's Diary, 1/19/43.

110 *Brooke's night:* Brooke, p. 358.

110 *"Canterville Ghost":* Kennedy's Diary, 1/14/43; Kennedy, p. 282.

SIX: DAY ONE: THURSDAY, JANUARY 14

111 *Minutes of the American Meeting:* AFHRA, Doc. No. 119.151-1, pp. 8–12.

111 *HMS* Victorious: Whitehill papers, Box 69, unlabeled notebook, p. 7; Michael Apps, *Send Her Victorious* (London: William Kimber), 1971.

112 *Brooke spent an hour and a half:* Brooke, p. 358.

112 *Conference room:* "Notes on Anfa Camp," n. 111–13; Slessor, pp. 444, 447; JACB 1/20, pp. 48–49; Murphy, p. 165; Pogue, *Organizer*, p. 19; Austin, p. 73; Imperial War Museum photos, IWM A 14042, 14134, 14139, 14141, 14142.

113 *Dykes and Deane, Notes and Minutes:* Dykes, pp. 205, 221; Danchev, *Very Special*, p. 118; JACB 1/20, pp. 76–77.

114 *captured in verse:* Dykes, p. 7.

114 *Minutes of the CCS meeting: FRUS*, pp. 536–56.

114 *"veiled antipathy":* Ismay, p. 285.

115 *"mathematical basis":* Slessor, p. 444; JACB 1/20, p. 59.

115 *"contempt for inadequacy":* Fraser, p. 83.

115 *Brooke's mannerisms, Dykes's mimicry, Jacob's admiration:* JACB 20/1, pp. 78–79; Danchev, *Very Special,* p. 123.

115 *"delicious talent for mimicry":* Roberts, p. 62, quoting Kennedy's diary; Fraser, p. 69.

116 *"thrown violently . . . shattering":* JACB, 20/1, p. 66.

116 *"killing Germans and chasing Italians": Patton Papers,* p. 161.

116 *great value to Italy's surrender . . . fifty-four divisions and 2,250 planes:* Bryant, p. 451; JACB 1/20, p. 66.

117 *"river of blood":* Sherwood papers, Box 40, "Interview with King," p. 2.

117 *"a good sea":* Leasor, p. 259.

117 *"twice shy about that particular dog":* Slessor, p. 434.

118 *rubber boat:* Harry Hopkins, vol. 2, p. 778.

119 *"bombshell":* Wedemeyer, pp. 177–78.

119 *caused Hitler to pull warplanes:* Gilbert, vol. 7, p. 267.

119 *Profile of Pound:* Brooke, pp. xliv–xlvi; Wedemeyer, p. 107; Roberts, pp. 43–44; Colville, pp. 177, 179; *Marshall Interviews,* p. 608; Leahy, p. 163; Danchev, *On Specialness,* p. 71.

120 *Profile of Portal:* Richards, passim; Parton, *Memoir,* p. 224; Danchev, *Very Special,* p. 124; Colville, pp. 186–88; Brooke, e.g., pp. 325, 332; JACB 20/1, p. 86; Pogue, *Ordeal,* p. 271.

122 *"angular and stiff" . . . "covering of horn":* JACB 20/1, pp. 85–86.

122 *"educate them":* Hastings, p. 288.

122 *"grand fellow":* Pogue, *Organizer,* p. 7.

123 *Arnold enjoyed:* Arnold, p. 463.

123 *Dill having told the British Chiefs of Staff that King:* Danchev, *Very Special,* pp. 121, 177, n. 35.

123 *"'Uncle Ernie'":* JACB 20/1, pp. 58–59.

123 *"The defensive anywhere":* Cooke papers, Box 24, Memorandum for Admiral King, December 21, 1942.

123 *"truly American":* Wedemeyer, p. 182.

123 *watched the British squirm:* Wedemeyer, pp. 180–81, 184.

124 *A British memorandum had concluded:* Cooke papers, Box 24—"American-British Strategy," 11/7/42, p. 3

124 *"wicked men":* McCrea, p. 139.

125 *Brooke's blood pressure:* Brooke, p. 359.

125 *"talked so damn fast":* Buell, p. 275.

125 *"trying to bounce them":* Ismay, p. 317.

125 *"it made me very hot":* Casablanca Conference, p. 4.

126 *"a trembling people":* Marshall Interviews, p. 615.

126 *what remained to use elsewhere:* JACB, 20/1, pp. 60–63.

126 *"hidden motives"* . . . *"this fear":* Roberts, p. 345.

126 *"sticking their noses":* Dykes, p. 207; Roberts, p. 99. See JACB 1/20, pp. 62–63.

127 *Libby still remembered:* Libby Oral History, p. 227. Libby attended this meeting (*FRUS*, p. 547) but not King's discussions with Churchill. Years later he mistakenly recalled that King confronted Churchill rather than Brooke.

127 *"particularly stuffy":* Wedemeyer, p. 184.

127 *"profane remark"* . . . *"very intently":* Cooke papers, Box 11, "Speeches, Writings and Interviews," "Casablanca Conference," p. 4.

127 *"position of a testator":* JACB 20/1, p. 61.

128 *Slessor guides the planners:* Slessor papers, AIR 75/11, Slessor Memorandum, "Casablanca Conference: Conduct of the War in 1943," 18 January 1943 ("Slessor memorandum").

128 *leaving little time:* JACB 1/20, p. 48.

128 *"no intention of studying":* JACB 20/1, p. 61.

128 *"to instruct them on the line":* Brooke, p. 359; CAB 120/76, Stratagem 23.

128 *"walk with John Kennedy":* Brooke, p. 359.

129 *mysteriously rosy light:* Arnold, *Global Mission*, p. 394.

129 *Arnold briefs Smart:* Smart, pp. 38–39.

129 *"a little assistance from the Americans":* Tedder, p. 388; JACB 1/20, p. 47.

129 *"reluctant tail":* Murphy, p. 168.

129 *"it is believed that":* JACB 20/1, pp. 78–80.

130 *"unexpected American views":* CAB 120/76.

130 *"the President arriving":* Kennedy, p. 281.

130 *"An amazing day":* Suckley, p. 198.

130 *Gambian poverty:* Log of the Trip, p. 11; McIntire, p. 149; Durno, p. 41; McCrea, pp. 134–35.

130 *FDR's arrival at Casablanca:* Log of the Trip, p. 12; Sherwood, p. 673; Suckley, p. 198; McCrea, p. 135; Durno, p. 42; Arnold, p. 670.

131 *"delightful villa":* Suckley, p. 198.

131 *"I hope you'll hurry up":* McIntire, p. 149.

131 *screaming newspapers:* Elliott Roosevelt, p. 85.

131 *Roosevelt and Churchill reunited:* FRUS, p. 557; Sherwood, p. 673; McCrea, p. 138; Churchill and Churchill, *Speaking for Themselves*, p. 473.

132 *FDR's opening party:* Log of the Trip, p. 13; Sherwood, p. 674; Elliott Roosevelt, pp. 66–70, 77; McCrea, pp. 136–38; *American Airpower*, vol. 1, pp.

464, 525, n. 104; Churchill and Churchill, *Speaking for Themselves*, pp. 473–74; Reilly, p. 154; Butcher's Diary, p. A-171; Butcher, pp. 238–39; Brooke, pp. 359, 446.

132 *"whiskey to soda"*: Slessor, p. 330.

133 *"with a swing"*: CAB 120/76, Stratagem 23, p. 1.

133 *"Under their hearty and friendly manner"*: Hastings, p. 288.

133 *"take you or reject you"* . . . *"mental superiority"*: JACB 20/1, pp. 86–87.

133 *Berlin radio* . . . *"White House"*: FDRL, Cuneo papers, Box 110, "Churchill at Casablanca" folder; *New York Times*, 1/27/43, p. 3, col. 5; Churchill and Churchill, *Speaking for Themselves*, p. 473; Hamilton, pp. 65–66, 130–31; Robert Hopkins, p. 57.

SEVEN: DAY TWO: FRIDAY, JANUARY 15

135 *Birds:* Brooke, p. 359; Kennedy's Diary, 1/15/43.

135 *The sultan and Noguès:* AFHRA Doc. No. 119.151-1, pp. 51–57; King's Flight Log Book, p. 13; Elliott Roosevelt, pp. 77–78, 87; Log of the Trip, p. 13; *FRUS*, p. 558; *Patton Papers*, pp. 111, 136–37.

135 *"it would not be desirable"*: FRUS, pp. 558–59.

137 *even Eisenhower:* Pogue, *Organizer*, p. 31.

137 *"the cross-Channel thing"*: Marshall Interviews, p. 614.

137 *Minutes of the British meeting:* CAB 99/24, pp. 101–3.

138 *Churchill's gray suit and remarks:* Kennedy's Diary, 1/15/43; Kennedy, pp. 281–82; Churchill, p. 474.

138 *"rompers"*: www.sartorialnotes.com/2017/02/01/churchill's-romper-suit-siren-suit.

138 *"Zoot suit"*: Whitehill papers, Box 69, unlabeled notebook, p. 7.

138 *"gullible people"*: JACB 20/1, p. 64.

138 *"claustrophobia"*: Slessor, p. 444.

139 *"knock their heads together"*: Kennedy's Diary, 1/15/43.

139 *"lubricator"* . . . *"thought the world of him"*: Handy Interview, pp. 90–94 ("Sir John"); JACB 20/1, p. 81.

139 *"bringing the young things together"*: Danchev, "Dilly-Dally," p. 35.

139 *Profile of Butcher:* Butcher papers, Finding Aid, "Correspondence File: January 1943," passim; Durno, p. 44; Dykes, p. 135; Butcher, 239; Roberts, p. 487.

139 *Profile of Macmillan:* Charmley, passim; Murphy, pp. 163–64; Funk, *de Gaulle*, p. 55; Eisenhower, *Papers*, vol. 2, p. 886, n. 1; Kennedy, p. 282; Codman, p. 80.

140 *On the flight to Casablanca:* Macmillan, *Blast of War*, p. 191; Macmillan, *War Diaries*, p. 7; Eisenhower, *Crusade*, p. 135; Butcher, p. 237.

140 *Patton met their plane:* Patton Papers, p. 154.

140 *embraced his British staff:* Patton Papers, p. 123; Richards, p. 215; Ismay, p. 291; Portal Oral History, pp. 6–7.

141 *Butcher's tour:* Butcher, pp. 237–38.

141 *Eaker and Parton:* Parton, *Memoir*, pp. 228–31.

141 *"a deadening effect":* FO 660/86, "Situation in French North Africa," pp. 1–3.

141 *Eden's and Churchill's French positions:* Eden, pp. 360–61.

142 *Macmillan told Murphy:* Pendar, p. 226.

142 *lunch in the president's garden:* FRUS, p. 563; Elliott Roosevelt, p. 78; FDRL Map Room Papers, Box 165, "Casablanca Conference" folder, telegram, Matthews to Hull, 1/8/43, with note by FDR.

143 *"'off the record'":* Churchill and Churchill, *Speaking for Themselves*, p. 473.

143 *Minutes of the CCS meeting:* FRUS, pp. 563–73.

143 *"hostile shot":* Patton Papers, p. 133.

143 *flu . . . exhaustion . . . bags:* Butcher's Diary, p. A-154; Butcher, p. 235.

143 *green ink . . . "lamentable":* Fraser, p. 204.

143 *"won't run":* Mackesy, p. 49.

144 *"daring side":* Butcher's Diary, p. A-156.

144 *Brooke liked Ike:* Brooke, pp. 418, 600, 669.

144 *"as a general is hopeless":* Brooke, p. 351.

144 *Eisenhower's grilling:* FRUS, pp. 567–69; *Hinge of Fate*, pp. 677–78; Eisenhower, *Crusade*, p. 136; *Eisenhower Diaries*, p. 89; Bryant, pp. 447–48; Brooke, p. 359. See JACB 1/20, p. 74.

146 *Brooke thought his case:* Brooke, p. 359.

146 *Eisenhower's talk with Roosevelt:* Sherwood papers, Box 40, Eisenhower interview folder; Log of the Trip, p. 14; FRUS, p. 523; Elliott Roosevelt, p. 79; Sherwood, p. 677; Eisenhower, *Crusade*, pp. 136–38; McCrea, pp. 139–40; FDRL, Map Room Papers, Box 165, "Casablanca Conference" folder, Marshall to FDR, 1/6/43 and enclosed Eisenhower memo; Ambrose, p. 219 ("favored the efficiency").

147 *"would be catastrophic":* FDRL, Map Room Papers, Box 165, "Casablanca Conference—27 Nov. 1942–14 Jan. 1943," Eisenhower to Marshall, 1/5/43; Marshall to FDR, 1/6/43.

148 *"slickers":* Eisenhower Papers, vol. 2, p. 711.

148 *Macmillan at Villa Mirador:* Macmillan, *Blast of War*, p. 195.

148 *Murphy at the White House:* Log of the Trip, p. 14; *FRUS*, p. 523; Murphy, pp. 168–70; Elliott Roosevelt, pp. 79–80.

149 *"how abhorrent":* Murphy, p. 168.

149 "mes fiefs": CHAR 20/92/24-28.

149 *Profile of Murphy:* Crawford, p. 103; Murphy, passim; Pendar, p. 19; Elliott Roosevelt, p. 79; Funk, *de Gaulle*, pp. 8, 31–35.

149 *"disguise you":* Murphy, p. 102.

150 *Profile of Franklin Jr.:* McCrea, p. 139; Suckley, p. 199; Elliot Roosevelt, pp. 66, 82; *FRUS*, p. 524.

150 *"Emperor of the East and the Emperor of the West"* . . . *"very smart":* Macmillan, *War Diaries*, pp. 7–8.

150 *luxuries in wartime Britain:* Harriman papers, Box 163, "Service with the British: A Guide Book for AAF Officers," p. 1.

150 *"colossal"* . . . *"terrifying":* Dykes, p. 136.

150 *Jacob on food: "mixing of the clans . . . Yanks changed their ways . . . a genial warmth":* JACB 20/1, pp. 53–54.

151 *Shorty:* Unpublished papers of Louise Anderson Locke ("Anderson Papers").

151 *Harriman watched friendships:* Harriman notes, p. 6.

151 *"superbly beautiful"* . . . *pebbles:* Macmillan, *War Diaries*, p. 9.

151 *"Mutual respect":* JACB 1/20, pp. 81–83.

151 *informal work:* Parton's Diary, 1/14/43, 2/23/43, interview, 11/28/43; Gilbert, p. 297.

151 *even King dropped his growls:* Cunningham, p. 515.

151 *Dill befriended:* Danchev, *Very Special*, p. 125.

151 *deep in conversation:* Kennedy, p. 284.

151 *"someday we have got to go across":* Gilbert, pp. 914–15.

152 *"military suicide":* Parton's Diary, 3/21/43.

152 *"neutral pitch"* . . . *"gradual education":* JACB 20/1, pp. 81–83.

152 *Profile of Alexander:* FRUS, p. 523; Keegan, pp. 104–7; Elliott Roosevelt, p. 80; Codman, p. 72; Brooke, p. 647; Coleville, pp. 194–95.

153 *Profile of Tedder:* Eisenhower Diaries, pp. 84, 91; Tedder, passim.

153 *"I was rather disappointed":* Tedder, p. 393.

153 *Alexander, Tedder, and Eisenhower's discussion:* FRUS, pp. 573–78; Elliott Roosevelt, p. 101; *Hinge of Fate*, pp. 676–78.

154 *slippery slope:* Wedemeyer, pp. 163–64.

155 *"bawled him out"* . . . *"success":* Butcher's Diary, p. A-176.

155 *"chose to show displeasure"* . . . *"such nonsense":* Parton, *Memoir*, pp. 218, 231,

337; Eaker, pp. 121–22; Parton, *"Air Force Spoken Here,"* p. 23; Parton, "General Ira Eaker, Creator," p. 33.

155 *"finishing the liquidation":* Gilbert, p. 294.

155 *Roosevelt's plans to visit troops:* FRUS, pp. 524, 558; Elliott Roosevelt, pp. 82–84; Arnold, *American Airpower*, vol. 1, pp. 464, 525, n. 104; Arnold, *Global Mission*, pp. 394–95.

156 *Kansas Republican congressman's speech:* Elliott Roosevelt, p. 84.

156 *Three sons' deaths: New York Times*, 2/12/44; Roberts, p. 484; Thompson, p. 184.

156 *"bitter mood" . . . "anything but easy":* Brooke, p. 360.

157 *Profile of Cunningham:* Colville, p. 181; Dykes p. 196; King, p. 461.

157 *tommy gun:* Libby Oral History, pp. 71–72.

157 *"aide's table" . . . "not quite":* Butcher's Diary, p. A-172.

157 *Eisenhower and Patton:* Butcher, pp. 239–40; *Patton Papers*, pp. 154–55; Marshall, *Organizer*, p. 182; Libby Oral History, pp. 71–72 ("Tommy gun").

157 *nightmare born of war:* Butcher, p. 240.

EIGHT: DAY THREE: SATURDAY, JANUARY 16

158 *yellow alert . . . "terrific weapon":* Wilson papers, unnumbered pages.

158 *"so comfortable in Casablanca":* Roosevelt, *Public Papers*, p. 57.

158 *reset the Tunisia campaign:* FRUS, pp. 580, n. 3, 580–81; Kennedy, p. 282; Brooke, p. 360.

159 *Later in the day:* Eisenhower, *Crusade*, pp. 137–38.

159 *"fortunate indeed": Hinge of Fate*, p. 677.

159 *Macmillan, Murphy, Eisenhower, and Roosevelt:* Log of the Trip, p. 15; *FRUS*, pp. 524, 579, 809; Macmillan, *Blast of War*, p. 195, Macmillan, *War Diaries*, p. 9; Murphy, p. 166; Elliott Roosevelt, pp. 84–85.

160 *"President's tendency" . . . "near him": Marshall Interviews*, pp. 590, 620.

160 *Minutes of the American meeting:* AFHRA Doc. No. 119.151-1, pp. 13–21.

161 *he too had just told Marshall:* AFHRA Doc. No. 119.151-1, p. 15.

161 *"convert the Americans":* Tedder, p. 391. See JACB 1/20, pp. 64–65.

161 *"We all believed":* King's Flight Log Book, p. 12.

162 *The CCS minutes:* FRUS, pp. 580–93.

163 *"put their money on Portal" . . . "best mind of the lot":* JACB 20/1, p. 87; Marshall, *Organizer*, pp. 4, 6.

163 *the ablest too:* Coleville, p. 187.

163 *"He berated me like a pickpocket":* Pogue, *Organizer*, p. 4.

165 *"let the cat out":* Wedemeyer, pp. 177–78.

165   *"have our shirts"*: Spaatz papers, Box 97, "Casablanca" folder.

166   *Kennedy thought . . . "We felt"*: Kennedy, p. 283.

166   *Jacob on Marshall:* JACB 20/1, pp. 84–85.

166   *Tedder wrote:* Tedder, pp. 388, 396.

167   *"were not above learning"*: CAB 65/25, War Cabinet No. 8 of 1942.

167   *"dog tired"*: Brooke, p. 360.

167   *"extraordinary integrity"*: Roberts, pp. 390–91, citing Brooke interview.

167   *"almost impossible"*: Brooke, p. 360.

167   *"Greeks" . . . "too clever"*: Hugh Dalton, *The Second World War Diary of Hugh Dalton* (London: Cape, 1986), pp. 693, 722.

168   *"suspicious . . . treacherous"*: Marshall Interviews, pp. 593, 599.

168   *Arnold, Eaker, and Andrews:* Eaker papers, Eaker Correspondence, 1 Jan–March 1944, Eaker to Stratameyer, 1/30/43.

168   *invoking an RAF pilot:* Eaker papers, Box I-1, "8 AF, CG (Eaker)" folder, "Relations Between British and American Forces," September 11, 1942.

168   *Parton works with Eaker:* Parton's Diary, 1/14/43; Parton, *Memoir*, pp. 220, 231–32; Parton, "General Ira Eaker, Creator," p. 33; Slessor, p. 401 (Patton's pistol and helmet).

168   *"The Case for Day Bombing"*: Air Force Historical Research Agency, "Eighth Air Force: Growth, Development and Operations, Air Force Plans," Exhibit 3, AFHRA CD A5835, Reel A5835, p. 1.

168   *Roosevelt's lunch:* FRUS, p. 524; Log of the Trip, p. 140; Elliott Roosevelt, pp. 85–86.

169   *Churchill's lunch with King:* King's Flight Log Book, p. 14; Buell, p. 277; King, p. 425.

169   *told Arnold he had a rough time . . . poked:* Arnold, *Global Mission*, p. 395; Arnold, *American Airpower*, vol. 1, p. 465.

169   *British walks, "great hunt"*: Dykes, p. 80; Wilson, p. 86; Brooke, p. 360; Codman, pp. 74–75.

170   *"Goddamn liar"*: Harmon, p. 109.

170   *Roosevelt's meeting with the Joint Chiefs:* FRUS, pp. 524, 594–600; AFHRA Doc. No. 119.151-1, pp. 58–65; Elliott Roosevelt, p. 87; Harriman notes, p. 6.

171   *"cobwebs"*: Marshall Interviews, p. 626.

171   *"typical fascist"*: Dykes, p. 220.

171   *Churchill meets with his Chiefs of Staff:* CAB 99/24, pp. 103–4.

172   *The WAACs and their presidential dinner:* Anderson papers; Hall papers, Box 1, "Interview—Mattie on Casablanca," "Interview—Alene Drezmal, 1977"; Durno, pp. 48–64.

174   *Marshall's good deed:* FRUS, pp. 525–26; Butcher, p. 240, McCrea, p. 140; Reilly, pp. 153–54.

174   *"except King would have gone crazy":* Marshall, *The Papers*, vol. 4, pp. 246–48.

174   *Patton's dinner:* Brooke, pp. 360–61; *Patton Papers*, p. 155.

174   *Churchill wired Eden:* Dixon's Casablanca Diary, January 16; Funk, *de Gaulle*, p. 68, n. 13.

174   *"his root":* Dixon's Casablanca Diary, January 16.

174   *"some pomp":* Murphy, p. 171.

175   *"small hill":* FRUS, pp. 579–80, 809–11.

175   *"bellows" . . . "quiet":* JACB 20/1, pp. 80–81.

175   *daily intelligence briefing:* David Stafford, *Roosevelt and Churchill: Men of Secrets* (New York: Overlook Press, 2000), pp. 202–3.

NINE: DAY FOUR: SUNDAY, JANUARY 17

176   *not a good day for France:* Eisenhower Diaries, p. 86; Arnold, *American Airpower*, vol. 1, p. 465; Brooke, p. 361.

176   *Butcher's breakfast:* Butcher's Diary, p. A-175; Butcher, pp. 240–42.

177   *Eisenhower and Butcher returned:* Butcher, pp. 242–43.

177   *"laboriously planned":* Eisenhower, *The Papers*, p. 910.

177   *Minutes of the American meeting:* AFHRA Doc. No. 119.151-1, pp. 22–26.

178   *"can't get away":* Roberts, pp. 531–32, citing papers of Lawrence Burgis.

178   *"To our great surprise":* Kennedy, p. 283; Brooke, p. 361.

178   *Marshall confessed he was bluffing:* Marshall Interviews, p. 593.

178   *"long harangue":* Brooke, p. 361.

179   *"and were wishing":* Brooke, p. 361.

179   *"distinct from the egret":* Brooke, p. 361.

179   *"birds leave no time":* Kennedy, p. 201.

179   *"bad wicket":* FO 660/85, Chronological Account of Anfa Negotiations, p. 1; Impressions of ANFA Conference.

179   *Eden's meetings with de Gaulle:* FRUS, pp. 809–10, 814–16; de Gaulle, vol. 2, p. 83; Eden, pp. 361–62.

180   *70 million pounds:* Murphy, p. 170.

180   *"les Anglo-Saxons":* Murphy, p. 182.

181   *"angry crabs":* Butcher's Diary p. A-163.

181   *Profile of Noguès:* FRUS, p. 525; Log of the Trip, p. 15; Macmillan, *Blast of War*, p. 197; Patton's Diary; Crawford, p. 37; Middleton, p. 250; *New York Times*, 4/22/71, p. 44; Roosevelt, *Public Papers*, vol. 12, p. 85; Leahy, p. 137.

182   *"poor devils":* Middleton, p. 148.

182   *Roosevelt with Noguès:* Log of the Trip, pp. 15–16; *FRUS*, pp. 525, 606–9; Elliott Roosevelt, pp. 87–89; Macmillan, *Blast of War*, pp. 197, 201.

183   *"Is he a good man"* . . . *"agreeably enough":* Macmillan, *Blast of War*, p. 198; Elliott Roosevelt, p. 88.

183   *Churchill's French:* Gilbert, p. 278; Brooke, p. 374.

183   *Patton's observations:* Patton's Diary; *Patton Papers*, p. 155.

184   *Churchill's lunch with Roosevelt: FRUS*, pp. 525, 532, 609, 704; Log of the Trip, p. 17; Elliott Roosevelt, pp. 117–18; *Patton Papers*, p. 157. Churchill later said he had no memory of this "free and unguarded" conversation. He did not deny it. *Hinge of Fate*, p. 685.

184   *Churchill sent Stalin a cable: FRUS*, p. 643, n. 2.

184   *Giraud's arrival:* Arnold, *American Airpower*, vol. 1, p. 466; Funk, *de Gaulle*, p. 66; Kennedy, p. 284; *Patton Papers*, p. 156.

185   *Roosevelt's meeting with Giraud: FRUS*, pp. 609–12; Log of the Trip, p. 17; Durno, p. 20; Clark, pp. 147–48; Elliott Roosevelt, pp. 88–91; Murphy, pp. 169–70, 181 ("generals got up early"); Funk, *de Gaulle*, p. 67; Funk, "'Anfa Memorandum,'" p. 249.

186   *Churchill's meeting with Giraud:* Clark, pp. 147–48; Codman, p. 74; Kersaudy, p. 24, quoting Giraud, pp. 91–93.

187   *Minutes of the British meeting:* CAB 99/24, pp. 105–6.

188   *Eisenhower cabled Hopkins: FRUS*, pp. 811–12.

188   *Roosevelt's dinner: FRUS*, pp. 526, 613; Log of the Trip, pp. 91–92; minutes of the American meeting, 1/18/43, AFHRA Doc. No. 119.151-1, p. 28; Elliott Roosevelt, pp. 91–92; Kennedy, p. 284; Buell, p. 277.

188   *Churchill cabled his War Cabinet:* AIR 8/1076, Stratagem 56; *Hinge of Fate*, p. 676.

TEN: DAY FIVE: MONDAY, JANUARY 18

189   *"lovely cool morning":* Kennedy's Diary, 1/18/43.

189   *Minutes of the American meeting:* AFHRA Doc. No. 119.151-1, pp. 27–31; Arnold, *Global Mission*, p. 396.

189   *starving the Pacific:* Cooke papers, Box 11, "Speeches, Writings and Interviews," "Casablanca Conference," p. 3.

189   *"insufferable"* . . . *arguably paralyzing:* Hastings, pp. 279, 289.

190   *"You must remember":* Danchev, *On Specialness*, p. 42.

190   *Cooke, Wedemeyer: FRUS*, pp. 755–57.

190   *Cooke and other King staff on pressuring both enemies:* Cooke papers, Box 24, "American-British Strategy," 11/7/42, pp. 2–6: "Strategical Policy of the

United States for the Conduct of the War," 11/27/42; "Determination of Suitable, Feasible, and Acceptable Course of Action," 12/10/42; Captain R. L. Conolly, "Memorandum for Admiral King," 12/21/42; Cooke, "Memorandum for Admiral King," 12/28/42; Cooke, "Additional Memorandum for Admiral King on Basic Strategic Concept for 1943," 12/28/42.

190 *Minutes of the CCS Meeting: FRUS*, pp. 613–26. See also Slessor, p. 445.

191 *"cheese-paring parsimony":* Morgan, p. 137.

192 *"dormant" . . . "idle":* See JACB 1/20, p. 65.

192 *"Tempers were getting a little frayed":* Slessor, pp. 445–46.

192 *"Gatling gun":* Leasor, pp. 168–69.

193 *"he means business":* Wilson, p. 22.

194 *"hand grenades" . . . "common sense":* Wilson, p. 768.

194 *planning field . . . battlefield:* Portal Oral History, p. 6.

196 *Jacob on Cooke:* JACB 20/1, p. 48.

196 *Brooke, Dill, and Slessor:* Brooke: p. 362; Danchev, *Very Special*, p. 126; Slessor, pp. 444–46; Slessor papers, AIR 75/11, Slessor Memorandum.

196 *"great nuisance":* Bryant, p. 446 n.

198 *Slessor's compromise:* Slessor papers, AIR 75/11, Slessor Memorandum; Slessor, pp. 442–43, 446; Kennedy, p. 283; *FRUS*, pp. 760–61, Brooke, pp. 361–62.

198 *"Not one American soldier":* Dill, p. 122.

199 *Brooke and Dill on compromise:* Brooke, pp. 361–62; Danchev, *Very Special*, pp. 130, 180, n. 84. Slessor's accounts in his papers and his book differ slightly with each other and Brooke's.

200 *"Major Giraud":* Price, p. 185.

200 *furious at de Gaulle . . . options:* Dixon's Casablanca Diary, January 18; Macmillan, *Blast of War*, p. 198.

200 *Somervell and Giraud: Patton Papers*, p. 156; Patton's Diary; Codman, p. 73.

200 *Roosevelt's lunch with Churchill:* FO 660/88, "Anfa Conference Second Phase," p. 3; Impressions of ANFA Conference, p. 3; Macmillan, *Blast of War*, pp. 198–99; McCrea, pp. 138–39; Funk, *de Gaulle*, p. 68.

200 *"Above all . . . cross-purposes":* JACB 20/1, p. 32.

201 *"refused to run":* Macmillan, *Blast of War*, pp. 198–99.

201 *"Frankenstein monster":* FO 660/88, Impressions of ANFA Conference, p. 3.

201 *Macmillan advised Churchill:* Dixon's Casablanca Diary, January 18.

201 *"Where is the bride?":* FRUS, p. 627.

201 *"We delivered our bridegroom":* FRUS, p. 816.

201 *"gardenia":* Durno, p. 21.

201 *"We made a bad error":* *Eisenhower Diaries,* p. 89; Ambrose, p. 223; Leighton and Coakley, pp. 58–59.

202 *Compromise accepted:* Slessor papers, AIR 75/11, "Conduct of the War in 1943," and handwritten notes; Slessor, p. 446; Brooke, pp. 361–62, 464–65, 616; Kennedy's Diary, 1/18/43; Kennedy, p. 283; Buell, p. 279; Danchev, *Very Special,* pp. 126–28, 131–32.

203 *Marshall, King, and Cunningham: Marshall Interviews,* p. 621; King, p. 461; Cunningham, p. 465.

204 *Mountbatten told Hopkins and Harriman:* Harriman notes, p. 6; Harriman, p. 182.

204 *guard-changing ceremony:* Log of the Trip, pp. 18–19; *FRUS,* p. 526; Patton's Diary; Elliott Roosevelt, p. 93.

204 *Plenary session: FRUS,* pp. 627–37; CAB 120/75, "Anfa 2nd Meeting—Villa No. 2, Casablanca"; CAB/75, Stratagem 98; *Hinge of Fate,* pp. 683–86; Brooke, p. 361; Bryant, pp. 457–58; Wedemeyer, pp. 186–87; Elliott Roosevelt, pp. 93–94.

204 *prised open:* JACB 20/1, p. 90.

204 *white-leather chairs . . . oval table:* See the photograph spread.

204 *it made Turkey personal:* Murphy, p. 166.

207 *Cunningham fearless and tongue-tied:* Brooke, p. xliii; Harry Hopkins, vol. 2, p. 674; Colville, pp. 176 and 181.

210 *"final spring of the tiger":* Normanbrook et al., p. 86.

210 *"We were not invited":* Kimball, vol. 2, p. 98.

211 *"a most satisfactory meeting": Hinge of Fate,* p. 684.

211 *"translated the generalities":* Kennedy's Diary, 1/18/43; *FRUS,* pp. 760–63.

211 *Robert Hopkins showed his pass: FRUS,* p. 527; Robert Hopkins, pp. I, 43–45; Butcher's Diary, p. A-174; Butcher, p. 240; Elliott Roosevelt, p. 118.

212 *Brooke's dinner with Giraud:* Brooke, p. 362.

212 *Brooke on the French:* Brooke, p. 363.

212 *"in his fantasy of egotism":* CHAR 20/127, Stratagem 78, Churchill to Eden, 1/18/43.

ELEVEN: DAY SIX: TUESDAY, JANUARY 19

214 *Churchill sent Clement Attlee:* Gilbert, p. 300.

214 *Arnold told Hopkins:* Sherwood, pp. 681–82; *FRUS,* p. 648, n. 1.

214 *Hopkins and Wilson:* Wilson, pp. 86–87.

215 *Minutes of the American meeting:* AFHRA Doc. No. 119.151-1, pp. 32–36.

215 *"our position with the Bear":* Gilbert, p. 302.

215   *"The shirt is gone":* Spaatz papers, Box 97, "Casablanca" folder, Wedemeyer to
         Handy, 1/19/43.

215   *Arnold and Kennedy:* Arnold, *American Airpower*, vol. 1, p. 466; Kennedy, pp.
         283–84.

215   *"trifling amendments":* Compare *FRUS* pp. 760–61 with pp. 774–75.

215   *Minutes of the CCS meeting: FRUS*, pp. 637–41, 774–75, 782–85; *Hinge of
         Fate*, p. 691.

215   *Harriman and Poniatowski: FRUS*, pp. 641–42; Sherwood, p. 682; Harriman,
         p. 185.

216   *Roosevelt's meeting with Giraud:* Log of the Trip, p. 21; *FRUS*, Plate 8 and pp.
         527–28, 644–46; McCrea, pp. 136–37; Sherwood, pp. 683–84; Elliott Roo-
         sevelt, p. 95.

218   *harbor tour:* Log of the Trip, p. 21; *FRUS*, pp. 528, 644–47; *Patton Papers*, p.
         157; Elliott Roosevelt, pp. 95–96; Sherwood, p. 684.

218   *"Air Commodore Frankland":* Churchill, *Speaking for Themselves*, p. 474, n. 2.

218   *Churchill and Arnold:* Arnold, *American Airpower*, vol. 1, p. 467, *Global Mis-
         sion*, pp. 396–97.

218   *got it backward:* Slessor, pp. 429–31; Portal Oral History, p. 5.

219   *Churchill and Eaker: FRUS*, pp. 528, 666–67; *Hinge of Fate*, pp. 678–80;
         Eaker, pp. 123–24; Oral History with General Eaker, U.S. Military History
         Institute, Carlisle, PA, Senior Officers Debriefing Program, pp. 30–33; "The
         Case for Day Bombing," AFHRA CD/Reel A5835; Parton, "General Ira
         Eaker, Creator," p. 33; Parton, *"Air Force Spoken Here,"* pp. 221–22; Arnold,
         Global Mission, pp. 375, 396–97, Arnold, *American Airpower*, vol. 1, p. 467.

219   *"Ring Bell":* Parton, *Memoir*, p. 228.

219   *"We won't do much talking":* Arnold, *Global Mission*, p. 375; Parton, *Memoir*,
         p. 229.

220   *Parton's bombing study:* Parton papers, "Principle [*sic*] Lessons Learned on the
         First Ten Daylight Heavy Bombardment Raids Over Enemy Territory."

221   *"We had won a major victory": FRUS*, p. 528; Arnold, *Global Mission*, pp.
         396–97.

221   *Minutes of the CCS meeting: FRUS*, pp. 647–55; Kennedy, pp. 284–85; King,
         p. 424; Danchev, *Very Special*, pp. 124–25.

221   *Giraud's presentation:* Harriman notes, p. 7; Slessor, p. 447; Kennedy's Diary,
         1/19/43; Kennedy, pp. 284–85; JACB 1/20, pp. 87–89; Mangold, p. 37;
         Middleton, pp. 244–45; Codman, pp. 73–74; Danchev, *Very Special*, pp.
         124–25; Arnold, *American Airpower*, vol. 1, p. 467; FO 660/88, Impressions
         of ANFA Conference, p. 3; Smart, p. 41; King's Flight Log Book, 1/22/43.

224   *"not made many mistakes":* Kennedy, p. 285.

224   *Profile of Randolph:* Log of the Trip, p. 22; *FRUS*, p. 528; Churchill and Churchill, *Speaking for Themselves*, pp. 465, n. 3, 475; JACB 20/1, pp. 113–15; John Colville, *The Fringes of Power: Downing Street Diaries, 1939–1955* (London: Hodder & Stoughton, 1985), pp. 178, 265; Elliott Roosevelt, pp. 96–97.

225   *Churchill's Marrakech plans:* Durno, p. 46; Brooke, p. 363; *Hinge of Fate*, p. 694; Bryant, p. 453; Fraser, pp. 324–25.

225   *Churchill's dinner:* Log of the Trip, p. 21; *FRUS*, p. 643; Sherwood, p. 683; Robert Hopkins, p. 46; Erik Larson, *The Splendid and the Vile* (New York: Crown, 2020), p. 497.

226   *Eden and de Gaulle:* De Gaulle, vol. 2, pp. 83–84; 128; Kersaudy, p. 245; Macmillan, *Blast of War*, pp. 196–97; *Hinge of Fate*, pp. 680–81; de Gaulle, vol. 4, pp. 127–28; Dixon's Casablanca Diary, January 20.

226   *"YBSOB":* Butcher papers, "Anfa Cables (Outgoing) [January 14–26, 1943] (1); Murphy, p. 138.

226   *Patton's dinner, Villa Maas:* Log of the Trip, pp. 21–22; *FRUS*, p. 528; Arnold, *American Airpower*, vol. 1, p. 469; Durno, p. 71; Elliott Roosevelt, pp. 97–99; *Patton Papers*, p. 157; McCrea, p. 140.

226   *Patton, FDR, and Churchill:* Log of the Trip, pp. 21–22; *FRUS*, p. 528; Sherwood, p. 683; Parton's Diary, 1/19/43; Elliott Roosevelt, pp. 97–99; *Patton Papers*, p. 157; McCrea, p. 140; Dulles and Ridinger, p. 5, n. 10 ("reliable source").

227   *After Churchill left . . . "mention India!":* Elliott Roosevelt, p. 71.

TWELVE: DAY SEVEN: WEDNESDAY, JANUARY 20

228   *scrambling for more staff . . . pinned a medal:* Patton Papers, p. 157.

228   *"let the dog see the rabbit":* Slessor, p. 401.

228   *"stimulate our friends":* Hinge of Fate, p. 684.

228   *cable to Attlee and Eden:* Eden, p. 363.

229   *"loll about":* Ismay, pp. 289–90.

229   *Minutes of the CCS meeting:* FRUS, pp. 777–81.

229   *"exhausted animal":* Hastings, p. 279.

230   *Command arrangements:* Brooke, p. 365; Churchill, *Speaking for Themselves*, p. 476; Ismay, pp. 288–89; Bryant, p. 454; Ambrose, p. 220 ("burning inside"); Tedder, p. 396 ("rubbed in").

230   *Murphy came to the White House:* Log of the Trip, p. 22, *FRUS*, p. 529; Elliott Roosevelt, pp. 102–3; Suckley, p. 199. See Leahy, p. 143.

230 *"No come no pay":* Roll, p. 254.

230 *Minutes of the CCS meeting: FRUS*, pp. 663–65. See also Brooke, p. 64.

231 *"half-baked thoughts":* Brooke, p. 332.

231 *Three bird debuts . . . "dumped Giraud":* Brooke, p. 364.

232 *"You Are My Sunshine":* Log of the Trip, pp. 35–36.

232 *"threw his hat on the sofa":* Log of the Trip, p. 23; *FRUS*, p. 666; Kersaudy, p. 244, quoting Giraud, pp. 98–99; Elliott Roosevelt, p. 103.

232 *Churchill's dinner: FRUS*, p. 529; Churchill and Churchill, *Speaking for Themselves*, p. 475; Potter, pp. 25–26; Gilbert, p. 304, Elliott Roosevelt, pp. 103–4; CAB 120/76, Churchill to Eden, 1/22/43.

232 *traveling map room:* Potter, pp. 2–3; 25–26; Elliott Roosevelt, p. 104.

233 *Patton's dinner and guest book:* Patton's Diary; *Patton Papers*, p. 157.

233 *"I have seldom had a harder week":* Fraser, p. 321.

233 *"JOAN OF ARC":* CHAR 20/127, Stratagem 112, Churchill to Eden, 1/20/43.

233 *De Gaulle agrees to come:* De Gaulle, vol. 2, pp. 83–84 ("no particular haste"); Dixon's Casablanca Diary, January 20.

233 *Sammy Schulman:* MacVane, pp. 174–75.

233 *"The back of the work":* Brooke, p. 364.

THIRTEEN: DAY EIGHT: THURSDAY, JANUARY 21

235 *Minutes of the American meeting:* AFHRA Doc. No. 119.151-1, pp. 41–44; King's observations, Whitehill papers, Box 69, unlabeled notebook.

236 *Minutes of the British meeting:* CAB 99/24, pp. 110–11.

236 *McCrea's morning:* McCrea, pp. 140–42, *FRUS*, pp. 530–31.

236 *Patton and the sultan:* Patton, *War*, pp. 25, 31–32.

237 *"Hail to the Chief":* Issac D. White Papers, U.S. Army Heritage and Education Center, Carlisle, PA, Oral History of General Isaac D. White, p. 162.

238 *Roosevelt and the troops:* Log of the Trip, pp. 22–28; *FRUS*, pp. 499, 505, 529–30, 838; Durno, pp. 74–76; all YouTube films are cited in the bibliography; *Picture Post* magazine, 2/13/43; McCrea, pp. 142–43; Clark, pp. 149–51; *Patton Papers*, pp. 157–58; Reilly, p. 160, McIntire, p. 153; Harriman, p. 181; FDRL, OF 4675 World War II, "Casablanca Conference Crimea Conference," John Lee to FDR 5/22/43, "Tom" to "Dear Mom," 4/13/43; Pendar, pp. 144–45; Elliott Roosevelt, pp. 104, 107–8; Sherwood, p. 685; Robert Hopkins, pp. 49–50; Harmon, pp. 109–10; Burns, p. 321; Atkinson, p. 290; Hamilton, pp. 102–3.

239 *Letters:* FDRL, OF 4675 World War II "Casablanca Conference Crimea

Conference" and "Casablanca Conference," Misc. Comments folder; OF 200-2-P-OF 200-2-U Trips of the President, "Casablanca Conference Jan. 9–31, 1943."

240 *Minutes of the CCS meeting:* FRUS, pp. 667–82; Arnold, *American Aviation,* vol. 1, p. 467. See Overy, *Why the Allies Won,* p. 117.

241 *Escort capacity:* Cooke papers, Box 24, "American-British Strategy," 11/7/42, p. 4.

241 *The Casablanca Directive:* FRUS, pp. 781–91.

242 *Portal did not consider U-boats:* Portal Oral History, pp. 9–11.

244 *Churchill and the British chiefs and planners:* CAB 99/24, pp. 112–15; CAB 120/76, Stratagem 179, p. 1; Brooke, pp. 365–66; Kennedy's Diary, 1/21/43 and 1/22/43; Kennedy, p. 285; JACB 20/1, pp. 70–72 ("look big" . . . "piddling" . . . "obstinate"); Handy Interview, p. 135 ("sun lamp"); Ismay, p. 122 ("machinery of negation"); Howard, *Grand Strategy,* pp. 266–67; Fraser, p. 326; Casablanca Conference, pp. 5–6.

246 *Churchill sent Attlee and Eden:* FRUS, p. 830.

246 *Harriman on Giraud:* Harriman notes, p. 7.

246 *"better change"* . . . *"able to swing it":* FRUS, p. 530; Elliott Roosevelt, pp. 107–8.

246 *"rough stuff"* . . . *"Turkey":* Hinge of Fate, p. 686; Ben-Moshe, p. 699.

246 *"bride arrives"* . . . *"recovery from the effects":* FRUS, pp. 831–32.

FOURTEEN: DAY NINE: FRIDAY, JANUARY 22

247 *War correspondents:* Butcher's Diary, pp. A-183–84; Durno, pp. 81–82; Middleton, p. 248; MacVane, p. 173; Austin, pp. 72–73.

247 *Hopkins advised him to postpone . . . "shut in a room":* FRUS, pp. 820–21; Arnold, *American Aviation,* vol. 1, p. 468.

248 *Hopkins found Churchill in bed:* Log of the Trip, p. 29; FRUS, pp. 530, 679–80; Sherwood, pp. 687–88.

248 *The British meeting:* CAB 120/76, Stratagem 179, p. 1.

248 *Minutes of the CCS meeting:* FRUS, pp. 680–86.

248 *draft report to Stalin:* FRUS, pp. 782–85.

249 *Marshall haggard:* Parton's Diary, 1/19/43.

250 *someone else would have to be found:* Kennedy's Diary, 1/22/43; Kennedy, p. 285.

250 *"unbroken German forces" . . . "unbeatable":* Cooke papers, Box 24, "American-British Strategy," 11/7/42. See AIR 9/168, "American-British Strategy in 1943."

251 *"culmination of all my efforts":* Brooke, p. 367.

251 *"We came, we listened":* Wedemeyer, p. 192.

251 *"relays"... "smarter than hell":* Handy Interview, pp. 179–84; Roberts, p. 337.

251 *The group picture: FRUS,* pp. 530–31, photos after p. 483; Sherwood, p. 688; Kennedy's Diary, 1/22/43; Kennedy, p. 286; Elliott Roosevelt, p. 108.

252 *Medal of Honor:* Ismay, p. 289; McCrea, p. 144.

252 *Mountbatten and his eccentrics:* Sherwood, pp. 688–89; Wedemeyer, p. 109; Pogue, *Ordeal,* p. 311; Dykes, p. 158; King's Flight Log Book, p. 6; King, pp. 486–87; Kennedy's Diary, 1/19/43; Lorne W. Gold, *The Canadian Habbakuk Project* (Cambridge, UK: International Glaciological Society, 1993).

253 *Marshall lunched with FDR:* Log of the Trip, p. 30; *FRUS,* p. 531; Elliott Roosevelt, pp. 108–9; Sherwood, p. 689.

254 *De Gaulle arrived:* Macmillan, *Blast of War,* p. 198; Murphy, pp. 173–75; de Gaulle, vol. 2, p. 84; Mack's Account, p. 1; Dixon's Casablanca Diary, January 22; Codman, pp. 79–80; Kersaudy, p. 247.

254 *white villa inflamed... "a flagrant insult":* Murphy, pp. 165, 173–74; de Gaulle, vol. 2, p. 84; Codman, pp. 81–82.

255 *De Gaulle's lunch with Giraud:* Kersaudy, p. 247; Macmillan, *Blast of War,* p. 200; Sherwood, p. 689; Mack's Account, p. 1.

255 *"desperate conflict... shotgun wedding":* Macmillan, *Blast of War,* p. 199; Macmillan, *War Diaries,* pp. 7, n. 11, 10.

256 *Macmillan's and Mack's first approach to de Gaulle:* FO 660/85, Mack to Strang, 1/28/43, and Mack's Account, p. 2; Dixon's Casablanca Diary, January 22; de Gaulle, vol. 2, p. 86; Macmillan, *Blast of War,* p. 201.

257 *Minutes of the CCS meeting: FRUS,* pp. 687–93.

257 *"Continental Operations in 1943": FRUS,* p. 785.

257 *Wedemeyer had wired:* Matloff and Snell, *1941–1942,* p. 381.

258 *a combined planners not: FRUS,* p. 789.

258 *"What a bunch":* Arnold, *American Airpower,* vol. 1, p. 469.

258 *too complicated:* Patton's Diary, 1/22/43.

258 *"bad hater":* Wilson, p. 87.

258 *Churchill's meeting with de Gaulle: FRUS,* p. 532; CAB 120/76, Stratagem 198, p. 2; Mack's Account, p. 2; Dixon's Casablanca Diary, January 22; de Gaulle, vol. 2, pp. 86–87; *Hinge of Fate,* pp. 681–82; Sherwood, p. 690; Harriman, p. 186; Wilson, p. 88.

259 *"considered it cock-eyed":* Harriman notes, p. 7.

261 *"very mild approval":* Mack's Account, p. 2.

261 *Roosevelt's dinner for the Sultan:* Log of the Trip, pp. 29–30; *FRUS,* p. 531;

Sherwood papers, Box 7, McCrea folder, McCrea to Sherwood, 12/8/49, p. 4; McCrea, pp. 144–46; Sherwood, pp. 689–90; Crawford, pp. 35–36; MacVane, pp. 180–81; Macmillan, *Blast of War*, p. 201; Elliott Roosevelt, pp. 109–12; de Gaulle, vol. 2, p. 93; Harriman, p. 191; Pendar, p. 145; Patton's Diary, 1/22/43; Patton, *War*, p. 13; *Patton Papers*, pp. 151, 158; Murphy, p. 173; Robert Hopkins, p. 50; McIntire, p. 152; Leahy, p. 144; Robertson, p. 73; Susan Gilson Miller, *A History of Modern Morocco* (New York: Cambridge University Press, 2013), pp. 142–43.

261 *"bright as a button"*: Codman, p. 84.

262 *"worse for drink"*: Jacob in Normanbrook et al., pp. 182–83.

264 *Churchill returned to the White House:* Sherwood, p. 690.

264 *Murphy's and Roosevelt's talks with de Gaulle:* Sherwood, pp. 685–86; Murphy, p. 174; de Gaulle, vol. 2, pp. 87–89, 92; Reilly, pp. 157–58; Pendar, pp. 141–42; Elliott Roosevelt, pp. 113–14; Kersaudy, pp. 249–56; Suckley, p. 199; Macmillan, *Blast of War*, pp. 201–2; Wilson, pp. 88–89; Mack's Account, p. 2; Dixon's Casablanca Diary, January 22.

265 *Roosevelt's effect on de Gaulle was hypnotic:* Wilson papers, unmarked page.

268 *Roosevelt, Churchill, and the diplomats:* Mack's Account, pp. 2–3; Elliott Roosevelt, p. 113.

FIFTEEN: DAY TEN: SATURDAY, JANUARY 23

269 *Patton's medal:* Patton's Diary, 1/23/43; Patton, *War*, p. 34; *Patton Papers*, p. 158; Puryear, Edgar F., Jr. *19 Stars.* (New York: Presidio Press, 2003), p. 269.

269 *drop-ins:* Log of the Trip, pp. 31–32.

269 *Hopkins's meeting with the grand vizier:* FRUS, pp. 532, 701–4.

270 *Book inscription:* Elliott Roosevelt, p. 116.

270 *Catroux, Giraud, and Murphy:* FRUS, pp. 700–701, 705; de Gaulle, vol. 2, pp. 89–92; Murphy, p. 175; Mack's Account, pp. 3–4; Dixon's Casablanca Diary, January 23; Elliott Roosevelt, p. 118.

270 *"imperial villa"* . . . *"unwilling to grasp"*: Log of the Trip, p. 32; FRUS, p. 532; Macmillan, *Blast of War*, pp. 199–200; Elliott Roosevelt, p. 118.

271 *Minutes of the CCS meeting:* FRUS, pp. 697–700, 791–800.

271 *"I would never have written"*: JACB 20/1, pp. 83–84. See Arnold, *Global Mission*, p. 398.

271 *King was a happy man . . . gone along with Marshall . . . wise:* FRUS, p. 630; Cooke papers, Box 11, "Speeches, Writings and Interviews," "Casablanca Conference," p. 1; Sherwood papers, Box 40, interview with King, p. 2; Wilt, p. 528; Stoler, Mark A. *The Politics of the Second Front: American Military*

Planning and Diplomacy in Coalition Warfare 1941–1943. (Westport, CT: Greenwood Press, 1977), p. 25.

271 *"It was not": The War Reports,* pp. 155–56.

272 *"skin of our teeth":* Morgan, p. 26.

272 *"wonderfully good conference":* Kennedy's Diary, 1/23/43.

272 *"feeling much better":* Sherwood, p. 691.

272 *"speed and weight":* Gilbert, p. 308.

272 *Giraud's lunch with de Gaulle:* de Gaulle, vol. 2, pp. 89–92; Mack's Account, pp. 4–5; Dixon's Casablanca Diary, January 23; Funk, *de Gaulle,* pp. 74–75.

273 *"not ten percent": FRUS,* p. 705; de Gaulle, vol. 2, p. 92.

274 *Wilbur and de Gaulle: FRUS,* pp. 705–7; Hopkins papers, Box 330, "Book 7: North Africa, Pre-Casablanca—Moscow Conference," Wilbur memo, 1/23/43; Sherwood, pp. 686–87; de Gaulle, vol. 2, p. 93.

274 *De Gaulle and Macmillan:* de Gaulle, p. 397; Mack's Account, p. 5; Dixon's Casablanca Diary, January 23.

274 *Brooke and Marshall on de Gaulle:* Brooke, p. 263; Pogue, *Organizer,* p. 400.

275 *late-night talk with Murphy and Macmillan:* Mack's Account, p. 5; Dixon's Casablanca Diary, January 23; Macmillan, *Blast of War,* p. 202.

275 *Plenary meeting:* Log of the Trip, p. 32; *FRUS,* pp. 532–33, 707–19; Kennedy's Diary, 1/23/43 ("phenomenally lovely"); Ismay, p. 290; Arnold, *Global Mission,* pp. 399–400; King, pp. 422–24; Elliott Roosevelt, p. 118; Brooke, p. 367; Buell, p. 280.

275 *"being measured":* U.S. Army Heritage and Education Center, Carlisle, PA, Interview of General Jacob E. Smart, pp. 153–54.

277 *huge colored arrows:* Slessor, p. 403.

278 *"Churchill was rather stubborn":* King's Flight Log Book, p. 14.

279 *"subtle deals" . . . "that naïve":* Wedemeyer, pp. 106–7.

279 *Colosseum:* John Colville, *The Fringes of Power: Downing Street Diaries, 1939–1955* (London: Hodder & Stoughton, 1985), p. 282.

280 *tube alloys: FRUS,* p. 803; *Hinge of Fate,* pp. 474–75; CHAR 20/127, Stratagems 196 and 198, p. 3 ("extinction"); Brooke, p. xxxii.

281 *Minutes of the CCS meeting: FRUS,* pp. 719–22.

281 *Brooke on the conference's results:* Fraser, p. 321; Brooke, pp. 367–68.

281 *Churchill and Marrakech: Hinge of Fate,* p. 694; Pendar, p. 147.

282 *Roosevelt's dinner and the evening's work:* Log of the Trip, p. 32; *FRUS,* pp. 533, 707, 801–5, 836, n. 1, 842–49; Dixon's Casablanca Diary, January 23.

282 *an old SOB: Patton Papers,* p. 159.

282 *lifted a glass:* Log of the Trip, p. 33; *FRUS,* p. 533; Elliott Roosevelt, p. 119.

SIXTEEN: THE DENOUEMENT

283 *"breaking up at the end of term"*: JACB, 20/1, p. 96.

283 *"weighed a bit"*: FDRL, Box 133, Executive Office of the President—McCrea, John L., unnumbered handwritten narrative.

283 *Churchill wrote Clementine:* Churchill and Churchill, *Speaking for Themselves*, pp. 474–75.

284 *"tumbled" bed . . . "sensible alterations"*: JACB, 20/1, pp. 98–101.

284 *"the messengers"*: de Gaulle, vol. 2, p. 93.

284 *draft communiqué: FRUS*, pp. 822–23; Mack's Account, pp. 6–7.

284 *De Gaulle's reply:* Mack's Account, p. 6; de Gaulle, p. 93; Macmillan, *Blast of War*, p. 202; *FRUS*, p. 839.

285 *Murphy, Hopkins, Roosevelt, and Macmillan: FRUS*, pp. 723, 839–49; Sherwood, pp. 686, 691–93.

285 *"I don't think the President"*: Charmley, p. 559, citing FO 660/86, Macmillan memorandum.

285 *rounds of failed negotiations:* Mack's Account, pp. 3–5; Dixon's Casablanca Diary, January 23–24; Funk, *de Gaulle*, p. 77.

286 *Giraud's conversation with Roosevelt and associated documents:* Funk, "'Anfa Memorandum,'" passim; *FRUS*, pp. 823–28, 840; Sherwood, p. 693; Elliott Roosevelt, p. 119; Thompson, p. 107; de Gaulle, vol. 2, p. 94; Leighton and Coakley, pp. 514–15; Pogue, *Organizer*, pp. 230–33; Funk, *de Gaulle*, pp. 79–83.

287 *"slapdash methods"*: Macmillan, *Blast of War*, pp. 194–95, 209; Murphy, pp. 165, 169.

287 *Churchill's meeting with de Gaulle: FRUS*, p. 840; de Gaulle, vol. 2, p. 94; Mack's Account, p. 6; Sherwood, p. 693; Thompson, p. 107.

288 *participants' accounts . . . irreconcilable:* See the source note immediately below. Hopkins's version is logical, consistent with Thompson's, nearly contemporaneous, and comes from a straight-talking source.

288 *FDR, Churchill, de Gaulle, and Giraud confer:* Log of the Trip, pp. 32–33; *FRUS*, pp. 533, 725, n. 1; 829, 840; Thompson, pp. 107–8; de Gaulle, vol. 2, pp. 94–95; Sherwood, p. 693; Macmillan, *Blast of War*, p. 203; Murphy, p. 175; Elliott Roosevelt, p. 119; Funk, *de Gaulle*, p. 81; Mack's Account, pp. 6–7; Dixon's Casablanca Diary, January 24. For Macmillan's overview of the French imbroglio, see FO 660/86, Macmillan to Eden, 1/24/43.

290 *The press conference:* Anderson papers, original stenographic transcript and reminiscences; Wilson papers, manuscript, p. 31; Log of the Trip, p. 33; *FRUS*, pp. 534, 725–31, 829, n. 1, 833–49; *New York Times*, 1/27/43, pp. 3,

col. 6, and 6, col. 1; *Hinge of Fate*, p. 693; de Gaulle, vol. 2, p. 95; Sherwood, p. 693; Churchill and Churchill, *Speaking for Themselves*, p. 475; McCrea, pp. 146–47; Harriman, p. 187; Macmillan, *Blast of War*, p. 203; Elliott Roosevelt, pp. 120–21; Murphy, p. 165; King, pp. 425, 483; Reilly, pp. 158–59; Thompson, p. 108; Robert Hopkins, p. 53; Moorhead, pp. 148–51; Middleton, p. 254; Austin, pp. 72–73; Butcher, p. 428; Gilbert, p. 269; Grigg, p. 75; Burns, pp. 322–23; Hamilton, pp. 130–33 ("Goebbels").

292   *its declaration had been excised:* Ben-Moshe, p. 704.

295   *Patton, Noguès, and Michelier:* Log of the Trip, p. 33; *FRUS*, p. 534; Patton's Diary; *Patton Papers*, p. 160.

295   *leather portfolio: New York Times*, 1/27/43, p. 3, col. 6.

295   *No consultations on unconditional surrender and reactions to its announcement:* Smart, p. 42; Slessor, p. 447; *Marshall Interviews*, p. 616; King's Flight Log Book, p. 14; Leahy, p. 145; Howard, *Grand Strategy*, p. 285.

295   *dispersed across the globe:* Arnold, *Global Mission*, p. 400; King, p. 426; Brooke, p. 368; Wedemeyer, p. 193; Smart, p. 42; Parton, *Memoir*, pp. 230, 232; Kennedy, p. 286.

295   Bulolo *steamed for home:* Potter, p. 26.

295   *officers threw parties:* Anderson Papers, Louise Anderson's Diary.

296   *their joint communiqué:* Funk, de Gaulle, p. 82; De Gaulle, vol. 2, p. 95; Macmillan, Blast of War, p. 203; FO 660/88, Impressions of ANFA Conference, p. 3 ("saved from the wreck"); Mack's Account, p. 7.

SEVENTEEN: MARRAKECH

297   *Motorcade to Marrakech:* Log of the Trip, pp. 33–34; *FRUS*, pp. 534–35, 840; JACB 20/1, p. 101; *Hinge of Fate*, p. 64; Sherwood, p. 694; Macmillan, *Blast of War*, pp. 203–4; McCrea, p. 148; Pendar, p. 146; Harriman notes, p. 3; Harriman, p. 191.

298   *Marrakech and the Taylor Villa:* Log of the Trip, p. 35; *FRUS*, pp. 534, 840; floor plan, FDRL, Box 20, Secret Service Records, File 6-1, Trips of the President, 1934–1943; Harriman notes, pp. 3–4; *Hinge of Fate*, pp. 694–95; Sherwood, p. 694; Moran, p. 89; Pendar, pp. 131, 135–37; 145–47, 158; JACB 1/20, pp. 102–4; Brooke, p. 368; Durno, p. 92; Robert Hopkins, pp. 56–57; Thompson, p. 131; Churchill and Churchill, *Speaking for Themselves*, p. 476; FDRL, McCrea papers, handwritten narrative; Atkinson, pp. 295–96, 300.

298   *The tower:* Log of the Trip, p. 35; *FRUS*, pp. 535, 841; *Hinge of Fate*, p. 695;

Sherwood, p. 694; Pendar, pp. 147–48; McCrea, pp. 148–49; Moran, pp. 89–90; McIntire, pp. 154–55.

298 *"beauty prize"* . . . *"so generously"*: Pendar, p. 147; Moran, p. 90.

299 *"world of good"* . . . *"sobbed with the loneliness"*: Brooke, pp. 368, 447–48.

299 *"put his back into it"*: JACB 20/1, p. 87.

299 *Profile of Pendar:* Parton's Diary, 2/23/43; Harriman notes, p. 4; JACB 1 20, p. 103; *New York Times,* 12/8/72, p. 48; Howard, *Grand Strategy,* p. 147.

299 *Pendar's dinner:* Log of the Trip, p. 36; *FRUS,* pp. 535, 731–32; 841; Pendar, pp. 131–40; 145–52, 158; *Hinge of Fate,* p. 695; Harriman notes, pp. 4–5; Harriman, p. 191; Sherwood, p. 694; Moran, p. 90.

301 *"high dudgeon"*: Harriman, pp. 188, 190.

301 *Late-night work: FRUS,* pp. 732, 805, 841; Pendar, pp. 152–53; Kennedy, p. 276; Suckley, p. 199 ("Winston hours"); Sherwood, p. 694; Harriman notes, p. 5; Harriman, p. 192; McIntire, p. 155; JACB 20/1, p. 108; CHAR 20/127, Stratagems 252, 255, 361.

EIGHTEEN: HOMEWARD BOUND

303 *"Drove to the field"*: Sherwood, p. 694; Harriman, p. 192.

303 *Churchill to the airport and back:* Pendar, pp. 153–55; *Hinge of Fate,* p. 622; McCrea, pp. 149–50; McIntire, p. 155; JACB 1/20, p. 108; Brooke, pp. 223, 369; Moran, p. 90.

305 *summoned Brooke* . . . *"duty calls"*: Brooke, pp. 369–70; Bryant, pp. 460–61; *Life* magazine, 11/6/50, p. 99 (Mrs. Taylor's bedroom); *Hinge of Fate,* pp. 703–4; Pendar, p. 155.

306 *De Gaulle rejected an American Liberator:* Mack's Account, p. 7; Kennedy, p. 287; de Gaulle, vol. 2, p. 95.

306 *"subversives"*: *New York Times,* 1/27/43, p. 1, col. 3.

306 *"kill someone"*: Patton's Diary, 1/26/43; *Patton Papers,* pp. 161, 163.

306 *Ismay's note:* CAB 120/75, Ismay to Eisenhower, 1/23/43.

307 *Death of Dykes and Stewart:* JACB 1 20, pp. 96, 124–26; Harriman papers, Box 163, "Meiklejohn Report" folder, Report of the Harriman Mission, p. 204, "Chron File Feb. 1943," Harriman to Hopkins, 2/2/43; Dykes, pp. 2–3, 16; Harriman, p. 192; Bernard Fergusson, *The Watery Maze: The Story of Combined Operations* (London: Collins, 1961), p. 218; Polley, p. 290; Marshall, *The Papers,* vol. 3, pp. 519–20.

307 *Roosevelt's journey home:* Log of the Trip, pp. 40–51; Durno, pp. 92–102; McCrea, pp. 151–53; Sherwood, p. 695; McIntire, p. 157; Eleanor Roosevelt,

pp. 81–82; FDRL, Map Room Papers, Box 165, naval aide's files, A/16 Casablanca Conference, November 27, 1942–January 14, 1932, Memorandum for File, 3/31/43, McCown to McCrea, 2/6/43; Leahy, pp. 144–45; Burns, p. 324 ("FDR left behind").

309 Roosevelt briefed . . . "talking in England": Eleanor Roosevelt, p. 282; Leahy, p. 145.

309 Churchill in Turkey: Hinge of Fate, p. 708; Brooke, pp. 73–76.

309 Churchill and Brooke in Tripoli: Brooke, pp. 378–79.

309 Churchill addresses the Commons: "Mr. Churchill's Speech in Parliament on Feb 11," Bulletin of International News 20, no. 4 (February 20, 1943): 152–54; Eaker, p. 124.

AFTERMATH

311 "stick pins into them": Roosevelt, Public Papers, vol. 12, pp. 82–83.

312 tentative outline . . . true north: Atkinson, pp. 270, 299; Wilt, pp. 518, 523, 528–29.

312 six ensuing conferences: The following pages' thumbnail treatment of the post-Anfa conferences and the progress of the war closely track and draw heavily on the far more thorough and nuanced accounts in Roberts, cited below.

312 "we got organized": Handy Interview, pp. 233–34.

312 planning system: Cline, p. 219.

312 "together and ahead": Marshall, The Papers, vol. 3, pp. 634–35.

312 Trident: Roberts, pp. 357–93; Pogue, Organizer, pp. 193–213; Rawson, pp. 73–122; Wedemeyer, pp. 215–17.

313 at least twenty staff officers: Weiss, p. 85.

313 Tunisia: The War Reports, pp. 93–98; Roosevelt, Public Papers, vol. 12, p. 46.

315 The war on the U-boat: Overy, Why the Allies Won, pp. 54–60; Bryant, pp. 489–91.

315 Quadrant: Roberts, pp. 391–409; Pogue, Organizer, pp. 245–62; Rawson, pp. 123–46.

315 crushing news . . . "painful" . . . "irreconcilable": Brooke, pp. 420, 426–27, 441–42.

316 "the root of the matter . . . Mediterranean strategy": Brooke, pp. 443, 445, 447.

316 choose itself: Roberts, p. 403.

316 "poisonous" . . . fist: Brooke, p. 444; Roberts, pp. 404–5.

316 Pykrete demonstration: Brooke, pp. 347, 438, 445-46; King, p. 487; www .dailymail.co.news/article-6211223/Unseen-Churchill-letter-reveals-brazen -Lord-Mouontbatten-nearly-shot-dead-RAF-chief.html; Leasor, p. 76.

317   *Sextant:* Roberts, pp. 418–43; Pogue, *Organizer,* pp. 297–309; Rawson, pp. 147–56.

318   *"stink"... "nebulous" second front:* Brooke, pp. 465, 475.

318   *every Mediterranean goal:* Roberts, pp. 425–26, 435–36.

318   *Having overtaken them:* Roberts, pp. 428–32; Wilt, p. 526.

318   *the British brought five goals . . . explicit direction:* Roberts, pp. 428–32; Wilt, p. 526.

318   *insults . . . "socked him":* Danchev, *Very Special,* p. 119.

318   *talk with Roosevelt . . . "uncommonly little":* Brooke, p. 477.

319   *Chinese generals . . . Brooke implied:* Brooke, pp. 478–80; Roberts, pp. 437–38.

319   *"lining up"... "acquisitive"... "adjust":* Roberts, pp. 439–41.

319   *"father and mother of a row":* Brooke, p. 481.

319   *the Dill Rule:* Roberts, pp. 441–42.

319   *Tehran:* Roberts, pp. 433–51; Pogue, *Organizer,* pp. 309–23; Rawson, pp. 157–200.

320   *"asylum or a nursing home":* Brooke, p. 485.

320   *"seemed puzzled":* Brooke, pp. 483–87

320   *"rough SOB":* Pogue, *Organizer,* p. 313.

320   *Uncle Joe:* Roberts, p. 445.

320   *rocked the prime minister:* Normanbrook et al., pp. 33–36, 209–10.

320   *Roosevelt's anticolonial talks with Eden, Churchill, and Stalin:* Dulles, pp. 10–16.

321   *A third of the Luftwaffe . . . another twenty divisions:* Roberts, pp. 410–11, 413–14, 459.

321   *Fifteen percent:* Roberts, p. 459.

321   *"has been forced upon us":* Roberts, p. 479.

322   *"His Majesty's anxieties":* Churchill, *Closing the Ring,* p. 621.

322   *three Luftwaffe fighters:* Roberts, p. 488.

322   *"the Boche refused":* Brooke, p. 558.

322   *"Afterwards you lose sight":* Roberts, p. 489, quoting Handy.

322   *the Germans outfought the Allies:* Roberts, pp. 354–55.

322   *more divisions in the field . . . "his role":* Normanbrook et al., p. 32; Roberts, pp. 468, 493.

322   *had little effect:* Roberts, p. 508.

323   *Octagon:* Roberts, pp. 512–26; Pogue, *Organizer,* pp. 432–37; Rawson, pp. 216–30.

323   *"nothing would have saved":* Roberts, pp. 514–15.

323 *"ever-increasing"*: Roberts, p. 518.

323 *"Churchill offered . . . self-supporting"*: Roberts, pp. 519–24.

323 *Churchill denies Dill a peerage*: Brooke, pp. 464–65, 617.

324 *Dill's funeral . . . "fully realize"*: George C. Marshall Foundation, Doc 4-570; Danchev, " 'Dilly-Dally,' " p. 35.

325 *"harmonious conclusion"*: Roberts, pp. 541–42.

325 *"life in my body . . . Dear old Winston"*: Dulles, pp. 16–17.

325 *snookered Churchill too*: Roberts, pp. 548–58.

325 *"unproclaimed victory"*: Murphy, pp. 175–84.

325 *ghostwritten memoranda*: Macmillan, *Blast of War*, p. 207; CHAR 20/127, Stratagem 323; Funk, " 'Anfa Memorandum,' " pp. 251–54; Funk, *de Gaulle*, pp. 83–100; Charmley, pp. 559–60.

326 *Arming the French*: Leighton and Coakley, pp. 515–16; Murphy, p. 141.

326 *"trouble for the Boche"*: Durno, pp. 28–30, 103.

326 *"crockery"*: FDRL, Map Room Papers, "FDR Corresp. to Churchill, December 1942–March 1943.

327 *Giraud and his family's fate*: Murphy, pp. 178–81, 184; Charmley, pp. 563–67; Durno, p. 103; Katherine Marshall, p. 151; *Closing the Ring*, p. 699; Brooke, pp. 621–22.

327 *De Gaulle rode with Churchill*: Thompson, p. 147; Harold Nicholson, *Diaries and Letters, 1939–1945* (London: Collins, 1967), p. 412.

327 *Unconditional Surrender*: Ben-Moshe treats its announcement at Anfa comprehensively and contributes an interesting theory on how it came about.

327 *"stay won"*: Sherwood, pp. 695–97; Chase, p. 263.

328 *nothing to fear*: Chase, pp. 264–66.

328 *boosted Allied morale*: See, e.g., Pogue, *Organizer*, p. 34.

328 *"He was a maniac"*: Gilbert, p. 310.

328 *Wedemeyer's memoirs refuted*: Wedemeyer, pp. 186–87; Pogue, *Organizer*, pp. 33–34.

329 *Some historians think*: e.g., Grigg and Wedemeyer.

329 *"so many ifs"*: Roberts, p. 402.

329 *"different quartet"*: Roberts, p. 557.

329 *The British, he goes on, were right*: Roberts, pp. 422–26, 451.

330 *Brooke told a BBC audience*: YouTube, "The Alanbrooke Diaries."

330 *"the impossible"*: Overy, *How the Allies Won*, p. 245.

330 *"Ice Cream Front" . . . "chair-borne infantry"*: Crawford, pp. 25–26.

330 *Mrs. Taylor*: Murphy, p. 155.

331 *Mohammed V and Hassan II:* Susan Glaser, *A Modern History of Morocco.* (Cambridge, UK: Cambridge University Press, 2013), pp. 30–52, 135–212.

331 *Churchill* was *moved to tears:* Thompson p. 157.

331 *"physical blow":* Meacham, p, 344.

331 *"forced along by the crowd":* Thompson p. 157.

331 *middle-class boys:* Normanbrook et al., pp. 74–75.

331 *"for fear of breaking down":* Brooke, p. 712.

332 *"this era of mediocrity":* Kersaudy, p. 413.

332 *"special relationship"* . . . *"iron curtain":* Winston S. Churchill, *The Sinews of Peace*, Randolph S. Churchill, ed. (London: Cassell, 1948), pp. 93–105.

332 *Angelina Jolie: New York Times*, March 4, 2021, Sec. C, p. 5.

332 *Marshall's memoirs and papers:* Pogue, *Ordeal*, p. xi.

332 *"hold a candle to him":* Slessor, pp. 362–63.

332 *everyone stood up:* Grigg, p. 67.

333 *At his initiative:* Brooke, p. 702.

333 *"ostentatiously turn his back":* Colville, p. 84.

333 *Montgomery called Brooke:* Brooke, pp. xxiv–xxv; Bryant, p. 18.

333 *"ornithologist":* Brooke, p. xxvi, quoting Raymond Fletcher, "Books and People," *Tribune*, November 6, 1959.

Bibliography of Works Frequently Cited

PRIMARY SOURCES

Interviews and Oral Histories

Interview with Thomas T. Handy for Dwight D. Eisenhower Library.

Oral History of Admiral Ruthven E. Libby (United States Naval Institute, Annapolis, MD).

Oral History of Robert Murphy (Columbia University Oral History Project, New York, NY).

Reminiscences of Charles Frederick Algernon Portal, October 1968 (Columbia University Oral History Research Office, New York, NY).

Interview of General Albert C. Wedemeyer (U.S. Army Heritage and Education Center, Carlisle, PA).

Manuscripts

"American-British Strategy in 1943," AIR 9/168.

The Case for Day Bombing, Eaker to Churchill (Air Force Historical Research Agency, Maxwell Air Force Base).

George E. Durno, "Flight to Africa: A Chronicle of the Casablanca Conference Between President Roosevelt and Prime Minister Churchill" (FDRL).

Harold Mack to William Strang, 1/28/43, followed by Mack's account of negotiations with de Gaulle and Giraud at Anfa, FO 660/85.

Log of the Trip of the President to the Casablanca Conference—9–31 January 1943 (FDRL).

Operation "Symbol," Brigadier E. I. C. Jacob, Churchill Archives, JACB 1/20.

Photographs taken at Casablanca (National Archives, College Park, MD).

Pierson Dixon, "Anfa Camp Casablanca Diary of Events; de Gaulle–Giraud Negotiations," FO 660/86.

Pierson Dixon, "Impressions of ANFA Conference: French Question," FO 660/88.

President's Trip to Casablanca, Gary H. Spaman to Frank J. Wilson, June 26, 1945 (FDRL).

Archival Papers

Papers of Louise Anderson Locke (privately held).

Papers of General Henry H. Arnold (LOC).

Papers of Harry C. Butcher (Eisenhower Library).

Papers of Sir Winston Churchill (Churchill Archives).

Papers of Admiral Charles M. Cooke (Hoover Institution Library & Archives, Stanford University, Palo Alto, CA).

Papers of George Hall (Eisenhower Library).

Papers of Governor Averell Harriman (LOC).

Papers of Harry Hopkins (FDRL).

Papers of General Sir Edward Ian Claude Jacob (Churchill Archives).

Papers of General Sir John Noble Kennedy (Liddell Hart Centre for Military Archives, King's College, London, UK).

Papers of Admiral Ernest J. King (LOC).

Papers of General George C. Marshall (George C. Marshall Institute, Lexington, VA).

Papers of Captain John L. McCrea (FDRL).

Papers of James Parton (Houghton Library, Harvard).

Papers of General George S. Patton Jr. (LOC).

Papers of Robert E. Sherwood (Houghton Library, Harvard).

Papers of Air Marshal Sir John Slessor (National Archives, London).

Papers of Major General Carl A. Spaatz (LOC).

Papers of Walter Muir Whitehill (Massachusetts Historical Society, Boston, MA).

Papers of Frank Wilson (University of Wyoming, Laramie, WY).

Books

Arnold, H. H. *American Airpower Comes of Age: General Henry H. "Hap" Arnold's World War II Diaries*, two vols, vol. 1, John W. Huston, ed. Montgomery, Al: Air University Press, 2002.

———. *Global Mission.* New York: Harper & Brothers, 1949.

Austin, A. B. *Birth of an Army.* London: Gollancz, 1943.

Brooke, Alan. *War Diaries, 1939–1945: Field Marshal Lord Alanbrook*, Alex Danchev and Daniel Todman, eds. London: Phoenix Press, 2002. (Original pub. London: Weidenfield & Nicholson, 2001.)

Butcher, Harry C. *My Three Years with Eisenhower.* New York: Simon & Schuster, 1946.

Casablanca Conference (Morocco). Washington, DC: Joint History Office, Office of the Chairman of the Joint Chiefs of Staff, United States Department of Defense, 2017.

Casablanca Conference January 1943, Papers and Minutes of Meetings. Washington, DC: Office, U.S. Secretary, Office of the Combined Chiefs of Staff, 1943.

Churchill, Winston. *The Second World War*. Boston: Houghton Mifflin, 1948–1953.

———. *Their Finest Hour* (1949).

———. *The Grand Alliance* (1950).

———. *The Hinge of Fate* (1951).

———. *Closing the Ring* (1951).

Churchill, Winston, and Clementine Churchill. *Speaking for Themselves: The Personal Letters of Winston and Clementine Churchill*, Mary Soames, ed. London: Doubleday, 1998.

Clark, Mark. *Calculated Risk*. New York: Harper & Brothers, 1950.

Codman, Charles. *Drive*. Boston: Little, Brown, 1957.

Crawford, Kenneth G. *Report on North Africa*. New York: Farrar & Rinehart, 1943.

Cunningham, Andrew Browne. *A Sailor's Odyssey: The Autobiography of Admiral of the Fleet, Viscount Cunningham of Hyndhope*. New York: Dutton, 1951.

De Gaulle, Charles. *The War Memoirs of Charles de Gaulle*, 5 vols., vol 2, *Unity 1942–1944*, and vol. 3, *Unity 1942–1944, Documents*. New York: Simon & Schuster, 1959.

Dykes, Vivian. *Establishing the Anglo-American Alliance: The Second World War Diaries of Brigadier General Vivian Dykes*, Alex Danchev, ed. London: Brassey's, 1990.

Eden, Anthony. *The Eden Memoirs: The Reckoning*. London: Cassell, 1965.

Eisenhower, Dwight D. *Crusade in Europe*. Garden City, NY: Doubleday, 1948.

———. *The Eisenhower Diaries*, Robert H. Ferrell, ed. New York: W. W. Norton, 1981.

———. *The Papers of Dwight David Eisenhower*, 4 vols., vols. 1 and 2, Alfred Chandler, ed. Baltimore: Johns Hopkins University Press, 1970.

Foreign Relations of the United States: The Conferences at Washington, 1941–1942, and Casablanca, 1943. Washington, DC: U.S. Government Printing Office, 1968. (Minutes and key documents produced at the Casablanca Conference.)

Giraud, Henri. *Un Seul but, la Victoire*. Paris: Julliard, 1949.

Harmon, E. N. *Combat Commander: Autobiography of a Soldier*. Englewood Cliffs, NJ: Prentice-Hall, 1970.

Harriman, Averell, and Elie Abel. *Special Envoy to Churchill and Stalin, 1941–1946*. New York: Random House, 1975.

Hopkins, Harry. *The White House Papers of Harry L. Hopkins*, 2 vols, vol. 2, *January 1942–July 1945*, Robert E. Sherwood, ed. London: Eyre & Spottiswoode, 1949.

Hopkins, Robert. *Witness to History: Recollections of a WWII Photographer.* Seattle: Castle Pacific Publishing, 2002.

Ismay, Hastings Lionel. *The Memoirs of General Lord Ismay.* New York: Viking, 1960.

Kennedy, Sir John Noble. *The Business of War: The War Narrative of Major General Sir John Kennedy.* London: Hutchinson, 1957.

King, Ernest J., and Whitehill, Walter Muir. *Fleet Admiral King: A Naval Record.* New York: W. W. Norton, 1952.

Leahy, William D. *I Was There.* New York: Whittlesey House, 1950.

Leasor, James. *War at the Top: Based on the Experiences of General Sir Leslie Hollis.* London: M. Joseph, 1959.

Macmillan, Harold. *The Blast of War, 1939–1945.* New York: Harper & Row, 1967.

———. *War Diaries: Politics and War in the Mediterranean, January 1943–May 1945.* New York: St. Martin's Press, 1984.

MacVane, John. *Journey into War.* New York: Appleton-Century, 1943.

Marshall, George C. *George C. Marshall Interviews and Reminiscences for Forrest C. Pogue*, Larry I. Bland, ed. Lexington, VA: George C. Marshall Research Foundation, 1996.

———. *The Papers of George Catlett Marshall*, 7 vols., Larry I. Bland and Sharon Ritenour, eds. Lexington, VA: George C. Marshall Research Foundation, 1981–2003.

Marshall, Katherine Tupper. *Together: Annals of an Army Wife.* New York: Tupper & Love, 1946.

McCrea, John L. *Captain McCrea's War: The World War II Memoirs of Franklin Roosevelt's Aide and USS Iowa's First Commanding Officer*, Julia C. Tobey, ed. New York: Skyhorse Publishing, 2016.

McIntire, Ross. *Twelve Years with Roosevelt.* New York: Putnam, 1948.

Middleton, Drew. *Our Share of the Night.* New York: Viking, 1946.

Montgomery, Bernard Law. *The Memoirs of Field-Marshal the Viscount Montgomery of Alamein.* Cleveland: World, 1958.

Moorhead, Alan. *The End in Africa.* New York: Harper & Brothers, 1943.

Morgan, Frederick Edgeworth. *Overture to Overlord.* Garden City, NY: Doubleday, 1950.

Murphy, Robert. *Diplomat Among Warriors.* Garden City, NY: Doubleday, 1964.

Normanbrook, Lord, John Wheeler-Bennett, John Martin, Ian Jacob, and Leslie

Rowan. *Action This Day: Working with Churchill*. London: St. Martin's Press, 1968.

Patton, George S., Jr., *The Patton Papers, 1940–1945*, Martin Blumenson, ed. New York: Da Capo, 1996.

———. *War As I Knew It*. Boston: Houghton Mifflin, 1995.

Pendar, Kenneth. *Adventure in Diplomacy: Our French Dilemma*. New York: Dodd, Mead, 1945.

Price, G. Ward. *Giraud and the African Scene*. New York: Macmillan, 1944.

Reilly, Michael F., as told to William J. Slocum. *Reilly of the White House*. New York: Simon & Schuster, 1947.

Roosevelt, Eleanor. *This I Remember*. New York: Harper, 1949.

Roosevelt, Elliott. *As He Saw It*. New York: Duell, Sloan & Pierce, 1946.

Roosevelt, Franklin D., compiled by Samuel I. Rosenman. *The Public Papers and Addresses of Franklin D. Roosevelt*, vol. 12. New York: Harper & Brothers, 1950.

Sherwood, Robert E. *Roosevelt and Hopkins: An Intimate History*. New York: Harper & Brothers, 1948.

Slessor, John. *The Central Blue: Recollections and Reflections*. London: Cassell, 1956.

Stimson, Henry L., and McGeorge Bundy. *On Active Service in Peace and War*. New York: Harper, 1948.

Suckley, Margaret. *Closest Companion: The Unknown Story of the Intimate Friendship Between Franklin Roosevelt and Margaret Suckley*, Geoffrey C. Ward, ed. Boston: Houghton Mifflin, 2012.

Tedder, Arthur William. *With Prejudice: The War Memoirs of Marshal of the Royal Air Force, Lord Tedder*. Boston: Little, Brown, 1966.

Thompson, Walter. *I Was Churchill's Shadow*. London: C. Johnson, 1951.

The War Reports of General of the Army George C. Marshall, Chief of Staff, General of the Army H. H. Arnold, Commanding General Army Air Forces [and] Fleet Admiral Ernest J. King, Commander in Chief, United States Fleet and Chief of Naval Operations. Philadelphia: Lippincott, 1947.

Wedemeyer, Albert C. *Wedemeyer Reports!* New York: Holt, 1958.

Wilson, Sir Charles McMoran. *Churchill, Taken from the Diaries of Lord Moran*. Boston: Houghton Mifflin, 1966.

SECONDARY SOURCES
Books

Adams, Henry H. *Harry Hopkins, a Biography*. New York: Putnam, 1977.

Ambrose, Stephen A. *Eisenhower: Soldier General of the Army: President Elect, 1890–1952*. New York: Simon & Schuster, 1983.

Atkinson, Rick. *An Army at Dawn*. New York: Henry Holt, 2002.

Brodhurst, Leo. *Churchill's Anchor: The Biography of Admiral Sir Dudley Pound*. South Yorkshire, UK: Pen & Sword, 2000.

Bruer, William B. *Feuding Allies: The Private Wars of the High Command*. New York: Wiley, 1995.

Bryant, Arthur. *The Turn of the Tide: A History of the War Years Based on the Diaries of Field-Marshal Lord Alanbrooke, Chief of the Imperial General Staff*. Garden City, NY: Doubleday, 1957.

Buell, Thomas B. *Master of Sea Power: A Biography of Fleet Admiral Ernest J. King*. Boston: Little, Brown, 1980.

Burns, James MacGregor. *Roosevelt: The Soldier of Freedom*. New York: Harcourt Brace Jovanovich, 1970.

Cline, Ray S. *Washington Command Post: The Operations Division*, vol. 8 of *United States Army in World War II*. Washington, DC: Office of the Chief of Military History, Department of the Army, 1951.

Collier, Richard. *The Sands of Dunkirk*. London: Collins, 1961.

Colville, John. *Winston Churchill and His Inner Circle*. New York: Wyndham Books, 1981.

Cray, Ed. *General of the Army: George C. Marshall, Soldier and Statesman*. New York: Simon & Schuster, 1991.

Danchev, Alex. *On Specialness: Essays in Anglo-American Relations*. London: Macmillan, 1998.

———. *Very Special Relationship: Field Marshal Sir John Dill and the Anglo-American Alliance, 1941–1944*. London: Brassey's, 1986.

Davis, Kenneth S. *FDR, The War President, 1940–1943: A History*. New York: Random House, 2000.

Davis, Vernon E. *The History of the Joint Chiefs of Staff in World War II*. Washington, DC: United States Department of Defense, 1972.

Downing, John P. *At War with the British*. Daytona Beach, FL: J. P. Downing, 1980.

Ehrman, John P. W. *Grand Strategy*, vol. 5, *August 1942–September 1943*. London: Her Majesty's Stationery Office, 1956.

Fraser, David. *Alanbrooke*. New York: Athenaeum, 1982.

Funk, Arthur Layton. *Charles de Gaulle: The Crucial Years, 1943–1944*. Norman: University of Oklahoma Press, 1959.

Gilbert, Martin. *Winston S. Churchill: Road to Victory, 1941–1945*. Boston: Houghton Mifflin, 1986.

Grayling, A. C. *Among the Dead Cities: The History and Moral Legacy of the WWII Bombing of Civilians in Germany and Japan*. New York: Walker, 2006.

Grigg, John. *1943: The Victory That Never Was*. New York: Hill & Wang, 1980.

Hamilton, Nigel. *Commander in Chief: FDR's Battle with Churchill, 1943*. Boston: Houghton Mifflin Harcourt, 2016.

Hastings, Max. *Winston's War: Churchill, 1940–1945*. New York: Alfred A. Knopf, 2009.

Hayes, Grace P. *The United States Joint Chiefs of Staff: The War Against Germany*. Washington, DC: U.S. Government Printing Office, 1949.

Higgins, Trumbull. *Winston Churchill and the Second Front, 1940–1943*. New York: Oxford University Press, 1957.

Hindley, Meredith. *Destination Casablanca: Exiles, Espionage, and the Battle for North Africa in World War II*. New York: PublicAffairs, 2017.

Howard, Michael. *History of the Second World War*, vol. 4, *Grand Strategy: August 1941–September 1943*. London: Her Majesty's Stationery Office, 1972.

———. *The Mediterranean Strategy in the Second World War*. London: Weidenfeld & Nicolson, 1968.

Jackson, Julian. *De Gaulle*. London: Allen Lane, 2018.

Jackson, William, and Lord Bramall. *The Chiefs: The Story of the United Kingdom Chiefs of Staff*. London: Brassey's, 1992.

Jones, Matthew. *Britain, the United States and the Mediterranean War, 1942–44*. New York: St. Martin's Press, 1996.

Keegan, John, ed. *Churchill's Generals*. New York: Weidenfeld, 1991.

Kersaudy, François. *Churchill and de Gaulle*. New York: Athenaeum, 1982.

Kimball, Warren F., ed. *Churchill and Roosevelt: The Complete Correspondence*, 3 vols. Princeton: Princeton University Press, 1984.

Leighton, Richard M., and Robert W. Coakley. *Global Logistics and Strategy: 1941–1943*. Washington, DC: U.S. Government Printing Office, 1953.

Lord, Walter. *The Miracle of Dunkirk*. New York: Viking, 1982.

Mangold, Peter. *An Almost Impossible Ally: Harold Macmillan and Charles De Gaulle*. London: I. B. Taurus, 2006.

Matloff, Maurice. *Strategic Planning for Coalition Warfare, 1943–1944*. Washington, DC: Center of Military History, 1959.

Matloff, Maurice, and Edwin M. Snell. *Strategic Planning for Coalition Warfare, 1941–1942*. Washington, DC: Center of Military History, 1953.

McFarland, Stephen L. *America's Pursuit of Precision Bombing, 1910–1945*. Washington, DC: Smithsonian Institution Press, 1995.

Meacham, Jon. *Franklin and Winston: An Intimate Portrait of an Epic Friendship*. New York: Random House, 2003.

O'Sullivan, Christopher. *Harry Hopkins: FDR's Envoy to Churchill and Stalin*. Lanham, MD: Rowman & Littlefield, 2015.

Overy, Richard J. *The Bombers and the Bombed: Allied Air War Over Europe, 1940–1945*, New York: Viking, 2013.

———. *Why the Allies Won*. New York: W. W. Norton, 1995.

Parton, James, *"Air Force Spoken Here": General Ira Eaker and the Command of the Air*. Bethesda, MD: Adler & Adler, 1986.

Pogue, Forrest C. *George C. Marshall*, 4 vols. New York: Viking, 1963–1986.

———. vol. 1, *Education of a General, 1880–1939* (1964).

———. vol. 2, *Ordeal and Hope, 1939–42* (1965).

———. Vol. 3, *Organizer of Victory, 1943–45* (1973).

Potter, John. *Pim and Churchill's Map Room*. Belfast: Northern Ireland War Memorial, 2014.

Rawson, Andrew. *Organizing Victory: The War Conferences, 1941–1945*. Stroud, UK: The History Press, 2013.

Richards, Denis. *Portal of Hungerford. The Life of Marshal of the Royal Air Force Viscount Portal of Hungerford*. London: Heinemann, 1977.

Richardson, Charles. *From Churchill's Secret Circle to the BBC: The Biography of Lieutenant General Sir Ian Jacob*. London: Brassey's, 1991.

Roberts, Andrew. *Masters and Commanders: How Four Titans Won the War in the West, 1941–1945*. New York: Harper, 2009.

Robertson, Charles L. *When Roosevelt Planned to Govern France*. Amherst: University of Massachusetts Press, 2011.

Roll, David L. *George Marshall: Defender of the Republic*. New York: Caliber, 2019.

Sangster, Andrew. *Alan Brooke: Churchill's Right-Hand Critic: A Reappraisal of Lord Alanbrooke*. Oxford, UK: Casemate Publishers, 2021.

See, Kwang-Yew. "The Downfall of General Giraud: A Study of American Wartime Politics." *Penn History Review* 18 (December 2010): 36–50.

Smart, Nick. *Biographical Dictionary of British Generals of the Second World War*. Barnesley, UK: Pen & Sword, 2005.

Stoler, Mark A. *Allies and Adversaries: The Joint Chiefs of Staff, the Grand Alliance, and US Strategy in World War II*. Chapel Hill: University of North Carolina Press, 2000.

———. *The Politics of the Second Front: American Military Planning and Diplomacy in Coalition Warfare, 1941–1943*. Westport, CT: Greenwood, 1977.

Thorne, Christopher. *Allies of a Kind: the United States, Britain, and the War Against Japan, 1941–1945*. London: Hamish Hamilton, 1978.

Weiss, Steve. *Anglo-American Strategic Negotiations, 1938–1944*. New York: St. Martin's Press, 1996.

Wingate, Ronald. *Lord Ismay: A Biography*. London: Hutchinson, 1970.

Articles and Chapters of Books

"Ack-Ack Fire at Casablanca." *Life*, March 15, 1943, pp. 33–36.

Beaumont, A. "The Bomber Offensive as a Second Front." *Journal of Contemporary History* 22, no. 1 (January 1987): 3–19.

Ben-Moshe, Tuvia. "Explaining an Historical Puzzle: Freudian Errors and the Origin of the Declaration on the Policy of 'Unconditional Surrender' in the Second World War." *Political Psychology* 14, no. 4 (December 1993): 697–709.

Biddle, Tami Davis. "Winston Churchill and Sir Charles Portal: Their Wartime Relationship, 1940–1945," in Peter W. Gray and Sebastian Cox, eds., *Air Power Leadership: Theory and Practice* (London: The Stationery Office, 2002).

Bond, Brian. "Alanbrooke and Britain's Mediterranean Strategy, 1942–1944," in Lawrence Freedman et al., eds., *War, Strategy and International Politics* (Oxford: Clarendon, 1992), pp. 175–93.

"Casablanca Conference." *World War II* magazine 52 (1975).

Charmley, John. "Harold Macmillan and the Making of the French Committee of Liberation." *The International History Review* 4 (November 1982): 553–67.

Chase, John L. "Unconditional Surrender Reconsidered." *Political Science Quarterly* 70, no. 2 (June 1955): 258–79.

Danchev, Alex. "Britain: The Indirect Strategy," in David Reynolds et al., eds., *Allies at War* (New York: St. Martin's Press, 1994), pp. 1–26.

———. "The Combined Chiefs of Staff and the Making of Allied Strategy in the Second World War," in L. Freedman and R. O'Neill, eds., *War, Strategy, and International Politics: Essays in Honor of Sir Michael Howard* (Oxford: Clarendon Press, 1992).

———. "'Dilly-Dally,' on Having the Last Word: Field-Marshal Sir John Dill and Prime Minister Winston Churchill." *Journal of Contemporary History* 22 (January 1987): 21–44.

———. "Field Marshal Sir John Dill: The Early Years." *Journal of the Society for Army Historical Research* 67, no. 269 (Spring 1989): 28–39.

———. "A Special Relationship: Field-Marshal Sir John Dill and General George C. Marshall." *Journal of the Royal United Services Institute* 130, no. 2 (June 1985): 56–61.

———. "Waltzing with Winston: Civil-Military Relations in Britain in the Second World War." *War in History* 21, no. 20 (July 1995): 202–30.

Dulles, Foster Rhea, and Gerald E. Ridinger. "The Anti-Colonial Policies of Franklin D. Roosevelt." *Political Science Quarterly* 70, no. 1 (March 1955): 1–18.

Eaker, Ira. "Some Memories of Winston Churchill." *Aerospace Historian* 19, no. 3 (Fall, September 1972): 120–24.

Emerson, W. "Franklin Roosevelt as Commander in Chief in World War II." *Military Affairs* 22, no. 20 (Winter 1958–59): 181–207.

Funk, Arthur Layton. "The 'Anfa Memorandum': An Incident of the Casablanca Conference." *The Journal of Modern History* 26, no. 3 (September 1954): 246–54.

Holland, Edward C. "The Effects of an American Sense of Morality on the Evolution of Strategic Bombing Campaigns," in *Fighting with a Conscience* (Maxwell Air Force Base, Montgomery, AL: Air University Press, 1992).

Love, Robert William, Jr. "Ernest Joseph King," in Robert W. Love, ed., *The Chiefs of Naval Operations* (Annapolis, MD: Naval Institute Press, 1980).

Mackesy, Piers. "Sir John Kennedy at the War Office, 1940–1944." *Journal of the Society for Army Historical Research* 76, no. 305 (Spring 1998): 43–51.

Miller, John. "The Casablanca Conference and Pacific Strategy." *Military Affairs* 13, No. 4 (Winter 1949): 209–15.

Morton, Louis. "Germany First: The Basic Concept of Allied Strategy in World War II," in *Command Decisions*, Kent Roberts Greenfield, ed. (Washington, DC: U.S. Government Printing Office, 1960).

Painton, Frederick C. "Giraud's Brilliant Escape from a Nazi Prison." *Reader's Digest*, September 1943, p. 39.

Parks, W. Hays. "'Precision' and 'Area' Bombing: Who Did Which and When?," in *Airpower: Theory and Practice*, John Gooch, ed. (London: Frank Cash Publishers, 1995).

Parton, James. "General Ira Eaker, Creator of the Eighth Air Force." *Air Power History* 39, no. 3 (Fall 1992): 31–34.

———. "Lt. Gen. Ira C. Eaker, USAF (Ret.): An Aide's Memoir." *Aerospace Historian* 34, no. 4 (Winter/December 1987): 226–35.

Polley, N. G. T. "Brigadier Guy Stewart." *Journal of the Society for Army Historical Research* 76, no. 308 (Winter 1998): 289–90.

Reynolds, Clark G. "Admiral Ernest J. King and the Strategy for Victory in the Pacific." *Naval War College Review* 28, no. 3 (Winter 1976): 57–64.

Sainsbury, Keith. "'Second Front in 1942': A Strategic Controversy Revisited." *British Journal of International Studies* 4, no. 1 (April 1978): 47–58.

Sanders, H. "King of the Oceans." *United States Naval Institute Proceedings* 97 (June 1971): 54–59; and 100 (August 1974): 52–59.

Sebrega, John J. "The Anticolonial Policies of Franklin D. Roosevelt: A Reappraisal." *Political Science Quarterly* 101, no. 1 (1986): 65–84.

Smart, Jacob. "The Casablanca Conference, January 1943." *Air Power History* 46, no. 3 (Fall 1999): 36–43.

"Why 'Europe First'? Cultural, Economic and Ideological Underpinnings of America's 'Europe First' Strategy, 1940–1941." Army Hertitage.org.

Wilt, Alan F. "The Significance of the Casablanca Decisions, January 1943." *The Journal of Military History* 55, no. 4 (October 1991): 517–29.

Wouk, Herman. "Decision at Casablanca." *Air Force Magazine*, January 2003.

Wright, Donald. "That Hell-Hole of Yours." *American Heritage* 46, no. 6 (October 1995): 47.

Films Available on YouTube

"The Alanbrooke Diaries." BBC interview of Alanbrooke by General Sir Brian Horrocks, 1958.

"Churchill-Roosevelt Casablanca Conference AKA Churchill-Roosevelt Casablanca Meeting (1943)." British Pathé.

"FDR Goes to Africa for the Casablanca Conference—1943/Today in History/14 Jan. 19." British Movietone News.

"US Navy Newsreel 1943 Casablanca Conference WWII President Roosevelt & Winston Churchill 55374."

"WWII Casablanca Conference—1943," British Movietone News.

Photo Credits

Endpaper: US Army Newsmap collection, Volume 1 Number 42 G 3201.S7 coll .U5 Newsmap, Library of Congress

INSERT
1. National Portrait Gallery, London
2. United States Army Center of Military History Photographs, Wikimedia Commons
3. The National Museum of the United States Navy (NMUSN), courtesy of the Library of Congress (LOC)
4. National Archives and Records Administration (NARA), Wikimedia Commons
5. Franklin D. Roosevelt Presidential Library and Museum
6. NMUSN, courtesy of NARA
7. NMUSN, courtesy of LOC
8. NMUSN, courtesy of NARA
9. LOC
10. NMUSN, courtesy of LOC
11. NARA
12. NMUSN, courtesy of LOC
13. FDR Library
14. Royal Air Force, Wikimedia Commons
15. NARA
16. Papers of Louise Anderson Locke, courtesy of Patricia Gardetto

THROUGHOUT
Pages xiv–xv: Maps by Don Hawkins

Index

THE WOR

Legend

United Nations

Axis and Axis Occupied

Relations with Axis Broken

Neutrals